105

THE

MANAGEMENT

OF

BUSINESS

AN INTRODUCTION

THE
MANAGEMENT
OF
BUSINESS

AN INTRODUCTION

EARL P. STRONG

Assistant Dean and Professor of Management

College of Business Administration

The Pennsylvania State University

HARPER & ROW, PUBLISHERS

New York

T O

Mid and Lou Ellen

658 St 88

CONTENTS c · 1

PART II · ANALYSIS OF THE FRAMEWORK OF MANAGEMENT

PART III · ANALYSIS OF THE TECHNICAL KNOWLEDGES AND SKILLS OF MANAGEMENT

PART V · ANALYSIS OF THE LEADERSHIP CHARACTERISTICS OF THE MANAGER

PART VI · ANALYSIS OF INFLUENCES ON MANAGEMENT

The first part of this book, consisting of six chapters,
is available in a paperbound edition under the title,
A Concept of Management.

PREFACE

Management today is far different from what it was a generation ago. Within that span of time, it has changed its style from the tough, hard-nose manager to the human-relationist, and then to the pressure-for-results executive of the fifties, each being a product of the times. The present era, including the next decade, finds the manager dealing in the realm of *situations.* The pendulum has swung from the Horatio Alger ideal of a successful executive to the professional manager who is oriented toward results and organizational responsibility.

In our time the first requirement in learning about management is to gain a conception of its breadth, what it does, and how it does it. This means that the manager of the present and future decades must understand varied situations and how to use his organization effectively in those situations. His failures will be the basis for developing his self-insight as he faces new situations.

This book presents management in its broadest perspective. In the limited space available it cannot and does not attempt to delve deeply into all the ramifications of the field, but the author hopes that from its study the reader will acquire a clearer concept of management.

The book is organized to achieve the maximum utilization of the reader's time and effort. As a teaching technique, it uses the "concentric circle" method, the first circle being an introduction to or overview of the field of management as presented in the first six chapters of Part I. The remaining five parts present an analysis in detail of the points made in Part I.

For one person to have written such a comprehensive book without the assistance of others would have been almost impossible. The author is indebted, therefore, to a number of people who have contributed generously of their time and thoughts to the writing and makeup of this work.

Particular recognition is due the following, who made contributions to its contents: Professor Harold P. Zelko, Professor of Speech, The Pennsylvania State University; Dr. Monroe Newman, Professor of Economics, The Pennsylvania State University; Lt. Richard M. O'Brien, United States Army Command and General Staff College, Fort Leavenworth, Kansas; Dr. Norman George, University of Dayton; Mr. Robert D. Smith, College of Business Administration, The Pennsylvania State University; and to Mrs. Miriam D. Pierce, Assistant Engineering Librarian, The Pennsylvania State University. In addition, gratitude is expressed to the Allegheny Power System and its subsidiaries for permission to use tested materials from its management manual, which was originally prepared by Dr. William P. Davidson, Professor of Business Administration, the Ohio State University, and Dr. James H. Healey, President, Management Associates, Inc., Columbus, Ohio.

Recognition is also given to those persons who assisted so diligently in the preparation of the manuscript for publication; namely, Mrs. Eva T. Burke, who directed its preparation, Miss Lou Ellen Strong, and Mrs. Janice Dahlberg.

E.P.S.

University Park, Pennsylvania
May, 1965

Building Men*

How do you train him?
There he stands before you,
Clean and lanky,
With a look of bright morning on his face.
Appealing
In the way that morning is,
And youth is,
And the hopefulness of youth.

And then you realize
The awful responsibility
That is yours
To train.
To train and build,
And nurture and lead.
You realize how much of business is training,
How much of modern industry is building men,
Inspiring men,
And leading them to achievement.

Well, here is good timber
But what are you going to build of it?
And how do you go about the building process?

This is the answer:
You give him of yourself.

Urge him learn his craft, of course,
And learn it well,

* Reprinted by permission from THINK Magazine,
copyright 1960 by International Business Machines
Corporation.

Whatever it is—law, accounting, engineering.
Tell him he must labor hard, to learn it well.
That, of course,
Goad him to dip into classic tomes
And newer letters
To touch base often
In academic halls
And move about in tasks foreign and unfamiliar.

But this young man needs more.
Judgment he needs,
And understanding,
And maturity.

For these, he looks to you
And you must give them to him.
Let yourself rub off on him,
Let him sit beside you as you work,
To work with you,
To study with you,
To be perplexed with you,
To analyze with you,
And to dream with you.

Give him the impossible task to do,
The unanswerable question to answer.
There is no better way to train—
Whether you be Socrates training Athenian youth,
Or an American man of business
Teaching some young hopeful the craft of management
In mid-century industrial America.

—ROBERT W. MURPHY

PART I

INTRODUCTION TO THE
CONCEPT OF MANAGEMENT

Part I presents a broad view of the subject matter of management from a conceptual standpoint. Here management is considered as a totality. By studying Part I carefully, the reader will obtain an overview of management and will pass through the first ring in the group of concentric circles comprising this book's coverage of the subject. There is no detail in this part pertaining to the elements or functions of management; the remaining parts of the book are devoted to a treatment in depth of various functional areas. By progressing through the introductory outer ring first, the reader's conceptual understanding of management relationships will be sharpened so that the later parts will be more meaningful and useful.

1

THE MANAGEMENT PROCESS

There are several ways in which the word "manage" is commonly used. By exploring a few of its commonly accepted usages, we may clarify the function of the manager.

A few common expressions are:

"I'll manage *somehow*."

"I'll manage *it*."

"I'll manage *him*."

"I'll manage *them*."

"*I* manage."

"I'll manage *somehow*" is a grim, dogged phrase. It denotes "getting by somehow," which is what some managers do. Managing *can* be just getting by. Some businesses are run in a by-the-skin-of-the-teeth, cliff-hanging way.

You or I would not long support such management. You would be more comfortable with a company that reflects, "I'll manage and *this* is how." "This is how" implies aim, purpose, goal.

The work of the manager begins with the establishment of objectives. It probes the present to determine where we are and forecasts future objectives in terms of next month and next year. "This is how" schedules the steps that must be taken to get the business from the present to next year. Alternatives are charted. Agreement is reached. The date to move ahead is set.

Through taking purposeful action regarding the company's

major asset—its future—the manager assumes one of his functions. Rather than "managing somehow," he *plans*.

"I'll manage *it*" is another dogged phrase. It implies a management surprised by a deadline, a management that now must "throw some odds and ends together" to "get by."

Managing a business is not just planning. It includes breathing life into the plan by bringing together people, materials, and machines in a relationship that comes to life. And all of this must be done on schedule.

So the work of managing includes both planning and *preparing* to do, both planning and *organizing*.

"I'll manage *him*" often means, "When I've finished with him, he'll be alive, but he'll be suffering." "Managing him" implies fear, force, threat. Its objective is sullen, grudging agreement. It represents power *over* others.

There is no place in a modern, progressive business for this concept. One man is now "over" another only in terms of the blocks in an organization chart. The power of management exists *with* or *through* people, but not *over* them. It has its source in methods of leading, motivating, teaching, influencing, counseling, coaching, appraising, delegating, setting an example. This is the work of the manager.

So, in addition to planning and organizing, the manager channels the creative power of people toward company objectives. The manager plans, organizes, and *motivates*.

"I'll manage *them*" means, "I'll knock their heads together until they see eye to eye." This is a relic from past days. People do what makes sense to them. If they understand what is going on around them, seeing eye to eye is not too difficult.

To get employees to see things in the same way at the same time calls for effective communication, whose purpose is to inform them what to do.

The work of the manager, then, is planning, organizing, motivating, and *directing*.

"*I* manage" smacks of blind authority. It brings to mind images of the Caesars, of Russia, of the worst of the small-town constables. There is something of the "divine right" to manage about the phrase. This certainly is out of date.

There is only one reason why the manager of today holds his job; that is because he is good at it. Rather than "*I* manage," he stresses "I *manage*," meaning, among other things, that he establishes the financial requirements of his part of the organization and manages to live within his budget. He is accountable for quality and quantity and *manages* to maintain them. He is responsible for meeting deadlines and *manages* to meet them.

This he does by setting standards and by measuring and comparing. He establishes systems to send and receive data promptly He is in tune with the internal language of figures. He draws meaning from these figures that enables him to meet deadlines and maintain standards, to replan and redirect.

The manager, then, plans, organizes, motivates, directs, and *controls*. These are the broad aspects of his work. He adds foresight, order, purpose, integration of effort, and effectiveness to the contributions of others. That is the best use of the word "manage." That is the work of the manager.

What do managers "manage"? What do they plan, organize, motivate, direct, and control? In general terms, the six M's: men, money, materials, machinery, markets, and minutes—the resources common to any organization, be it a church, a lodge, the government, or a business firm.

So the manager does not merely direct work he once used to do. There is more to it than that. Whether he manages an apple stand on a corner or runs a Westinghouse or General Motors, he plans, organizes, motivates, directs, and controls through the use of certain management tools. These include the following:

Objectives—the goals, aims, and purposes of his company and his part of the company

Ethics—the quality of conduct desired in reaching company objectives

Policies—the principles and guides to action that direct the work toward these objectives

Organization structure—the network of decision centers, backed with the proper authority, that best accomplishes the work

Leadership—his own and that of others, that manages with understanding, objectivity, and aggressiveness

Systems, procedures, and methods—the orderly structuring of routine that maximizes production and minimizes waste

Position descriptions—the summarization of the responsibilities and authorities of the various positions in the organization

Morale—the climate which encourages employees to use their skills and machines to do their best work

Standards—the yardsticks and ways of measuring and reporting all the information—and there are many, many kinds—that keeps the entire productive system "in orbit"

Learning about these tools or elements of management can widen one's horizons, and the process of fitting them all together is an interesting challenge. Growth in management is a long-term, never-ending process. Defining the functions of management doesn't take long. But possessing the ideas, trying them, proving them again and again is a continuing self-development job for the best of us.

Growth goes on in many ways. There are fine points to polish and new skills to learn. There are knacks to reading faster, communicating better, thinking more precisely. There are skills to conference leading and ways to coach and interview and question more effectively.

As growth continues, the manager's curiosity and interest extend beyond his work place, to suppliers, customers and stockholders, communities, counties, and states, for his work must relate constructively to the needs and hopes and feelings of all the people his company "lives with" as a friend, neighbor, and citizen.

The manager himself probably does not think of his functions, knowledges, skills, and viewpoints as "work." Calling them a way of life or a living philosophy might be more to the point. For the manager adds to the values of his world through his own personal growth and development.

QUESTIONS AND PROBLEMS

1. Trace the management process in solving a simple problem, such as taking a short vacation trip.
2. Give examples of objectives, morale, and standards.
3. Is the progress of a manager ever static? Explain.
4. Give an example of poor management out of your own experience.
5. Give an example of good management out of your own experience.

READING REFERENCE

Davidson, William R., and James H. Healey, *Power Management,* Allegheny Power Co., and Its Subsidiaries, 1962.

2

THE CONCEPTUAL APPROACH TO MANAGEMENT

The student of management theory and practice today is indeed fortunate. He finds himself in an economy, both national and international, that is fully aware of the place of the individual manager in the organizational structure. Since 1950 there have been rapid strides in our understanding, knowledge, and appreciation of the part management plays in an expanding and sophisticated economy. In short, the field of management has identified the information (learning *about* management), skills (learning *how* to manage), and the wisdom (learning *why*) essential to the totally trained and developed manager.

Fully to appreciate the scope and opportunities in the field of management, the student of the subject must not stop with the study of specialized areas, but should learn to view the over-all field from the vantage point of a generalist. To be sure, many successful managers have developed from successful subject-matter specialists, but with our present knowledge and experience, today's student has the advantage of seeing *all* of the picture, not just a part of it. True, he may wish to specialize in one phase of business and become, perhaps, a sales manager or controller or factory superintendent. Even so, he can become more effective in his specialization by acquiring a conceptual appreciation of the entire management field.

It is important, therefore, that the student of management

see the field in its entirety, recognizing its various parts, how they interact and are synchronized into an effective working whole. In addition, he should see where the manager fits into the picture and his importance to the success of the enterprise. Lastly, he must see the enterprise in relation to the outside influences that affect its success.

To appreciate the place of conceptual skill in the over-all field, let us examine what several authorities have to say on the subject. One identifies the three essential skills of a manager as follows:

1. Technical skill—"specialized knowledge, analytical ability within that specialty, and facility in the use of the tools and techniques of the specific discipline."
2. Human skill—the ability of the manager "to work effectively as a group member and to building co-operative effort within the team he leads."
3. Conceptual skill—"the ability to see the enterprise as a whole; it includes recognizing how the various functions of the organization depend on one another, and how changes in any one part affect all the others and it extends to visualizing the relationship of the individual business to the industry, the community, and the political, social, and economic forces of the nation as a whole. Recognizing these relationships and perceiving the significant elements in any situation, the manager should then be able to act in a way which advances the over-all welfare of the total organization."[1]

Another authority identifies conceptual skill as "the ability to develop and understand concepts—systems of ideas or organized ways of thinking about the structure, function, and relationship of things."[2]

Conceptual skill, says Houston, is also "the ability to *use* . . . concepts . . . to apply or transfer them to a variety of similar or related situations so as to aid in understanding and analysis of these situations and in planning or projection of future action, including conjecture as to the possible effects of such action."[3]

Peter Drucker says that management will be able to do its work only if it learns to "convert into system and method what has been done before, by hunch or intuition, to reduce to principles and concepts what has been left to experience and 'rule of thumb,' to substitute a logical and cohesive pattern for the chance recognition of elements."[4]

Professor Charles H. Judd, of the University of Chicago, says, "The end goal of all education is the development of systems of ideas which can be carried over from the situations in which they were acquired to other situations. Systems of general ideas illuminate and clarify human experiences by raising them to the level of abstract, generalized, conceptual understanding."[5]

The concept of management presented in this book includes technical knowledges and skills, administrative skills, facilitating elements, individual characteristics, and outside influences and the coordination of these elements in such a manner as to facilitate getting the work done in line with the objectives of the group and of the organization.

It is well known that learning is the result of messages received by the mind, which proceeds to organize and interpret them. It forms a *structure* of information, a mental picture, image, or concept through which it can interpret and utilize that information.

In the presentation of the information about management in this book, the organized structure or image concept that emerges is analogous to a man (the manager) whose success in riding a bicycle is dependent upon the synchronization of its parts. (See Fig. 1) This analogy should give the reader a concept of the organization as continually moving forward toward a specific goal, under the motive power generated by the individual manager in his particular area (department, division, or company), running on the roadway of current economic, social, and political forces, and surrounded by the landscape of employee and customer attitudes.

A PHILOSOPHY IS BASIC TO DETERMINING GOALS AND OBJECTIVES

A sound philosophy of business management has been slow in developing and even now is far from adequate. Management has few problem areas in which research could not produce more fruitful results.

The early beginnings of management theory have become overgrown with a jungle of approaches to the subject. From the orderly analysis of management at the shoproom level by Frederick Taylor and the reflective distillation of experience from the general management point of view by Henri Fayol have sprung numerous "schools." They include the management process school, the empirical school, the human behavior school, the social system school, the decision theory school, and the mathematical school.[6] Further sources of confusion are semantic differences, the a priori assumption, the misunderstanding of principles, and the inability or unwillingness of management theorists to understand each other.

In approaching management theory, then, keep in mind that one must make his own selection of what he thinks is a workable philosophy in his particular situation.

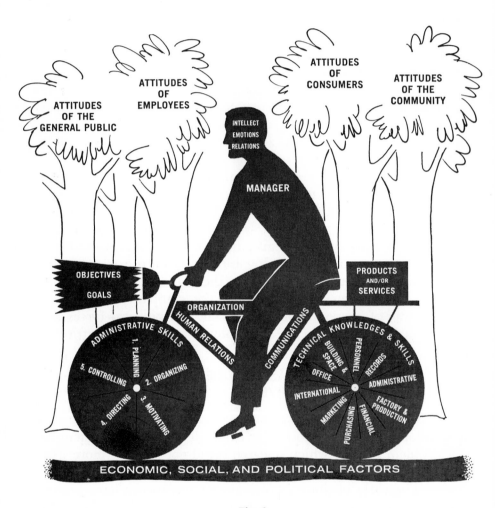

Fig. 1

Too often, those face to face with daily problems that require immediate solution tend to shy away from theory and philosophy. This is a pity since our solutions to problems are often related directly to the theory we hold.

Some years ago, an English physician wrote: "To theory, sooner, or later, the subtlest craftsman has to bow his head; for, even while his hand is on his tools, by theory contingencies and complications are being detected and eliminated and processes shortened and economized."[7]

What is needed is to see the entire vista of managment; then the complexities which dog one in his daily chores suddenly take on a simplicity of design. Having seen the pattern, one is better able to look into its parts, and to understand their relationship to other parts. To understand and apply this relationship is the key to the success of a manager.

A philosophy—of life in general, of one's own life, of the management task, of relations with others—is a basic necessity. If a personal philosophy is unsatisfactory or negative, the consequences can be catastrophic. Successful managers and executives usually have sound philosophies of life and, as a result, sound philosophies of management.

The basic philosophy of an organization is actually the guide to better management. Such a philosophy should be stated and made clear, not only to the managing heads of an organization, but to the employees. Without it objectives cannot be clearly set up and the people within the organization will operate without real goals. Basic operating policies need to be stated in writing so that all personnel know what they are and will be guided by them.

Whether the operation of the organization is centralized or decentralized need make no difference in carrying out a management philosophy. Long-range planning for future growth grows out of a statement of principles, policies, and programs.

Many organizations do not have a philosophy of management; some do not even have an organization chart showing the interrelationships of personnel and their functions. Such a chart is a *must* to good organization. The part played by each person should be clearly described so that there is little or no overlapping of functions.

It sometimes takes a great deal of courage to tell one individual not to do something that is someone else's duty. Nevertheless, it has to be done. One organization in which a study was made recently had a great deal of overlapping, and management took action only after a great deal of prodding. The organization is already operating more smoothly and the morale of employees and middle-management people has greatly improved.

Part of the basic philosophy of management is the realization that it is management's job to facilitate getting the work done. Too often, management unwittingly hinders work progress. A case in point came up recently when a company vice president rejected a plan to place a new-type temperature gauge on a piece of production machinery. This gauge would have enabled the plant superintendent to check the temperature of the machine automatically, saving much time and wear on the machinery. Management rejected the gauge, not because of the money involved, but because of lack of support for the plant superintendent's ideas. The sequel was the breakdown of the machine, which had to be replaced at a very high cost. In this particular case, the situation had not been studied thoroughly by management and a snap decision was made. The effect on the plant superintendent was great. He felt that he had been let down, that his ideas were not valued, and that future suggestions for improvements would not be welcome. Frustration and dissatisfaction spread to others who had observed what had taken place. In short, management had blocked rather than facilitated work progress.

One of the techniques set up by progressive business organizations to facilitate work is to determine definite objectives. These are made clear to all persons in the organization, especially to various levels of management. They are stated in terms of individual goals, which, when put together, become part of the over-all objectives. Everyone in the organization knows exactly what is expected of him, and what the organization's major objectives are. Management knows exactly where effort needs to be directed, how much effort needs to be made, and who is performing best.

The concept of a philosophy of management is well illustrated by a formal statement prepared by one of the nation's best-known students of the field of management, Professor Ralph C. Davis, of Ohio State University:

The term "philosophy" means to the undersigned a body of related knowledges that supplies a logic for effective thinking for the solution of certain kinds of problems. A management philosophy supplies the basis for the solution of business problems. An executive with no philosophy can have only limited capability for creative thinking, regardless of his basic intelligence. The development of this philosophy of management began about twenty-five years ago. It was undertaken for practical rather than academic reasons; the undersigned wanted, for himself, a better basis for problem-solving thought in the field of Management. He still believes that the development of a sound philosophy of management for oneself is probably the most practical self-development project that an executive can undertake.

The following . . . is a reasonably accurate statement of the basis of his management philosophy:

1. This management philosophy is based on the right of private property and the concept of a free market economy. It is, accordingly, a philosophy of economic decentralism. This philosophy tends to be opposed, therefore, to:

a. Philosophies of socialism, since they are basically philosophies of economic and political centralism that tend to diminish the freedom of the individual and the exercise of individual initiative.

b. Centralized controls of the economy by central government, beyond the necessary minimums, since these weaken the right of private property.

c. Monopoly, either of capital or labor, since this monopoly tends to destroy a free market economy.

d. Any measures designed to prevent the formation of private capital, without which there can be no system of private capitalism. These measures include confiscatory taxation, social pressures that are exerted deliberately to promote "dis-saving," "planned inflation," and various others that tend to prevent private capital formation. A free market economy can only operate effectively under a system or private capitalism. Such measures lead to the substitution of state capitalism for private capitalism and the development of a socialist economy.

2. This philosophy emphasizes the prior obligation of private enterprises, their owners and employees, to contribute substantially to a standard of living that is increasing continuously through time. It is based, therefore, on the concept that the primary objectives of the business organization are those economic values that are needed or desired by its customers. This is, accordingly, a philosophy of economic service by private enterprise to the public interest.

3. The acceptance of this service obligation by owners and managers is necessary for the validation of the concepts of private property and private profit. It is not necessary, however, that this acceptance be completely voluntary. It is sufficient that it be accepted under the duress of competition and a minimum of supporting governmental regulation. This is a philosophy of intelligent selfishness, accordingly.

4. This philosophy commits owners and managers to the active promotion of social and economic progress. It is accordingly a philosophy of progressive conservatism.

a. It does not sanction attempts by owners or managers to "turn back the clock," since it recognizes the economic and social obligations of private ownership to contribute to progress in an expanding economy. It is not reactionary management philosophy, accordingly.

b. This philosophy does not sanction attempts by politicians or academic theorists to bet the fruits of past technical and managerial achievements of private enterprise on the nose of some untested economic, political, or social hypotheses. It is not a radical management philosophy, accordingly.

5. This philosophy recognizes the importance of big rewards for big results. It does not seek to chisel away the fruits of success, whether they be in the form of profits, bonuses, incentive pay, salaries, wages, fringe benefits, or various intangible values, provided that these are earned under competitive conditions. It is, accordingly, a philosophy of positive motivation. This philosophy recognizes, therefore, the validity of the profit objective in private enterprises, on the basis of:

a. The concept of a profit as a reward of private capital for the successful acceptance of business risk in the rendering of an economic service, under competitive conditions in a free market. It recognizes, consequently, that a profit is the principal objective of the businessman, even though customer service is the primary objective of the business organization.

b. The concept of profit making as a necessary function in the processes for the formation of private capital.

6. No organization can be better than its leadership, over a period of time. The work of management is the work of executive leadership. It is the mental work of planning, organizing, and controlling the activities of others in the joint accomplishment of a common objective. The executive must have the rights of decision and command that are necessary for effective leadership anywhere, as well as the concomitant obligations of leadership. This philosophy recognizes that an uncontrolled exercise of executive authority is neither in the public interest nor in the interest of private enterprise. It is a leadership philosophy in this respect.

7. This philosophy also emphasizes the importance of confidence in the purposes of executive leadership as a basic factor in the development of good organizational morale, and in the maintenance of sound business relations of all kinds. It emphasizes, therefore, the importance of ethical principles in the formulation of business policies. It is a moral philosophy in this respect.

8. This philosophy requires the recognition by owners and managers of Labor's right of collective bargaining. It is a labor-management philosophy in part.

a. It recognizes that the loss of a property right in one's services is coincident with or follows the loss of property rights in one's goods. A denial of the right of collective bargaining, and its concomitant right to organize, leads to socialism. The socialist state owns or controls the means of production. These means include operative Labor and Management, as well as land and capital. There can be no true collective bargaining under socialism.

b. It does not recognize any right of labor to a profit share because of the service obligations set up in a contract of employment. One cannot sell one's services, and retain title to them at the same time. It does recognize the right of capital to dispose of its profits or losses in any legitimate manner.

9. This philosophy emphasizes the concepts of delegation, decentralization, individual initiative and individual accountabilty. It recognizes the obligation of the individual to contribute to the accomplishment of the primary service objectives of his organization, as well as his right to a reasonable satisfaction of his personal objectives. It emphasizes the importance of the individual, while recognizing the importance of group coordination and cooperation. It is a philosophy of individualism, in this respect.

10. This philosophy breaks down the problem of management in a free-enterprise economy into its basic elements. It analyzes the principal factors, forces, and effects in the management process. It develops a logic of effective thinking, in terms of business objectives, policies, functions, factors, and relationships, that is applicable to the solution of managerial problems anywhere. It is a scientific philosophy of management in this respect.[8]

MANAGEMENT PRINCIPLES

The development of management principles has been retarded, in part, by the failure to recognize, until recently, that management is a function distinct from technical work. Emphasis has been wrongly placed upon knowledge of a particular functional activity of the business, e.g., sales, production, and the like, as a measure of managerial ability. It is true that specialized knowledge of specific operations is helpful to the executive in a particular job in a particular organization; yet it is not technical knowledge and ability that are most needed by the manager, but rather the ability to use and coordinate the technical skills possessed by others.

This idea that management is, itself, a specialized activity was broached by Henri Fayol as early as 1908. It was Fayol's concept that the elements of management were universal; that management knowledge could be recorded and classified and transferred to others. This assumption, that the management function can be taught, is the basis of today's management development programs deliberately aimed at the education of "generalists." Until recently the major contributors to a theory of business management were business executives; now the work of the social scientist has been applied to the functions of the business manager. Important contributions have been made by the sociologist, the political scientist, the psychologist, the economic theorist, and others.

Management today requires that we see the whole picture— our own organization, the economy around us, and the relationship of our operation to national and international problems and issues. We are an important functional part of our community, our profession, and our own particular work.

QUESTIONS AND PROBLEMS

1. What is your understanding of a concept? Write out your concept of business management.
2. Why is personal philosophy so important to the manager and to his organization?
3. What contribution did Henri Fayol make to management?
4. Why has management structure been so confusing in the past? What is your understanding of it?
5. Write out a statement of your philosophy of life. Conceptualize it and then visualize it in written form.

REFERENCE NOTES

[1] Robert L. Katz, "Skills of an Effective Administrator," *Harvard Business Review*, January-February, 1955, pp. 33–42.

[2] George C. Houston, *Management Development: Principles and Perspectives*, Richard D. Irwin, 1961, p. 104.

[3] *Ibid.*, p. 104.

[4] Peter F. Drucker, *The Practice of Management*, Harper & Row, 1954, p. 374.

[5] Charles H. Judd, *Education as Cultivation of the Higher Mental Process*, Macmillan, 1936, p. 201.

[6] Harold Koontz, "The Management Theory Jungle," *Journal of the Academy of Management*, December, 1961, p. 174.

[7] Col. Lyndall Urwick, *Advanced Management*, Society for the Advancement of Management, February, 1956.

[8] Ralph C. Davis, "A Philosophy of Management," mimeographed paper distributed at the 1958 sessions of the Ohio State University Executive Development Program.

3

THE CENTRAL FRAMEWORK OF MANAGEMENT

Much has been written about the three central connecting bars (organization principles, human relations, and communications) that support the three other elements in our bicycle analogy—the front wheel, the back wheel, and the manager. (See Fig. 1.) The bars of this triangle are sometimes referred to as the "holy three," for without them no organized activity could exist for long. It is up to the manager to use them effectively. How well he does so depends upon his basic understanding of their place in the over-all structure of management.

TOP BAR—ORGANIZATION PRINCIPLES

The line organization is one in which authority and responsibility flow in a direct line from the chief executive to the lowest employee. At each successive level, authority and responsibility are alike in kind but more limited in scope than at the level immediately above. Each executive is responsible for the actions of all below him; each person in the line has only one immediate superior. The line organization has complete responsibility for operations and the authority to command when necessary. Line executives are assisted by staff officers whose authority is to provide ideas, counsel, and service. The staff officer does not command unless this authority has been specifically delegated to him.

The relationship of the staff to the line organization is a

delicate one, fraught with difficulties unless both parties thoroughly understand it and strive to promote the general welfare. It is very important that staff responsibilities be clearly defined; and it is highly desirable that both line and staff officers be carefully trained in the theory behind line-and-staff organization. In addition, dynamic leadership by the line officers is required to keep the relationship balanced. It is very easy to retain the structure yet change the facts of the relationship over a period of time. The people down the line who are most involved will be aware of it, and suffer considerable emotional distress; yet their voices may never be heard by the people responsible for correcting the situation. The final responsibility for keeping the staff organization in a balanced relationship rests with the line officers. Aggressive individuals tend to get more recognition than is their due unless management is constantly alert to see that the people who perform their duties quietly but effectively are given consideration.

Determinants of Organization Structure

The following list of organization principles is widely quoted and has been used effectively by many enterprises.

1. Principle of organizational objectives. The objectives of an enterprise are of major importance in determining the structure of the enterprise.
2. Principle of unity of objectives. The organization as a whole and every part of it must contribute to the attainment of the organizational objectives.
3. Principle of the primacy of organizational objectives. An organization may fail when important individuals or groups within it place their personal interests ahead of the organization's interests.
4. The scalar principle. A fundamental organization requirement is a chain of direct authority from superior to subordinate throughout the organization.
5. Principle of unity of command. Each individual in an organization should have but one immediate, direct superior.
6. Principle of definite supervisory channels. For any given enterprise, the various organization units should be connected by clearly defined supervisory channels so that the activities of each can be properly supervised by a single unit of the organization level immediately higher.
7. Principle of organization levels. The number of levels of authority should be kept at a minimum.
8. Principle of functions. Functions are the main entities around which a manager builds an effective organization structure.

9. Principle of simplicity. Only functions which are absolutely necessary, related in a plain and forthright manner, and accompanied by clear statements of the authority and responsibility of persons charged with performing them should be incorporated in the organization.

10. Principle of functional similarity. Duties should be grouped and assigned in accordance with their functional similarities.

11. Principle of the span of management. There is a limit to the number of personnel and activities that one individual can manage effectively.

12. Principle of delegation. Authority should be delegated to the greatest extent possible, consistent with necessary control, so that coordinating and decision-making can take place as close as possible to the point of action.

13. Principle of definition. The duties, authority, responsibility, and relationships of everyone in the organization should be clearly and completely defined, preferably in writing.

14. Principle of parity of authority and responsibility. Authority and responsibility should be coextensive. A person should not be given a responsibility unless he is given enough authority to discharge it.

15. Principle of fixed responsibility. For any given period, an individual will accomplish most when responsibility for the completion of a definite task is fixed upon that individual.

16. Principle of complete assignment. Responsibility and authority for every activity necessary for effective operation of an organization should be definitely assigned to someone.

17. Principle of ultimate responsibility. The responsibility of a higher authority for the acts of his subordinates is absolute. The process of delegation relieves the responsible executive of none of his responsibility, authority, or accountability.

18. Principle of residual responsibility. There are certain basic responsibilities in any position of executive leadership which cannot be delegated; they "reside" in the position.

19. Principle of cross-contacts. Managers at any level in the organization may contact other managers, make decisions, lay plans, or take cooperative action upon any subject within the scope of their authority and responsibility, provided (a) the contact be made only with the knowledge and consent of the immediate superiors; (b) before the agreed-upon action is taken, it be approved by the immediate superiors.

20. The exception principle. Each manager at each level should make all decisions within the scope of his authority, and only those matters which he is not competent to decide (because of authority limitations) should be referred to his superior for decision.

21. Principle of increasing organization relationships. As new personnel are added to an organization structure, the number of

organization relations increases at a much greater rate than do the number of persons added.

22. Principle of personnel placement. Maximum organization effectiveness requires effective personnel placement; each individual should be carefully selected and placed so that the requirements of the job and the makeup of the individual represent the best possible combination.

23. Principle of informal organization groups. Within most organization structures, informal organization groups exist and affect operations in the entire organization.

24. Principle of organization balance. The development of the various functions and organizational units must conform as closely as practicable to their *relative* importance.

25. Principle of continuity. One of the obligations of management is to provide effective continuity to the operations of the organization.

26. Principle of dynamic organizing. Organizing should take into account changes in the organization, whether these changes be in goals, scope, content, or personnel.[1]

Ten Commandments of Good Organization

There are two kinds of efficiency. One kind is produced through the exercise of mere discipline. This is but a simulation of true efficiency, which springs, as Woodrow Wilson said, from "the spontaneous cooperation of a free people." If you are a manager, it is your job, in the final analysis, to create and develop this voluntary cooperation among the people you supervise. No matter how powerful a combination of money, machines, and materials a company may have, it is a sterile thing without a team of willing, thinking articulate people to guide it. The following ten commandments of good organization will help to create a climate in which such a team can develop.

1. Definite and clear-cut responsibilities should be assigned to each executive.
2. Responsibility should always be coupled with corresponding authority.
3. No change should be made in the scope of responsibilities of a position without a definite understanding to that effect on the part of all persons concerned.
4. No executive or employee, occupying a single position in the organization, should be subject to definite orders from more than one source.
5. Orders should never be given to subordinates over the head of a responsible executive.
6. Criticisms of subordinates should be made privately.

7. No dispute or difference between executives or employees as to authority or responsibilities should be considered too trivial for prompt and careful adjudication.
8. Promotions, wage changes, and disciplinary action should always be approved by the executive immediately superior to the one directly responsible.
9. No executive or employee should ever be required or expected to be at the same time an assistant to and a critic of another.
10. Any executive whose work is subject to regular inspection should, whenever practicable, be given the assistance and facilities necessary to enable him to maintain an independent check on the quality of his work.[2]

How to Judge Effective Organization[3]

To judge the effectiveness of an organization, we must study the character of its administration. A diagnosis of administration naturally deals with its defects, but it must be remembered that most of these reflect defects of personnel, and that a few may result from uncontrollable influences. Some defects may result from a combination of factors, whose separate influence cannot be distinguished.

If we cannot trace the results of enterprise directly to their ultimate causes, we can at least look for clues in defects of administration. After that, it may be possible to trace a clue to its ultimate cause. Defects can be classified into eight groups. However, to identify the defect is only to begin the diagnosis, and remote causes in organization are therefore suggested.

1. **Failure to act.** Enterprise implies action, constant action, and failure to act is a serious defect of administration. It occurs when a man omits some part of his responsibility, often continuously, or when for a period he fails to perform his entire responsibility.

Partial omission occurs frequently. A production man will neglect his housekeeping; a salesman will neglect a particular customer or class of customer; an accountant will neglect to reconcile details with his general ledger; the man responsible for making a contract will neglect to get legal advice. The degree to which such failures are prevalent in an enterprise will speak quite eloquently of the character of administration.

Partial omission may result from a variety of defects in structure. Perhaps the first to be suspected is a failure to define the man's responsibility properly so that he will understand his duty; perhaps his responsibility is too great so that he lacks time to perform it completely; perhaps the neglected duty is inconsistent with his major duty—always a temptation to neglect. On the other hand, the failure may spring from defective relationships; perhaps, not understanding his obligation, the man may think he is free to use his own discretion; perhaps his supervisor may be neglecting to guide him. There are other possibilities.

Omission to perform an entire responsibility for a period, if due to organizational cause, reveals failure to appreciate the need to designate an alternate to act during absences.

On the other hand, many failures to act may be chargeable either to defects of personnel or to unavoidable obstacles. Organization may be excellent, both in structure and in the understanding of relationships, yet because of the defects to which human nature is liable, a man may simply fail to do his duty. A particular omission may be something that just could not be helped.

2. Delay in acting. This serious defect differs only in degree from failure to act, but is probably much more prevalent. It is so easy to persuade oneself that decisions should not be made hastily. Delay in acting can infect and become characteristic of an entire enterprise. There is some reason to believe this to be one of the disadvantages suffered by an old, established enterprise as compared with a young and growing one. It certainly can be expected in an enterprise that is "overorganized."

Administration is especially exposed to this defect when organization places its reliance on action by groups or committees, or on any other form of joint action. Consultation takes time and waits upon common convenience. Overlapping responsibilities have much the same effect: each man may wait for the other to act.

On the other hand, delays may result from slack personal habits or ineffective supervision.

3. Wrong actions. Doing the wrong thing is often a defect of personnel rather than of organization; yet wrong actions can spring from an overload of work that induces hasty decisions. Wrong actions chargeable to incompetence may be the result of not adequately describing a job so that a competent man could be found to fill it.

4. Lack of quality of effort. It is difficult to determine whether administration maintains a reasonable level of competence, and lack of quality may be its most common defect. This naturally suggests lack of quality in personnel. Nevertheless, it can come also from any of the organizational causes of inadequate supervision. Lack of quality may also reflect a definition of responsibility that requires too great a diversity of duties and thereby demands too great a diversity of talent.

5. **Lack of quantity of effort.** The work a man does may be of acceptable quality, yet he may not do enough of it. This is a common defect of personnel. The most obvious cause is poor definition of responsibility. It may also come from too many stages of delegation—so great a distribution of responsibility that there is too much supervision in proportion to the actual doing. Like most other defects, it may also come from lax supervision.

More than other defects in administration, the failure to produce may result from poor morale, and poor morale may stem from organizational as well as personnel causes. Most men want to know what is expected of them and who expects it. If a man is told to do too many things that seem inconsistent with his understanding of his duties, his interest is likely to flag. Misorganization can impair morale in many ways, and lack of quantity of effort usually results.

6. **Waste effort.** Waste effort can come from not defining jobs, so that a man tries to do work that someone else is doing or should do. It can also occur if supervision fails to restrain those who like to go adventuring into other men's work.

7. **Excessive quantity of effort.** Best recognized of all administrative defects is failure to devise the simplest way of doing things. When actions must be taken jointly, the quantity of effort is usually extravagant and the waste of talent is proportionate. Since this often occurs at the higher levels of administration, it is a waste of the best talent. Overlapping responsibilities have something of the same effect. Another cause of excessive effort is failure to understand coordinate responsibilities. When the actions of one department depend upon those of another, economy of effort suffers unless both departments understand each other's problems and needs and seek prompt reconciliation whenever there is a hitch in relations.

8. **Excessive quality of effort.** Enterprise must expect to pay for effort in proportion to its quality; if quality is excessive, payment will be excessive. It is a mistake to give a job to a man whose ability exceeds its need.

While this defect can be due to faulty personnel selection, it is perhaps more likely to be due to faulty definitions of responsibility. If some duties of a job demand skill or experience disproportionate to the demands of the rest of the duties of that job, the man who fills the job must possess the qualities required for the more exacting duties. His ability will be excessive in relation to the less exacting duties. Much the same result occurs if a supervisor delegates any of the more important parts of his own responsibility.

After the defects of administration have been diagnosed, there still remain those which are traceable to organization. This further study will compare possible organizational causes with other possible causes.

Tenets of Better Organization

Said the late Harry Arthur Hopf, great management authority who formulated the organization credo presented below, "It is my conviction that if progress is to be made in organization, executives must subscribe wholeheartedly to the truth of these tenets and always act upon their implications."

1. To adhere to the substance of organization, rather than to worship the form in which it is cast
2. To view organization as a means to an end, rather than as an end in itself
3. To recognize the values inherent in improvisation, rather than to rely exclusively upon the virtues attaching to organization
4. To insure liberation of human energies, rather than their suppression or regimentation
5. To respect the authority of knowledge, rather than the authority of position
6. To strive to maintain loyalty on the part of executives to their subordinates, rather than to stress the reverse
7. To develop well-rounded and intellectually well-balanced executives, rather than one-sided and narrow specialists
8. To imbue executives with a spirit of tolerance toward one another, rather than to permit the existence of intolerance
9. To inculcate in the minds of executives the wisdom of rendering themselves dispensable, rather than of cherishing the illusion that they are indispensable
10. To sacrifice almost any other value than to injure the foundations upon which inspiring leadership rests

LEFT BAR—HUMAN RELATIONS

The second bar of the central framework of management is concerned with people—people in the organization who are managed and for whom the manager is responsible. Someone has said, "The most important person in the world to an individual is his boss." The manager may be able to make or break him, and he knows it. However, a good manager is not a "boss," but a leader whom people like to follow; he is a good manager because he practices good human relations with others. One of the major goals of efficient management is to get more work done without increasing the number of workers. Achieving this can lie partially in the improvement of human relations.

Objectives and Philosophies of Human Relations

There are two objectives for human relations: to achieve the maximum understanding of why people act the way they do and to make the greatest possible ethical use of that understanding in dealing with them. Two vastly different philosophies have evolved for approaching these objectives: the military tradition of fifty years ago and certain radical social science theories.

The traditional military method was centered on motivation through fear. It was based on the idea that people are lazy by nature and won't act unless driven to it by fear of the consequences if they don't. This system works; in the hands of a strong person it gets a lot of work done. It assures compliance, but it does not foster cooperation.

The other extreme is based on the philosophy that people want to do the right thing and that all that is necessary is to give them the opportunity.

There is a middle course which is infinitely preferable to these two extremes. It yields more work, better work, and happier work. It is harder to do well; but its increasing use in industry shows clearly that it is practical as well as theoretically sound. It involves the acceptance of four principles:

1. People differ a lot from each other and so can't be treated alike. This means that each person working in an organization is observed as he responds to praise, to reproof, to added responsibility, to assistance and requests for assistance, to easy going and rough going; then he is treated accordingly.

2. You get more and better work out of a man by helping him to feel important than you do by making him feel afraid. No force will bind persons together so firmly as helping them to feel more important. The surest way of getting a man to do what you want is to get him to want to do it; and the surest way to do this is to raise his prestige.

3. Actions result more often from habit or emotion than from logic. We must not be satisfied with observing what the other fellow does, but we have to be on the lookout for habit-conditioned and emotional

behavior. Emotional problems cannot be solved with logical solutions.

4. You have to like people to get along well with them. To be helpful to people, you must like them, and you have to be enthusiastic about people to study them enough to do a decent job under the first principle listed above.[4]

An interesting insight into the art of managing is given us by Thomas R. Reid, Director of Civic Affairs, Ford Motor Company:

I've always liked to simplify the executive function and describe it as quickly as possible by saying it is a triangle. In the lower corner of that triangle see a picture in your mind of the phrase, "Makes Judgments." All day long an executive makes judgments. He says, "yes"; he says, "no"; he says, "maybe"; he says, "I don't have enough facts, I'll let you know later." . . . That is the primary function of an executive —to make judgments.

But if an executive did nothing but make judgments, he'd be a pretty poor excuse for a real, driving, energetic sort of fellow we're looking for in business today.

So look at the other corner of that triangle now and write in "Initiates Action." It isn't enough just to make judgments that somebody else brings to you for decision—you've got to bother the other guy by sending him something to worry about. You initiate some actions which then give him a judgment to make, to decide whether what you've initiated is any good, or whether it needs changing. He gets into the act by making judgments on an action you've started.

The self-starter process of initiating action, plus the receiving process of making judgments, constitutes the main body of work of the executive.

There's one corner left on the triangle. That's the top corner where everything comes to a head. In your mind's eye write, "Gets Results" there. All your superiors—the fellows that own the stock and manage the business—care about the executive function is whether you get results. And you do or you don't.

Now put them together. You make judgments, you initiate actions, in order to get results. The only blank space left in the triangle is the white area in the center—that's the most important part of all. Let's label it, in your mind's eye, "The Field of Human Relations." Every judgment you make, every action you initiate in order to get a result as an executive must be by, through, with, and for, people.

There's no way to get around it; you move through the field of human relations in order to get any results as an executive. The fellow that overlooks that fact is doomed for failure in business. That fellow that learns it early is off to a running start to success.[5]

Three Ways to Lead and When to Use Them

Democratic leadership—in which the leader draws ideas and suggestions from his group by discussion and consultation. Group members are encouraged to take part in setting policy. The leader's job is largely that of moderator.

Autocratic leadership—in which the leader assumes full responsibility for all action. He mainly seeks obedience from the group in following his orders. He determines policy and considers decision-making to be a one-man operation—he being the man.

Free-rein leadership—in which the leader is more or less an information booth. He plays down his role in the group's activity. He's on hand mainly to provide materials and information, with a minimum of control.[6]

Psychologists and sociologists haven't been content to describe the different types; they have also compared and evaluated them and have generally decided that democratic leadership is best. But autocratic leadership will be successful in certain situations where other types fail; and free-rein leadership, under the right conditions, can produce more successful results than either of the other kinds, despite the fact that it is usually written off as useless. So let's stop talking about the "best" method and begin to talk about the "most appropriate" method. Then the emphasis is where it belongs—on fitting the approach to the conditions, not to some abstract, arbitrary rules. The three approaches are not mutually exclusive. Note how Mr. X, a successful superintendent, uses them:

He *consults* (using the democratic method) with his five foremen on the best way to push a special order through their departments with a minimum upset to regular production.

He *directs* (using the autocratic method) his secretary to get a report on all overtime worked on the special order each Monday before noon until the work is done.

He *suggests* (using the free-rein method) to his assistant that it would be a good idea to figure out ways in which they can handle special orders a little more smoothly in the future, leaving details of planning to his assistant.

Why did he use the method he did in each case? Here are the guides he used.

Rank or job knowledge. The job a man does helps us decide which approach will get results. When Mr. X discussed the special order with the foremen, he was acknowledging their specialized knowledge and their status. He didn't consult with his secretary about getting overtime reports, but he undoubtedly would consult her on such matters as a new filing system or a method of scheduling his appointments, matters about which she is expert.

Personality. In general, you will find that certain types of personality respond best to certain types of leadership. The aggressive, hostile person does better under an autocratic leader. His latent hostility must be firmly channeled to direct his work to constructive ends. The insecure person, who tends to be dependent on his superior, also does better under the firmer hand of the autocratic leader.

The aggressive, cooperative type will work better under democratic or free-rein leadership. He will head in the right direction when he's on his own.

The individualist, the solo player, is usually more productive under the free-rein type of leadership if he knows his job.

Situation or problem. Any critical situation calling for fast, decisive action can usually be handled best by autocratic methods.

When the leader faces circumstances he doesn't understand or problems he can't solve, then democratic consultation and discussion with members of the group is quite logical.

Type of group. For stable groups that can work well together, democratic leadership is most effective. A shop superintendent has five foremen, old line men who have learned their jobs from the ground up. Each is capable of taking sound, independent action. They work well together, without friction.

For groups that are essentially untrained and undisciplined, autocratic leadership may be best. This is the kind of group you may find in a new department in a rapidly expanding plant. The leader must exercise firm and decisive authority to weld the group rapidly into a producing unit.

For the highly trained or professional staff, free-rein leadership is preferable. Tool designers are a good example. They work much of the time on their own. Some cross-communication is needed among them, but the leader doesn't have to provide much guidance, since knowledge of methods and techniques required for their work is their stock in trade.

Test yourself on the problem in Table 1. Don't try to give the "best" answer. Give the one that seems natural or logical to you—what you would do if faced with the same problem.

TABLE 1. How Flexible a Leader Are You?[7]

	Democratic	Autocratic	Free-Rein
1. Which leadership technique would you favor in dealing with:			
a. Timid people?	_____	_____	_____
b. Hostile, aggressive individuals?	_____	_____	_____
c. The brilliant prima donna?	_____	_____	_____
d. A man who is strongly co-operative?	_____	_____	_____
e. The scatterbrain?	_____	_____	_____
2. Which technique would you use to plan and inaugurate changes affecting your own subordinates?	_____	_____	_____
3. Under which technique are communications held to a minimum?	_____	_____	_____
4. Which is best for leading a highly trained group?	_____	_____	_____
5. If you were leading a newly-organized group:			
a. Which technique would you use to get across your orientation information?	_____	_____	_____
b. Which would you use to help them adjust to one another?	_____	_____	_____
c. Which technique is best suited to bring out the capabilities of the group?	_____	_____	_____
6. In which leadership technique can you substitute group pressure for discipline?	_____	_____	_____
7. Which technique would you choose:			
a. To whip up group solidarity to a new high?	_____	_____	_____
b. To replace competitiveness among group mem-			

TABLE 1.   How Flexible a Leader Are You? (*Continued*)

	Democratic	Autocratic	Free-Rein
bers by a spirit of coopera- tion?			
c. To make the best use of the brainpower of the group?			
d. To replace apathy with interest?			

RIGHT BAR—COMMUNICATIONS

The third bar in the management framework is effective communications with all those in the organization. Communication is sharing meaning: ideas are converted into symbols in the mind of a "transmitter"; they are then "sent" in a variety of ways to a "receiver," who converts the symbol into an idea as he happens to see it. A Dutch management consultant named Luijk, who studied the executive working pattern, found that 60 percent of an executive's day is spent communicating. Dr. Hugh F. Seabury, of the State University of Iowa, puts the figure as high as 75 percent.[8]

Communicating is done through actions, spoken words, and printed or written symbols, and may be conscious or unconscious. Meaning is shared in business through physical actions— smiles, frowns, a shrug of the shoulders, a red face; through changes in habits, such as coming in early and staying late; as well as through talk, graphs, and written forms of communication. We communicate *across* to integrate plans, coordinate work, compare methods or results. We communicate *down* to inform, motivate, direct, redirect, evaluate, or keep in touch. We communicate *up* to report progress and problems, offer solutions, "let them know we're here."

Where do all the misunderstandings, flare-ups, foul-ups, and hold-ups come from? The answer isn't easy, and it doesn't come in one piece. Primarily, the answer will be found with the senders and receivers of communications, rather than with the media. Various investigators have made suggestions for coping with these problems. Here is a cross-section of these suggestions.

Rudolph Flesch in his series of books on communication urges the "transmitter" to (1) use short words, short sentences, short paragraphs; (2) pick a single main idea theme and build around it; (3) personalize the ideas: use names, places; use "you" and "I"; and (4) be liberal with examples, illustrations, "for instances."

Norbert Wiener in the area of cybernetics urges: Insist on feedback—be sure your message got through by getting a receipt. In face-to-face communicating, this means questioning and listening.

Count Korzybski makes the following suggestions:

1. Guard against the inadequacy of words to provide total description. Words are symbols that represent meaning, but they do not give a complete description.
2. Beware of overgeneralizing. There are differences between any two things. Which are we talking about?
3. Be specific about time. "Things" change. When we talk about a company, do we mean as it is today, as it was in 1950, or in 1940?
4. Be careful in discussing things that both "transmitter" and "receiver" cannot see or touch. What is meant when one reports that a machine "is in good condition" or that it "broke down"?
5. Be most careful if neither communicant can see or touch what is being discussed. Abstract ideas are very difficult to delineate.[9]

To these suggestions may be added a few others. Be sure that your use of a word helps the listener or reader get the particular meaning you intend. One word can have several meanings. Be sure that you are using the proper word for the specific public you are addressing. People understand words as *their backgrounds* dictate. Each word-symbol has a special private nondictionary meaning for each of us. S. I. Hayakawa has pointed out the importance of self-images in communications. One's self-image is constructed over a life span. It may or may not be accurate, but the individual does not want to change it. If your message attacks the receiver's self-image, he'll reject what you say—he'll ignore or deny or discredit it, or refuse to try to understand it. In *Death of a Salesman,* Willie Lohman was brought face to face with the fact that he was no longer a star salesman. He couldn't change his image; he refused to look at the record. He accused the younger salesman of short cuts and unethical practices. Part of a man's frame of reference is his image of himself; treat it tenderly.

The self-image idea allows us to swing to some ideas generated by Kurt Lewin and "group dynamics" that relate to communications: (1) When working with others, think in terms of what *they* want; what they *feel* is important. Being totally concerned with what *you* want may put you on a wavelength all your own. (2) Lead, and accept leadership, objectively. Be neither hard-boiled nor soft-headed. Recognize the barriers of rank, vocabulary, and background, and work constructively and considerately *with* people to reach a common meaning.

An all too common attitude of executives in regard to communicating "important information" is illustrated by the following incident related by a well-known industrial relations executive, Alexander R. Heron:

One corporation executive in an intimate conference rejected the idea of encouraging, or even permitting, foremen to answer employee questions about such things as company finances, for instance. Did he not want employees to ask questions and obtain information of this kind? Of course, he did. But he explained that his corporation's capital structure, for one thing, was too complicated for a foreman to understand or to explain correctly; "I welcome such questions from employees," he said, "but I want them to bring their questions to me, not to some foreman."

Another member of the group asked him, "Can you explain this complex capital structure so that the employee can understand it?"

"Yes, of course," he answered.

"Then why can't you explain it so that the foreman can understand it?"

The corporation executive started to answer, then laughed. Six months later he was committed to a program of sharing information with employees through the channel of the regular line organization—even the complicated financial information.[10]

That gossip through the "grapevine" can play a constructive role in company communications is the principal message contained in the following excerpt from a book by Herbert A. Simon:

A great deal of the informal communication in any organization is far less deliberate than the activities of cliques or even the conversations of executives who lunch together. In addition to these there is the great mass of communication that goes under the head of "gossip." In most organizations the "grapevine" probably plays, on the whole, a constructive role. Its chief disadvantages are, first, that it discourages frankness, since confidential remarks may be spread about; second, that the information transmitted by the grapevine is often inaccurate. On the other hand, in addition to transmitting information that no one has thought to transmit formally, the grapevine is valuable as a barometer of "public opinion" in the organization. If the administrator listens to it, it apprises him of the topics that are subjects of interest to organization members, and their attitudes towards these topics. Even for this latter purpose, of course, the grapevine needs to be supplemented by other channels of information.[11]

The higher the executive in the chain of command, the more remote he often is, or feels he is, from the operations level of his organization. President Eisenhower has been quoted by Foreign Correspondent Louis P. Lochner as thanking Mr. Lochner for bringing certain information about the conduct of his troops to his attention. Mr. Eisenhower said:

You know, there is nobody so lonely as the man on top. He cannot personally attend to everything and must rely on the men below to keep him informed. But how difficult it is for him to learn the full truth!

Some have an ulterior motive in not reporting all the facts. Others believe the man on top is so burdened with a multiplicity of cares that they do not want him to receive additional unpleasant news.

Still others fear the man on top cannot take it and will "break" the informant. Thank you for giving me an unvarnished account.[12]

QUESTIONS AND PROBLEMS

1. Describe your understanding of the "holy three."
2. How would you go about using the Ten Commandments of Good Organization?
3. How can you judge effective organization? What are the causes of poor organization and solutions?
4. What is your reaction to the tenets of organization as set out by Harry Hopf?
5. What is the place of human relations in a business organization?
6. Write a short case (two hundred words) describing a situation where good human relations were involved.
7. Peter Drucker has referred to communications as the number one problem of management. Explain this statement.
8. Can there be communications without words? Explain. Demonstrate.
9. Is it true that the higher a manager is in the organization, the easier is his problem of communication? Explain.
10. Which is better, written or oral communication? Why?

REFERENCE NOTES

[1] Source unknown.
[2] American Management Association.
[3] Alvin Brown, "Judging the Effectiveness of Organizations," *Advanced Management*, January, 1955, pp. 13-15.

[4] Earl P. Strong, "Organization Management in the Atomic Age," Part V, *The Pennsylvania Business Survey*, November, 1962, p. 8.

[5] Thomas R. Reid, "Management Is a Triangle," *Manpower Management*, General Foods Corp., 1955.

[6] Auren Uris, "How Good a Leader Are You?," *Factory Management and Maintenance*, July, 1951.

[7] Earl P. Strong, *op. cit.*, p. 9.

[8] William R. Davidson and James H. Healey, *Power Management*, Allegheny Power System and its Subsidiaries, 1959, p. 147.

[9] Alfred Korzybski, *Science and Sanity*, Institute of General Semantics, 1948.

[10] Alexander R. Heron, *Sharing Information with Employees*, Stanford University Press, 1942.

[11] Herbert A. Simon, *Administrative Behavior*, Macmillan, 1947, pp. 161–162.

[12] Louis P. Lochner, *Always the Unexpected*, Macmillan, 1956, pp. 281.

4

THE KNOWLEDGES AND SKILLS OF MANAGEMENT

THE SUPPORTING POWER WHEEL (Rear Wheel)

Every organized activity has its "wheel" of technical knowledges and skills which the manager must understand or have access to. A business organization will have such divisions as administrative, factory and production, sales, personnel, purchasing, financial, building and space, office, and research. A government agency may have divisions including controllership, procurement, claims and registration, and processing. A chamber of commerce may have such divisions as retail promotion, industrial development, tourist attractions, urban redevelopment, transportation, and regional planning. The manager need not necessarily be expert in all the phases or divisions of his activity, but he should have the courage to realize he does not know everything and be willing to turn to others for information.

His main job is the *coordination* of these various divisions of information and technical knowledge so that all phases of activity are given the attention they deserve when they need it.

The terms "organize," "organizing," and "organization" will be used a great deal in this book. "Organization" will be used to designate a bar in the framework, "organizing" as one of the administrative skills, and "organize" with reference to the area of technical know-how.

Coordinating and Synchronizing the Parts

In a study made several years ago by Dun & Bradstreet of the reasons for failure of 9,162 businesses, it was found that 96 percent of them failed because of incompetent or inexperienced management. Subsequent studies have revealed similar findings. Of particular note is the fact that 13.5 percent of the businesses failed because the management had an unbalanced experience— that is, their managers were not well grounded in the various areas of business, such as sales, purchasing, finance, personnel, and office procedures. From every study made of the situation, it would seem imperative, then, that anyone who takes on the management of a business should thoroughly understand all its functions.

While it is true that we are living in an age of specialization, there is a welcome in any organization for a person with an overall view, an eye for the goal, an ability to coordinate the activities of others toward a major purpose. In administration he is often called an "administrative generalist." A good manager is usually a "generalist," and he knows how to weigh the relative importance of each operation in the organization.

As organizations grow large and problems become complex, there is of necessity increased specialization. Activities are divided and subdivided and certain people give concentrated attention to circumscribed activities. They become experts. At the same time, the physical and intellectual distance between the specialized work of each individual becomes greater. If they are to "keep up" on their subject, experts will find little time for general considerations. It is the responsibility of the administrative generalist to blend the divergent views of experts into a workable pattern. He must see to it that each expert adjusts his specialized work to the major purpose of the organization. In order to do this, he must look at things, not from the standpoint of his own specialized knowledge, but in the light of the total program.

A good organization, then, either has at its head a single manager, qualified in all the subject areas of management, or, in the case of very large companies, a single administrator who delegates the management responsibilities to subject-matter specialists who carry out the functions specified by him. The number of breakdowns within a subject-matter area depends entirely upon the size of the business and its organizational structure.

Integration of All Subject Areas

There are a number of reasons why subject areas should be well integrated. First, good integration will help to meet competition better since improved organization will result in more effective production. Next, through proper integration greater service can be rendered to customers, while more efficient production will yield greater profits.

The successful manager must become proficient in the integration of all subject areas, whether or not he likes them equally. Some businessmen say that they do not like the financial side of their businesses, that they do not like figures. But they will *have* to like figures if they are to remain in business and be successful.

It is a mistaken idea that small business is essentially different from big business. The subject areas are identical in both. The difference is one of degree, scope, and volume of business. It is contended, therefore, that a person who owns and operates his own business, or who manages the business of another, must be a better all-round businessman than the manager of a large business. This throws upon the small businessman the heavy responsibility of constant study and effort to understand management in all its aspects. Failure results when he merely opens the doors of his business to the public, hoping that customers will come to him and that management will "take care of itself."

Authority, Responsibility, and Delegation

The one-man-band type of manager is a common phenomenon in American business. He is invariably so busy that it is difficult to get an appointment with him, and harder still to keep his attention. The telephone interrupts; people run in and out with papers, problems, questions. His attention is dispersed over a host of minor details.

Strangely enough, the one-man-band executive always sees himself as a student of organization and a practitioner of delegation. He proves it by displaying elaborate organization charts in handsome bindings. He doesn't seem to realize that delegation on paper is only theory, that true delegation involves people.

Every executive is confronted daily with many situations in which he has to ask himself, "Should I do it myself or should I delegate it?" Students of the field of management say the answer to this question is a major indication of whether the executive is able or otherwise. It has been said about delegation:

The successful executive does nothing himself that anybody of lower rank can do competently. He delegates his authority and reserves for himself: (1) only those matters which he alone is capable of handling; (2) the responsibility for coordination; (3) the task and the time to consider ways in which his company might be doing better and his company making more money; and (4) the task and the time to develop his department heads.[1]

These four factors are the actual keynotes to the success of a business executive. All managers need to consider them in carrying out their daily business routine, and should give them special consideration in developing others in their organizations.

Before a manager can delegate, however, he must have accepted the philosophy that he can multiply his own effectiveness only through the process of delegation. Authorities agree that whether an executive will delegate depends on three factors: (1) Does top management encourage him to delegate? (2) Has he accepted the need to delegate? (3) Has he developed his department heads so that they are competent and willing to take delegation?

In considering the first point, we are told that most executives have had to work on their own attitudes so that they could accept the necessity for delegation. Even able men have such erroneous attitudes as:

"I can do it better."

"I must keep my hands on everything."

"Management looks to me to know all the answers."

"It is traditional for me to do this."

"I must protect my power, prestige, and security."

"I must be careful not to work myself out of a job."

The successful executive has learned that these attitudes are stumbling blocks to personal and company progress.

The most frequent explanation for failure to delegate is: "The man down the line is not competent." If he is not competent, then why isn't he? The following reasons are often given:

"I (or somebody before me) selected the wrong man for the job."

"He is too new on the job for this assignment."

"He doesn't have the technical knowledge."

"He needs training."

"He is too busy, so I'll do it myself."

"He does not take to responsibility."

"He may not handle it properly, and we can't afford to make mistakes."

Each of these can be a valid reason for not delegating, but

what can be done to bring those upon whom management must depend to accept more responsibility so that top management can have time to handle those matters which it alone is capable of handling? The answer is *training*.

One of the most effective methods for management training is coaching on day-to-day assignments. Such coaching is usually done by the executive in close cooperation with his assistant or assistants, and is usually confined to a specific period of time each day. In one organization the executives who are coaching junior executives set aside a period of one hour each day, during which the junior executives watch the senior executive operate. Likewise, the senior executive observes the junior executive carrying out his regular duties, as well as those which the senior has given him to perform. By self-criticism, as well as mutual criticism, development takes place, confidence is built, and ultimate efficiencies in management operation are gained.

The future of management development, therefore, depends largely on the attitude that company executives take toward the process of delegation, for management will be effective only to the extent that delegation is practiced.

THE SUPPORTING GUIDE WHEEL (Front Wheel)

The area of the manager's administrative skills may be designated as "the guide wheel." These skills were first identified in the year 1907 by Hopf, a German management expert, but were not widely recognized or adopted until relatively recent times. They are: (1) planning, (2) organizing, (3) motivating, (4) directing, and (5) controlling. They are used and practiced by a manager to solve problems that occur in the technical know-how area (rear wheel). For example, an organization proposes to undertake a promotional campaign. The problem is to devise the most successful campaign it has ever had. The solution is to *plan* the campaign thoroughly, *organize* it effectively, *direct* wisely the people involved in carrying it out, and constructively *control* the campaign at all points. In practice, these skills are used by accident in most cases. To be thoroughly effective, however, they should be developed and practiced purposefully.

Planning

Planning is the study of the future, immediate or distant, and the evolution of a series of courses of action to meet it. Each course of action will synthesize considerations of past performances and/or occurrences, the present situation, and a forecast of the future.

Henri Fayol, the management pioneer, said, "The preparation of the plan of action is one of the most difficult and most important matters of every business and brings into play all departments and all functions, especially the management function." Planning is predominantly a management function, but there are occasions in the normal operation of a business when the lowest-echelon employee may have to pause in his physical efforts to decide upon a course of action. There is scarcely a business activity that does not call for planning in some degree.

The scope of planning is organization-wide. It includes such basic topics as the formulation and clarification of objectives and policies, the determination of essential programs, the development of procedures for operations, and the resolution of essential functions.

Organizing

Organizing is the process of *integrating* into a coordinated structure the activities required to achieve the objectives of an enterprise; *staffing* this structure with qualified, competent personnel; and *supplying* them with the physical factors necessary to perform their functions.

There are three phases in organizing a business or any form of association.

The first is the formulation of an organization structure. This is an assembly, with each part in its proper place, of the phases of work considered necessary to fulfill the objectives of the enterprise. The grouping of the separately defined functions into an integral unit, frequently crystallized as an organization chart, is the first phase of organizing.

The second phase is the selection of competent personnel who will satisfy the main specifications for each position represented in the organization structure.

The third stage of organizing is providing each individual with the physical factors—tools, materials, equipment—needed to perform satisfactorily the functions of his position.

With the competent manning of a well-planned structure and with each employee provided with the necessary tools to discharge his obligations, organization becomes the means for effective group action.

Motivating

Motivating is the process of indoctrinating personnel with unity of purpose and the need to maintain continuous, harmonious relationships. Getting individual employees to subordinate their personal objectives to the objectives of the organization, and encouraging every member of the group to cooperate with every other member, results in a general willingness to "hear the other fellow out," to get expressions of opinion on pertinent matters from one's associates, and to engage in cooperative group action.

Organization can provide the framework for effective group relationships, and control can contribute to cooperation; but a basic willingness of all members to cooperate must be present. It is the function of management to create and perpetuate the conditions which foster this mental attitude.

Directing

Directing consists of instructing people in the detailed operations necessary to reach the organization's objectives. Basically, directing consists of two elements: (1) instructing people in what they are to do and (2) ordering them to do it.

In an operating situation, the factors are the leader, the people being led, and the physical and emotional content of the situation. Before direction can be effective, the specific situation must present a favorable climate for successful operations. In direction, then, it is necessary to review the planning that has been done; to look over the organization structure to determine the specific unit in which the work is to be accomplished; to review the job description so that the proper worker can be selected; and to review the job standards for that particular job. Direction involves preparing and issuing effective instructions and methods to develop subordinates, and maintaining an adequate program of three-way communications between the leader and the led, and among those at the follower level.

Motivating and directing may be summarized as the integrating of personal objectives with the primary service objectives of the organization. Coordinating is the facilitative function that aids in integrating the four basic functions. It is aimed at increased efficiency and effectiveness; but it also involves control, and control is likely to be considered by employees as antagonistic to good human relations and so it affects morale. The larger the organization, the more management must work through others in order to motivate and communicate effectively with people.

Controlling

Controlling is the process of regulating the various factors in an enterprise according to the requirements of its plans. It may take many forms. Regulatory devices include policies, organization charts, budgetary controls, standard operating procedures, and quality controls. Regulation may be oral, written, or a combination of both. Controlling sees that the directions of management are properly communicated and are carried out within the time allotted for performance. It includes the removal of interferences with the operation of business plans and the adjustment of conditions to prevent a recurrence of an unfavorable event or to perpetuate the occurrence of a favorable event. Control is concerned with results.

INFLUENCE OF MANAGEMENT LEVEL ON THE ADMINISTRATIVE SKILLS

At the higher levels of management, the principal managerial skill is planning; organizing is of secondary importance. At the first-line supervision level, however, the most important management function is controlling, with motivating a close second. Not only are planning and organizing of lesser importance, but they are of a different character, since the major decisions affecting them have already been made at the higher level.

QUESTIONS AND PROBLEMS

1. Is it true that the technical know-how in each organization will have differences? Why?
2. What is the job of the department manager in terms of the technical area of his own specialization? The job of the division manager? The job of the general manager?
3. Why is coordination of the parts so important to the success of the organization?
4. Who makes a good organization? What makes a good organization? Why?
5. Why is delegation so vital to all phases of the organization?
6. Why is delegation so poorly practiced? How can it be corrected?
7. Can the administrative skills be practiced without application to a problem arising in the technical area? Explain.

8. How do you use the administrative skills in your daily work and routine?

REFERENCE NOTE

[1] Earl P. Strong, "Organization Management in the Atomic Age," *The Pennsylvania Business Survey,* Pennsylvania State University, July, 1962, pp. 10–11.

READING REFERENCE

Newman, William H., *Administrative Action,* 2nd ed., Prentice-Hall, 1963.

5

THE MANAGER AND HIS PERSONAL CHARACTERISTICS

PERSONAL CHARACTERISTICS OF EFFECTIVE MANAGERS

A number of research studies have been made to determine the qualifications of effective managers. These have been summarized under three main headings: (1) the intellect, (2) the emotions, and (3) relations with others. Each area involves a number of personal characteristics that take certain modes of expression. These are listed in Table 2.

METHODS FOR DEVELOPING A MANAGER

No one can train another to be a manager. One must train himself. Here are some techniques generally accepted for helping people develop themselves.

Individual Methods

In coaching a subordinate, let him observe how decisions are made and operations are carried out. Not that he is going to operate in the same way; but at least he will pick up some of the tricks learned by people in the past. The coaching technique is very popular.

A second method is the use of an understudy or apprentice, who will actually share his superior's work. He is on the job, not

TABLE 2. Leadership Qualifications[1]

Main Areas	Personal Traits	Modes of Expression
1. Intellectual capacity	Perception	Interest, observation, listening, questioning, reading
	Imagination	Originality, vision, planning, creativity
	Judgment	Common sense, understanding, intelligence, foresight
	Expression	Oral, written
2. Emotional stability	Drive	Motivation, initiative, enthusiasm, ambition (industriousness), carefulness (accuracy), endurance
	Stability	Self-sufficiency, self-discipline, perseverance, adaptability, decisiveness, dependability, maturity, poise, high standards
	Integrity	Moral, intellectual, financial
	Courage	Risk-taking, faith in God, faith in self, faith in others
3. Relations with others	Friendliness	Cheerfulness, sincerity, tolerance, respect, trust, participation, courtesy, helpfulness
	Sensitivity to others	Weaknesses, strengths, wants
	Authority	Prestige, speed of decision, definiteness of decision, aggressiveness, delegation
	Responsibility to	Organization, superiors, peers, subordinates
	Inspiration to accomplishment	Discipline, teamwork, self-development, devotion to organization, devotion to leader

just for an hour or two, as with coaching, but for a full day at a time. He listens to all telephone calls, all conversations. He should be allowed to make some decisions, which should be followed so that he will gain confidence. He should also be permitted to make occasional mistakes, for only in that way will he learn.

Another development method is job rotation. A person circulates throughout the organization for a year, eighteen months, or two years, spending a month or two in every department. This achieves several results. First, it gives the trainee an over-all view of the whole organization. Second, it will help the company decide where he can be of greatest use to the organization. The method will work less well if the employee does not know why he is being shifted about. Make sure that he understands that it is for training purposes.

Permanent transfer to a given department within the organization is another development technique.

Assigning the trainee a work project is still another. His performance is observed and evaluated. How well does he plan? How does he organize his solution to the problem? How does he carry it out? A person can be checked very quickly on his present ability, if not on his potential, in this manner.

Having a trainee join professional societies is also useful. Here he has a chance to hear good speeches and participate in discussion groups.

Developing his reading with a recommended list of books is still another training device.

Public speaking engagements, public appearances, and participation in community activities are all usable training methods.

Giving him an opportunity to teach is also valuable training, for to teach a subject, one has to know something about it.

Evaluation of the trainee is an important part of the training process. The evaluator sits down and observes a person managing or taking command. There is one obstacle here, however. A man who is willing to be observed probably is a good manager to start with. The person who really needs the help and should be observed is the fellow who will not want it.

Counseling differs from coaching in that it involves actually working with people and pointing out their weak points. It takes courage to call a man in and say, "Look, you seem to have a problem getting along with people. I've been watching you for six months now, and you've been fighting with everybody you work with. What's the matter?" The man needs counseling; maybe the trouble is so deep he needs psychiatric help. Unless something is done, he may be dropped by the wayside. The good manager has got to draw this to his attention, no matter how unpleasant the task.

Group Methods

Several training methods involve developing more than one person at a time.

In the case study method a problem is assigned to a group

and each member is asked to read and think about it. Some time later the group reconvenes under the chairmanship of one of the men, who acts as leader. It's amazing the amount of discussion that can come out of such a group. The pooling of varying experiences and personalities is impressive; ten different people may have accumulated as much as two hundred years of experience. As a consequence of group thinking, a person may go back to his job with an idea that is worth much to him and his organization.

Other group techniques include conference leadership, in which employees are allowed to take over in order to develop leadership ability; role-playing; problem-solving; and university or college courses.

Committee work is a training method that has perhaps been overworked. But if well planned and executed, it can, of course, be of valuable help to management. Let the manager present real, substantial problems to his committee with the admonition, "Look, here is a problem we have. You represent a cross-section of our group. Now, talk it over among you, and give me your ideas. I need help." Such an approach may result in real aid to the manager. Unfortunately, however, the group is often not given the chance to consider a problem. The manager merely says, "Well, fellows, I have a problem, a real problem here. And here is my decision; this is the way we are going to do it!"

THE MANAGER AS A LEADER

Growth in management rests with the individual. It comes from *wanting* to grow. If the want exists and is coupled with a reasonable degree of intelligence, the process of growth will continue, and its rewards will follow.

Wanting starts with *belief*—belief in self, belief in people, belief in the value of the work to be done. Wanting is spurred by curiosity—a ceaseless, unending impulsion to seek out the better way, to find the new combination of people, of ideas, of machines and processes. The growing manager is impelled (not compelled) to do the job at hand the best way he knows and to range beyond that job, in his mind, in search for a still better way.

The growing manager's wanting is fortified by patience—empathy, if you will. He recognizes that his role is not *to do*, but *to see that it is done.* He works through people, reasonable people. What is reasonable to the manager today may not appear reasonable to others just yet. His willingness to be patient is based on understanding and respect for others. It is also based on a willingness to concede that his own job might have been done better. He might have taught more clearly; he might have led more enthusiastically; he might have planned more clearly.

To be an effective manager, then, one must possess a desire that is based on belief, spurred by curiosity, and made acceptable to others by an insightful patience.

A man of these qualities soon grows beyond routine or "operative" work. His wanting takes him out of reach of his machine or desk job. His knowledge is applied now to *managing* work rather than to *doing* it.

MANAGING SITUATIONS AND PEOPLE

Good management, however, depends not merely on the manager's personal characteristics and abilities. It also depends on (1) the situation and (2) the people in the situation.

The Situation

Name the ten greatest leaders you can think of, then mentally transfer each of them to the situation of one of the others. How well would Moses have done at the Battle of Waterloo? Could Albert Schweitzer run General Motors? Or could Charles Wilson have succeeded in the shoes of Buddha?

These questions sound ridiculous, and they are. But they are no more ridiculous than moving a manager from one type of activity to another without considering how he and the new situation will interact.

The People in the Situation

If this man seems right for a particular situation, consider his reaction to the man to whom he will report. Will they see eye to eye? How about the men reporting to the new manager? How will they get along? Are they new in their jobs? If so, is the new manager qualified to carry more than his share of the load? Is the new leader a "man's man" leading women? Is he a Northerner among Southerners? A big city boy in the country? It is good to have balanced teams and to knock the rough edges off by mixing things up a bit. But the difference between mixing and improper placement may be disastrous.

All three must be considered: the situation, the people in the situation, and the manager himself. To determine executive qualifications, we must decide what is required of a leader in a given situation with specific people. Then the man with the desire, the know-how, *and* the specific qualifications that the situation and people demand has executive qualifications. *That* man has the best chance of getting results.

TYPES OF LEADERSHIP

Several common types of leadership have been recognized and identified:

The autocratic leader. Doesn't "spoil" employees by praising them. Checks up constantly. He does the thinking; they do the work. Distrusts initiative. Work is done by commands—his commands.

Effect upon subordinates: Production under the hard-boiled leader is fair. It slips when he is not there in person to do the commanding. No one sticks his neck out. There is buck-passing and friction, "back-stabbing," lack of cooperation.

The Dutch uncle or paternalistic leader. He has taken authority personally. All work is done "for him." He is the source of all work standards. Those standards change as his mood changes. He wants people to be dependent. He wants a loyal and happy "family." He swaps his benevolence for the group's "loyalty" or dependence.

Effect upon subordinates: Production is fairly high as long as he is there to say what he likes. The group is passive, submissive, sheeplike. Little is done by members of the group to improve themselves. A few sense the "I'll be benevolent if you are dependent" theme and bitterly resent it.

The free-rein leader. He was a technician and a good one. He buries himself in his paper work. He sets no clear goals, makes no clean decisions. Avoids any sort of close relationship with his people—"They might take advantage of it." He doesn't direct. He is incapable of commanding. He feels if he lets things go, problems will disappear.

Effect upon subordinates: Productivity and morale are at rock bottom. The work is sloppy, the output low. Lack of direction has produced anarchy. No one knows what to do, what to expect. In this situation, they are not a "group"; they are individuals assembled in one place. There is no theme or goal around which to rally.

The goal-centered or consultative leader. He knows that

the means to reach the goal are people. He encourages and helps his people grow on the job. He is not democratic in the "majority rule" sense, but, *when it is possible,* he develops participation and shares decision-making with his people. Responsibilities are clear. Standards are firm, written, and understood. Praise and criticism are based on the standards, not on his personal feelings.

Effect upon subordinates: Of the four types, he produces highest quality, quantity, morale, and group cohesiveness. The identifying feature of the group is their ability to carry on without the leader. He has more time for managing, needs to spend less time "fire fighting." More members of this group develop and are promoted.

Probably most leaders exhibit characteristics of all the above types of leadership at one time or another. Every leader is probably autocratic at certain times, or on his favorite subject, or with respect to certain subordinates; goal-centered or consultative at other times, on problems with which he is only generally familiar, or with subordinates he likes and respects; and perhaps uses the "free-rein" or "Dutch-uncle" techniques on still other occasions. Most leaders, however, tend toward one of the four types of leadership; they use it more often than the other types.

ETHICS AND THE MANAGER

Most managers are not students of business ethics, but regard themselves as behaving in an ethical manner. Yet when it comes to determining what is "right" or "wrong" business conduct in a particular situation, heated arguments can be generated among equally sincere people.

Much of the difficulty arises out of the fact that many cultural influences have contributed to our "business ideals," which may be defined as the moral values of the society as they affect business activity.

The complex of moral systems that we have inherited has been outlined by Samuel H. Miller, Dean of the Harvard Divinity School, as follows:

The Hebraic culture, based on the Ten Commandments, with emphasis on the group in total "covenant"

The Christian system, based on the Beatitudes, with emphasis on redemption of the individual born into the Kingdom

The Medieval way of life, based on penance, with emphasis on the future life

The Renaissance culture, based on the individual and his freedom

The Industrial Revolution, based on the technical application of science to production and distribution

The scientific approach, based on the empirical method and the reign of law[2]

The combined influences of these various systems have resulted in "standards of business conduct" which are somewhat unstable and shifting. When an individual tries to be ethical, he has a more difficult task than is commonly assumed, owing to the fact that he cannot choose simply between "good" and "bad," but may have to decide among various "goods" or lesser "bads" as determined by one or more sets of influences.

Ethics is not a set of rules or a code or regulations imposed by authority. The ethical man is one who sees reality, respects it, discloses it, and fulfills it. As stated by Dean Miller in the article cited above,

He does not import it, like a foreign flavor for a domestic product. ... If it be true that the ethical is built into reality at every level, then our task is to uncover the peculiar nature of it at each level. The secular interpretation of this nature would be that man makes the most of his world when he is in accord with reality and fulfills its possibilities. The religious interpretation is that God's will is done when man relates himself to the task of bringing Creation to its fullest expression.[3]

Thus an ethical manager must have regard, not only for the realities of transforming natural resources and raw materials into usable products, but also for the potential fulfillment of persons. The more the manager contributes to the opportunity for people to fulfill themselves, the more they accomplish, and with energy, enthusiasm, and an *esprit de corps*. The less fulfilled they are as persons, the less has the manager recognized the realities of the relationships among people, and the more the work suffers.

In any well-managed business firm, and throughout some whole industries, standards of ethical conduct tend to emerge, through the free association of leaders and the manner in which their actions are perceived. They may result in what are known as organization or industry standards of business conduct. Such standards tend to exist whether or not they are formally recognized as such. Ideally, they should be related to the objective of the firm.

High standards of conduct common to a group of managers in a company have important practical values for the individual manager, the company, the industry, and the public. Such values have been summarized by Professor Ralph C. Davis, as follows:

1. They foster the development of a mutuality of confidence within the business organization, since they facilitate the determination of proper business activity with due regard for the rights of all concerned.

2. They facilitate the determination of courses of business action that will permit the achievement of business objectives without danger of the loss of public confidence and patronage.

3. They facilitate the prompt, amicable adjustment of differences between individuals or groups within the industry or concern, by providing a body of criteria governing proper conduct to which assent has been secured previously.

4. They facilitate the preservation of the conditions that are necessary for equality of opportunity in business based on individual abilities and qualifications.[4]

UNDERSTANDING EMPLOYEES

That a good manager must meet with those who work for him on their own grounds is aptly stated by Professor Paul Pigors of the Massachusetts Institute of Technology:

Often executives, uncomfortably aware of disunity between themselves and their employees, call out: "Let's get together on this." Such a plea usually means: "Come over here and look at this thing from my point of view. Get behind me and let's pull together." But why should an employee, especially if he is suspicious, respond to any such invitation?

When communication between executives and employees is really a meeting of minds, it occurs at a place remote from the chosen habitat of most top officials. The location preferred by the typical V.I.P. is the seclusion of his office. There he is carefully insulated from the wintry blasts of criticism that circulate so freely in the worker's world.

The desire to be so insulated is wholly human. Most of us would achieve it if we could. Sharing this feeling as we do, we easily recognize that it is smarter not to tell the Boss what he does not want to hear. If his whole immediate environment is ruled by this simple maxim, the Boss can remain in what amounts to a mentally air-conditioned room. But if he is really interested in communication, he will have to open his door from time to time and walk out toward the world where employees live. Then he will have some chance to get together with them on their own ground. He can, at least, go halfway to meet them.

When an executive starts to do this, he usually finds that he underestimated the distance that separates them. And if he actually gets there, he may be surprised at the difference in the view. But at least having once located the worker, he will henceforward find it easier to talk to him when he wishes to do so.

What is more important, he may even be able to hear what the worker has to say. But until an executive knows where the employee is, communication down the line and across to the union is likely to miscarry. Remarks not accurately aimed but only shot out into the air are as unlikely to prove effective as a telephone conversation that is initiated by someone who has not bothered to dial the number. Moreover, the possibility of getting a reply from the other party is eliminated if he is not even on the line.

It is high time that top management stopped depending upon anyone else—employees, union leaders, or even personnel men—to do the understanding. This is one job that each executive has to do for himself.

Each of us who is concerned with achieving understanding in human relations finds that he must begin by looking at things as they are. The real facts are often less agreeable to contemplate than the way things ought to be. But if we want to get on with other people, we have to begin by being realistic.[5]

QUESTIONS AND PROBLEMS

1. Rate yourself by using the "Leadership Qualifications" table. Use a five-way breakdown of outstanding, excellent, good, fair, and poor.
2. After determining those qualifications in which you are relatively weak, what are you going to do about them? Outline a plan for improvement.
3. Who must develop *you* as a manager? Why is this true?
4. Set up a plan for your personal development as a manager after listing your strengths and weaknesses. Use Table 2 as a guide.

REFERENCE NOTES

[1] Earl P. Strong, *Increasing Office Productivity*, McGraw-Hill, 1962, pp. 268-269; *Organization Management in the Atomic Age,* Institute Department, U. S. Chamber of Commerce, 1962, pp. 38-40; and "Organization Management in the Atomic Age," *The Pennsylvania Business Survey,* Pennsylvania State University, September, 1962, p. 13.

[2] Samuel H. Miller, "The Tangle of Ethics," *Harvard Business Review,* January-February, 1960, p. 59.

[3] *Ibid.,* p. 61.

[4] Ralph C. Davis, *The Fundamentals of Top Management,* Harper & Row, 1951, p. 122.

[5] Paul Pigors, *Effective Communication in Industry,* National Association of Manufacturers, 1949.

READING REFERENCE

Houston, George C., *Manager Development,* Irwin, 1961.

6

THE MANAGEMENT ENVIRONMENT

THE PASSING LANDSCAPE (ATTITUDES OF PEOPLE)

Another important facet of the philosophy of management is its attitude on various matters affecting the work and lives of the people employed by the organization.

Our attitudes and feelings impel us to action and, to a large extent, govern our actions. For this reason, the attitudes and opinions of employees, supervisors, and top management should be a major concern of an organization in its efforts to foster cooperation among those groups responsible for production. Attitudes are elusive, fluid, and difficult to interpret. Useful and practical methods have been developed, however, for measuring the attitudes of groups toward specific policies and working conditions, and for the purpose of determining the prevailing level of job satisfaction and areas of content and discontent. These techniques include the employee survey, personnel counseling, and suggestion systems. They are a supplement to, and not a substitute for, personal contacts. A wise management will make a conscientious effort to gain an understanding of its employees' attitudes and feelings through the application of one or more of these techniques and utilize this knowledge in the formulation of its policies and the elimination of employee dissatisfaction.

From the management standpoint, attitudes break down into five types: (1) attitude of the worker toward management; attitude of the worker toward his immediate supervisor; (3) attitude of the worker toward the work task; (4) attitude of the worker toward fellow employees; and (5) attitude of the worker toward the public. Each of these is briefly discussed below.

Attitude of the Worker toward Management

This attitude is least easily defined because no one ever "sees" the company and frequently employees aren't sure who "management" is. Such things as wages are highly important to the employee, yet they are determined by people whom he rarely if ever sees. He is likewise affected in important personal ways by the acts and decisions of people who are unknown to him. Attitudes toward management are related to the whole field of communications— communications between management and the employee. Yet employees are eager to know about their company. In an employee-opinion survey conducted by one firm this question was asked: "Would you like more information about the plant and the company?" Of all the employees, 88 percent said "yes" and only 6 percent said "no." We all want to be a part of the group, to feel that we *belong*.

Attitude of the Worker toward His Immediate Supervisor

The humane supervisor who has respect for his employees is better liked than one who is eternally "pushing" for production regardless of human welfare. Employee-centered supervisors get higher production from their employees than do production-centered supervisors. (A Prudential Life Insurance Company study showed that 86 percent of the high-production supervisors were employee-centered, whereas only 30 percent of the low-production supervisors were employee-centered.)

Attitude of the Worker toward the Work Task

Some people like their jobs and others do not. Partly, this is a matter of ability; generally speaking, *we like to do that which we can do well*. Physical environment may also play a role in attitude determination. Some people would rather work outdoors, others indoors; some would rather have sedentary types of jobs, others active ones. All of these things play a part in the employee's morale.

Attitude of the Worker toward Fellow Employees

Most people want to work with people who like them and whom they like. Where there is cohesion among employees and where the employees see the goals of the company and their own goals in the same light, productivity is increased. Also, pride in the work group is related to productivity.

Attitude of the Worker toward the Public

In some types of organizations this attitude is not important, but in an organization which requires that the employee come in contact with the customer, or the public, it becomes extremely important. In a retail store, for example, the clerk who waits on customers has the responsibility of reflecting the entire management of the organization. Too few retail clerks and, needless to say, too few in management realize that the "point of contact" with the public is of prime importance. If the "point of contact" is strong enough and if service is rendered the customer, then a sale is made. The human element is extremely important in this transaction. It is of even greater importance that it reflect the true attitude of management.

THE ROADWAY (ECONOMIC, SOCIAL, AND POLITICAL FACTORS)

Economic, social, and political situations constantly affect management decisions profoundly. In making both his present and future decisions, the manager must take into account the outside forces that influence his business activities. A slight downturn in the economy, for example, can postpone or permanently cancel a decision to build a new plant or to introduce a new product. Social and political changes also affect certain managerial decisions.

Part of the complexity of managing a business enterprise springs from the unpredictability of economic, social, and political forces. The least any manager can do is to make an effort to understand them, learn to cope with them, and, in fact, learn to take advantage of them. This means that he must make a daily effort to keep up with contemporary events in his locality, state, nation, and the world in order that his managerial decisions will take into account current trends at all times.

PERSONAL AND ORGANIZATIONAL OBJECTIVES[1]

Every organization comes into existence to achieve some purpose. This is true whether it is a Friday baseball game, a fishing trip, a charter flight to Tahiti, a corner magazine shop, a church, a lodge, a sorority, or a business enterprise of great scale. Basically, someone sees a need in some segment of society which does not appear to be met by existing organizations. He influences others to join him in establishing an enterprise which will meet that need. If he foresees that man will want a new way to convey himself from spot "X" to spot "Y," he will examine the *values* expected from the new mode of transport, and strive to create a mechanism by which these values can be achieved. In this way, man's desire for faster, more comfortable travel brought about the jet aircraft.

All organizations exist to provide values to some segment of society. The values may be economic, such as a new source of low-cost lendable funds. They may be artistic, such as a new form of musical reproduction like multiplex stereo. They may be intangible and social, such as a recreational center, or tangible and basic to survival, such as food, shelter, and clothing.

Only by keeping in touch with the shifting value systems of customers can any organization assure its survival. The interurbans came into existence because of a need for a better form of personal and parcel transportation than that provided by the horse and wagon or the railroads. The businessmen who ran the interurbans *as a form of transportation* recognized the values of the new gasoline-powered "wagons." They shifted their economic resources out of interurbans into busses or into other customer needs, including the rising use of electrical energy to power a seemingly endless variety of household and business equipment. The interurban managers who loved the trolley car as an end product probably went out of existence with them.

Personal Objectives

The resourceful businessmen who recognize new customer needs are not unselfish in the creation and distribution of products to satisfy those needs. They develop business organizations not only to serve customer needs but to serve themselves as well. For the investment of their funds they rightfully expect a return. This should be high enough to compensate for the additional risks of their business as contrasted with other, less speculative investments. As individual investors, then, they expect a reasonable *profit*. They also expect that their funds will be protected against depletion by the preservation of the property values underlying the investment.

Businessmen anticipate that if they serve the organization in an employee capacity as well as in an investment capacity, they will receive the monetary and nonmonetary rewards customary for their form of service. Thus they believe they are entitled to receive managerial salaries appropriate to their industry and level of service. They believe they should receive reasonable protection against unwarranted discharge.

The suppliers of new organization also have personal objectives. Among these are continuity of patronage consistent with services rendered, fair prices, reasonable notice redelivery dates, and freedom from unethical demands such as rebates, etc.

Employees expect that their personal objectives will be respected by the organization and its management. These are many and varied, including fair wages, good working conditions, job security, respect for their dignity as human beings, and personal recognition.

The community housing a business organization normally has interests in its operation. These include employment opportunities for its citizens, avoidance of operating conditions unfavorable to its health and welfare, and support by the company of community projects.

Society in general poses personal objectives for business organizations operating within it. These include the protection of the health of its citizens, protection against monopolistic behavior detrimental to the society, protection of the rights of its citizens who are employed by business organizations, and a financial contribution, appropriate to the success of the organization, to the operations of the government of the society.

Everyone associated with a business organization has personal objectives. The organization cannot, however, ever allow itself to subvert its customer-value objectives to the personal objectives of any group associated with it. Continuous attention to the economical creation and distribution of customer values is the only real insurance any firm has of its survival. Typical of statements of business managers who recognize this truth is that of Harry T. Klein, writing about the Texas Company:

If we were to isolate the one factor, above all others, that transformed the tiny company of 1902 into the industrial giant of 1952, while hundreds of competitors failed and are forgotten, I should say it has been Texaco's settled policy of thinking first of quality of product and service to the customer, and only second to the size of its profit. . . . it is the starkest kind of business realism. In a highly competitive industry such as ours, the highest rewards are reserved for those who render the greatest service.[2]

Long-Run Organizational Objectives

In the very long run—one hundred years or so—a business organization has only one basic objective: *to live.*

In the long run—twenty years or so—a business organization has only two true organizational objectives: the creation and distribution of tangible and intangible customer values.

However, to achieve these, any organization must recognize the existence and validity (at least to the persons involved) of the personal objectives of those associated with it. As a consequence, the stated objectives of all well-managed organizations contain both organizational and personal objectives.

An example of one company's statement of long-run objectives is the creed of the Cleveland Electric Illuminating Company:

We Believe the first obligation of the Company and the employees is to supply the public with the best modern utility service at reasonable rates.

We Believe in keeping the Company a first-class place to work; paying fair and just wages and salaries; providing the employees with such benefits as vacations with pay, sick leave with pay, paid holidays, pensions, and life insurance; and continually endeavoring to maintain good working conditions.

We Believe in the Company doing all it can to assure employees of security, opportunity, and recognition of work well done.

We Believe in the Company and in every employee helping to develop the fullest and finest teamwork.

We Believe in the Company and the employees constantly striving for safety in all operations.

We Believe in safeguarding the investment in the Company, paying a fair return to the investors for the use of their capital, and maintaining a record of earnings which will enable the Company to attract new capital to continue to expand its services.

We Believe the Company has immense opportunity for growth, and that its growth will create new and larger opportunities for the employees.

We Believe in the Company and the employees participating in leadership in community-building.

We Believe in the Company and its employees doing their full part to defend the American way of life from its enemies, and so to preserve freedom and justice.[3]

A suitably formulated and framed statement of company objectives is but a starting place for any management philosophy. These long-run objectives must be supplemented by intermediate (one-to-five-year) and immediate (this year) objectives. These must be established not only at company-wide level, but for each function, each unit, and, finally, each position. The employee may know the goals of his position as a part of company goals, or he may know only the immediate position objectives. At lower levels, this is adequate for work direction.

In summary, a manager must assume *all* the responsibilities that go with his title. An effective leader of people understands the true difference between directing the activities of the group and working with the individual members of that group.

While production remains the manager's primary responsibility, that production depends upon the person even more than it does on the machine. The true leader must be able to tell his workers what is to be done, when it is to be done, who is to do it, and how it is to be done. People expect to receive directions, orders, and assistance that will enable them to work intelligently and effectively. Someone said not long ago that management is nothing more than communications. Almost every problem in management can be traced to lack of communication. Employees say, "Oh, is this what you meant? Well, if you had told me that in the first place . . ."

In present-day management philosophy, the manager has become a professional person. He is no longer the man who does the work; he sees to it that the work is done through others. His job is managing people, not things.

QUESTIONS AND PROBLEMS

1. Describe your attitude toward the field of management. How can you improve it?
2. Why is the field of attitudes so complex?
3. List some additional attitudes that are not listed and described in this chapter.
4. Can we be sure of the economic roadway? What changes occur from day to day? Give at least two examples.
5. Write out your personal objectives. Your personal management objectives. Your organizational objectives.

REFERENCE NOTES

[1] William R. Davidson and James H. Healey, *Power Management,* Allegheny Power Co., and its Subsidiaries, 1962.

[2] Harry T. Klein, *The Way Ahead,* Texaco, Inc., April 7, 1952, p. 3.

[3] *Management Creeds and Philosophies,* Research Study No. 32, American Management Association, 1958, p. 103.

PART II

ANALYSIS OF THE
FRAMEWORK OF MANAGEMENT

Part II deals in depth with organization, communications, and human relations, which, like the three parts of the frame supporting the other parts of a bicycle, form a support for the framework of management. These parts have been presented in Part I as the top bar (organization principles), the left bar (human relations), and the right bar (communications). These three factors are basic to the operating of any organized activity, whether it be a business, a social club, a civic association, a government, or a fraternity. They become, in our context, a focal point for further study. Their importance cannot be overstressed, and they should be considered of paramount value in developing competence in the field of management.

7

ORGANIZATION PRINCIPLES

Organization structure with its attendant principles truly carries the burden of the activity with which management works. In an organized activity, organization structure makes it possible to recognize the problems that arise in the technical knowledges and skills (the rear wheel in the bicycle analogy) and to find their solution through the application of the administrative skills (the front wheel). As with a bicycle, the front wheel (administrative skills) is the guide for the rear wheel (technical knowledges and skills). Thus the technical knowledges and skills are without purpose and remain ineffective without the administrative skills to guide them through their problem-solving techniques. The two wheels, then, depend upon the organization structure to hold them together so that they can operate together in an integrated and coordinated manner.

Over the years, a body of organization principles has evolved. Some of these principles can be traced back to the earliest records of mankind. For example, in Exodus 18 appears the famous passage in which Moses receives counsel from Jethro, his father-in-law. Jethro is concerned about how Moses can effectively extend his leadership to his followers. He points out that Moses cannot hope to administer justice to all his followers individually. The mass of details would soon overwhelm him. He admonishes Moses first to train ten of his most immediate followers, who in turn would train ten more followers, and so on, until the echelons of organization included all. These deputies would take care of the more routine decisions at each of their levels of the organization. Only those decisions of unusual nature and import would be referred to Moses himself. It was necessary, as a more recent management philosopher put it, for Moses to "extend his personality."

This famous Biblical passage illustrates, in one short commentary, several very fundamental principles of organization management which we know now by such terminology as "delegation," "span of management," and "the principle of exception."

The organization principles discussed in this chapter are basic to practically every decision and action of the manager.

AUTHORITY AND RESPONSIBILITY

Most of our management principles involve some aspect of authority and responsibility. Lines of authority and responsibility form the web which ties the organization together into a unit rather than a disjointed and uncoordinated maze of parts. For example, the relationship between the production supervisor and his men hinges on the question of authority. The supervisor has authority to assign particular people to particular jobs and to schedule when they will begin work on a new job order. Likewise, the sales manager has authority to assign salesmen to sales territories.

But authority carries with it responsibility. The production supervisor is responsible for seeing that the work is completed on time. He is responsible for seeing that the product is of the quality specified. The sales manager has the responsibility of taking action to see that sales goals are reached.

But the nature of authority and responsibility is not nearly so clear-cut as it may first seem. Since these concepts are so important to understanding basic organization principles, we shall consider them in more detail.

AUTHORITY

What is authority? What do we mean when we say a president, a superintendent, or a supervisor has authority? Usually we answer this in legalistic terms. Authority is the *right* to command It is the right to require certain kinds of performances. The foreman is empowered to assign work, sometimes to issue tools, to decide when work will be started on an order. The office manager has the "right" to hire a girl for the typing pool.

Authority is never unlimited. Much of the foreman's authority has been taken away, particularly in the realm of labor relations. The foreman can take disciplinary action only within the limits of certain well-defined rules if workers are represented by a union and work under a labor contract. The president of a firm may need the approval of the board of directors to spend a sizable sum of money enlarging plant facilities.

Authority is limited in another way. A manager may have the authority to ask for the full cooperation of his subordinates. But how effective is this authority when, for example, workers operating punch presses decide they want to work only so hard or so fast? Workers at any level of the organization can face dismissal if they openly defy *legitimate* directives. But an individual can easily withhold full cooperation without openly violating any directives.

To a very considerable extent, then, *effective* authority depends upon the degree of *acceptance* by subordinates.

Realities of the situation have caused managers to look more and more at authority from the "bottom up." Sometimes they must take pains to make sure acceptance of an order or plan is assured before proceeding. Managers are taught to be aware, for example, that any change in a work pattern tends to meet resistance. Suppose, to cite a common occurrence, a supervisor decides he must reassign several of his workers to new or different jobs. Moving an individual from one job to another always raises questions in his mind. Why is he being moved? Is it because he hasn't done well on his regular job? Will he be able to make as much money on the new job? Will he be able to perform the new job as well as his present one, which he has grown accustomed to and feels comfortable with? The supervisor may have the right to move him, but he can resist. Maybe he can't openly defy the supervisor's order, but he *can* make little effort to learn the new job. He can purposely perform less effectively, perhaps in the hope of being assigned back to his old job.

Reasons for Acceptance of Authority

Most of the time, members of an organization do accept authority, although with varying degrees of enthusiasm. The reasons are probably many, but a few stand out as primary.

Cultural respect for authority. Authority is accepted as part of our way of life. We have been taught from early childhood to respect legitimate authority. We recognize that organized society requires that orders and directives must be followed when they come from a proper source.

Sanctions. Another reason for acceptance of authority is the awareness that sanctions can be invoked. In industry, these sanctions are usually in the form of something that can be withheld. If the worker or manager openly defies orders, he may lose his job, be disciplined by temporary loss of employment, or lose the opportunity for promotion.

Respect for special knowledge. Often a manager or staff specialist has no *formal* authority over other members of the organization. Perhaps he has only authority to advise and make suggestions. But his advice tends to be followed anyhow because he possesses special knowledges or skills which others respect.

Status. An individual may enjoy a high degree of status in the company because of his special knowledge, because he has the reputation of being unusually capable, or because everyone knows the top boss thinks highly of him. Whatever the reason, he can often exercise *effective* authority even though he has no formal authority over anyone except his immediate subordinates.

The Concept of Zone of Indifference

Employees are more affected and concerned by orders and directives under some circumstances than under others. Recently, some management writers have called attention to what they call a "zone of indifference." The basic idea is that there are certain types of situations in which the employee raises no question about an order or instruction given, but carries it out almost automatically. Apparently, he is "indifferent" to this exercise of authority, in that he has no reason for feeling any reaction about complying.

Take, for example, a "utility" man. He performs a variety of tasks depending upon where he is needed. He is unconcerned if he is assigned a task today that is different from what he did yesterday. He has come to expect this, obviously. He is "indifferent" about a new assignment since this is for him a normal event.

The importance of the "zone of indifference" concept is not difficult to see. Knowing when a subordinate is likely to be indifferent about a directive and when he is likely to be seriously concerned is useful information to the manager. In the one case, he need only issue the order. In the other, he may make a special effort to explain why the order was issued, pointing out that the employee's job status or potential earnings will not be affected adversely (if, of course, that is the case).

RESPONSIBILITY

Authority always carries with it responsibility. The supervisor is responsible for seeing that costs are kept within bounds, that quality specifications are met, that the products are produced on time. The plant manager is responsible for seeing that over-all production goals are met and for supervising directly the echelons of managers just below him. The operative employee is responsible for meeting minimal production standards and for the proper care of the machines and tools assigned him.

Responsibility is an obligation to perform certain functions and achieve certain results. Sometimes that obligation is spelled out in specific terms, as in the case of producing a prescheduled number of products. Often the responsibility is general. The supervisor has responsibility for maintaining good labor relations. But what are good labor relations? Are labor relations good when harmony is achieved at the expense of good production and quality? Do good labor relations mean the supervisor must be "liked" by his employees? Responsibility stated in general terms is not always clear. Recent surveys have indicated that when the general responsibilities of production supervisors are examined in specific terms, there is wide disagreement between the supervisor and his superior over what he is responsible for and where his responsibility ends.

Responsibility must be matched by authority. If the manager is to be held responsible for achieving certain results, it is only reasonable that he have enough authority to bring these results about. Many supervisors feel, for example, that they cannot be held entirely responsible for good labor and personal relations with their employees. Often they have little influence over working conditions. Their authority to hire, fire, and discipline usually is very limited. Their arguments are not without justification.

One puzzling question is whether or not responsibility can be delegated. Ultimately, no manager can divest himself of responsibility. The plant manager may hold his superintendents responsible for meeting production goals, but in the final analysis he remains responsible for the over-all results. But to say that responsibility cannot be delegated seems contradictory, for isn't everyone in the organization given some responsibility?

The apparent contradiction can be clarified only by thinking of responsibility in terms of accountability. The plant manager, for example, is accountable to *his* superior for over-all results.

At the same time, his superintendents are responsible to him for achieving the goals assigned them. We should think of responsibility, therefore, in terms of accountability.

DELEGATING AUTHORITY

Delegating authority is probably the most fundamental process of organization management. The top man in an organization has the authority to do everything required to achieve the company's purpose. But the very reason for an organization is the inability of *one* person to do everything and make every decision that is required. He must, in effect, "multiply" himself. This means giving someone else the authority to make some decisions and perform some functions.

The delegation process takes place throughout the organizational hierarchy down to the lowest level of operative employee. The question is often raised, is any authority delegated to the operative employee, one who operates a lathe or types letters? In a theoretical sense, we might say "yes." The individual is endowed with the right to perform certain physical functions and to make certain decisions with regard to the use of equipment and materials. But, generally, when we talk about delegating authority, we mean managerial authority.

Importance of Delegation

Delegating is often the most critical factor in a manager's effectiveness. It may be his only means of making some jobs manageable if he has too many details to look after. A supervisor may spend so much time filling out production and cost reports that he has little time for major problems, such as planning work schedules in advance to avoid last-minute emergencies, and training new and relatively new workers. His only hope is to let someone else perform some of his functions.

Why Many Managers Don't Delegate Very Much

In spite of the acknowledged importance of delegation, many managers delegate very little or poorly. It is often apparent why. Aware that they will be held accountable for results, they simply don't trust others to make decisions for them. A manager may feel, "It's my responsibility. It's my neck if things don't go right, not my subordinates'."

Some managers argue that they simply do not have the

caliber of people who can make the kind of decisions required. "They don't know enough about their own jobs, let alone make some of the decisions I have to make." The refrain is only too familiar.

Others use the argument that they can do things more quickly themselves. "By the time I've trained someone to the point where I think he can handle the job, I've spent more time than if I did it myself."

The reluctance to delegate can often be traced back to a manager's previous experience. Most managers reach their position through promotion from a lower organizational level. The new function calls for different, often radically different, types of activities. In his new position the manager may be insecure. Instead of delegating some of his less important functions to subordinates, he tends to retain them if they are similar to the type of work to which he is accustomed. For this reason some managers never completely make the transition to their new role.

Reluctance to delegate is often attributed to a manager's own superior. If his boss's version of good management practice is that the manager himself should make all the decisions and exercise close supervision, the atmosphere is hardly conducive to delegation.

Finally, the lack of effective delegation may be simply a matter of not knowing how to delegate. Effective delegation is an art requiring a high degree of skill. It is not just a matter of releasing authority and forgetting about it. The delegator must judge how well the decisions for which he himself is responsible are being made. He must often decide whether or not to support the decision of a delegatee which he believes to be unwise. He must consider under what circumstances he may wish to reassume authority he has specifically entrusted to his subordinate, and how his withdrawal of support may affect the subordinate's effectiveness in making similar decisions in the future.

Good Delegating Procedures

No manager can hope to delegate effectively without first analyzing his own function in considerable detail. What kind of decisions does he make? What specific activities does he perform? How much time does he generally spend on each activity? Which activities are routine and which require separate judgments? To find the answers, it may be necessary to do a job and time analysis of his functions over a period of two weeks or more.

His functions and decisions must be broken down into small units, then grouped into larger and lesser units. The grouping generally should be on the basis of similarity of functions. For example, the filling out of all production, labor, and cost forms might be grouped under the unit of reporting. Time sequence might be a more valid basis for grouping other functions. Still another basis is the relative difficulty and importance of functions. Grouping activities that require about the same level of skill will greatly facilitate the delegation process.

SOME GUIDES TO DELEGATING

Having broken his activities down into detailed units and regrouped them, the manager is now ready actually to delegate. Some guides will be helpful in deciding how and to whom to delegate.

Delegate the More Routine Functions

Those functions which require more or less routine types of judgment and decisions should be delegated first. The delegatee can be guided by stock answers or policies laid out by the delegator. He can perform the function with a relatively small amount of information and training.

Delegate to the Lowest Possible Level

It is desirable to involve as many subordinates in the delegation process as possible. This can be done by delegating those functions which require the least level of skill to those of lowest ability sufficient to handle the activity. This is why it is useful to group together activities requiring relatively equal skill. If the levels of skill required for an assignment are uneven, subordinates of relatively high ability will necessarily be performing some functions that could be handled by those with less capability. This may also have the effect of eliminating many from the delegation process, which is undesirable since delegating authority is an excellent means of training and developing all employees.

Delegate Functions That Can Be Performed Independently

Generally, it is best to delegate those activities which can be performed independently, without the necessity of consulting and coordinating with others. Differences that cannot be resolved without some judgment being made should probably be left to the department head. An illustration will help clarify this important point.

An important function of the supervisor usually is assigning work. This is particularly true in the case of job-order shops. If job assignments can be routinized, decided in advance by rules and procedures applicable to most problems that are likely to arise, the function of assigning work may well be delegated to a subordinate. But if work in the department fluctuates greatly, requiring frequent increases and decreases in the number of employees, job assignment will be much more complicated. A number of simultaneous changes in assignment may be necessary. Overtime may be involved. Conversely, layoff or interdepartmental reassignments may be necessary. Such decisions require a high level of judgment. They require coordinating several moves. This means decisions which seem adverse and unfair to some, and feelings will have to be mollified. Obviously, in such cases the job assignment function should remain in the hands of the head of the department.

Delegating is an effective and necessary managerial tool, but it is no panacea, nor is it easy to implement. It requires follow-up, for once a function has been delegated, a manager must constantly evaluate how effectively a subordinate performs. Generally, he must be ready to stand behind the decisions made by the delegatee, but he cannot permit too many errors. The best means of avoiding this is to train the subordinate thoroughly in advance. But if he has to withdraw or reassign the authority, he may find himself with more rather than fewer problems. He has then defeated one of the prime purposes of delegation.

But proper delegation results in great benefits. It frees the manager to devote more time to more important functions. It provides opportunities for developing the abilities of subordinates. It means more effective managerial supervision for the entire department.

THE SPAN OF MANAGEMENT PRINCIPLE

Closely related to delegation is the span of management principle. This can be stated simply: There is a limit to the number of subordinates that a manager can effectively manage. To overextend that limit results in inadequate supervision and control. In the opposite case, control may be too close, and the number of echelons unnecessarily increased, magnifying the problem of communications up and down.

The "Tall" versus the "Flat" Organization

The span of management will, of course, greatly affect the structure of an organization. A short span of management—relatively few subordinates for each manager—produces a "tall" organization of many levels. Some large companies have more than twenty echelons in their hierarchy. They feel this is necessary for proper control and supervision.

Others feel the "flat"-type organization makes for better management. The number of echelons is reduced, shortening the line of communications. With the proper training and careful selection of high-caliber managers, the larger number of subordinates reporting to one manager need not present problems. Sears, Roebuck and Company is an advocate of large spans of management and few echelons. The company feels strongly that this policy has proved its value.

Some Studies of the Problem

There is no clear-cut basis for saying that one type of organization structure is better than the other. Situations and conditions differ from organization to organization, and it would seem that these factors should determine the span. A study by the American Management Association revealed wide variation in actual practice.[1] Another study of J. H. Healey indicated that, while there is a wide range of variability, the number of subordinates does tend to run from three to eight, depending upon the size of the company.[2] One of the most interesting studies of the span of management is that of A. V. Graicunas, who developed a mathematical analysis for determining its limits.[3] Few analyses have been made of the span of management at the operative level. The different processes would make generalizations difficult if not impossible. But the same basic concept applies, that there is some limit to the number of subordinates who can properly be managed.

Determining the Proper Span of Management

The most practical approach is to consider what guides may be used in determining the proper span for a particular situation. One of the first determinants will be the nature and variety of functions performed by subordinates. In a drill press department, for example, most of the people will be performing the same function. This means policies and procedures will generally apply uniformally to everyone in the department, so instructions can be given to all in one or only a few communications.

Similarity of function is a basis for enlarging the span of management at any level. The sales manager can supervise a large number of salesmen, particularly if each handles a relatively limited line of standard products and distribution channels are the same in all territories. The manager can decide many problems in advance by establishing uniform policies and procedures.

Assembly line activities also generally involve very simple and routine operations. This greatly reduces the amount of training required and the frequency with which production problems are likely to come up. For the same reason, the span of management of a sales manager supervising field salesmen selling relatively simple products will likely be greater than that of a sales manager in charge of sales engineers. The selling and servicing functions in the latter case are much more complicated, and problems requiring the counsel and decisions from the department head will arise much more frequently.

The span of management will vary with the capabilities of the managers themselves. Are they skilled in delegating? Do they do an effective job of organizing their own activities? Are they capable of decision-making without having to go to their own superiors too often? Affirmative answers increase their spans of management.

Where close control is necessary, the span will be shortened. In industries, such as electronics and missile development, where a high degree of reliability is required in the functioning of all components, the work has to be supervised very closely.

Effective use of staff assistance will help expand the span of management. The staff specialist can usually perform certain functions much more efficiently than the line manager, freeing the latter for other activities.

All these factors must be considered in determining the proper span of management in a particular situation rather than blind adherence to a rigid rule of thumb.

ORGANIZATIONAL BALANCE

Every manager naturally tends to feel his function is of the greatest importance to the organization. The sales manager will argue that without sales volume the business cannot survive. The production manager responds that without products competitive in cost and quality sales are impossible. For the design engineer, all things revolve around his function. That all these functions are important is evident. But *how* important, relatively? This is a question that must be decided, for the most part, by top management.

The task is a never-ending one. The relative importance of the various organizational elements changes, often rather rapidly. The company's customers are the primary reason for this. Their tastes and values change. In the early days of television, for example, the emphasis was on quality and styling in TV cabinets. The best grades of wood, beautifully finished, made the TV set an outstanding item in the living room decor. But soon the emphasis shifted to functional aspects. The public demanded sets at lower prices which took up less space. Design and production economy became primary, and the work of design and process engineering consequently grew in stature.

Organizational balance also reflects economic conditions. The transition from a predominantly production economy to a selling economy has naturally enhanced the importance of the sales function. The influence as well as the size of the sales organization has grown in most companies. More and more, top executives come from the sales department. Not too many decades ago, the "public be damned" philosophy could prevail with relatively little consequence to the company's market position. Today high-salaried, public relations specialists head spawning departments whose function is to project a favorable company "image." Perhaps the newest developing organizational element is the government affairs staff specialist and department. Executives are becoming increasingly aware of the role of busines in politics, with the result that many companies openly acknowledge the need for more attention to the political environment.

Weighing the Balance

Somewhere, somehow, the relative importance of each organizational element must be judged. Before the era of scientific management, tradition often provided the main, or even the only, basis for deciding. Now job analysis and functionalization have made possible a more logical basis for structuring the organization.

The criterion for measuring an element's relative importance is easy enough to state: What contribution does it make toward achieving the firm's service objectives? Is the importance of a particular department great enough, in comparison with other departments, to merit its present size and stature? What is a job worth in comparison with others? Can we afford top-caliber people commanding high salaries?

INFLUENCES THAT TEND TO THROW THE ORGANIZATION OUT OF BALANCE

The factors that tend to throw an organization out of balance are often quite formidable, and dealing with them is no simple task. But simply being aware of their existence can help management stop undesirable trends.

The Personality Factor

One obvious factor is the personality of the men occupying key positions. Strong personalities often succeed in acquiring authority and influence not justified by the relative importance of their functions. Strong staff executives often go far beyond their usual role of counsel and perform certain auxiliary functions. On the other hand, domineering line managers sometimes run roughshod over legitimate staff control procedures. Clearly both extremes are to be avoided. Staff should not exceed its proper function of advising and performing certain well-defined control functions. Line managers, on the other hand, should respect the principle which states that the advice and services of staff personnel should be sought before decisions are made in an area to which they might make a contribution.

Tendency toward Staff Growth

The tendency toward disproportionate staff growth has been particularly marked in recent years. No doubt this is largely attributable to the difficulty of measuring the contribution of certain staff functions. Management development seems to have been passing through a faddist stage. The hasty installation of office automation before it was justified resulted in a larger, not smaller, clerical staff. In some instances, large operations research departments were established before line managers ascertained whether they would result in sufficient savings to justify the increased overhead.

There is no doubt that in many instances rapid technological developments necessitate staff expansion. But such expansion can easily get out of control when top management does not quite understand the relative potentialities of staff's contribution.

THE SHORT-RANGE VIEW

Many managements tend to view all organizational elements from a short-range point of view. Conditioned to making day-to-day decisions whose results are usually immediately apparent, it is difficult for them to commit themselves to programs and plans whose values are not immediately discernible. Perhaps no better example can be cited than the area of management development. Almost to a man, top executives will agree that the single most critical factor in a company's survival and growth is the caliber of its management. Yet outlays in time and effort for formal programs to develop managers tend to fluctuate violently with business conditions. Apparently, this is one of the most variable of variable costs. It would seem much wiser to plan a more modest program to begin with, with reasonable assurance that it would be relatively little affected by short-term business fluctuations.

STEPS TO DEVELOP OR RESTORE ORGANIZATIONAL BALANCE

It is virtually impossible to attain perfect organizational balance. For the most part, this must be engineered at the higher levels of management. But lower echelons can contribute on a smaller scale.

Clarifying and Spelling Out Objectives

Odd as it may seem, the prime objective of many companies, especially larger ones, are stated in such general terms that they provide no realistic basis for planning. A division of one large aircraft company which had diversified into several other fields found, to its dismay, that its top and middle executives could not agree on their prime goals and objectives. Specifically, they could not agree on what markets they were trying to serve, what their prime service values should be, and in which areas they were equipped and staffed to be competitive. Under these circumstances, how could top management judge the relative importance of departments, make allocations of resources, and decide what weight to give various departments and key executives in reaching even fundamental decisions?

The first step, then, in working toward a balanced organization is to develop objectives which are specific enough to serve as a basis for guiding subsequent decisions.

Position Descriptions and Job Evaluation at All Levels

Most organizations provide no job descriptions or job evaluation above a relatively low managerial level. The argument usually given is that it cannot be done with any degree of precision. There is some validity in this, but not much. The lower we go in an organization, the less choice the individual has in *how* he can achieve his goals. The production supervisor's function is largely reduced to standard procedures. The sales executive, on the other hand, has much more latitude. It is much more difficult to describe specifically what he should be doing.

The solution is to define higher-level positions more in terms of *goals* and *objectives*. Some functions can be identified, such as a top executive's responsibility for supervising his immediate subordinates. The prime factor in evaluating positions should be the position's contribution to the success of the organization. It is not so easy to stick rigidly to this concept, for personal and intangible factors often enter the picture. But this at least provides a guide or bench mark.

Organization Charts and Organization Manuals

Careful attention to charts indicating lines of authority and responsibility and manuals describing authority relationships can contribute greatly to achieving organizational balance. When top management is forced to consider who should report to whom, who should be responsible for what, and similar questions, they cannot avoid evaluating the relative value of various positions and departments with consequent consideration of size as well as structure.

An example illustrates the point. An organization may be pondering where the position of chief purchasing agent should be located. Should he report to the production manager, to the general manager, perhaps even to the president? Should all purchasing be centralized or decentralized? The answers can be determined only after considering a number of other factors. For example, if materials constitute a large percent of unit cost, and prices fluctuate widely, then the purchasing function requires both a high degree of skill and considerable authority, since the purchasing executive will need latitude in deciding when to buy large quantities. Clearly, then, he should be an executive of high caliber. This, then, is a strong argument for placing the position at a very high level organizationally.

Staff-Line Ratios

Maintaining statistics on staff-line ratios can be quite valuable. Ratios can at least chart trends. An increasing ratio of staff to line is a cue to examine closely the need for larger staff departments. Furthermore, in some industries statistics are available for comparison. In a large multi-plant corporation, ratios can be compared among the various plants or divisions. If one division seems out of line, this is at least reason for taking a close look at the situation.

Periodic Auditing

A periodic audit of structure and staffing should provide an effective tool for achieving organizational balance. It can be a reminder that excessive staffing should be avoided and that authority and responsibility within the department should be updated and clearly recorded.

DECENTRALIZATION AND CONTROLS

The Meaning of Decentralization

It is an axiom of traditional economics that as an organization increases in size, it finally reaches a point where managerial efficiency diminishes. One answer to the problem is decentralization. Some managements make decentralization part of their philosophy. The General Electric Company, for example, has been a strong proponent of decentralization as a corporate way of life.

Sometimes there is confusion over just what is meant by decentralization. To some, it means geographical dispersion. The firm with headquarters in one city and several plants in a number of different cities gives the appearance of being highly "decentralized." But geographic location is not the central factor. The vital element of decentralization is the division and delegation of authority to make managerial decisions to units lower in the organization.

But what do we mean by "units" in this case? To some, the "unit" can be one person, making decentralization practically synonymous with delegation. Thus when the production manager allows the planning department to decide the over-all scheduling of production, this is a form of decentralization.

Others would limit the meaning of decentralization to a

complete group of activities and functions. Decentralization, in this view, would be the segregating of *all* the production activities for one or more products, and the delegating of over-all authority and responsibility to one particular production or plant manager. Decentralization may also be on a functional basis. For example, machine and foundry operations may be separated, with over-all authority and responsibility charged to one general or plant manager.

Decentralization means the division of a group of functions and activities into relatively autonomous units, with over-all authority and responsibility for their operation delegated to a head of each unit.

How Much Control to Maintain

The question that immediately arises, of course, is how complete shall the authority delegated to the head of the organizational unit be? Shall the production manager have the authority, say, to purchase all materials and supplies?

Decentralization is never complete. Some degree of control is always maintained. The production manager may be authorized, for example, to make expenditures for new equipment up to a certain figure, with anything over that requiring approval from higher up.

Probably the most nearly complete degree of decentralization is achieved in the "profit center" type of situation. Here, the unit head has almost complete decision-making latitude, his responsibility being simply to show acceptable results in terms of profit performance.

Deciding on the degree of decentralization is one of corporate management's most perplexing problems.

Advantages of Decentralization

Some of the advantages of decentralizing are readily apparent. Pushing authority "down the line" means that those closest to a situation can make the decisions bearing on it. Those directly concerned with meeting production schedules, for example, are in a better position to determine how many employees should be hired. Design engineers working directly and exclusively for a manufacturing division have the necessary direct communications with production to better evaluate the feasibility of some of their design specifications.

Decentralization provides a valuable means for developing

people, particularly managers, through a wider range of decision-making authority.

Decentralization facilitates communications. In a highly centralized organization, decisions affecting lower levels are made several echelons above. Communications tend to get snarled and distorted as they travel down. Particularly in the case of verbal communications, those at the end of the communication line receive different versions of the original directive. Even if the communications are transmitted in written form, remoteness of the source makes it difficult to check an unclear or incomplete directive. Furthermore, the upward flow of communications, always difficult, is even more distorted when the chain of command is a very long one.

Finally, decentralization is likely to result in more effective supervision. The production supervisor who cannot make important changes in work assignment, schedule production, take disciplinary action, or recommend promotions is likely to have little influence with his work group.

Disadvantages of Decentralization

But the disadvantages must be considered, too, and often they will clearly outweigh the advantages. Decentralization requires a higher level of personnel at the lower echelons.

Too much decentralization may prevent the cost-saving efficiencies of specialization. For example, a centralized production planning and control department, staffed by qualified specialists, can plan and schedule production much more efficiently. Work can be scheduled and coordinated so as to cause the least amount of idle operations and confusion. Centralized purchasing permits buying in larger quantities, at substantial savings, as well as a more systematic study of sources of supply.

Centralization makes maximum use of a small number of exceptionally talented people, spreading their talents more broadly. For example, during World War II, one large aircraft manufacturer with an unusually brilliant engineer on the headquarters staff, gave him almost complete authority to make certain critical technical decisions at the plant level.

Sometimes decentralization of certain functions is made difficult or impossible by external factors. Company- or industry-wide bargaining with labor unions may have to be confined to a high level in the organization. Legal and government requirements may require certain financial decisions to be made for all units of the firm by one centralized department.

Decentralization versus Centralization

The question of centralization or decentralization is not a black-or-white issue. It is always a matter of degree. Some functions lend themselves to centralization more readily than others. A strong and militant union may necessitate centralization of labor relations policy-making and contract administration, while at the same location production planning and scheduling may be largely in the hands of the first-line supervisor.

The nature of the production process will often determine the degree of decentralization. Continuous production calls for centralized planning and controlling. Heavy equipment investment generally means capital expenditures are determined high up the line for all units and departments.

The diversity of the company's product will be a strong factor. A large number or dissimilar products calls for decentralization of production in most cases. This in turn calls for decentralization of the sales organization, especially if the various products are marketed through different distribution channels.

In any case, the degree of decentralization is something that should be periodically reviewed. Changes in the company's product objectives or market conditions will often warrant review of the present organizational structure.

ELEMENTS OF COORDINATION

The work of coordination is a never-ending one, requiring the attention and skills of all managers. Sometimes it is a matter of smoothing relations among subordinates. Sometimes it involves working out problems with another department. Often, it is a combination of both.

The task of coordination is essentially a matter of seeing that activities are performed in the proper sequence and at the proper time. A batch of machined parts must be ready for the next department. The operation performed by the preceding department must be within the quantity and quality specifications called for. The sales department must be able to rely on the availability of sufficient quantities of the final product at the right time to meet its sales quotas.

Fundamentals in Coordination

Certain basic conditions are fundamental for effective co-ordination. For the most part, these conditions depend on top management, at least for initial implementation. But all members of the organization have a responsibility for seeing that they prevail.

Clearly established and understood objectives. Two departments cannot hope to coordinate their activities if they are working at cross purposes. Both the engineering and production departments, for example, must understand the company's over-all product objectives. Producing goods of high quality at low cost seems clear enough, but the two do not necessarily go hand in hand. Beyond a certain point, higher quality can be achieved only at greater cost. Conversely, costs can be reduced only at the sacrifice of quality. Somewhere a balance must be effected. And both departments must clearly understand what bench marks have been set.

Precise and well-understood plans. Plans that are not spelled out in sufficient detail will result in decisions by those who do not have enough information to make them. To use an extreme example, the foreman of a department performing one of the operations on a product may not know enough about the next operation to appreciate just how accurately the part must be shaped, ground, or sheared for the next department to perform its job. Likewise, the foreman is not in a position to know how much quality is needed to meet competition.

Organization Structure

The design of the organization's structure should be based on consideration of the problems of coordination. Departments must be grouped in such a way that the work moves smoothly from one phase to another. Too much specialization can result in unwieldy problems of coordination. This factor will be an important consideration even within a department. For example, in a maintenance department there are advantages in having one electrician who handles all electrical repair jobs. On the other hand, the problems of coordination may be greatly reduced if each worker is able to perform all or most maintenance functions since each can then be assigned to an area. This greatly reduces the problem of communications and avoids situations where maintenance assistance is not available as soon as needed.

Aids to Coordination

A variety of techniques and practices can help reduce the problem of coordination. Some of these involve time and expense, but their value may well be worth it.

While there has been a great deal of criticism over too much reliance upon "committee management," there is little controversy over the value of committees as a device for achieving coordination. In deciding what standards of quality should be set for the firm's product or service, a product committee can be most useful in reconciling the views of production, engineering, and sales, and assuring that the decision reached will be accepted by those who must live with it.

Channels of Communication

Coordination requires effective channels of communication. This means, often, that the regular channel of the chain of command must be supplemented with other media. Conferences are a good example. The conference enables the higher-level manager to communicate with all interested parties at once. But, more important, the conference involves two-way communication. At the superintendent's production meeting, for example, the foreman of department A learns what part of the plan is the responsibility of the foreman of department B. Furthermore, this is an opportunity for him to check the things they are dependent upon each other for. Foreman A may learn, for example, that foreman B is running into trouble that may cause some delay in getting materials or parts to foreman A. This information enables foreman B to prepare for the difficulty or work out a solution with foreman A.

Various other channels of communication may be used, depending on the nature of the communications. In some instances, good, clear, written directives may suffice. The manager should remember, however, that written communications are a one-way proposition. Unless the receiver takes the time to check with the sender, or vice versa, the sender can never be completely certain that it has been understood or, for that matter, even received.

In the final analysis, person-to-person communication is most effective. It provides the superior and subordinate or peer the opportunity to check with each other on their understanding of the matter discussed.

Use of Staff

Many staff functions are established for the prime purpose of smoothing coordination. A staff person or department can do a thorough job of collecting all pertinent data and seeing that everyone affected or involved receives the information.

Clear Definition of Authority and Responsibility

Many problems of coordination can be reduced by a little more effort to define clearly the authority and responsibility of each member of the organization. "That's not my job" or "I thought Harry was taking care of that" are comments heard only too frequently. Some managers feel that the effort to define a subordinate's authority and responsibility in some detail is a waste of time. Some informal research in tracing the causes of the breakdown of coordination should convince them otherwise. Clear understanding of authority and responsibility requires constant review. Conditions change and job definition must reflect this. Quite often a written job description becomes so outdated that everyone recognizes it is meaningless. An individual's function has changed and often no one, not even the person himself, is any longer quite sure what his specific responsibilities are.

SUMMARY

The management function is a complex one since it deals with human beings, the uncertainties of the future, and varying conditions in the market and environment. It is not a precise activity; it has not been reduced to a science. But some basic principles have emerged and have been refined. These principles provide general guides only, but they are useful if a manager understands and applies them judiciously. Most management principles are based on a concept of authority. Organization structure is built on authority relationships. Decentralization and the exercise of control involves choice in the methods of exercising authority.

The basic management principles deal largely with how functions and activities are grouped and related to each other. There are various approaches to grouping and establishing the relationships. The best approach depends on such conditions as the type of industry, the nature of the manufacturing process, the degree of control necessary, and the abilities and qualifications of the members of the organization. It should be remembered, furthermore, that these conditions change.

Following the management principles discussed here does not guarantee success in an organization. But it is very difficult to achieve success, or, at least, to maximize the organization's potential, without them.

QUESTIONS AND PROBLEMS

1. What is authority in management?
2. What is responsibility in management?
3. Can either of these be delegated? Explain why one can be delegated and the other cannot.
4. Give the reasons for our acceptance of authority.
5. What are the reasons for managers not delegating as much as they should?
6. What are the guidelines for proper delegation?
7. Explain the principle of span of control in management.
8. How can organizational balance be accomplished?
9. What is the relationship between objectives and organizational structure?
10. When an organization is decentralized, what is its most difficult problem?

REFERENCE NOTES

[1] Ernest Dale, *Planning and Developing the Company Organization Structure,* Research Report No. 20, American Management Association, 1952.

[2] James H. Healey, *Executive Coordination and Control,* Ohio State University, 1956.

[3] A. V. Graicunas, "Relationship in Organization," in L. Gulick and L. Urwick, eds., *Papers on the Science of Administration,* Institute of Public Administration, 1937, pp. 181–187.

READING REFERENCES

Allen, Louis A., *Management and Organization,* McGraw-Hill, 1958.
Holden, Paul E., Lounsbury S. Fish, and Hubert L. Smith, *Top-Management Organization and Control,* McGraw-Hill, 1951.

8

HUMAN RELATIONS

Today's manager is concerned with *people,* and the more expert he becomes in understanding them and in building the best working climate, the more successful he will be.

In the last century the term "Industrial Revolution" was applied to an era when our mighty industrial and business organizations were founded and machinery was developed that made mass production possible. The worker had few rights, minimum information and sophistication, and seemed content to be bossed and directed. In recent decades management has become people-centered, and we have been going through a "human revolution" characterized chiefly by the individual's achieving greater rights, more information and sophistication, and the recognition that he, too, is a human being.

During World War II training in human relations was one of four areas of management development for which courses were developed by the Training Within Industry group of the War Manpower Commission. In the course, "Job Relations Training," the major principles taught, under the heading "A Supervisor Gets Results Through People," were:

1. People must be treated as individuals.
2. Let each worker know how he is getting along (communications).
3. Give credit when due.
4. Tell people in advance about changes that will affect them.
5. Make the best use of each person's individual ability.
6. Handle problems by careful analysis of the facts.[1]

At this time many companies intensified their in-service training programs, among them General Motors, which aptly titled one of its courses "Man to Man on the Job," to emphasize the importance of relationships in the work scene. The preface to the booklet of this title, written by one of the company vice presidents, has this to say:

Today, I think we all agree that most of our production bottlenecks are caused by the human element, and not by mechanical elements. . . . Industrial employees cannot be led or driven as a herd of cattle, for this is contrary to human nature. . . . To my way of thinking, there are no tricks to getting along with people, regardless of the various courses that are advertised to give us a sort of hypnotic power over those we want to captivate.[2]

This was written in 1943. Today there is probably more written in the professional and management journals on the human factors in management than on any other single subject, save perhaps communications. And one of our major professional groups for management development, the American Society of Training Directors, has come to the conclusion that "Human relations and communications are synonymous."[3]

At a later date, and under the interesting title, "Human Relations: Boon or Bogle?," another writer, trying to put human relations in management in proper perspective, emphasizes the manager's leadership abilities:

An underlying element of his approach to other people is an attempt to understand them, which involves a high degree of acceptance of people as they are. . . .

He has an awareness and sensitivity to differences between his outlook and another man's, coupled with an ability to maintain his own individual point of view in the face of such differences. . . .

He has an ability to respond to and understand not only the logical content of what other people say but also the feelings and sentiments implied in their behavior. . . .

He has awareness of himself and of the impact of his behavior on other people. . . .[4]

In the famous Hawthorne studies at the Western Electric Company, which many cite as the first modern research effort to find out what motivates people to work harder, the researchers set out to measure the effects of changes in physical conditions on worker morale and productivity. To their amazement, they found that any change in, for example, lighting, work tables, rest periods, or uniforms, improved production whether it was favorable or unfavorable. The researchers concluded that the primary factor in bringing about increased production was the feeling of the workers that *they were being recognized as people* and singled out for *participation* in the experiment.

Since the Hawthorne studies, there have been countless others linking production to morale, and one study has brought together in a single volume much of this research and the conclusions of those who have tried to find in it a degree of consensus as to the human relations behavior that will accomplish the best results.[5]

It is well to realize that a dogmatic and uniform set of principles does not exist, for people are not machines; they vary in their conduct and feelings, and react differently to different practices. However, we can set forth some guiding principles as flexible guides, to be adapted and used with judgment by the manager in any given instance.

SOME GUIDING PRINCIPLES

1. Members of any work group must be treated as individuals. The effort to regard every subordinate as an individual who must be treated in terms of his particular feelings, wants, and background has given rise to the concept of *people-centered* rather than work-centered management. This is to say that a manager will usually get more production from his subordinates if he spends more of his time on communication and human relations problems, and the practice of leadership and motivational principles than on production itself. Research has shown that managers who practice close supervision of production and even "pitch in" to help do the work actually get less out of their work groups than managers who maintain more "distance," encourage group spirit and individual effort, and leave employees more on their own.

2. Opportunities for participation and recognition must be available. In our chapter on communications, we point out the modern practice of consultative management of allowing the subordinate to share in the decision-making process. This participation has proved to be a major factor in building morale and in motivating individuals to do their best. At the same time, it is important to give recognition to work well done so that workers will feel their extra effort is appreciated. Today much less attention is paid to reprimanding employees and much more to counseling

with them, so that poor work may be turned into better performance in the future.

3. Teamwork and group effort must be encouraged. One of the major conclusions of the Hawthorne studies was that workers like to come together in informal groups, which they tend to develop if given sufficient freedom and a feeling of self-confidence. Again, studies have shown the superior value of group effort to that of persons working individually without a feeling of cohesive group objectives. Further, when groups are allowed to work out their own procedures, set production goals, and even set standards, a degree of competitiveness with other groups develops that results in increased productivity. An interesting example is that of the Hormel Packing Company, which has developed an exceedingly permissive work climate in which committees are appointed to work out answers to specific problems. The results of this program are described in a book aptly titled *Toward a Democratic Work Process.*[6]

4. A democratic and permissive climate must be developed. In substance, this means a change from the old practices of bossism and order-giving to the practices of leadership. A democratic climate includes giving subordinates opportunities for participation in work goals and standards, a share in decision-making, and similar practices which recognize workers as people. Much has been written on leadership as a requisite for today's manager, and we devote a section of this book to it.[7]

5. Motivation must be a constant goal. We have learned that the individual who is ordered to do something will both resent the order and probably do no more than the instructions cover. If, on the other hand, he is made to *want* to do his job in a superior way, perhaps because he has been praised for previous work or has been given an opportunity to help plan the work ahead, he is apt to do a far superior job. And in so doing, he will motivate his fellow employees to do likewise, for attitudes and enthusiasm are contagious. Since there has been so much research effort to link motivation and productivity, it is not surprising that a new book has recently appeared dealing in detail with the research and conclusions in this field.[8]

6. Attitudes must be developed in positive directions. Work attitudes are the result of many things, including work environment, pay, and other material rewards. Though the manager can perhaps do little about these, he can do much about his own relations with his subordinates and other personal factors which

affect their attitudes. These might be summarized as follows: (1) attitude of the worker toward the management of the company as a whole; (2) attitude of the worker toward his immediate supervisor; (3) attitude of the worker toward the work task; (4) attitude of the worker toward his fellow employees; and (5) attitude of the worker toward the public.[9]

LEADERSHIP AND HUMAN RELATIONS

It might be said that if you practice all the advice in this book you will be a good manager and a good leader. But leadership is not a set of mechanical or external skills. It is rather a deep-seated combination of character, moral conduct, reputation developed over a period of time, respect for the feelings and sensitivities of others, and a balanced combination of confidence and humility. The overconfident braggart is not a leader, nor is the weak, submissive person.

The leader knows himself, analyzes his strengths and weaknesses, and tries to develop his abilities as well as his attitudes. Above all, in his personal relations with others he is enthusiastic, animated, and dynamic. And he can be all these without being bossy and directive. Yet too many managers think that the only way they show enthusiasm is to order people around in an arrogant manner.

Here are some contrasts between the behavior of the boss and the leader:

The Boss	*The Leader*
Drives and orders	Coaches and advises
Depends on his authority	Depends on confidence and goodwill
Engenders fear	Inspires enthusiasm
Says "I"	Says "we" and "you"
Fixes blame and fault	Solves problems
Knows all the answers	Consults and seeks advice
Makes work a drudgery	Makes it a game
Directs individual effort	Inspires group effort
Sets all goals and standards	Asks his group to help
Says "Go"	Says "Let's go!"

It is interesting to observe that the manager is pulled in many directions by his multiple roles, all of which he must blend together in order to achieve the maximum efficiency. He has conflicting roles in that he must always be aware of his relations with his own superior at the same time that he considers how to deal with subordinates. It is difficult for a manager to practice the leadership qualities we are discussing here if he works in a climate of strict authoritarian bossism and this is the way he is treated by his superior. Yet he should do all he can to change this climate. A real leader, at whatever level, will try to disseminate upward through the line of the organization the kinds of influences that will induce higher management to act in like manner. No level of management exists as an island unto itself.

UNDERSTANDING PEOPLE AND SATISFYING NEEDS

Leadership is conceived as a dynamic functional relationship between leader and led in which the leader is attempting to satisfy the varied needs of his particular followers.[10]

There are several key words in this quotation that symbolize the manager's responsibilities in developing the best possible relationships with his co-workers. "Dynamic functional" implies that all relations with others are changing and fluid. They must be adapted to the situation at hand and must not be mere mechanical, external acts or gimmicks that are used for all occasions. They must be adapted to the specific relationship.

"Varied needs" implies that needs change with different individuals. The word "particular" is also important here, for it places emphasis on the fact that people are different and must be treated, each in his own way, as individuals. In a situation, for example, where a supervisor had to make two similar work assignments, he called in foreman A and simply handed him the assignment with the comment that he "should get busy with it." He then called in foreman B and handed him the same assignment with the same terse comment. But it was obvious that B did not feel ready to accept the assignment. He needed more than an order to make him feel confident that he could do the job. Had the supervisor realized that he was dealing with two different persons, each with certain characteristics, he would have approached B on a much different basis. He would have asked questions about his present assignments, his experience with the type of work in the new one, built his confidence in his ability to do the job, and even offered words of encouragement and assistance.

One of the strange paradoxes about people is that they are at once both different and the same. We come from a vast variety of backgrounds and experiences. And there is no question that the habits we develop in the home and with friends do carry over into the work scene. If we are domineering and autocratic with our children, we may also be with our workers. Though we may try to change and modify our behavior to suit the role we are playing, we are not all good actors in changing from "Jekyl" to "Hyde," and our real characteristics tend to show through.

Our education, both formal and informal, our recreational hobbies, our political preferences, and our club and church affiliations—all these add up to a frame of reference against which we judge and measure all matters that confront us. Probably the failure to recognize that each individual is conditioned by the particular frame of reference he has developed is the cause of most human relations breakdowns.

In terms of material things, $100 may seem a very large sum of money to a clerk-typist or other worker whose weekly salary is less than $50. The same sum may be no more than an evening's expense account for the president of a company or a successful entertainer whose annual salary exceeds $100,000. Both measure the worth of the $100 against the frame of reference which is their basic standard of living. Other frames of reference are more emotional, such as loyalty to our church or to the United States as a democracy. Any subject that is mentioned by another which "rubs" this attitude the wrong way is going to affect our behavior toward that person.

When an attitude grows very strong, it becomes a prejudice, which in turn can become a stereotype. We are now talking about attitudes which we feel so deeply as to defy rational judgment in any situation where they are affected. One's religion is likely to be viewed in this manner. But we can also develop such deep-rooted feelings about our way of life, or our habits both in and out of the work scene. Intense loyalty to one's company or organization or even strong attachment to certain co-workers or a piece of machinery can develop into a stereotype.

When, as a manager, you approach a subordinate on a subject about which he has strongly developed feelings, you will have the best chance of handling the situation if you know his predetermined frames of reference, attitudes, or prejudices. The more you can find out about these in advance, the more successful will be your approach to him.

This is why the *communication of change* is such a difficult objective for managers. Most of us have developed established habit patterns and attitudes. In general, we tend to favor the status quo. When something is proposed that will take us out of the normal channel of doing things, we tend to resist the change.

Considerable motivation must be present to make change attractive to most people. In practice, this means ascertaining a man's degree of receptivity to a new assignment, telling him *why* the change is being proposed, and pointing out its advantages over the old method. The failure to tell "why" is often the reason why subordinates do not readily take hold of a new assignment with enthusiasm. There is a "principle of least effort" within most of us which urges us not to expend more energy than necessary to do a particular job. Yet a person who initially would object to a new assignment because it will make more work for him will probably brag about his execution of it to fellow workers once he realizes its value and superiority over the old.

We have emphasized how coming from different backgrounds makes us different people. But we also have pointed out the paradox that as human beings we are all alike. This likeness is evident in the fundamental human drives and needs which we all possess and which so largely motivate our behavior. The difficulty is that we vary in the degree of intensity or meaningfulness with which we react to them. It behooves every manager to realize that people are motivated by these basic drives, sometimes referred to as vital appeals, basic emotions, or psychological needs.

Some writers classify them in ascending order, from those that are necessary for survival to those that are creative in nature. The outstanding social psychologist, Gordon Lippitt, of George Washington University, has listed this "Hierarchy of Needs" in reverse order:

5. Creative and growth goals
4. Ego and self-development
3. Social acceptance and relations
2. Security—economic and material
1. Physiological needs

It is, of course, obvious that the most basic need is acquiring the physical necessities to exist. These would include bodily health and food, with at least a minimum of shelter. Economic security is that degree of monetary income the individual feels he must have, first to exist and then to enjoy the comforts of life. For most persons in the work scene these two basic needs are satisfied by persons other than the immediate supervisor or manager. The manager may be able to influence the pay level of the employee, but this would usually be a matter for the personnel office.

It is in the third area, that of social relations and the fundamental drive of all of us to be accepted and to feel comfortable in our relations with other people, that the manager has most influence. He also affects the individual's desire for self-development and growth, satisfying the need for personal recognition, praise for a job well done, encouragement for the future, and hope for advancement and the opportunity to do new and creative things.

In the above hierarchy of needs, most people would regard physical wants and economic security as most important and put them before the others. It is well to keep in mind that this is not necessarily so with all individuals. In the following list, self-preservation is shown first, but to some persons, and to many under specific situations of danger, the last one shown, that of protection of one's loved ones, may be the most dominant:

1. Desire for life, self-preservation, and physical well-being
2. Desire for property and economic security
3. Desire for social recognition, reputation, and approval
4. Desire for aesthetic things and pleasant surroundings
5. Desire for protection of loved ones, friends, and human beings in general

Motivation, then, as a part of leadership's human relations goal, is a constant effort to stimulate and satisfy basic drives.

Many of our present-day studies of individual and group behavior include the relationship of productivity to high morale. It is hard to define morale or to be certain what brings it about, but we are quite sure that to the extent that managers practice the kinds of relations we are proposing, morale will be affected in a positive way. Yet some act of higher management or the personnel office, or some apparently minor decision may destroy the good morale that has been built up over a period of time. For example, the decision to shorten coffee breaks from fifteen to ten minutes may lower morale beyond the reach of anything management can do in the way of good "human relations." These kinds of actions are often beyond the manager's control, but he should be alert to their effect on morale and do what he can to explain or "soften" their announcement.

Morale is not a factor that can be turned on and off mechanically by higher management, although some pleasant announcement may do much to raise it. Sometimes management wrongly assumes that it can simply tell employees they should have better morale and they will automatically have it. In a situation where a group of several hundred clerical workers were quite discouraged over recent company reverses, the manager chose to call a meeting at which he spent a half-hour repeating that it was simply wrong to have low morale and that everyone should immediately change his attitude. Those in attendance left the meeting with chins closer to the floor than they had been before.

HANDLING SPECIFIC HUMAN RELATIONS SITUATIONS

Human relations are improved or worsened by the countless interpersonal contacts between manager and employee, and the ultimate test of their success is usually the quality of the communication between the two or more persons involved. Let's look at some attempts to solve human relations problems in typical situations, and also make some suggestions.

Counseling

This is the effort to advise by working out *mutual* solutions to problems. The essence of counseling as a human relations goal is that it is based on the principle of respect for the employee and not on the outdated principle of the "boss" telling him what's wrong, "bawling him out," and directing him to do things differently. It is in line with modern management concepts of the open door, a democratic approach to problem-solving, and a permissive climate.

The manager should be able to sit down and counsel with his people in a manner which respects their position and feelings and which works toward the mutual benefit of both parties and the organization as a whole. Such an interview might discuss a work production schedule or problem, what appears to be a mistake made by the employee, a complaint or grievance by the employee, a personal matter about which the employee seeks advice, or some other problem. Most counseling interviews follow a pattern something like this:

Greeting and common ground remarks
Attention directed to the problem at hand
Analysis of the problem
   Causes, origin, history
   Current extent and implications
   Factual information obtained

Consideration of possible solutions
  Free and permissive offering of these
  Postponing judgment and evaluation
Arriving at best solution
  Discussing standards and objectives sought
  Considering pros and cons
Agreeing on specific decisions and courses of action

It should be pointed out that this sequence would not necessarily always follow these exact steps. There may be several parts to the problem or several different problems to discuss. A parallel pattern might develop in which a part of a problem is analyzed and explored, then solutions offered and a best solution found, after which the interview would move toward another part of the problem and its solution.

Nondirective counseling has been developed as the best method of conducting such an interview. Simply defined, this is the attempt on the part of the manager to avoid direct and dogmatic statements, to avoid making early judgments, to avoid evaluative comments at least in the early stages of the counseling, and to encourage maximum participation by the employee.[10]

Questions are the primary tool in counseling. They are used for two basic purposes: (1) to seek information in the form of facts, explanations, and data; and (2) to seek opinion in the form of judgment, attitudes, and feelings. Here are some suggestions in the use of questions:

Relate questions to the other person's interests.
Relate questions to his frame of reference and knowledge.
Avoid too many questions calling for simple "yes" or "no" answers.
Avoid "leading" questions which supply your answer or opinion.
Avoid accusing words in questions, such as "wrong," "ignorant," "uninformed," and "sloppy."
Follow general and abstract questions with more specific ones dealing with a narrower phase of the subject.
Keep questions short, clear, and uncomplex.
Make clear transitions in changing to a new subject.
Avoid an unpleasant "cross-examination" manner.
Don't interrupt in the middle of an answer.

In arriving at a decision, try to get the other person to confirm the judgment you think should be reached. Sometimes you may have to take the dominant part in doing this, but as much as possible this should be joint accomplishment, with the employee feeling that he has helped reach the decision.

Performance Appraisal Interviews

This practice has replaced the old one of calling an employee in only when something had gone wrong for which he should be corrected or reprimanded.

Most companies today have a regular program of performance appraisal or merit rating in which all levels of employees are rated by their superiors, usually on a form or in some written statement which becomes a permanent record. But management has learned that these are not very useful until they become the subject of an oral discussion between the rater (manager) and the person rated (employee). Further, we have learned that this interview is not very valuable and may do more harm than good if the manager chooses simply to point out weaknesses and wrongdoings and makes corrective suggestions too directly. There is almost always some area of satisfactory performance that can be discussed first. Other areas should then be treated as problems for analysis, leading toward mutual agreement on courses of action that will lead to better performance. The real purposes of the appraisal interview are, therefore, several: to promote increased understanding between manager and employee; to point out areas of good performance for praise and recognition; to ascertain reasons for weaknesses; to find methods for improving and bringing about better future performance; and to bring about a totally improved climate in which the employee feels more confident and communicative in future interpersonal relations.

Handling Arguments and Differences of Opinion

First, we do not suggest that the way to get along with others is always to agree with them, even though we know that this might lead to better human relations. But it surely would not lead to a democratic way of life, either in the work scene or in our total society. Democracy thrives on controversy and differences of opinion.

But you will not develop good human relations by regarding the other person as your "opponent" or by taking issue with him too strongly. You really never win an argument; it leaves both persons the worse for wear, and it is doubtful whether it settles anything. So the best way to win an argument is to avoid it. This does not mean that you should not maintain and advance your opinions or take issue with the other person. But *it is the way you do it that counts,* and here are a few suggestions:

1. Listen carefully to what he has to say. Most of us are so anxious to get back at the other person with our reply that we don't really listen to what he is is saying. If we do listen, it is usually out of self-interest and within our own frame of reference, instead of trying to realize that what he is saying does make sense to *him*. Try to determine whether he is simply trying to explain something or is presenting a point of view, opinion, or feeling. It is in the latter areas that we get into most trouble.

As you get ready to reply, apply the Golden Rule of Human Relations: Speak with others as you would like them to speak with you. We all tend to look for ways in which we can refute our opponent's point rather than for areas of agreement. More often than not, there is part of what he says with which you can agree. In answering him, then, look for the points you have in common rather than taking issue with all that he has said.

2. In replying, don't look upon him as your opponent. Remember that he is also working for the same company, and, in the case of a subordinate, under your supervision. He is not your enemy; he is a co-worker. It takes two to make a fight, and he is not any more anxious to start one than you are. Keep your attitude one of *conciliation* rather than opposition.

3. Avoid strong disagreement. When you start your reply, it is better to omit the word *"dis*agree," for when he hears this he immediately becomes defensive, steels himself to your statement, and thinks chiefly of how he will "disagree" with you in turn as soon as you are finished. The most conciliatory way to reply is to state and advance your position.

4. Restate his position as you understand it, before you state your own and your degree of difference. The very act of doing this leads you to understand his point more clearly and to realize that it may not be a bad one after all. It also allows you time to cool off, like the old admonition to "count to ten before you reply."

After you have stated his point, then indicate where you stand in relation to it, perhaps in this vein: "Jim, I understand your point to be . . . and I like these aspects of your proposal. . . . I wonder, however, when we consider the company as a whole instead of just our department, whether it will work. Let's explore another way of looking at it and perhaps arrive at a solution that will satisfy all of us."

5. Support your position. You should then introduce all the persuasion, reasoning, and evidence you can muster to show

that your point of view is sound and will work. In doing this, try to be less dogmatic and direct when you touch on matters you know will bring up feelings and attitudes in him contrary to yours. We are not suggesting that it is more important to please him than to make your point. You have more than a right to maintain your position. Sometimes you have an obligation to do so.

6. Keep your manner pleasant. Your facial expression can be pleasant and friendly. Your voice can be kept under control. Studies show that the pitch of a shrill, excited voice in itself can deeply affect the emotions and feelings of another person. It also makes rational listening very difficult.

Finally, we must remember that there never will be strict rules governing the business of getting along with people. Since people differ from each other, so must we differ in the way we handle them. The most we can hope for are signposts that point out the general direction our behavior should take.

SUMMARY

Everything you do as a manager must be done through people. Though this is an age of automation and technology which places heavy emphasis on the machine, people must run them and probably always will. In recent years, through research in human relations, we have learned that it is no longer possible to boss, direct, and order others to do our bidding. We must lead, motivate, and build a climate and atmosphere in which people want to do their best, not simply because they are told to do so, but for their own satisfactions.

In business, people must be treated as individuals, and given opportunities to participate and to develop cooperative team efforts. Motivation is management's major tool in reaching these objectives. Leadership must be developed that emphasizes consideration of others and the satisfaction of their basic wants.

All human relations are based on contact with others in the work scene. It therefore behooves today's manager to be a student of communications and to apply his skill as a communicator at all times.

QUESTIONS AND PROBLEMS

1. As manager of a small department in a company, you decide to hang up a sign bearing a short message that will make everyone conscious

of the importance of good human relations. What would you put on such a sign?

2. Assume that you have sent to the personnel office a performance appraisal of an employee under your supervision. Outline the plan for a twenty-minute interview with him in which you will go over the appraisal and counsel him in his work.

3. Assume that you are to confront an employee or a manager of another department about a situation on which he holds an opinion that is quite different from yours. Attempt to conciliate and discuss the best solution that the two of you can reach in a five-minute exchange.

4. Hold a panel discussion with two or three other members of your group on man's basic drives and their bearing upon good human relations. Which drives are most dominant in most people? What does motivation have to do with satisfying these drives?

REFERENCE NOTES

[1] War Manpower Commission, *Job Relations Training* (manual), Washington, D.C., 1944.

[2] General Motors Corporation, *Man to Man on the Job*, 1943, pp. 3, 4, 9.

[3] American Society of Training Directors, *Training Directors Journal*, November, 1956, p. 51.

[4] Donald R. Schoen, "Human Relations: Boon or Bogle?," *Harvard Business Review*, November-December, 1957, pp. 43-45.

[5] H. Landsberger, *Hawthorne Revisited*, Cornell University Press, 1958. For other works compiling research studies in human relations, see C. M. Arensberg, *et al.*, *Research in Industrial Human Relations*, Harper & Row, 1957; and Donald and Eleanor Laird, *The New Psychology for Leadership*, McGraw-Hill, 1956.

[6] Fred Blum, *Toward a Democratic Work Process*, Harper & Row, 1953.

[7] The Laird book cited in note 5 is a very interesting, condensed, and practical treatment of over one hundred major research studies dealing with human relations and leadership.

[8] Saul W. Gellerman, *Motivation and Productivity*, American Management Association, 1963.

[9] Earl P. Strong, "Attitudes Are Important to Management," *Pennsylvania Business Survey*, Pennsylvania State University, February, 1955.

[10] Carl Rogers, *Counseling and Psychotherapy* and *Client-Centered Therapy*, Houghton Mifflin, 1942 and 1951.

READING REFERENCES

Argyris, Chris, *Interpersonal Competence and Organizational Effectiveness,* Dorsey Press, 1962.

Bursk, E. C., *Human Relations for Management,* Harper & Row, 1956.

Davis, Keith A., *Human Relations in Business,* McGraw-Hill, 1957.

Dubin, R., *Human Relations in Administration,* Prentice-Hall, 1951.

Gellerman, Saul W., *Motivation and Productivity,* American Management, 1963.

Hoslett, Schuyler D., *Human Factors in Management,* Harper & Row, 1951.

Lawrence, Paul R., *et al., Organizational Behavior and Administration,* Dorsey Press, 1961.

Maier, N. R. F., *Principles of Human Relations,* Wiley, 1952.

McGregor, Douglas, *The Human Side of Enterprise,* McGraw-Hill, 1960.

9

COMMUNICATIONS

Communication plays such a major part in good management today that some would go so far as to say that management *is* communication. The title of a recent book by a General Electric executive, *Managing by Communication,* suggests this "wedding" of communication with management. The author leaves little room for doubt when he says, "The past decade should be chronicled by historians as the age in which businessmen discovered communication as their principal tool."[1] Indeed, none of the traditional management objectives, including planning, organizing, motivating, directing, and controlling, can be accomplished without communication.

FACTORS INFLUENCING COMMUNICATION IN BUSINESS

It is difficult to appraise this extraordinary phenomenon or to single out the causes that brought it about. Business has been in a state of constant change since World War II, partly because of its rapid growth and partly because of the increased demands of the individual. It is well to remember that "business" is part of a world climate which has brought all peoples closer together. The uncertainties of our time intensify our need for information from all corners of the earth. And for most of us this information is at our fingertips, through the mass communications media; we don't have to pry it out of an unwilling boss.

This has resulted in several circumstances which affect the

concern of modern business with communication. First, we have available the means of receiving information we feel is vital in our daily living. Second, we have become more informed and more sophisticated in our knowledge of local, national, and international affairs. Third, as a people we interact more, spending more time together talking things over.

All these factors are operative in business. Modern business has to be regarded as part of the total social climate of our day. At the same time, certain developments place heavy demands on industrial communication: increased size, expanding technology, growing competition, more powerful unions, and research in the social and human sciences.

Growth in size places heavy burdens on communication because of increased numbers of people, more levels of management through which communication must flow, and more distance and locations to be covered.

Complexity and technology have made greater the need for clear explanations of difficult subject matter. This factor has also placed a greater challenge on decision-making and encouraged the seeking of advice and counsel from experts and subordinates. This in turn has increased the need for communication upward, placing a higher premium on listening and on conference leading and participating.

Competition has always been a major factor in accomplishing the goals of any business. Modern business has recognized more and more that good customer relations depend on a healthy internal communication climate, not merely on the plush carpet of the public relations office.

The unions have grown in size and stature in the last several decades and have hastened the recognition by management of the worker as an individual. This has led to increased emphasis on keeping him informed and giving him more participative opportunities.

Research in the social sciences and the human factors of management may exert a greater influence than many realize. As we noted in the previous chapter, since the famous studies at the Western Electric Hawthorne plant, there have been countless attempts by researchers to link the human factors of morale, motivation, recognition, and participation to productivity.[2] One of the major conclusions of these studies is that all management's human relations goals are accomplished through good oral communication.

MODERN MANAGEMENT CONCEPTS INFLUENCING ORAL COMMUNICATION

The increasing demand for better oral communication has placed heavy emphasis on interaction, group cooperation, and increased personal contacts. Some estimate that 75 percent or more of a manager's total communicative time is spent on the oral communication skills of speaking and listening. One writer sums up the manager's need to communicate as follows: "No matter whether the manager's job is engineering, accounting, or selling, his effectiveness depends on his ability to listen and to read, and his ability to speak and to write."[3] Others put it this way: "The foreman's chief task is to serve as a communication center."[4] "The present goals of industrial management are teamwork, cooperation, and great enough participation to make all employees feel a part of the social work group. Communication has reached a major position in the achievement of these goals."[5]

The major modern management concepts and practices which place heavy emphasis on oral communication include the following:

Leadership. This is the combination of attitudes, personal qualities and skills, and management practices which distinguish today's democratic manager from yesterday's autocratic boss. It encompasses the desire to motivate, encourage, guide, consult, and allow for permissive opportunities to participate by subordinates.

Recognition. This is the attitude of management which regards all employees as *people,* gives them proper credit and respect, and allows them greater participation and interaction.

Participation. Recognition brings more opportunities to participate in problem-solving, decision-making, and achieving organization goals.

Consultation. Today's manager seeks the judgment, opinions, knowledge, and experience of others in order to make better decisions and to keep informed. Partly this is because the subordinate is a more capable and informed person than he used to be. At the International Business Machines, Endicott, New York, plant a few years ago, the plant superintendent had a series of "consultative conferences" with six hundred supervisors over a period of six months, which resulted in the issuance of a company statement that consultative management was a major management practice.

Delegation. Today's tendency to delegate more responsibilities to subordinates requires clear explanation of the assignment, clear reporting back, and other communication obligations.

Teamwork. Here the effort is to develop group cooperation in achieving production or other objectives. Studies show that a number of persons working on the same objective will accomplish it better when they feel they are working together as a team.

Counseling. Sitting down with subordinates to work out solutions to problems, to evaluate and encourage work performance, and to advise on other matters is a practice used more and more by today's manager. The increased emphasis on merit ratings has made the counseling interview following this rating a major management responsibility.

Decision-making. Sharing in decision-making, particularly on matters of direct concern to subordinates, increases the manager's responsibilities as a group leader in many ways.

Climate developing. This management objective encompasses all the others. In order to develop a wholesome, democratic, work environment, the manager must practice them all to the extent that the company's management philosophy permits.

The skill and practice of a manager as a communicator, therefore, depend on at least three major influences: (1) the climate, philosophy, and general practices of management in the organization as a whole; (2) the manager's own philosophy and practices, including his personal traits and habits; and (3) the specific principles and techniques of communication required in the particular situation.

ORGANIZATIONAL COMMUNICATION

Managers spend the major part of their workday—some surveys reporting as much as 80 to 90 percent—communicating. Internal organizational communication is usually discussed in terms of direction of flow. The external or public relations aspects of business communication are also of vital concern.

Internal Communication

Internal communication flow must go in three major directions: downward, upward, and horizontally. Whereas most communication does flow in these directions, considering the multiple relationships that exist in any organization, and especially in today's large ones, it is a mistake to think only in terms of these three. The participative objective, which is becoming increasingly important in the development of a democratic work climate, calls for more interpersonal communication and greater emphasis on group and conference activity. The formal organization chart, therefore, does not depict the actual flow of informal communication, despite the constant effort that should be made to communicate through channels.

Downward communication. This has as its major goal the conveying of information and knowledge intended to explain, clarify, and motivate. Management has always done a better job of this, chiefly because most policy and instruction originate at the top and have to be sent downward. And the more management clings to the older tradition of ordering and directing rather than consulting and participating, the more the downward channels will be used.

Downward communication is made difficult by such barriers as the number of levels that must be gone through, status differences, motivational differences, geographical distance, and the problem of determining what people want to know. Most management realizes it should overtell rather than undertell. The organizational pyramid is also being examined today to determine whether the number of levels can be reduced. There is a trend toward reducing the levels and broadening the lower bases, partly to make communication lines shorter. Studies show that loss in understanding an original message which started at the top of the organization and passed through five levels may be as much as 75 percent. Messages that deal primarily with informational and factual material rather than inferences and opinions, are tied to reader-listener interests, and try to motivate and show reasons "why" are less apt to be distorted as they pass from one level to another.

Upward communication. This has increased since modern management began giving greater attention to suggestions from below and more sharing in decision-making. The result has been a heightened interest in the skill of listening as well as conference leading. The increase in participative objectives has also brought *v* more emphasis on feedback and the exchange of information and opinion between levels. Some company presidents have written books whose titles imply an emphasis on both upward and participative communication.[6]

Horizontal communication. This involves coordination between departments of the line organization and between staff and line functions. Formerly one of the weaker aspects of internal communication, it is now receiving more attention, chiefly through increased use of the conference. In the area of staff functions, it is interesting to note the engineer's increased need for communication in explaining technical matters to line personnel. Studies conducted at Purdue University and at the Pennsylvania State University show that engineering graduates regard communicative ability as the most important of all skills. The Penn State study makes this conclusion: "The outstanding need of the engineer in terms of the survey is in the Communications area. Almost eight out of every ten engineers indicated a need or deficiency in one of the communicative skills."[7]

External Communication

External communication includes the public relation goals of the organization and the sales or customer relations goals, which are closely allied. We are finding that companies with good internal communications usually have better customer relations. A well-informed salesman, waitress, or bank clerk will do a better job of selling or serving the customer; and if he has a feeling of belonging to a good organization, which is the result of good internal communications, he will be better motivated to accomplish the organization's goals.

Many companies are making a major effort to improve their public image by increased speaker activities to community groups. Company speakers bureaus now make available to all kinds of organizations speakers who are usually members of management or staff officers. Among these are the American Telephone & Telegraph Company, General Electric, General Motors, United States Steel, Trans-Canada Airlines, and Smith, Kline & French Laboratories. In the AT & T Bell System, over 2,500 speakers talked to audiences totaling over eleven million people in 1963.[8]

THE MANAGER'S RESPONSIBILITIES AS A COMMUNICATOR

All of this obviously adds up to a major responsibility on the part of the manager to become a better communicator, for communication is integrated with everything he does. He must also realize that it is his responsibility to improve the organizational climate of management as a whole, so that communication will flow more freely. His first step toward improvement as a communicator should be to adopt modern practices of leadership, consultation, delegation, recognition, participation, shared decision-making, counseling, and so on. Then he will be ready to practice some of the techniques for developing communicative skills which we discuss later in this chapter.

Many companies are issuing statements of policy on communication to management personnel in order to spell out the company's philosophy, practices, and methods of communicating. Such companies as United States Steel, General Electric, and Johnson & Johnson have put such policies in the form of booklets. Others have done this by a letter or memorandum from executive management to all personnel.

An interesting summary of a manager's responsibilities as a communicator is contained in a policy bulletin on "Company Communications" issued to all levels of management by the Progress Manufacturing Company, through its executive vice president, Harold Yoskin, in the form of a letter:

Communication is playing a more and more important part in the successful operation of our business. . . . We have more people to inform, more people to listen to and to help us solve our problems, and more things to talk about. . . .

For a manager to be a good communicator, he must have the skills of speaking and listening effectively, leading meetings, talking things over informally in interviews and in personal relations, and writing effectively. . . .

I urge all of you to give thought to your own personal communications working toward these goals:

1. Be sure that you plan for communication whenever you start anything new or make a change. Who needs to know? When? How? How much?
2. Keep your superior informed at all times.
3. Establish and keep open the channels of communication with other managers.
4. Pass on to your subordinates whatever information they should have.
5. Make clear all oral explanations, instructions, and delegations.
6. Take time out for frequent contacts with your employees and make clear to them that they should feel free to come to see you on problems and to make suggestions.
7. Listen sympathetically and always with an attempt to understand the other person.
8. Hold meetings with your subordinates at regular intervals of about once a week, to keep them informed, to give them opportunities to express themselves, and to solve problems and develop a total group spirit of cooperation.

9. Answer written memos and letters promptly and clearly. Initiate and write letters, memos, and reports when needed. Send copies to appropriate persons.

10. At your next meeting with your group, discuss this Policy Bulletin on communications and how you and your group can best carry it out.[9]

In considering your responsibilities as a communicator, it is well to keep in mind the continuous nature of communication. The issuance of a policy in itself accomplishes nothing unless it is carried out, starting at the top where it is issued and throughout the organization. Nor is it wise to develop a communications "program," which implies some specific activity for a limited period of time. We are not dealing with a program but with a combination of attitudes, philosophies of management, policies, and skills. Another mistake of top management is to assume that everyone is skilled enough to carry out his communication responsibilities. Attention must be given to training and development. This thought was well expressed by the Director of Employee Relations of the E. I. du Pont de Nemours & Company:

The effectiveness of management in oral communication depends to a considerable extent upon the ability of management representatives. This ability, however, is not something necessarily native to the person's own qualifications; he can be trained to do a more effective job by the proper methods. It is my opinion that by far the greater number of effective management efforts in the field of oral communication have been obtained by training than by native ability per se.[10]

The amount of training being done in business, professional, government, and other in-service programs in the areas of oral communication is indicated in several other recent studies.[11]

Some companies use memo blanks with an admonition at the top such as: "Don't say it—Write it!" This slogan was changed by the Du Pont Company, after a study of their communications in major laboratories, to read: "Talk it over—Then write it down!" The trend in today's management is to talk things over more than ever before and then to make a written memo for a more permanent record or for distribution to others. Certainly the warning, "Don't say it," is not within present-day management philosophy.

The major methods of communicating used in an organization and the corresponding communication skills that need to be developed could be listed as follows:

Communication	*Skill*
Oral:	
Talks to groups	Speaking to groups
Informal contacts—conversation and telephone	Speaking with and listening to others
Interviews	Interpersonal relations
Conferences and meetings	Leading and participating in conferences
Instructing	
Written:	
Letters	Writing
Memorandums	Writing
Company bulletins and manuals	Reading
Reports	Writing and reading
Bulletin boards	Reading

THE NATURE OF COMMUNICATION

The act of communicating with others is far from a simple process. If we stop to consider some of the misconceptions about it, we may better understand what the communication process really is. Let's look at them:

1. Communication is a simple process. Actually, it is just about the most complex activity that human beings undertake. This is because human beings have quite complex psychological attitudes, reasoning processes, emotions and feelings, frames of reference, prejudices, and so on. When one person tries to communicate with another, all of these are operative and are apt to form barriers to understanding.

2. Communication is one-way: from one person *to* another. But it must be remembered that when you initiate and send a message, the other person receives and interprets it according to *his* wishes and *his* meaning. In this sense, communication must be regarded as a *two-way* and even a *circular process,* in which the sender must take into account the reaction and feedback of his receiver. This in turn will influence his continued act of communicating, until the interacting relationship results in a mutual exchange of meaning which the listener now accepts.

3. Words themselves have meaning. We have learned that they do not, that they are merely symbols used in an attempt to communicate meaning. And the meaning inferred from them is that which the receiver wants to attach to them, not necessarily that which the sender intended.

4. People are all alike. If this were so, we could assume that the same communication would be interpreted identically by everyone. But people differ in their backgrounds, education, job interests, personal interests, tastes, attitudes, emotional involvement, and their use of the reasoning process. Equally important are the images of ourselves that we convey and the delusion that the image we think we convey is the same as the image the other person has of us. Nor can we divorce what he thinks of us from the meaning he will infer from what we say. In this connection, we know that our facial expressions, gestures, general attitude, and even dress can make a difference in the conveying of meaning.

5. People are all different. It would at first appear that this is the reverse of the preceding misconception, but in a sense both statements are true. People are not all different in their basic drives and wants, and all communication should take into consideration which of these are operative in a given instance.

6. Good communicators, particularly good speakers, are born, not made. Actually, the record is full of examples which disprove this misconception, from Demosthenes, Patrick Henry, and Daniel Webster to Franklin Roosevelt, Harry Truman, and John F. Kennedy, all of whom worked hard to become more effective speakers.

7. A speech is an oration, a performance, a public display. Perhaps a century ago, when the average American was less informed and went to hear a speaker as a combination information source and public entertainer, a speech was so regarded. But today the average American audience is more informed, knowledgeable, and sophisticated. It would give the elocutionary and studied gesture of yesterday's "performer" a cool reception. We prefer speakers who are truly communicators, who want to exchange ideas with us, talk things over, and do not appear above us.

8. Reading a speech from manuscript is the best procedure. This may be the surest way to fail if it is not well done. The manuscript speech must be carefully prepared and practiced so that the speaker can read it in as close to a natural conversational manner as possible. Today's speaker uses the extemporaneous method for more effective communication, preparing well, making an outline, and presenting his ideas in language that is adapted to his audience and the immediate situation.

With all these barriers and misconceptions, one may wonder how we are able to communicate meaning at all. Actually, the barriers are not so high nor our differences so great that we cannot overcome them and achieve communication. We will now turn our attention to some basic principles of good communication which we can learn and practice.

DEVELOPING YOUR ABILITY AS A COMMUNICATOR

First, you must accept the idea that you can improve your ability and effectiveness, through self-practice as well as through organized instruction. If your company or organization has in-service training in communication, you should try to attend these sessions. If you can attend other training groups, such as those conducted by colleges and universities or other adult education groups, do so. If you are a college undergraduate, take as many courses in communication as you can before you graduate.

Second, accept the concept that communication is a circular, two-way process. It is not self-expression or exhibitionism. All communication must be other-person-centered, not self-centered. In communicating with another, always adapt your message to *his* status, *his* interests, *his* understanding, *his* attitudes.

With these basic factors in mind, you are ready to apply the more specific principles of good communication:

1. Have a purpose. Most discourse has one (or both) of two major purposes: (1) to inform and make clear (impart information); and (2) to persuade by influencing attitudes, beliefs, feelings, or actions (strengthen or change convictions). These purposes can be more easily accomplished when you are the sole speaker, as in making a speech or giving instructions. When you are a member of a conference, or a leader, or one of two persons in a conversation or interview, the other participants will help shape (or distort) your objectives if the effort is not cooperative. It is not enough simply to have a broad or general purpose; this must be narrowed down to the specific purpose you want to accomplish regarding the subject, the listeners or readers, and the situation.

2. Analyze your listeners or readers. You should try to find out all you can about your audience's interest in the subject, degree of present knowledge, ability to comprehend, and their attitudes and beliefs. Here you must take into consideration the fact that people are not all alike, but have different abilities, interests, and attitudes.

3. Organize your thoughts. You must consider the best possible arrangement and sequence of the main ideas you want to convey. This is important in a speech, a conference, an interview,

or in writing a letter or report. You might use a historical or time sequence, a space or geographical sequence, or some other logical arrangement when your purpose is to inform; or a problem-solution, need-satisfaction, or climax sequence when your purpose is to persuade. Organization is also facilitated by clear transitions as you move from one point to another, from introduction to main development to conclusion.

4. Develop your subject interestingly. Communication may be interesting because it affects vital needs of the audience, because it is clearly organized, or because it is developed with materials that are attention-getting. Occasionally, one speaks just to hold attention, as in the purely entertaining after-dinner speech with no serious message, or in animated social conversation at a cocktail party. But serious messages should be made interesting by the employment of certain principles of attention. We know that we attend more closely to material that is concrete and specific, unusual or novel, recent or proximate, vital to our basic drives, and includes reference to real people and human interest situations. That is why references to specific places, people, and things are a fundamental device to help explain, make clear, and hold interest. Similarly, we use analogies and comparisons so that the listener will transpose his knowledge of the familiar to what is unfamiliar in your point. And we support our opinions with the testimony of authority, statistics, and facts.

5. Develop your own personal effectiveness. Aristotle, who was one of the greatest rhetoricians of all time, expounded considerably on the "ethos" of the speaker, or his "ethical-proof" value. To him, the speaker's reputation, stature in the community, honesty, moral conduct, sincerity, and enthusiasm were qualities that influenced the listener's reactions. This could be stated another way: If you like a person as an individual, you will tend to like what he says, and you will tend to interpret what he says in terms of what you believe to be his meaning and intent.

Another important aspect of this concept is that the speaker's effectiveness is not determined by the immediate setting alone. The listener will refer what he says to a total frame of reference which includes all their previous relationships. That is why an attitude of utmost sincerity will not work if over a period of time you have developed a reputation for insincerity. The same holds true if you want the other person to offer advice or supply information, when in the past you have been consistently autocratic and directive.

Your "ethical-proof" value is, of course, apparent in the immediate situation. The way you handle the subject itself, the degree of clarity in your statement, the logic of your organization, and the depth of your knowledge will all show through. If you give the impression of "really knowing what you're talking about," the listener will tend to believe and understand your position.

SPECIFIC AREAS OF TRAINING AND DEVELOPMENT

In the business scene today, training to improve communications may be divided into these major areas:

Executive seminars on communication. Some companies set up regular meetings at the executive level to discuss communication problems, methods of communicating company policy, and the development of specific communication skills, such as speaking, listening, interviewing, and participating in conferences.

Middle management seminars. These are concerned with communication problems at this level and methods of improvement.

Courses in specific skills development. These include the ability to prepare and present a speech, give instructions, lead a conference, interview and counsel, and achieve good interpersonal relations. Such courses are becoming an integral part of in-service training in companies like General Motors, General Electric, Esso, Mobil Oil, Du Pont, and Ford, as well as smaller organizations, government, and professional groups.[12]

SPEAKING AND LISTENING

The basic techniques for becoming a good speaker apply to all communicative situations. This is one reaon why courses in public speaking are well attended and continue to be basic to oral communication development. In recent years, the increased emphasis on two-way communication, and the greater participation of subordinates in decision-making has brought about a realization that listening ability can be improved. That listening is heavily influenced by personal attitudes is amusingly illustrated by an anecdote about W. C. Fields, whose doctor advised him to cut down on his drinking, as alcohol was affecting his hearing. Fields replied, "Doc, I like what I'm drinking so much better than what I'm hearing that I think I'll keep on with it."

Another observation is that you cannot separate speaking from listening. As you practice better speaking habits, you become conscious that one of your objectives is to improve the listening habits of others. You are also improving your own listening ability by becoming more aware of what to watch for in the speaking of others. Here are some guiding rules:

As a Speaker	*As a Listener*
1. Plan your remarks in terms of listener reaction. Have a purpose.	1. Anticipate the situation and the message of *this* speaker.
2. Organize your main thoughts clearly.	2. Look for main points of the speaker.
3. Keep your specific purpose in mind at all times.	3. Analyze the speaker's purpose.
4. Be listener-centered, not self-centered.	4. Be speaker-centered, not self-centered.
5. Avoid being too autocratic or dogmatic.	5. Consider speaker's right to be autocratic if in a superior position.
6. Use sufficient facts, evidence, and other proof.	6. Weigh speaker's facts and relate evidence to his conclusions.
7. Consider possible listener prejudices and attitudes.	7. Suppress your prejudices as you try to understand speaker's position.
8. If a change is proposed: Tell why. Show advantages. Seek listener suggestions. Be clear to *this* listener. Proceed slowly.	8. Be open-minded to new ideas: Find out why. Weigh the advantages. Make suggestions. Understand *this* speaker. Think before you reply.
9. Be enthusiastic and projective in your manner.	9. Be physically alert and attentive.
10. Look the listener in the eye.	10. Look the speaker in the eye.
11. Use language he understands.	11. Analyze language in terms of what the speaker means.

THE CONFERENCE

Some would say that the business conference is the most important communication tool in modern management. The National Industrial Conference Board, in their nationwide surveys of industry and business, *Communication within the Management Group* and *Communicating with Employees,* found that the conference was used more than any other medium to accomplish a combination of communication objectives. Other surveys and practices of specific companies confirm this conclusion. Esso Standard Oil has a course in "Conference Leadership," the Du Pont Company a course called "Discussion Leading," and Johnson

& Johnson a course called "Conference Leadership Training," to name just a few. All these training programs emphasize at least three uses of the conference: (1) to solve problems, consult, make decisions, and arrive at policy; (2) to keep people informed, explain policies, procedures, and give instructions; and (3) to provide a participative medium, recognition, and the development of group cooperation and climate.

We are not suggesting that the conference should be used to solve all problems and make all decisions. Actually, the majority of managers use the conference as a consultative medium in decision-making, drawing out facts and opinions from their subordinates, on which they later make decisions.

In developing your own knowlege and skill in the conference process, remember that you are much more a member of a conference than you are its leader. Too many courses emphasize only leadership training.

Here are some suggestions on leading a conference:

1. Establish the practice of holding conferences at a regular time each week.

2. Plan an agenda and distribute it in advance. Ask your group to suggest items for the agenda, perhaps at the previous conference or during the week.

3. Arrange the best possible facilities. A conference group should preferably sit around a table with the leader integrated into the group. Members should be face to face. Use name cards if they do not know each other well. Have pad and pencil at each place. Arrange blackboard or chart easel for displaying prepared material or for developing points during the meeting.

4. For your own use, make an outline, based on the agenda, planning the sequence, questions you will raise, information to be presented, visual aids, and handouts.

5. Plan questions carefully. These are your chief tool for achieving the participation of the members. The basic type of question is the general or "overhead" question thrown out to the group. The "direct" question is asked of a specific person and should be used when you are sure he is ready to respond. Questions should be clear and not too abstract or vague. The abstract or broad question should be followed by more specific ones. Questions have two basic purposes: to seek information or clarification, and to seek opinion or judgment. Know which objective you want when you ask a question. Do not comment on every answer to a question; encourage others in the group to do so.

6. When asked a question by a member, throw it back to the group for reply rather than answering it yourself. Try to develop a spontaneous discussion among the members, not a give-and-take between yourself and a single member.

7. Keep your manner alert, animated, and direct.

8. When you are trying to get a group's opinions on a problem, yet still want to make the decision yourself, be honest and explain this to your group.

9. Encourage the voluntary offering of possible solutions before you or the group starts to evaluate and apply critical standards.

10. Refrain from offering your own opinion, depending on the degree to which you can allow the group to decide. Do not offer your opinion at the outset of a problem-solution discussion.

As a conference member:

1. Come to the conference with an open mind and cooperative attitude.

2. Try to understand the leader's methods and objectives and his reasons for running the meeting as he does. If he does not keep the discussion under control, help him get it on the right track.

3. Participate spontaneously and don't wait to be called on by the leader. When you have information and facts to submit, offer them at appropriate times.

4. Do not try to monopolize the discussion at the expense of other members.

5. Speak up with animation and enthusiasm, addressing all members and not just the leader.

6. When you have to take issue with someone, first understand his position, look for areas of agreement, state your own position, and support it with evidence and reasoning.

INFORMAL CONTACTS, INTERVIEWING, COUNSELING

All the principles that apply to the communication process, speaking and listening, and conference participation apply equally to your informal contacts with others.

Informal contacts. A manager's informal contacts within the work scene can go a long way toward building a climate of social interaction and enhancing his own "ethical-proof" value among his subordinates and associates. Informal talks also serve to keep you informed of developments, feelings, and attitudes.

Interviews. Before an interview you should plan in anticipation of the subject, problems, and other matters that are likely to come up. Here are some suggestions for conducting the actual interview.

1. Put aside other business on your desk, and do not accept phone calls or other interruptions during an interview. Provide comfortable surroundings and a place for the other person to sit where you can look at each other without straining.

2. Put him at ease with a friendly few words on common-ground matters, leading into the main subject gradually. Then indicate the purpose of the interview, or ask him to do so if he has been the initiator.

3. If a problem is being discussed, get all the facts first. In a counseling situation, this is extremely important. If it is a work performance interview, following a merit rating, discuss strengths before weaknesses.

4. Ask questions and listen to the answers. Don't just ask them for the sake of doing so.

5. If you must disagree, do so pleasantly while giving the most possible recognition to his position.

6. Be aware of the passage of time, both for his sake and yours. It is difficult to strike a balance between setting a permissive climate, which tends to be time-consuming, and being so highly organized that you rush through the sequence of points to be taken up.

7. Be constructive in proposing solutions. Try to get him to suggest solutions.

8. Keep the sequence of problem analysis, weighing possible solutions, finding the best solution, coming to a decision as the pattern for most problem-solving interviews and conferences, as well as most counseling situations.

Counseling. Today's manager frequently finds himself in counseling situations with his subordinates and others. The essence of good counseling is to explore the problem at hand from the other person's point of view and knowledge of the facts, then to be as "nondirective" as possible in trying to draw out possible solutions and courses of action. Counseling should take place in an atmosphere of mutual trust; based on wholesome work relations over a period of time.

WRITING

Most of the principles of good oral communication also apply to good writing. All letters, memorandums, reports, and other documents should have a purpose, be clearly organized, and be adapted to the reader. Writing is usually addressed to a wider audience than oral communication. Today's letters and memos are moving away from the stiff and formal type of expression. Write or dictate a letter as though you were talking to the person who will read it.

In writing reports, first make an outline, indicating the main points to be developed, the supporting material under each point, and their best sequence. Then plan the introduction and the conclusion. Work for brevity and conciseness. When you are finished, make a digest or précis for those who do not have time to read the entire report.

You can perfect your writing by studying a good text (some are listed at the end of this chapter) or your company's handbook on writing, plus a dictionary, and don't be afraid to consult them when you are in doubt.

SUMMARY

Today's manager is primarily a communicator. His effectiveness will depend on the climate and management policies of his organization, his own manager philosophy and practices, and his knowledge and skill in applying the principles of good communication. His primary method will probably be oral, but this will be supplemented with written documents. The basic principles of good communication apply regardless of the medium: Have a purpose, clearly organized supporting ideas, constant adaptation to the other person, and a warm, communicative manner of presentation. Remember that communication is not external and mechanical; it comes from within and is based on a background of environment, attitudes, feelings, and awareness of those involved.

QUESTIONS AND PROBLEMS

1. Make an analysis of the communication policy and methods of some organization with which you are familiar. How could they be improved?
2. Compare the relative effectiveness of oral and written communication in the following objectives: giving instructions, announcing a policy, solving an employee problem or grievance, making a decision on a problem.
3. Prepare a 10-minute speech in which you will inform or instruct on a policy, plan, process, or other subject, with a specific listening group in mind.

4. Plan a 10-minute interview on a specific problem which you will conduct with another person in front of the class.
5. Plan to lead a 20-minute conference with a larger group or the whole class in which you will spend most of the time on problem analysis. If time permits, plan another conference with the same group in which you try to reach a solution and a decision.

REFERENCE NOTES

[1] Willard V. Merrihue, *Managing by Communication*, McGraw-Hill, 1960, p. 5.

[2] See Elton Mayo, *The Human Problems of an Industrial Civilization*, Macmillan, 1933; F. J. Roethlisberger and W. J. Dickson, *Management and the Worker*, Harvard University Press, 1938; and H. Landsberger, *Hawthorne Revisited*, Cornell University Press, 1958.

[3] Peter F. Drucker, *The Practice of Management*, Harper & Row, 1954, p. 346.

[4] Paul Pigors, *Effective Communication in Industry*, National Association of Manufacturers, 1949, p. 63.

[5] Harold P. Zelko and Harold J. O'Brien, *Management-Employee Communication in Action*, Howard Allen, 1957, pp. 1, 12.

[6] Such references as these are pertinent: Earl Planty and William Machaver, "Upward Communication, a Project in Executive Development," *Personnel*, January, 1952, pp. 304–319; and C. P. McCormick, *Multiple Management*, Harper & Row, 1938.

[7] Samuel S. Dubin and H. L. Marlow, "Continuing Education for Professional Engineers in Pennsylvania," monograph mimeo, Pennsylvania State University, 1964, p. 131.

[8] Harold P. Zelko, "Internal Communication and Customer Relations," *Public Relations Journal*, December, 1959, pp. 18-21; and S. M. Vinecour, "Speech as a Public Relations Tool," *Quarterly Review of Public Relations*, July, 1956, pp. 15-20.

[9] Progress Manufacturing Company, policy bulletin, "Company Communications," 1960.

[10] P. E. Lull, *et al.*, "Business and Industrial Communication from the Viewpoint of the Corporation President," monograph mimeo, Purdue University, 1954; also in "What Communication Means to the Company President," *Advanced Management*, March, 1955.

[11] Harold P. Zelko, "Speech and Conference Leadership Training in Industry," *Personnel*, September, 1950; and Mason A. Hicks, "Speech Training in Business and Industry," *Journal of Communication*, Winter, 1955.

[12] See company training manuals on communication subjects, under a variety of titles, and such surveys as National Industrial Conference Board, Studies in Personnel Policy No. 80, *Communication within the*

Management Group, and No. 129, *Communicating with Employees;* and those referred to above.

READING REFERENCES

Berlo, David K., *The Process of Communication,* Holt, Rinehart and Winston, 1960.

Cooper, Joseph D., *The Art of Decision Making,* Doubleday, 1961.

Dance, Frank E. X., *The Citizen Speaks,* Wadsworth, 1962.

Lee, Irving, *How to Talk with People,* Harper & Row, 1952.

Maier, Norman R. F., *Problem-Solving Discussions and Conferences,* McGraw-Hill, 1963.

Merrihue, Willard V., *Managing by Communication,* McGraw-Hill, 1960.

Oliver, Robert T., Harold P. Zelko, and Paul Holtzman, *Communicative Speech,* 3rd ed., Holt, Rinehart and Winston, 1962.

Redfield, Charles E., *Communication in Management,* University of Chicago Press, 1958.

Strong, Earl P., and Robert G. Weaver, *Writing for Business and Industry,* Allyn and Bacon, 1962.

Thayer, Lee O., *Administrative Communication,* Irwin, 1961.

Zelko, Harold P., *Successful Conference and Discussion Techniques,* McGraw-Hill, 1957.

Zelko, Harold P., and Harold J. O'Brien, *Management-Employee Communication in Action,* Howard Allen, 1957.

Zelko, Harold P., and Frank E. X. Dance, *Business and Professional Speech Communication,* Holt, Rinehart and Winston, 1965.

PART III

ANALYSIS OF THE TECHNICAL KNOWLEDGES AND SKILLS OF MANAGEMENT

The technical knowledges and skills in an organization make up the "power wheel" of management, just as the rear wheel of the bicycle is the power wheel of that vehicle. This is the realm in which the problems of management arise and in which lies, therefore, the real challenge to management—the solving of such problems. Since problems make up the "warp and woof" of the individual manager's job, he should not become disturbed when he is faced with not one problem but a myriad of problems piled one on top of another. The manager's job is to deal with problems. He is challenged by them; he should welcome them; and he must find solutions to them.

For the purposes of this book, an assumption is made that the "power wheel" is located in a production type of business organization and is a corporate entity with no fixed size. It could be small, medium, or large since the importance of technical knowledges and skills does not diminish or increase according to the sizes of the organization. We are choosing to examine a production type of business because it is a complex organization and is typical of a large majority of business enterprises. By working with this "maximum" as a basis, other types of organizations usually can be dealt with in an easier manner, since their organizational structure will be simpler.

Adaptations to the type of organization in which he is most interested or with which he is actually associated will need to be made by the reader. For example, the composite of technical knowledges and skills in the Bureau of Old-Age and Survivors Insurance of the U.S. Department of Health, Education, and Welfare consists of six major breakdowns: Personnel, Fiscal Budget, EE/ER Registration, Claims, Public Information, and Procurement. In the United States Air Force it consists of six also: Comptroller, Development, Matériel, Operations, Personnel, and Installations. In a large state university there are five major areas; namely, Administration, Academic Affairs, Research and Contracts, Development and Public Affairs, and Admissions and Records. A church organization was found to contain five major areas; in a professional law office there were three areas; in a medical center, four; in a retail store, seven.

The size of the business or organization will not necessarily affect the number of the major divisions of its operations, but the diversity of its operations will influence the number of major areas needed to cover the multiplicity of activities. Each type of business activity has its own organizational structure based upon its historical background and growth pattern. The structure may be different in every kind of business organization, but similarities often occur in the types of activities that are carried on within the organization, i.e., purchasing, selling, hiring of personnel, producing a product or service, etc.

Each of the major divisions used in the following discussion may be further broken down into divisions and/or departments, or even units, depending upon the organizational structure.

An organization's size is a matter of degree determined by volume of transactions handled, amount of goods manufactured, amount of goods shipped, etc., and the old "saw" that "We are too small to be bothered about good management practices" simply has no validity. There is always a place for good management! It is the first responsibility of a manager to know what technical knowledges and skills are required in his organization or division, whether he is general manager, a department manager, or a division superintendent.

In the pages that follow, a more detailed treatment of major areas of technical knowledges and skills is presented to demonstrate the activities that go on in various business divisions.

10

ADMINISTRATIVE MANAGEMENT

The subject matter of administrative management in a typical business organization consists of two distinct levels: (1) those matters that deal with top management issues, policies, and problems; and (2) those matters that deal with management problems at lower levels but which do not seem to fit into any of the other specialized fields. The result is a rather heterogeneous conglomeration of subject matter that at first sight may be confusing to the reader.

This chapter will acquaint the reader with some of the more important and typical problems found in the administrative management area. The problems presented here are common to the typical, medium-sized business organization. Larger organizations will, of course, have more problems; smaller ones will have fewer. Those discussed here appear in no particular order since at any given time one problem may be more important than another.

ORGANIZATION STRUCTURE

Since businesses are organized to achieve different objectives, their financial and manpower requirements will also be different. Therefore, in order for top management to determine the structure that is most appropriate for a particular business, it is first necessary to determine the needs of the organization.[1]

Types of Structures

Sole proprietorship. In this structure there is no legal distinction between the individual and the business, with the consequent unlimited liability of the owners for all debts incurred. The owner is not only obligated to the extent of his personal investment, but he may be required to give up his personal assets to satisfy business debts.

Partnership. This structure involves the same unlimited liability and personal responsibility as sole proprietorship. However, the liability and responsibility are shared by the members of the partnership.

Corporation. The corporation is considered a legal entity, owned by shareholders who are personally liable only to the extent of their investment. Any debts which cannot be satisfied out of the assets of the corporation result in a loss to the creditors; therefore the shareholders or owners of the corporation are considered to have only limited liability.

In addition to these three basic structures, there are many others which are mainly variations of them; their legal status, function, and desirability will vary accordingly.[2]

ORGANIZATION CHARTS

In order for a business to function efficiently, it is necessary that relationships between departments and individuals be firmly established so that the relative authority and status of each is clear to all concerned. Only then is the decision-making process (the function of management) able to operate as intended. This is not to ignore the fact that an informal system of relationships will exist regardless of what is indicated on an organization chart; however, the formal organization is the principal device for enabling a group to assemble in such a manner as to accomplish a specific objective, such as production, sales, etc.[3]

The organization chart serves to indicate graphically the principal levels of authority (top management, middle management, and supervisory management) and the relative authority within each level. It also serves to indicate the various functional groups or departments which have been established to accomplish the business objective, and the "span of control" (limits of supervision) which each supervisor or manager exercises.

An additional feature of the organization chart is the distinction it makes between "line" and "staff." The line elements in the organization both supervise other elements and are themselves supervised. Staff elements exercise no authoritative supervision over other elements in the organization, though they are supervised by a higher element. The line organization contains those operating units and departments concerned directly with operations, such as the sales department or production department. The staff organization consists of those units and departments which perform specialized services that are indirectly concerned with production and marketing; for example, the personnel department and the legal office.

POLICY DETERMINATION

To establish guidelines of action, management issues statements of policy which set forth in general terms the goals toward which all employees are expected to work, but do not normally indicate specific actions which should be taken.[4]

Policies may be established by top management which are applicable to the entire organization or they may be established by intermediate levels of management to apply to one department or section. An example of a top management policy statement might be: "All company employees are encouraged to further their formal education through off-duty study, toward which the company will contribute financial assistance." A department manager might establish a policy that "All work which leaves this department will be of the highest possible quality." Neither statement indicates specifications, but both establish general objectives.

No policy can cover the appropriate course of action for every situation. In certain situations it may even be necessary to take a course of action that is contrary to established policy. Such action is not normally desirable since it tends to weaken the authoritative value of other policies. Therefore it should only be taken after due consideration of the alternatives.

In order to insure employee awareness of company policies, many organizations publish a policy manual to clarify the company's position on key matters. Such a manual is generally more effective than oral statements, which are frequently misinterpreted.

PROCEDURES AND OPERATING MANUALS

Whereas a policy is a general statement or guideline indicating a desired objective, a procedure is the action or specific method to be employed to achieve the objective. For example, top management may make a policy statement that "Maximum safety precautions are to be observed at all times while on company premises." In order to implement this policy, a middle manager may draw up a list of procedures to be observed when operating production equipment, such as: "(1) Wear the specified protective clothing when operating machines. (2) Do not attempt to repair faulty equipment, notify the maintenance crew. (3) Unplug all equipment before leaving the shop."[5]

Procedures, like policies, are generally more effective if they are written. Many companies incorporate all statements of procedure in an operating manual.

PLANNING

Most businesses are continually changing in response to fluctuations in product demand, the addition of new products or services, technological developments, and other circumstances which modify the organization's goals or the methods in which they are achieved. It is highly advantageous for top management to anticipate as many changes as possible so that the organizational structure can be modified to integrate them smoothly into the business.

Many companies have full-time planning departments that continually evaluate the organization's current ability to accommodate anticipated developments. Recommended changes to meet future requirements are presented to top management for review and approval, after which a plan of implementation is established which will cause a minimum of disruption to everyday operations.[6]

The planning process should be the result of the careful analysis of data with respect to present conditions and future expectations. Since conditions and circumstances change, alternate plans or provisions should be made to satisfy all possible future developments.[7]

FORECASTING

The plans developed by a business are normally the result of predictions (forecasts) based on the nature and level of business activity, economic conditions, and company performance. Forecasts cannot be completely accurate since conditions are continually changing. However, under most circumstances they are accurate enough to permit management to choose between possible courses of action.[8]

Some of the functions for which forecasts prove to be valuable tools are:

1. Determining production levels. Sales forecasts indicate probable demand or sales potential for various products.

2. Determining materials requirements. Sales forecasts are very important here since many materials must be ordered months in advance to insure availability when required. Other forecasts may indicate the anticipated availability and cost of certain materials, thereby permitting their purchase at the most opportune time.

3. Determining facility and equipment requirements. Company plans for expanding the physical plant or purchasing new equipment are based largely on forecasts which take into consideration consumer buying motives. For example, it would not be wise to make a substantial investment in facilities and equipment to produce a product which is only a temporary fad.[9]

LEGAL CONSIDERATIONS

In order to maintain the free enterprise system, it is necessary to establish certain limitations on the power and authority (economic, political, and social) which business can exercise. It may seem like a paradox to speak simultaneously of limited business and free enterprise; however, history has demonstrated that legal controls over business are as necessary to maintain free enterprise as laws limiting individual prerogatives are to maintain a democracy.

Most organizations have legal departments or retain legal consultants for advice as needed. The nature of the legal problems faced by any business will be determined by its size, the type of product it manufactures, its rate of growth, and the nature of its labor supply. Most businesses require at least periodic advice on one or more of the following: monopoly and antitrust laws, patent or copyright laws, tax regulations, and labor legislation.[10]

PUBLIC RELATIONS

Company sales are frequently influenced by the opinion which customers have of the organization. The goal of public relations is to create a favorable impression of the company that will be reflected in higher sales. Public relations need not be directed toward customers and potential customers efforts alone, but may and usually do include all members of the community.[11]

The tools with which public relations work normally include the mass media of communications (radio, television, and newspapers), as well as special programs designed to attract the favorable public attention (guided tours of company facilities, sponsorship of community projects, and speaking engagements by company personnel).

MANPOWER UTILIZATION

Human labor is one of the key resources required to operate a business. However, human labor, like machines, has its limitations. Rare indeed, for example, is the talented purchasing agent who is equally skilled in advertising or any other area of the business. Rare also is the top-level manager who without previous training can step into a functional area of the business and perform effectively. With the growing complexity and specialization in modern business it becomes imperative that personnel be utilized in those jobs for which they possess the necessary qualifications, and this holds true regardless of the level of the job in the organization hierarchy.[12]

Job analyses, preferably written, indicate the duties, responsibilities, and degree of skill required for each job and its relationship to other jobs in the organization. From them it is possible to prepare "manning tables," which indicate the number of personnel required to achieve the desired production. In order to insure an adequate supply of executive talent, and avoid crash programs of reshuffling or recruiting, many organizations use replacement tables which indicate, by name, the line of succession for filling key positions.[13]

CONTROLS

In order to insure that the functioning of the organization does not deviate from plan, it is necessary to establish some method of comparing stated obectives with results actually achieved (controls) so corrective action can be taken where necessary or the soundness of either the organization or its plan can be re-examined.[14]

Business controls are numerous and complex. Some of the more common ones are policies, rules, procedures, reports, records, and budgets.[15] However, in order for controls to be of value, they must yield information which is capable of being analyzed or evaluated in terms of established standards. For example, the figures in a sales report are useless unless they can be compared with established standards which indicate either a profit or a loss. Without such standards management cannot determine whether it should plan additional production or stop production entirely.

A business cannot be controlled completely, however, mainly because of the limitations of the available measuring devices, especially in the area of human personality, attitudes, and motivation. Significant work is being undertaken to improve the measurement and control of the human aspects of business.

REPORTS

In order for management to make necessary modifications in operation, initiate corrective actions, and plan for future operations, it must receive feedback reporting progress in its various areas. Reports provide a two-way channel of communications through which information vital to the efficient functioning of the business can pass. In addition to management's requirements, stockholders desire information on the status of their investment, the government requires reports on the business' financial status for tax purposes, and numerous other organizations and associations require various information for special purposes.[16]

The nature, length, and complexity of reports vary widely. Some must be made out after each operation is completed, others are prepared daily, weekly, monthly, quarterly, and annually. They may vary in length from a mere check mark on a data processing card to documents containing many pages of data, computations, and analysis that require days or even weeks to complete. The significance of the information reported may be slight until it is consolidated by management and evaluated in terms of trends or deviation from established standards.[17]

STANDARDS OF PERFORMANCE

For administrative management to perform its decision-making function, it must have some way of interpreting the almost unlimited volume of information with which it is continually confronted. In the realm of product engineering, measurement and control standards are readily available. Administrative management, however, does not have precise instruments for evaluating individual performance and behavior; therefore it must turn to those aspects of the business which are measurable: sales volume, production costs, operating expenses, etc. Within each of these areas specific objectives or limits can be established which can function as standards of performance.

Such standards, however, are not absolute. For example, a salesman may be given a sales objective of two thousand units. If he fails to achieve this objective, management cannot hold him absolutely responsible since sales volume is determined by many factors outside the salesman's control. Management, however, must continue to establish such standards, if for no other reason than to serve as a basis or starting point for comparison and analysis.[18]

RESEARCH AND DEVELOPMENT

Research is concerned with the systematic evaluation and analysis of materials and methods for the purpose of obtaining information that will be of value in assisting the organization to achieve its basic objective. Development is the process of taking the information gained through research and integrating it with existing information so as to create a new product or procedure, or to achieve new uses for an existing product or procedure.

Research may be divided into two categories: (1) "basic research," which is conducted entirely for the purpose of gaining additional knowledge with no specific use in mind; and (2) "applied research," which utilizes the knowledge gained through basic research in the development of a new product or process, or the improvement of an existing product or process.[19]

Research and development are closely associated with product development, the principal distinction being that research and development are primarily concerned with the physical properties of the product or process whereas product development tends to be oriented toward their marketing potential. The value of research and development efforts can be better appreciated when it is realized that many products on the market today did not exist ten years ago. Therefore careful planning requires that action be taken now to insure the availability of a product for which there may be a demand in the future.[20]

PRODUCT DEVELOPMENT

Frequently, what was acceptable in the past proves to be unacceptable to meet present requirements; therefore it is only reasonable to assume that many ideas and procedures which are quite satisfactory for immediate needs will not be adequate to future ones. Farsighted management must continually evaluate the future sales potential of its product and determine whether it should be retained in present form, modified, or eliminated entirely. Concurrently, the farsighted management team will strive to develop new products to replace those which may be eliminated. Just as the buggy whip manufacturer of the early 1900s had to redirect his efforts toward a new product or face extinction with the advent of the automobile, so must the modern manufacturer redirect his efforts when faced with a decreasing demand for his product and/or services.

The reasons that products and services become obsolete are numerous and include the development of new materials, technological improvements, changes in consumer tastes, altered economic conditions, and political developments. The ways in which new products can be developed are also numerous. It may be necessary only to modify the existing product slightly, establish new uses for it, or package it more attractively. A seasonal manufacturer may desire to make a product that will enable him to achieve better utilization of personnel and equipment during the off-season, as, for example, a swim suit manufacturer who also makes ski clothes.[21]

PRODUCT PRICING

Contrary to popular belief, price determination is one of the most difficult aspects of executive decision-making, especially with respect to new or unique products or services. Unfortunately, pricing is not a simple matter of totaling production and marketing costs and adding a "reasonable" margin of profit.[22]

Before any attempt is made to establish a selling price, two basic principles must be considered: (1) Production costs are not static, but fluctuate in relation to production volume—the greater the volume, the lower the cost of production. (2) Consumer demand is not static, but fluctuates in relation to product price, quality, uniqueness, and competitive standing. Management must generally decide, therefore, whether it is more desirable to sell at a relatively high price and achieve a low sales volume or sell at a relatively low price and gain a high sales volume.

A key factor in such a situation would be the most efficient level of production at which the plant could operate. For example, assume that a plant could produce 2,000 units each week at a cost of $5.00 per unit. To produce in excess of 2,000 units would require the hiring of additional personnel and the purchasing of additional equipment, causing the production costs to exceed $5.00 per unit. Likewise, if production dropped below 2,000 units per week, the unit price would also exceed $5.00 per unit. The most favorable selling price, excluding other considerations, would therefore be that which would result in a sales volume of 2,000 units per week.

This is only a start in determining prices since many factors other than price influence consumer demand. But it does give the reader some idea of the problems involved in this field.[23]

GOVERNMENT CONTRACTS

Contracts with agencies of the state and Federal Government possess several characteristics not found in contracts between private organizations. Probably the most striking feature of the government contract is its size, especially in areas of national defense. Government contracts also necessitate work in fields for which no precedent or experience data may be available. Therefore the actual contract cost may not be determined until after the work is completed, a provision seldom found in other contracts. At the other extreme are the tight limitations which are placed on even routine contracts, in some cases requiring Congressional approval before established cost limits can be exceeded.[24]

Because of the exploratory nature of many government contracts, it is often determined, after work has been initiated, that further expenditure on the project is not feasible, and the contract is canceled at some intermediate stage of completion. This possibility makes government contracts unattractive to many contractors, even though complete compensation is normally given for any financial loss incurred.[25]

A common characteristic of more routine government contracts is the detailed specifications on each item, frequently necessitating the modification of a rather common item to conform to government standards. Since government standards and specifications are generally highly desirable, they have evolved into industry standards for many items.

GOVERNMENT REGULATION

Prior to 1900 there was little government control over the functioning of a business enterprise. Today there are few areas of business that are not subject to some degree of government control.[26] Some of these are:

1. Establishing the business (granting of charters, licenses, and permits)
2. Selection, utilization, and dismissal of personnel (labor legislation)
3. Location, construction, and utilization of facilities and equipment (zoning laws, building codes and smoke control, water purification and noise ordinances)
4. Volume, method, and quality of production (agricultural control and Pure Food and Drug laws)
5. Marketing and distribution of goods (FCC regulations on radio and TV advertising and ICC regulations on interstate commerce)

The present government regulations of business were not established merely to expand the role of government, but rather evolved to meet the problems created by the growth of big businesses, big unions, the development of mass production techniques and the growing impact of business on the entire economy. Faced with increasing pressure from lobbyists, Congress was forced to act to protect the rights of certain groups. However, this was often possible only by limiting the prerogatives of other groups. For example, many of the legislative gains made by labor unions were achieved by limiting actions that had historically been "management prerogatives." Many arguments have been aired both criticizing and supporting the growth of government regulations.[27]

INTERNAL SECURITY

Since most businesses are in competition with other enterprises and since competitive advantage is frequently based on the possession of secret materials or methods of operation, most organizations must exercise protective measures to insure that their secrets are not stolen. Security is important to the automobile manufacturer, who must safeguard his designs of future models so that they cannot be copied by his competitors, and it is important to the chemical manufacturer who is on the verge of developing a new substance, compromise of which could result in a competitor obtaining the patent rights first.

Regardless of the degree of security exercised, it is impossible to safeguard all information that would be of assistance to a competitor. Some is bound to leak from employees or suppliers or when a product is test-marketed. However, companies continue to safeguard all important data and information so that their competitive advantage can be retained as long as possible.[28]

FAILURE AND BANKRUPTCY

In 1962 there were 15,782 business failures recorded in the United States.[29] The reasons for business failures are numerous and include:

Insufficient funds—lack of money to obtain the resources necessary to operate efficienctly or to sustain the business during the initial period when expenses are high and income low or nonexistent

Technological limitations—failure to utilize new technological developments to achieve greater efficiency in production or to produce an improved and competitive product

Product obsolescence—decline in product demand because of a change in consumer tastes or the availability of a more desirable product

Managerial incompetence—believed by many to account for the greatest number of business failures.[30]

All too frequently, businesses which are basically unsound continue to operate at a profit, because of a prosperous economy or lack of competition.

SUGGESTION SYSTEMS

Company suggestion systems vary in form and method of implementation. Most systems, however, have two basic objectives: (1) They provide employees with a channel of communication with top management through which they can air their opinions and attitudes without endangering their job security or creating friction with their immediate supervisor. (2) They provide management with a source of information regarding work improvement and employee attitude and morale.

Most suggestion systems make provision for the employee to share financially in any savings his suggestion may engender. Where actual savings are intangible, many systems present a cash award to the suggestor.[31]

SUPERVISION

The supervisor is the individual directly responsible for converting policy, plans, and procedures into reality. In order to fulfill these responsibilities, he must be acquainted with two general areas: (1) the technical aspects of the job being supervised; and (2) the techniques of management.

The supervisor need not be proficient in each of the jobs

he oversees, but he should have a complete knowledge of its purpose, general method of operation, skills required for performance, and its relation to other jobs in the organization. He is expected either to handle all technical problems that arise or to obtain the necessary assistance to do so.[32]

Since the supervisor is also a manager, he is expected to deal with the human problems of those under his supervision. In particular, he is responsible for hiring, orienting, and training new personnel, reviewing and analyzing the work of all the workers under his control and taking corrective action where necessary; and, finally, he must be continually conscious of employee morale and motivation as possible indicators of hidden problems.

Supervisors operate in both areas of the business structure —administrative and productive. The specific knowledge and skills required of them will not be the same in both areas, but they must be equally acquainted with the techniques of management.

CONSULTING SERVICES

Many businesses periodically find it necessary or desirable to seek assistance or advice from outside the organization. Normally, they do so for one of three reasons: (1) Their regular staff is not qualified on the basis of experience, education, or training to perform the required function. (2) Their regular staff does not have the time to devote to the required function. (3) An independent or impartial opinion from outside the organization is desired.

Rapid developments in certain fields, such as data processing, operations research, and international business, have uncovered attractive areas of expansion for many businesses. If they lack personnel experienced in these areas, they may find it advantageous to seek help from outside sources on a part-time or consulting basis.

Likewise, in most organizations fluctuations in work volume result in periods during which the regular staff is fully occupied. In order to give due attention to additional problems or work requirements that develop at such times, many organizations seek temporary outside assistance to handle the additional work load.

Some problems may arouse serious differences of opinion among members of the organization or for some reason may require confidential or impartial analysis. The services of an outside consultant may be sought to analyze or resolve the issue.[33]

Among the many sources to which a company may go to seek

advice or assistance are government agencies, financial institutions (banks, insurance companies, and investment firms), universities (faculty and research organizations), professionals (lawyer, CPA's), and professional consultants (individuals and firms). The source selected will depend upon such factors as the degree of personal attention desired, the nature of the problem, and the amount of money the company is willing to pay.

Some companies ask the consultant to implement his recommendations to include the establishment of specific programs and the training of company personnel. The consultant may be paid a fixed fee for his services or according to some scale established in advance. Out-of-pocket expense for travel, living away from home, and special supplies and materials are not usually included in the regular rate or fee.

QUESTIONS AND PROBLEMS

1. What action should management take before deciding to seek the services of an outside consultant?
2. How should management determine the degree of control it should exercise over a department or section?
3. What relationship, if any, is there between organization, size, and financial structure?
4. What relationship should exist between sales forecasts and company development?
5. Of what value is manpower planning during a period of relative high unemployment? When unemployment is low?
6. How far in advance should organization plans be developed?
7. Is it ever a good practice for management to act contrary to established policy? Give an example.
8. Should price be established first and operating expenses tailored to fit the price, or vice versa?
9. How can the efficiency of public relations efforts be measured?
10. Should the first-line supervisor associate himself with management, labor, or both?

REFERENCE NOTES

[1] Joseph H. Bonneville, Lloyd E. Dewey, and Harry M. Kelly, *Organizing and Financing Business*, 6th ed., Prentice-Hall, 1959.

[2] Eli Schwartz, *Corporation Finance*, St. Martin's Press, 1962.

[3] E. J. Revalon, "How to Make Organization Charts Effective and Useful," *Office Management*, May, 1958, pp. 71–74.

[4] George Albert Smith and C. Roland Christensen, *Policy Formulation and Administration*, Irwin, 1955.

[5] E. Mezner, "Procedure Manuals Program the Work," *NAA Bulletin*, January, 1958, pp. 51-57.

[6] "How Management Tackles Advance Planning," *Management Methods*, January, 1958, pp. 14-15.

[7] S. Cassels and R. L. Randall, "Six Steps to Better Planning," *Nation's Business*, August, 1961, pp. 42-43.

[8] Raymond P. Kent, *Corporate Financial Management*, Irwin, 1964.

[9] W. Rash, "Ten Step Plan for Forecasting an Industrial Market," *Industrial Marketing*, March, 1961, pp. 40-43.

[10] William H. Newman and James P. Logan, *Business Policies and Management*, 4th ed., South-Western Publishing Company, 1959.

[11] J. T. Cunningham, "Evaluating Public Relations Effectiveness," *Public Relations Journal*, January, 1962, pp. 20-23.

[12] "Check Your Management Costs," *Nation's Business*, January, 1962, pp. 36-37.

[13] Dalton E. McFarland, *Management Principles and Practices*, 2nd. ed., Macmillan, 1964.

[14] Richard Eells, *The Government of Corporations*, Free Press, 1962.

[15] Raymond Villers, *Dynamic Management in Industry*, Prentice-Hall, 1960.

[16] A. R. Pell, "How to Write a Better Report," *Purchasing*, December 18, 1961, pp. 78-79.

[17] E. W. McNamara, "Method of Analyzing Reports," *The Office*, March, 1958, p. 128.

[18] D. Denton, "How to Make Standards Work for You," *Purchasing*, April 28, 1958, pp. 74-76.

[19] R. W. Cairns, "Bringing Basic Research to Market," *Management Review*, July, 1961, pp. 59-61.

[20] J. B. Quinn, "Long-Range Planning of Industrial Research," *Harvard Business Review*, July, 1961, pp. 88-102.

[21] J. W. Russell, "Developing New Products for Profit," *Management Review*, August, 1958, pp. 9-13.

[22] Eugene J. Kelley and William Lazer, *Management Marketing: Perspective and Viewpoints. A Source Book*, Irwin, 1958.

[23] "Price Possibilities," *Fortune*, August, 1961, p. 42.

[24] L. F. Mihlon, "Dangerous Business of Defense Contracting," *Factory*, August, 1961, pp. 92-97.

[25] Stuart F. Heinritz, *Purchasing: Principles and Applications*, 3rd ed., Prentice-Hall, 1959.

[26] E. W. Kinter, "How Much Control Can Business Endure?," *Journal of Marketing*, July, 1961, pp. 1-6.

[27] E. Burgard, "Menace to American Way of Life," *Advertising Age*, November 20, 1961, pp. 32-36.

[28] J. L. Buckley, "Your Company's Security Program: How Does it Rate?," *Office Executive,* September, 1961, pp. 17-20.

[29] *Statistical Abstract of the United States,* U.S. Department of Commerce, 1963.

[30] "Why Businesses Fail," *Banking,* October, 1958, p. 134.

[31] "Are Suggestion Systems Worth Their Cost?," *Personnel Administration,* September, 1961, pp. 52-55.

[32] W. B. Wolf, "Supervisor's Role in Organizations," *Supervision,* December, 1961, pp. 4-6; January, 1962, pp. 10-12; and R. Likert, "Effective Supervision—An Adaptive and Relative Process," *Personnel Psychology,* Autumn, 1958, pp. 317-332.

[33] Wilson Seney, *Effective Use of Business Consultants,* Financial Executives Research Foundation, New York, 1963.

READING REFERENCES

Haimann, Theo., *Management: Theory and Practice,* Houghton Mifflin, 1962.

Haynes, W. Warren, and Joseph L. Massie, *Management: Analysis, Concepts and Cases,* Prentice-Hall, 1961.

Henderson, Herman B., and Albert E. Haas, *Industrial Organization and Management Fundamentals,* Industrial Press, 1961.

Heyel, Carl, *Organizing Your Job in Management,* American Management Association, 1960.

Jerome, William Travers, III, *Executive Control—The Catalyst,* Wiley, 1961.

Jones, Manley Howe, *Executive Decision Making,* rev. ed., Irwin, 1962.

Jucius, Michael J., and William E. Schlender, *Elements of Managerial Action,* Irwin, 1960.

Krupp, Sherman, *Pattern in Organization Analysis: A Critical Examination,* Chilton, 1961.

McDonough, Adrian M., *Information Economics and Management Systems,* McGraw-Hill, 1963.

Roberts, Edward B., *The Dynamics of Research and Development,* Harper & Row, 1964.

11

FINANCIAL MANAGEMENT

In this chapter the reader will get an overview of financial management, one of the major "spokes" in the power wheel of the bicycle, as it is in business or any organized activity.

BUDGETING

Budgets perform two principal functions in the business organization: (1) they are a tool for planning,[1] and (2) they are a control device for performance.[2] Since a business is usually organized to achieve a long-range goal, new plants, modern equipment, and highly skilled personnel will be required in the future, and action must be taken well in advance to furnish the financial resources to meet these requirements. A portion of annual profits must be set aside for this purpose, and if this is insufficient, then additional sources of capital must be located. Many businesses are currently using facilities for which loans and bond issues are still outstanding; therefore a portion of their annual profits must be applied to meeting these outstanding obligations.

The budget is a master plan for insuring that (1) adequate resources will be available to accommodate future development; (2) sufficient resources will be available to accommodate outstanding obligations; and (3) current operating expenses are confined within specified limits. The budget is management's tool for allocating resources to the various areas of the organization. If management desires to place greater emphasis on research and development and less emphasis on expanding current product sales, it makes appropriate adjustments in the operating budgets of the respective departments.

The budget for an entire business is merely the summation of several component budgets prepared by the various elements of the organization. For example, the personnel department submits a budget to top management that will normally be divided into functional areas that show the relative emphasis placed on each area. It will reflect the amount of money required for recruiting, interviewing, counseling, testing, record keeping, and the other functions performed by the department. A similar pattern is followed by the other technical areas of the organization.

As we have said, a budget is a plan. Like most plans, this one is subject to change. When a department submits its budget, top management will review and possibly revise it to conform to desired objectives. But even after a budget has been approved, developments may occur which warrant its modification. Such modification should either have the concurrence of top management or be supported with strong justification.

COST CONTROL AND METHODS

A manufacturing enterprise exists to make a profit by manufacturing a product for distribution and sale to customers. A customer will normally seek a product at the lowest possible cost consistent with current standards of quality. If another manufacturer offers the same or similar product at a lower price, then a customer can reasonably be expected to select that product. Such competition will usually result in a decline in demand for the organization's product, which, in turn, means a decline in profits and a decline in stockholders' earnings. The situation may be further aggravated by increasing production costs.

Since management has little or no control over competition or the cost of labor and materials, it must therefore direct its attention to those areas where costs can be controlled and the product made more competitively attractive.

For example, substantial savings may be achieved by buying raw materials in larger volume. Improvements in the utilization of labor will result in greater efficiency of operation. These are examples of areas in which costs can be controlled.

Before costs can be controlled they must be identified. If production costs are increasing, is the increase due to material wastage, machine failure, or worker performance? In order to answer these questions management must have (1) performance data and (2) standards by which to evaluate performance. For example, management may have data indicating that a worker is producing forty units a day. This, in itself, is not sufficient for evaluating performance, but if established standards indicate that the worker should produce at least fifty units a day, management then has a basis for further investigation and corrective action.[3]

To facilitate control, costs are usually divided into (1) material, (2) labor, and (3) overhead (utilities, insurance, taxes, etc.). Material and labor costs may be further identified as (1) direct or (2) indirect. Direct material includes all the supplies and components used in the production process which become a part of the product, whereas indirect material includes those items consumed or utilized in support of production which do not become part of the finished product. Likewise, the labor used in production (equipment operators, foremen, inspectors, etc.) is classified as direct labor, whereas labor in support of production (salesmen, public relations, personnel, accountants, etc.) is classified as indirect labor. A principal reason for the distinction between direct and indirect costs is that direct cost can be evaluated in terms of of units of production, whereas indirect costs must be analyzed on some other basis. Direct costs are usually reduced by the implementation of better methods or improved equipment. Indirect costs, however, are usually controlled by the application of budgetary limitations.[4]

OPERATING ANALYSIS

The success of a business cannot be measured merely by considering one or two factors, such as sales volume or production expenses. The profitability and solvency of a business, a large business in particular, is the result of the application of management skills in many areas, each of which makes a contribution to both present and future success. Therefore, in order to obtain an accurate picture of the financial status, it is necessary to analyze and evaluate several areas of performance.

Performance can be judged good or bad only with respect to some established standard. In evaluating the functioning of a business, three factors are frequently used as standards: (1) market performance (economic, political, and social activity); (2) previous business performance; and (3) established goals (development plans, budget performance, etc.).

These standards are closely related; therefore each must be

considered when analyzing business performance. For example, an organization may have experienced a gross sales of $100,000 last year. This established a standard or basis of comparison for the current year's performance. However, in preparing the budget for the current year, management may have estimated a gross sales of $110,000, assuming that the product demand would increase over that of last year. This budget, therefore, established another standard for evaluating performance. If gross sales for the current year actually amounted to $90,000, this would indicate a decline in performance compared to both the previous year and this year's anticipated sales. At this point it may appear that management deficiency was the cause of the unsatisfactory performance. However, the whole country may have experienced a decline in economic activity caused by less consumer spending (as in a recession). When market conditions are analyzed, it may be discovered that the organization experienced only a slight decline compared to other firms in the same industry.

The above example attempts to illustrate that the functioning of a business organization is influenced by many variables. Consequently, the determination of its operating efficiency must be the result of the careful analysis of many factors.

Management has several tools at is disposal to assist in this analysis.

Charts and Graphs

The various types of charts and graphs in use today permit management to compare many factors at one time and thus study important relationships. Such charts and graphs include:

Bar charts. Important data is represented by horizontal or vertical bars, the magnitude of the data being directly proportioned to the length of the bar which represents it. Bar charts are very effective for showing relationships between comparable figures.

Line graphs. These present a clear picture of the relationship between two sets of data. One set of data is arranged along a vertical axis and another set along a horizontal axis. When the data are plotted on the graph and a line drawn through the plotted points, trends and relationships are easily determined.

Pie charts. When a whole unit is divided into a number of component parts, a pie chart provides an effective method of illustration. The whole unit is represented by the entire chart (pie), and each component is represented by a wedge (slice) of proportionate size.

Ratios and Averages

Ratios. A ratio is an arithmetic relationship between two separate values. For example, a company may wish to compare its dollar investment in advertising against sales volume. A careful analysis may reveal that for every additional dollar spent on advertising there was a ten-dollar increase in sales. The ratio used to express this would be 10:1. This ratio would serve to indicate the increase in sales which could be anticipated for each additional amount spent on advertising.[5] Some other common ratios are:

1. Inventory turnover ratio indicates the rate at which goods and materials are sold and replaced.
2. Ratio of net profits to net sales indicates the degree of success with respect to sales volume.
3. An "acid test" ratio, which is determined by dividing cash and receivables by current liabilities, indicates a company's ability to repay current debts.

Averages. An average serves to condense the performance of several factors into one representative factor. For example, management can determine the efficiency of individual salesmen by taking an average of the efficiency of all its salesmen.

FINANCIAL ANALYSIS

An analysis of an organization's financial condition answers the question, "What is the current financial status of the organization?" An analysis of operations answers the question, "Why is the organization's financial status what it is?" The former is concerned solely with dollar performance, the latter with the entire business and its environment.

Knowledge of an organization's financial status is important for the following reasons:

1. A continually declining financial position indicates to management that a problem exists in the functioning of the organization which must be corrected.
2. The financial position indicates the extent to which management may implement certain actions and attempt to achieve desired objectives.
3. Federal and state governments are interested in the financial status of an organization for tax purposes.
4. Banks and bonding companies considering a financial arrangement

with an organization desire to know the degree of risk that may be involved.

5. Creditors, stockholders, and others who have an equity in the business are interested in its performance.

There are two financial reports which summarize the financial status of the business organization: (1) the balance sheet and (2) the statement of profit and loss. The balance sheet indicates a company's net worth as of a certain date, such as at the end of a fiscal or calendar year. The profit and loss statement shows a company's performance over any given period of time.

The Balance Sheet

The three principal components of the balance sheet are: (1) assets, (2) liabilities, and (3) net worth.

Assets. These include cash, property, facilities, and equipment. Although many intangible items may be considered as assets, for financial purposes, they are not usually included on the balance sheet. Current assets include the cash on hand and any other assets which will shortly be converted to cash through the normal functioning of the business. Fixed assets include the equipment and property used in operating the organization. The value of such assets is continually changing due to normal depreciation. One such asset, land, is not subject to normal depreciation since its value may rise or fall. Most land, however, tends to increase rather than depreciate in value.

Liabilities. Included in a company's liabilities are the rights of creditors to share in the assets of the organization. Current liabilities include obligations to employees, banks, and suppliers. Such obligations are normally fulfilled in less than a year. Fixed liabilities include long-term obligations, not normally satisfied within a year, such as outstanding bond issues, loans, and notes of various types.

Net worth. The net worth of an organization is the extent of the owner's equity in the assets of the company. It is determined by subtracting liabilities from total assets (Net Worth = Assets − Liabilities).

The Statement of Profit and Loss

Whereas the balance sheet indicates a company's financial status as of a given date (i.e., the end of the fiscal year), the profit and loss statement indicates performance (income and expenses) during a given period of time, usually one or more months.

Income. To obtain the gross profit on sales, the cost of the goods sold is subtracted from the revenue obtained through sales. The cost of goods sold is obtained by subtracting the value of the ending inventory from the value of the beginning inventory for the stated period, plus the cost of any purchases that increased the inventory.

Expenses. The expenses of an organization are its cost of doing business. Included are such items as wages and salaries, supplies and materials, marketing costs, insurance, taxes, and depreciation. The total operating expenses are subtracted from the gross profit on sales, to give the net income from operations.

Other income and expenses. In addition to income from sales, an organization may have income from other sources, such as rental of property and equipment or investments of various types. One of the most common additional expenses is interest paid on notes and bonds. If additional expenses are greater than additional income, then the difference is subtracted from net income from operations to obtain the net income for the organization. If, however, additional expenses are less than additional income, the difference is added to net income from operations to obtain the net income for the organization.

SYSTEMS

There is no such thing as an ideal or perfect financial system. The effectiveness of a financial system is determined by how well it works for a given set of conditions. The system suitable for a large mass production manufacturer would probably not be satisfactory for a small job-lot producer. Even for companies which are similar in size and nature of production, it is probable that their systems of financial management would not be interchangeable.[6]

A financial system may consist of the most elaborate equipment and the most modern procedures, but if it fails to provide management with the information and data it requires in order to operate effectively, then it is of little value. In this sense, a financial system must be "tailor-made" to a particular organization.

A financial system is seldom recognized as such except on three principal occasions: (1) when a business is being organized or reorganized; (2) when there is a serious organizational problem; or (3) when the data and information required by management are not being furnished by the existing system. At these times management may give considerable attention to the entire financial structure of the organization in an attempt to determine what improvements can be made. It may seek the services of various experts and professionals in the field: accounting specialists, management consultants, data processing equipment manufacturers, and other business organizations.

When establishing a financial system, or when modifying an existing system to meet new requirements, it is necessary to conduct a step-by-step analysis of the entire business. A typical analysis would consist of two parts: (1) a general analysis to provide understanding of organizational plans and objectives and (2) a detailed analysis of the various functional areas to determine the specific procedures, materials, and equipment required in order to provide management with needed information and data.

The general analysis would include:

1. The product(s) manufactured
2. Special characteristics of the industry
3. The manner in which the company has been organized
4. The facilities owned by the organization
5. Significant changes or developments which have occurred in the past
6. Plans for future growth and development

Following this general analysis of the entire organization, a detailed analysis of its functional areas is conducted to determine the specific requirements of each and the part it plays in the over-all functioning of the organization. Particular attention would be given to the following areas:

Production. Procedures and operations studies are made to determine the various actions performed and the degree and type of control that is required by management. In order for a financial system to be effective, management must be able to determine the cost of production in advance, so that it can make sound decisions in allocating the organization's resources.

Sales. Effective management must have a reasonable estimate of expected sales volume and how much must be spent on market research, sales promotion, and advertising in order to achieve it.

Material and personnel resources. Management must have continuous information on the quantity, cost, and utilization of materials and labor. If material costs begin to increase rapidly, less expensive materials may have to be substituted. Likewise, if the increasing cost of labor decreases profits, emphasis may have to be placed on more efficient methods of operation.

Company assets. Management must know at all times

whether sufficient assets are on hand to meet current and future obligations and still retain an adequate balance for contingencies.

Only after all these steps have been taken can a suitable financial system be designed. Such a system should be capable of assembling, processing, and analyzing information on all vital areas of the business so that accurate data will be available when needed for effective decision-making.

AUDITING AND INTERNAL REVIEW

Auditing and internal review may be considered the "financial watchdog" of an enterprise, assuring that proper utilization is being made of its financial resources.[7] In particular, audits and reviews serve to: (1) promote operation in accordance with established standards and procedures; (2) insure the effectiveness of the controls established by management; (3) evaluate the effectiveness of the methods, procedures, and actions used to achieve organizational goals; (4) detect errors in implementation of organizational policies, procedures, rules, and directives; and (5) discourage criminal misuse of organizational resources.

Audits are concerned primarily with the financial aspect of business operation, whereas internal reviews include an analysis of subjective factors such as methods and procedures. Reviews are normally accomplished after an audit has been performed. Raw data is of little value until it is consolidated into a meaningful format in which related factors may be compared. For example, an increase of 10 percent in sales volume might be interpreted as favorable performance until a review of expenses indicated that it was achieved only by a considerable increase in marketing cost. Likewise, a business with a stable or even declining sales volume may actually be improving its financial posture by more efficient methods of operation. The internal review, therefore, provides a composite picture of the over-all functioning of the organization to include many factors (such as tax status or depreciation) which might otherwise be overlooked.

The responsibility for performing audits and reviews is frequently assigned to the central accounting office. Some organizations have a special section, under the direct supervision of the controller, for performing audits and reviews. After analyzing all the information and data submitted, the controller will then usually brief top management on the organization's performance. He may make recommendations for continuing or eliminating certain policies or courses of action. Corrective action is normally determined by the president or chief executive officer. Before making a final decision, he may wish to consult with certain operating officials of the organization. He may delegate routine actions, however, to the controller for execution.

Audits and reviews are normally performed on a regular basis, the minimum normally being once a year. In large organizations the auditor normally goes to the section or office being audited so that he can have access to all documents and records.[7] Since the volume of material for audit is normally quite large, a complete check is seldom performed. More frequently the auditor will make a random sampling and only go into a detailed check if the sampling reveals certain discrepancies.[8]

CREDITS AND COLLECTIONS

Most businesses do not operate strictly on a cash basis. The policy which an organization maintains in issuing credit and collecting outstanding accounts (debts) will depend on the nature and size of the business and the type of product sold. The large organization is usually in a better financial position to maintain a liberal credit and collection policy. Since this often means that a large proportion of its assets are in the form of accounts receivable, many small organizations prefer to invest their assets where they can earn a return on investment. If the financial status of an organization is such that it requires the use of all available assets to maintain existing operations, a conservative credit and collection policy would be mandatory.

The philosophy behind a liberal credit and collection policy is that customers will be more inclined to do business with those organizations from which they can obtain the best credit terms. A liberal credit policy is not, however, the same as a lax policy. On the contrary, all organizations, regardless of their credit terms, must thoroughly evaluate the credit position of all parties to whom credit is extended.[9]

INSURANCE

Business, like life itself, is filled with uncertainty. In practically every aspect of the business environment events can occur which would seriously threaten the financial solvency of an organization. In order to protect itself against such unforeseen events and to provide a relative degree of security, most businesses purchase various types of insurance to reduce or eliminate certain risks.

In the event that a business experiences a financial loss against which it is insured, then the loss will be absorbed (to the extent of the insurance policy) by the insurance company. Insurance may usually be obtained against any conceivable loss, although in some extreme cases it may be difficult to find a willing insurance company and the premium may be exceedingly high. In normal business situations, however, insurance is obtainable only for those losses which are measurable in dollars and cents. Such losses may be divided into two categories: (1) material and (2) human. Material losses include total or partial destruction of property as a result of "acts of God," that is, acts which are not attributable to human causes. Human losses include death and bodily injury and damage to or destruction of property which are attributable to human causes.

Types of Insurance

Property destruction insurance. In order to protect itself against a substantial financial loss resulting from the destruction of its physical facilities, an organization will acquire property destruction insurance of some type. The most common type is fire insurance. The policy will specifically state: (1) the period of time during which it is in effect; (2) the extent of the insurer's liability (usually the actual cash value of the property damaged or destroyed); (3) the specific causes of loss for which insurance is granted; (4) causes of loss which are not covered; and (5) factors which will serve to void or terminate the policy. In addition, the policy may be modified, by the attachment of "endorsements," to protect an organization's facilities against most types of naturally caused damage, including water and smoke, tornado and earthquake.[10]

Liability insurance. In the operation of a business there are many circumstances which may result in bodily harm to individuals or in damage to or destruction of their property. If it can be demonstrated that the organization was negligent in performing its duties, then court action can compel it to make a damage payment to the injured party. Such liability claims have been known to be extremely high and have had serious impact even on businesses which were financially sound. In order to protect themselves, most business organizations make substantial use of liability insurance.

Marine insurance. Marine insurance covers the principal means of transportation, including airplane, truck, and railroad shipments, in addition to ocean transportation. It insures the goods being shipped and not the carrier used. Virtually every conceivable source of damage to or destruction of goods in shipment may be insured by marine insurance: theft, negligence, unavoidable delays which result in spoilage, as well as the usual hazards of accidents, fires, and acts of nature.

Miscellaneous insurance. In addition, there are a number of insurance programs to cover certain situations not common to all business organizations. Included in this category are life insurance, hospital insurance, and workmen's compensation insurance, which are really variations on the basic insurance programs discussed earlier.

Two additional types of insurance are taken out under special circumstances: (1) surety insurance and (2) fidelity insurance. Surety insurance provides a guarantee that certain specified work will be performed according to an agreed plan and schedule, for example, that a new building will be completed according to contract. Fidelity insurance protects a company against the financial loss which may result from a criminal or dishonest act on the part of an employee, particularly if he handles considerable amounts of money or valuable equipment.

Many companies have established group insurance plans which offer employees an economical means of increasing their personal security and thereby their work performance.[11]

TAXES

Taxes are a matter of major concern to all business organizations for two principal reasons: (1) they represent a substantial portion of operating expenses, and (2) they have a significant influence over what actions an organization can and cannot take. For many organizations, taxes account for well over half of net taxable income. Faced with such a sizable figure, many business executives are inclined to ask, "For whom are we really working—the government?"

Federal Taxes

The Federal Government requires approximately $85 to $100 billion annually to maintain its various operations, the largest portion going for defense expenditures. In order to obtain sufficient resources to finance these expenditures, it has established various taxes and other revenue-generating mechanisms. The Federal income tax (both individual and corporate) accounts for approximately three-fourths of the total Federal income. Federal corporation taxes account for approximately one-third of the total Federal income or about $30 billion.

Corporate income tax. For tax purposes, corporations are divided into three categories: (1) regular corporations; (2) special corporations (life insurance companies and savings and loan associations); and (3) nonprofit corporations (religious, charitable, educational, and scientific organizations, and labor unions). Nonprofit corporations are not taxed; however, they usually must file an information tax return with the Bureau of Internal Revenue. Special profit-making corporations are taxed according to a separate schedule of rates from regular corporations. In 1964 Congress established tax rates at 30 to 22 percent for small corporations and 52 to 50 percent for large ones.

Excise tax. A duty levied on the manufacture, sale, or consumption of specific items is known as an excise tax. Unlike a sales tax, an excise tax is normally levied against the manufacturer. There is little doubt, however, that in the final analysis it is the consumer who really pays it, through higher prices. Although most excise taxes were established to regulate the consumption of certain items by increasing their selling price, the regulatory function is almost nonexistent today and consequently the tax serves mainly as a source of revenue.

Social Security tax. Under the Federal program of Social Security, certain employers must pay a tax on wages. Revenue generated from this tax is intended to support the benefits paid through the program. Federal income from this tax amounts to about $8 billion from both employers and employees.

Tariffs. Taxes on the importation of foreign goods are designed to discourage foreign competition with domestic products. Their revenue-producing value (less than one billion dollars annually) is slight compared with other sources.

Miscellaneous taxes. Included in this category are estate taxes, gift taxes, communication taxes, etc. Most of these, however, have no significant impact on business in general.

State and Local Taxes

Like the Federal Government, state and local governments also require revenue in order to maintain operations. Many state and local taxes are similar to Federal taxes; however, there are others which have no Federal counterpart.

Corporate income tax. More than two-thirds of the states now have some type of corporate income tax. These are substantially less than similar Federal taxes. A number of local governments have also established corporate income taxes.

Sales tax. Taxes levied on sales are normally paid by the consumer at the time of purchase. However, most businesses are also consumers; therefore they are also influenced by such taxes.

Property tax. A business generally has a substantial investment in property; therefore its property tax can be substantial. There are various methods of applying property taxes. Some communities tax only real estate, whereas others also tax business equipment and facilities.

Miscellaneous taxes. There are several other state and local taxes which are employed in certain areas. These include various assessments and taxes for specific functions, i.e., sales and wage taxes.

All these taxes are levied according to complex regulations and procedures. Because of the many variations and exceptions in the tax laws their elaborate analysis may be required before a business can decide on a course of action. For example, when considering several possible areas for the location of a new plant, a business must evaluate the tax laws of both the state and community in which he considers doing business. This holds equally true for all major business decisions, including the development of new products and markets, expansion of facilities, and new construction.

Many organizations retain a staff of tax and law specialists, who continually analyze new laws and court decisions in order to determine the most favorable course of action in specific situations.[12]

QUESTIONS AND PROBLEMS

1. How does auditing increase organizational efficiency?
2. What are the two principal functions of budgeting? Give an example of each.
3. Can budgetary controls be effectively used to control direct costs? Why?
4. What is the distinction between a liberal and a tight credit and collection policy?
5. Why is the financial position of an organization of interest to persons other than owners and management?

6. What is the distinction between the balance sheet and the profit and loss statement?
7. What type of business equipment and property should not be insured?
8. What standards should an organization use to evaluate its over-all performance?
9. Why would the same financial system not necessarily be suitable for two separate companies of approximately the same size which manufacture similar products?
10. Why are taxes important to a business other than the fact that they use up a substantial portion of total earnings?

REFERENCE NOTES

[1] D. E. Bacon, "You Can Plan Profits Through Budgeting," *The Office*, January, 1962, p. 112.

[2] G. A. Welsch, "Budgeting for Management Planning and Control," *Journal of Accounting*, October, 1961, pp. 37-44.

[3] H. Dayserling, "Selecting Your Costing Method," *Controller*, April, 1962, pp. 162-164.

[4] D. P. Jones, "Budgetary Controls," *Office Executive*, May, 1961, pp. 22-24.

[5] W. E. Westerdahl, "Comparing the Company with Its Industry by Ratios," *NAA Bulletin*, November, 1961, pp. 29-42.

[6] F. W. Wanner, "Meeting Competition Through Systems," *Systems and Procedures Magazine*, September, 1961, pp. 13-16.

[7] L. C. Richards, "Current Concepts of Internal Auditing," *NAA Bulletin*, April, 1961, pp. 55-60.

[8] L. H. Pilie, "How to Cooperate with the Auditors," *The Office*, January, 1961, p. 90.

[9] P. J. Hampton, "Whose Credit Can Be Trusted?," *Credit and Financial Management*, August, 1961, p. 13.

[10] J. J. Friedman, "How Much Plant Insurance?," *Dun's Review and Modern Industry*, January, 1962, pp. 42-44.

[11] G. N. Watson, "Group Insurance (Major Problem)," *Best's Insurance News* (Life Edition), June, 1961, p. 80.

[12] W. H. Hoffman, Jr., "Theory of Tax Planning," *Accounting Review*, April, 1961, pp. 274-281.

READING REFERENCES

Anderson, Richard C., *Management Practices*, McGraw-Hill, 1960.
Ettinger, Richard P., and David E. Golieb, *Credits and Collections*, 5th ed., Prentice-Hall, 1962.

Foster, Louis O., *Understanding Financial Statements and Corporate Annual Reports*, Chilton, 1961.

Lemke, B. C., and James Don Edwards, *Administrative Control and Executive Action*, Merrill, 1961.

Phelps, Clyde William, *Retail Credit Fundamentals*, International Consumer Credit Association, 1963.

Rowland, Virgil K., *Managerial Performance Standards*, American Management Association, 1960.

Schlaifer, Robert, *Introduction to Statistics for Business Decisions*, McGraw-Hill, 1961.

Steiner, George A., *Managerial Long-Range Planning*, McGraw-Hill, 1963.

Villers, Raymond, *Dynamic Management in Industry*, Prentice-Hall, 1960.

Welsch, Glenn A., *Budgeting, Profit Planning and Control*, 2nd ed., Prentice-Hall, 1964.

12

FACTORY AND PRODUCTION MANAGEMENT

The operation of a production-type industry centers upon the factory. This chapter deals with some of the common areas of operations and management that are related to such production.

PRODUCTION METHODS AND PROCESSES

All production processes may be classified as either "analytic" or "synthetic." Analytic processes consist of the refining or purifying of one basic substance into some useful form, as, for example, the refining of oil into gasoline. Synthetic production consists of the combining of several substances into a product, such as an automobile. Since analytic production is limited to a few major industries, such as petroleum, metals, and lumber, and their production methods are limited, discussion will be confined principally to synthetic processes.

Synthetic production is accomplished by one of two general operations or by a combination of them: (1) fabrication, in which basic materials or substances are assembled or combined, such as in the erection of a bridge from structural steel; and (2) modification, in which the properties of a material or substance are substantially altered, as in a chemical reaction or machining process.

Production equipment and machinery can be classified either by function or by operation. Those classified by function can be further subdivided into either general-purpose or special-purpose. General-purpose equipment is that which is capable of performing more than one type of work. Such equipment has the advantage of flexibility: it can manufacture a variety of products, and changes in product design can be accomplished with little or no retooling. Special-purpose equipment can perform only one function, and generally tends to be more expensive in both initial cost and maintenance.[1]

Production equipment and machinery may be classified by operation as: (1) manual, (2) semiautomatic, (3) fully automatic, or (4) automated.

Manual machines require control at every stage of the operation. The machine is activated and the material positioned and guided through the operation by hand. A semiautomatic machine will perform an operation unattended. However, it requires the worker to load the material, activate the machine, and then remove the material after the operation is completed. Fully automatic machines require no loading prior to each operation but instead will repeat the processing cycle until the supply of material is depleted or the machine deactivated.[2]

In automated equipment several machines may be linked together in order to complete an entire process unattended. The material is automatically fed into each machine and when the operation is completed, is automatically moved to the next, until the entire process is completed, at which time the end product is automatically discharged. Many automated machines also include an automatic control device whereby the machine adjusts itself according to predetermined instructions or the characteristics of the material being processed.

Types of Production

Continuous production. Continuous production is characterized by a constant flow of material with little variation in volume and product design. The assembly line is the typical example of modern-day continuous production whereby a product is moved through the plant by a conveyor belt, or similar device, and workers perform specialized functions at various stations along the line. The automobile assembly line is an excellent example of "synthetic" continuous production, whereby various parts of subassemblies are joined together to create a finished product. A lumber mill is an example of "analytic" continuous production whereby a basic material (a tree) is processed and refined to obtain a finished product (lumber).

Intermittent production. Intermittent production is characterized by an unsteady flow of material with frequent variation in volume or product design. An example would be a shoe manufacturing plant where the size, style, or color of a shoe might vary from one day to the next. Production would be accomplished in "job lots," i.e., a certain number of shoes of the same size, style, and color. Intermittent production has the advantage of permitting considerable flexibility; however, for high volume production it lacks the efficiency of continuous production.

METHODS STANDARDIZATION

The manufacturing process, in order to be carried out with the highest degree of efficiency, must be an organized and orderly combination of human effort and equipment. Both are costly resources, and it is nothing short of pure waste if either men or machines are not utilized to the fullest possible extent.

However, before it is possible to establish production controls and schedules, it is necessary to determine the rate at which a man or machine can produce. To conduct time studies it is necessary to establish a standard method of performance. For some operations it may not be possible to establish reliable standards because of special considerations. However, every effort must be made to keep these to a minimum so that the entire production process can be closely scheduled.[3]

It is apparent that method of standardization is an important prerequisite for determining personnel and equipment requirements. When management knows, in advance, the time required to perform an operation, it can anticipate and make arrangements to avoid bottlenecks or lags in the production process. Normally, such obstacles can be easily eliminated by making minor adjustments in personnel strength or in the type and number of machines available. In the event of an equipment failure, management can frequently reroute the flow of production to personnel and equipment not fully utilized and thereby maintain output at a constant level.

PRODUCTION CONTROL

One of the principal requirements of efficient production is completion of the production process in sufficient time to insure delivery to customers as scheduled. The complex coordinating and scheduling of the various aspects of the production process is known as production control, and it has as its objective the efficient and economical utilization of personnel, equipment, and materials.[4]

The actual production control function consists of several closely related processes which must be carefully coordinated and synchronized so that they work together as an integrated system. These include:

Production planning. The basis of production planning is normally the factors of time, quantity, and priority. For example, a large order urgently required by an important customer will normally take precedence over a relatively small routine order by a minor customer, even though the latter's order has been placed first. Once the time, quantity, and priority have been determined, the planning process is then concerned with specific estimates as to what is required in terms of equipment, personnel, and materials based on available information as to machine capacities, worker capabilities, and material consumption.

Scheduling. Not only must a starting and completion time be established for the total product, but each phase or step in the production process must also be scheduled so that orderly preparation of component parts and subassemblies will be accomplished as required. Scheduling also facilitates the measurement of progress since actual accomplishment can be compared with an established standard.

Routing. There is normally some degree of latitude as to the exact time and sequence in which the various production processes must be accomplished. Some plants may be working on several products concurrently. Therefore it may be necessary to change the normal routing plan to provide for the efficient utilization of equipment and personnel as well as to maintain a continuous flow of production. The routing plan should also give careful consideration to the distance the product must be moved between processes, as well as the time required to accomplish the move, handling equipment required, and storage requirements prior to and after each process. Unnecessary duplications in handling will increase production time and cost.

Materials control. The actual purchasing, receiving, storing, and handling of materials is not always the responsibility of production control. However, it is the responsibility of production control personnel to notify the appropriate departments of material requirements. Especially when certain materials are not normally maintained in stock or when an unusually large amount of material will be used, production control must make known its requirements in sufficient time to permit the timely receipt of the required material and to prevent a depletion of inventory required for other products.

Tools and equipment control. Efficient production requires the availability of proper tools and equipment. Serious and costly delays have resulted from the failure to obtain an inexpensive piece of equipment. Likewise, if production volume for a particular product is sufficiently great, special-purpose tools and equipment may pay for themselves many times over with their greater efficiency.

Inspections and quality control. In order to meet the established schedule, it is necessary to maintain some degree of supervision over procedures, timing, and product quality. This aspect of the production process will be discussed in more detail a little later.[5]

PRODUCT STANDARDIZATION

Product standardization often requires choosing between two objectives, both of which are highly desirable. These are (1) producing a standardized product and (2) producing to meet customer specifications.

Frequently a customer will place an order specifying not only product capability and quality, but dimensions, component parts, and materials. Converting equipment, obtaining new materials, retraining personnel, and planning the new production is time-consuming and costly.[6] The manufacturer is faced with the choice of producing a product to customer specifications or a standardized product which can be turned out with greater efficiency.

There is still another aspect to product standardization. Standardization of materials and parts is the keystone of mass production since it permits interchangeability of the individual parts of a product, thereby facilitating volume purchasing with an accompanying reduction in cost. To the consumer this means that parts and materials are readily available in the event that repair requires replacement. It would be a costly matter, for instance, if every time an automobile part needed replacing it had to be specially fabricated to certain specifications.

QUALITY CONTROL AND INSPECTION

The principal reason for quality control is customer satisfaction, especially since repeat business is generally desired. There are, in addition, codes and laws which specify minimum levels of quality which some products must maintain. This is particularly true of those that could endanger public health, safety, or well-being. Another reason for quality control is its close relation to cost control. Generally, the higher the quality standard, the higher the production cost. Therefore the level of quality normally falls between two limits: the minimum one established by customer demands, codes, and laws and the maximum one set by competitive production cost.

Quality control is not the function of a single department in the organization, but rather of all departments and workers. The engineer who designs the product must settle for reasonable standards of quality rather than utopian ideals. The purchasing department must obtain materials that fall within the accepted limits of quality; supervisors must see that workers have the necessary training, tools, equipment, and time to perform their operations properly; and the workers themselves must strive to the best of their ability to follow established procedures.

To insure that desired levels of quality are maintained, raw materials must be inspected to insure that they are of the quality ordered. Inspection must also be made during production to make sure that operations are performed correctly and that there is not an accumulation of inferior work. A final inspection is required to insure that all scheduled operations were performed and the finished product is in operating condition.

The nature of the product and the production process will determine where the inspections are performed. There may be a centralized inspection center where special equipment and testing devices may be used or inspection points in the production process, such as receiving and packaging. When the material to be inspected is not easily channeled through one central point, floating inspection teams may be established in order to travel to various areas.

The principal inspection methods include the following: (1) personal inspections (visual, testing, etc.), (2) special instruments and testing devices, (3) laboratory analysis, and (4) performance testing.

SALVAGE AND SCRAP CONTROL

Some amount of material loss is expected in normal procesing. However, less acceptable types of material loss also occur, such as: (1) worker spoilage due to lack of training, skill, or proper tools; and (2) improper functioning of equipment due to worn, damaged, or malfunctioning parts. Scrap in excess of anticipated allowances not only increases production cost but also depletes material inventories, thus delaying production.

In order to detect malfunctioning equipment and substandard employee performance, some control mechanism to record excess scrap is necessary. Records of scrap history, compiled for an entire process or for one operation, facilitate the prompt detection of excess scrap.

Wasted materials do not necessarily result in a total loss since they may be salvaged and reused or sold. Reusable materials can be separated from items for disposal and housed in suitable containers on the production floor.

SHOP RECORDS

In order to exercise effective control over production, accurate and complete records of both current and past performance are necessary to redirect the efforts of personnel or to change methods of operation as required.

Preproduction Records

Prior to production, records will be prepared indicating the general objectives to be accomplished (master schedule), material that will be required (bill of materials), sequence of processes (routing plan), and many other documents designed to notify interested personnel of actions to be performed. These records are intended to insure that all the resources required for production will be available when required so that there are no costly delays once production has been started.

Production Records

When production has been initiated, information and data (feedback) must be relayed to production control personnel so that they can evaluate actual performance in terms of schedules and plans. In this way necessary changes and adjustments to improve efficiency may be made while work is still in progress. Accurate records of material consumption must also be maintained so that areas of waste can be detected and eliminated, and additional material ordered if stocks are being depleted. Records of machine performance are compared to established standards and their efficiency determined. And, finally, records of appropriate personnel data must be kept, including hours worked, equipment operated, rate of production, and any other information considered necessary.[7]

Postproduction Records

Postproduction records are intended primarily to detect areas where future improvement can be made. Actual production time is compared to planned production time and an efficiency rating determined. Accident reports, scrap reports, and reports of unexpected delays or bottlenecks are analyzed and recommendations made on how similar circumstances can be eliminated in the future.

MATERIALS CONTROL SYSTEMS

All materials control systems consist of two parts: (1) physical requirements, including handling and storage; and (2) records showing the exact location and status of materials. Some degree of administrative control is required during each of the following phases of material flow: (1) procurement, (2) shipping, (3) receiving, (4) holding and storing, and (5) issuing.[8]

For most manufacturing processes, actual physical control does not begin until materials are received from a commercial carrier, when they must be assigned suitable storage space. For example, delicate and valuable materials should not be relegated to unsecured, outside storage where they will be exposed to the elements, while bulky, durable items requiring less security and protection are assigned inside storage.[9]

The physical control function does not terminate with the storage of materials, but continues through the entire production process, from the warehouse or storage area to the production area or intermediate holding areas.

The exact type of material control system will depend, not only on the nature of the product, but on the nature of the production process. Distinction can be made between two principal types: (1) mass production, in which material requirements are relatively stable and the rate of production is basically constant, and a minimum amount of coordination is required between the production control and purchasing departments; and (2) custom production, in which the product will vary according to customer orders and material requirements will also change. In this type of production, close coordination is required between the production control and purchasing departments. The majority of manufacturing operations fall between these two extremes.[10]

The importance of control records cannot be emphasized too strongly, especially in custom production, where established schedules and formulas are not available. The key document in the materials control system is the "Bill of Materials," which lists the materials and parts required to produce a particular product, and is necessary in initiating checks on inventory or for ordering materials that are not in stock.

MATERIALS HANDLING

Materials handling is of prime importance since production is contingent upon the availability of sufficient supplies and materials at the proper place and at the proper time. It is not uncommon for materials handling to consume 80 percent of production time, thus accounting for a significant part of total production costs. Management is therefore constantly interested in determining ways in which materials handling can be improved.[11]

In particular, improved methods of materials handling result in savings in several areas:

Manpower. Since labor accounts for a significant part of all production costs, material handling methods which require less manpower normally result in appreciable cost reduction. Manpower savings can result from the intallation of equipment capable of handling greater volumes, or from a reduction of the distance over which materials must be handled.[12]

Space utilization. Improving the flow of supplies needed for production will reduce needed storage and holding space, an important consideration where space is scarce or extremely costly. Excessive storage requirements also tend to create bottlenecks, resulting in extensive delays and poor utilization of equipment.[13]

Time. The entire production process is a closely scheduled operation. If production time is excessive, customers may seek other, speedier sources of supply. Since a major portion of production time is consumed in materials handling, there should be constant search for possible savings in time.

Condition of material. Improper handling of supplies and material can result in impairment of their appearance or functioning, making them unacceptable to the intended consumer.

The variety of materials handling devices is almost unlimited; some type of equipment exists to meet every possible requirement. The principal types are (1) industrial trucks, (2) hoists and cranes, and (3) conveyors. Most of this equipment is quite costly, and a careful analysis of requirements is necessary to insure wise investment. In particular, consideration should be given to: (1) size of material to be handled, (2) volume of material, (3) frequency of handling, (4) consistency of material type, (5) availability of space, and (6) special handling required.

PACKAGING AND SHIPPING

With minor exceptions, all manufacturing operations require that the finished product be packaged and shipped to the customer. Packaging is important to insure that the finished product will be received by the customer in the condition the manufacturer intended. Depending on the product, it can be a major and costly operation, as in the case of delicate electronic instruments and glass products. If the packaging cost is more than minor, existing methods should be reviewed to determine whether other procedures and materials will provide the same or better product protection with greater economy.[14]

Last, but certainly not least, careful consideration must always be given to the effects of packaging on the consumer, including ease of handling, storing, and unpacking, as well as aesthetic and marketing factors. If the packaged product requires an excessive amount of space, storage and handling will be difficult and costly. Also, if the package is difficult to open, this may have a negative influence on future product demand.[15]

In many cases where no further improvements can be made in the product itself, attention is turned toward improving the product container or package, such as developing a more compact package for easier storage, a container that has a built-in opening device, or one that is reusable or more readily disposable.[16]

JOB AND OPERATIONS ANALYSIS

In the highly competitive business world of today it is not possible for a company to stand on past performance alone. The successful company must continually analyze and review its performance, discard inefficient or obsolete techniques and procedures, and replace them with current and proven methods. Job and operations analysis are tools whereby management can monitor and analyze production to determine where improvement is needed and can effectively be implemented.[17]

It may be beneficial at this point to clarify terminology since many terms have different connotations. The term "job" is used to mean an assignment of work involving precise actions and responsibilities performed under specific circumstances.

An "operation" is the method by which a work assignment is performed, given the necessary equipment, material, and circumstances. It may take several operations to complete one job, or several jobs may be required to complete one operation.

A "process' is a set of operations necessary to manufacture a particular product or product component. A process includes not only personnel, equipment, and material, but also the sequence, routine, and timing required to coordinate the various operations with the maximum of efficiency.[18]

Job and operations analysis consists of studying a particular function in order to determine what actions are performed and their relationship to others in the organization. It identifies the requirements of the function, such as the skill and training necessary, as well as any special circumstances under which it must be performed.

The completed analysis serves as the basis for standardizing the job and operation performance, a necessary prerequisite in the preparation of job and production standards. Without accurate job standards it would be impossible to prepare meaningful job descriptions, necessary in filling job vacancies, completing performance evaluations and merit ratings, and establishing a sound wage and salary scale. Likewise, without accurate production standards, it would be difficult to determine requirements for labor, materials, and equipment, and it would be impossible efficiently to control work flow, quality, and wastage.[19] Therefore, whenever a significant change occurs in a job or operation, an analysis should be conducted and new job descriptions and specifications prepared and new production standards established.

WORK MEASUREMENT

Historically, production output has been the principal means for measuring work, and employees were held directly responsible for their own accomplishments. However, production is no longer an individual process whereby each employee produces a separate and distinct product. It is not uncommon for one product to be the result of the efforts of hundreds or possibly thousands of workers. Therefore it becomes completely unfeasible to attempt to correlate individual effort with productive output. Likewise, productive output indicates nothing about the internal functioning of the production process, such as the time required to process component parts of the finished product. Without this information it is impossible to determine whether an operation is being performed efficiently, whether there is an adequate supply of materials on hand, or whether the additional training of existing employees will solve a given problem. Most important of all, it is impossible to determine whether orders can be filled on schedule and at a production cost that will permit a reasonable profit margin.[20]

Realizing the limitations of productive output as an evaluating yardstick, it is necessary to consider other types of work measurement:

Estimates. This method is of varying value, depending on the degree of accuracy required and the ability of the estimator. It normally consists of a foreman, supervisor, or work planner observing an operation and setting standards based on personal experience.

Time study. This is one of the most widely used methods of work measurement. It utilizes a stop watch or motion pictures to measure the time necessary to perform a series of motions, sub-operations, and operations. Adjusted to compensate for normal interruptions, the end result gives the performance time of the average skilled worker under normal conditions.

Work sampling. This consists of sampling the production process to determine the amount of time required to produce various work units. The work unit selected may be an entire production operation or only a small part of the operation. The results obtained by work sampling may be compared with established standards in order to obtain an approximation of production efficiency.

Experience data. From records of the units produced and the man-hours they require, a unit-time figure may be calculated. If the same operation is performed at a later date, the unit-time figure may be consulted as a basis of comparison to determine its relative efficiency.

Predetermined time systems. When a production operation is divided into various elements and the elements further divided into basic movements, established data may be consulted in order to assign a time value to each movement. When the time required for each of the basic movements is totaled, a time value for the work element is determined. A total of the time values for the various elements will then result in a total time for the entire operation.[21]

TIME STUDY

Since the production process must be a highly coordinated and scheduled operation, it is necessary to have accurate measurements of the time required to complete its various elements; thus, the necessity for time studies.[22]

Time study is closely associated with motion study, although the two may be conducted as entirely separate projects. Whereas motion study is concerned with analyzing an operation in order to achieve the best method of performance, time study is concerned with measuring the operation so as to determine standard time, the basis for scheduling production and remunerating workers. If a time study is not made after a motion study, care must be exercised to insure that a standardized method of production is, in fact, utilized. Otherwise, the measured time will be "loose" and have little or no value in either scheduling or remuneration programs.[23]

An effective time study consists of four principal steps: (1) preparation, (2) timing, (3) determining normal time, and (4) determining standard time.

During the preparation phase it is necessary to determine the exact elements and subelements of the operation that are to be timed, the number of subdivisions being determined principally by the degree of accuracy desired. During this phase it is also necessary to select the operator to be timed and determine the number of timings that should be made. Since standard time is normally based on what the "average" worker can do, the study should measure the performance of a worker who appears to have average skill and ambition.[24]

The most common method of measurement is the stop watch, although micromotion studies by motion picture permit the timing of motions not easily observed by the eye. The latter are costly and time-consuming, and since most operations do not require such a high degree of accuracy, their use is limited.

During the analysis phase, the repeated timings are reviewed in an attempt to establish a "base" time and a "normal" time for the operation. The base time is an average of the repeated timings, after any unusually high or low times have been discarded. When the base time has been determined, it is multiplied by an adjustment factor and the result is termed "normal" time. The determination of the adjustment factor is the most subjective part of the time study and a topic of great controversy between the time study analyst and the worker. The adjustment factor is supposed to correct the actual measured time to correspond to the time that would be required by average skilled operators, working at a normal rate under normal conditions. The area of dispute is normally over what an average operator, a normal rate, and normal conditions are.

When normal time has been established, corrections or allowances must be made for interruptions that occur during a "typical" workday. Such allowances include the time required to obtain tools and materials, rest periods, personal needs of the workers, and other interruptions. The resulting time is termed standard time—the degree of performance which the average skilled worker is expected to maintain while working at a normal rate under standard conditions.

WORK SIMPLIFICATION

Work simplification is frequently associated with motion study and methods engineering. However, work simplification goes beyond the latter, to include the education, training, and motivating of workers necessary to implement improved methods.[25] Likewise, work simplification is not limited merely to implementing new methods developed by methods improvement specialists, but also includes those improvements developed by workers themselves. In fact, the principal emphasis of a sound work simplification program should be upon stimulating workers to review and analyze the various operations they perform with the intent of improving existing operations or developing completely new and more efficient ones.

A successful work simplification program, then, accomplishes three important tasks: (1) it makes the worker aware of the program, the contributions he can make to it, and the benefits he can derive from it; (2) furnishes the worker with the necessary training and instruction with which he can systematically analyze an operation and evaluate the relative advantages and disadvantages of process changes; and (3) establishes the organizational mechanism through which work simplification ideas can be fully implemented and their benefits derived.[26]

QUESTIONS AND PROBLEMS

1. What are two primary reasons for conducting job and operations analysis?
2. Under what circumstances would it be desirable to purchase specialized (capable of handling one type of item) materials handling equipment rather than general-purpose equipment?
3. Under what circumstances would methods standardization be difficult?
4. How does product standardization benefit automobile owners?
5. In what respect would the production control function be different for an organization producing one product from that of an organization which produces several products?
6. What factors should be considered before installing a fully automated production process?
7. How can a distinction be made between an acceptable and an excessive level of scrap?
8. Why can time study be considered a scientific method of determining standard time when, in reality, observation and judgment influence the outcome?
9. Why is productive output no longer a completely suitable method of work measurement? For what purposes is it still useful?
10. What should be the foreman's role in a work simplification program?

REFERENCE NOTES

[1] Edward V. Krick, *Methods Engineering, Design and Measurement of Work Methods*, Wiley, 1962.

[2] Richard W. Owens, *Management of Industrial Enterprises*, Irwin, 1961.

[3] Louis J. Rago, *Production Analysis and Control*, International Textbook, 1963, p. 203.

[4] Charles A. Koepke, *Plant Production Control*, 3rd ed., Wiley, 1961.

[5] Henry G. Hodges and Raymond J. Ziegler, *Managing the Industrial Concern*, Houghton Mifflin, 1963.

[6] Howard L. Timms, *The Production Function in Business*, Irwin, 1962.

[7] E. H. Niece, *Production Forecasting, Planning and Control*, 3rd ed., Wiley, 1961.

[8] Evan D. Scheele, William L. Nesterman, and Robert J. Himmert, *Principles and Design of Production Control Systems*, Prentice-Hall, 1960.

[9] Dean S. Ammer, *Materials Management*, Irwin, 1962, p. 428.

[10] "Seven Yardsticks to Better Material Handling Control," *Factory*, June, 1961, pp. 98-99.

[11] James M. Apple, *Plant Layout and Materials Handling*, Ronald, 1963.

[12] Dean S. Ammer, *op. cit.*, p. 430.

[13] "Evaluation of Work Station Layout (Analysis of Material Handling)," *Material Handling Engineer*, June, 1961, p. 70–75.

[14] "Cut Costs on Small Shipments," *Purchasing*, August 14, 1961, p. 87.

[15] Franklin G. Moore, *Manufacturing Management*, Irwin, 1955.

[16] G. Stahl, "Basic Guide to Industrial Packaging," *Industrial Marketing*, October, 1961, p. 122-127.

[17] L. H. Wiley, "Does Industry Need Tasks Qualifications Analysis?," *Personnel Administration*, March, 1961, pp. 23-30; and J. A. Sargent, "Job Requirements: Before and After," *Supervisory Management*, February, 1961, pp. 53-54.

[18] Howard L. Timms, *op. cit.*, p. 264.

[19] Leonard R. Sayles and George Strauss, *The Human Problems of Management*, Prentice-Hall, 1960.

[20] Virgil H. Rotroff, *Work Measurement*, Reinhold, 1959.

[21] William L. Westerman, Evan D. Scheele, and Robert J. Wimmert, *Principles and Design of Production Control Systems*, Prentice-Hall, 1960.

[22] Joseph Glasser, *Fundamentals of Applied Industrial Management*, William C. Brown Co., Dubuque, Iowa, 1962.

[23] Guy C. Close, *Work Improvement*, Wiley, 1960.

[24] Marvin E. Mundel, *Motion and Time Study, Principles and Practices*, Prentice-Hall, 1960.

[25] N. H. Broom, *Production Management*, Irwin, 1962.

[26] Bernard L. Lewis and William W. Pearson, *Management Guide for Work Simplification*, Rider, 1961.

READING REFERENCES

Baumgartner, John Stanley, *Project Management*, Irwin, 1963.

Campbell, James S., *Principles of Manufacturing Materials and Processes*, McGraw-Hill, 1961.

Feigenbaum, A. V., *Total Quality Control: Engineering and Management*, McGraw-Hill, 1961.

Glasser, Joseph, *Fundamentals of Applied Industrial Management,* William C. Brown, 1962.

Hansen, Bertrand L., *Quality Control: Theory and Application,* Prentice-Hall, 1963.

———, *Work Sampling: For Modern Management,* Prentice-Hall, 1960.

Holt, Charles C., Franco Modigliani, John F. Muth, and Herbert A. Simon, *Planning Production, Inventories and Work Force,* Prentice-Hall, 1960.

Krick, Edward V., *Methods Engineering: Design and Measurement of Work Methods,* Wiley, 1962.

Lambrou, Fred H., *Guide to Work Sampling,* Rider 1962.

Scheele, Evan D., William L. Westerman and Robert J. Wimmert, *Principles and Design of Production Control Systems,* Prentice-Hall, 1960.

13

MARKETING MANAGEMENT

Our technology has advanced to such a point that almost any conceivable product can now be manufactured in the quantity desired. Moving manufactured goods to the market place, however, is another matter. A selection of the problem areas found in marketing management is presented in this chapter.

THE MARKETING PROCESS

"Marketing" is an all-inclusive term that is applied to the process of transferring goods from a producer to a consumer. The marketing process, however, may begin long before a product is produced and it may continue after it has reached the consumer. For example, the production of a new product necessitates the investment of a considerable amount of money, time, and effort. Therefore, before entering into production, a manufacturer is greatly interested in the potential market for his product so that he can judge whether production will be profitable.

Likewise, after a consumer purchases the product, the producer is interested in whether the consumer is satisfied so that he will purchase it again and recommend it to others, or whether certain changes are necessary to insure consumer satisfaction and future product demand. This aspect of the marketing process, which involves evaluating the factors influencing product demand and determining what actions are necessary to encourage product success, or whether success is even possible, is known as market research.

Once it has been determined by market research that an adequate market does exist or can be developed, and production has been initiated, the producer's attention then turns to (1) informing the potential consumer that the product is available and (2) appealing to or creating a consumer need for it. This phase of the marketing process is known as advertising and sales promotion and consists of displaying the product to the consumer via one or more of the advertising media—newspapers, magazines, radio, television, direct mail, and outdoor advertising—and influencing him to purchase it by appealing to physical and psychological needs, such as health, love, and prestige.

The next phase of the marketing process is to make the product available for consumer purchase. The route that a product takes from producer to consumer is known as the channel of distribution. Its character depends primarily on the nature of the product and the volume to be marketed. It may be an extremely simple operation in which the producer sells directly to the consumer or a complex network, with several "middlemen" handling the product before it reaches the consumer.

Sales management is that aspect of the marketing process which consummates the actual transfer of goods from one step in the channel of distribution to another. The function of the individual salesman may be merely to take the action necessary to make the transaction legal, or he may be required to create a demand for the product by employing various advertising and sales promotion techniques.

TYPES OF PRODUCTS

In order to acquaint the reader with the terms used in marketing circles, the major types of products distributed by manufacturers are listed below:

Producers' Goods

Producers' goods are those products which serve as raw materials or component parts in the production of other products. A manufacturer of rubber, for example, turns out a producers' goods for the maker of floor mats.

Consumers' Goods

Consumers' goods are those products which are utilized only by the ultimate consumer. The manufacturers of automobiles, televisions, and luggage are makers of consumers' goods. Some manufacturers make both producers' and consumers' goods, as, for example, the manufacturer of rubber tires. Consumers' goods may be further subdivided into convenience goods, shopping goods, and speciality goods.

Convenience goods. Convenience goods are those products for which the consumer has no strong preference as to brand and for which he has little desire to compare competitive items. The consumer of convenience products places greater value on availability than on the product itself. That they are generally low-cost items adds to his reluctance to go out of his way to obtain a particular brand. Typical examples are candy and hardware, though some consumers may have such a strong preference for a particular brand that they will not purchase a substitute.

Shopping goods. Shopping goods are those items in the purchase of which a consumer will take time to compare competing brands with respect to price, size, quality, or some other feature. Since shopping goods normally have a higher price than convenience goods, the consumer is hesitant to spend his money until he is assured that he is getting the best value possible. However, in most cases he will confine his comparison to the brands available at the store he happens to be in at the time. For example, a shopper in a grocery store will choose between the available brands of catsup rather than shop from store to store in order to find the best possible brand. The principal basis of comparison for most shopping goods is price.

Specialty goods. Specialty goods are those items for which a consumer has a strong brand preference. They are normally items which involve a considerable investment of money and are retained for a long period of time. The consumer will therefore go to a great deal of trouble to insure a wise selection. His final selection, however, is not generally based upon an objective, point-by-point comparison of all available brands, but rather upon a single factor that has a strong appeal to him. In purchasing an automobile, for example, the consumer will be influenced by key attributes, such as style or brand name.

The reason why a consumer decides to buy a particular product at a specific time is a complex subject involving a great number of variables. Certain factors do stand out, however, permitting broad generalizations. These generalizations may prove untrue for an individual consumer; nevertheless, applied to a large group they are an effective tool in analyzing buying patterns.

SELECTION PATTERNS

Here are some of the major patterns that consumers follow in selecting the items they purchase.

Impulse Buying

A common instance of impulse buying is the consumer who goes to a grocery store to purchase one or two items and comes out with a ten-dollar order. Exactly what influenced the decision to purchase additional items is not certain, even to the consumer. Possibly she saw it advertised on television and seeing it in the store motivated her to try it out. She may have been influenced by subconscious motivations that compel her to purchase an item almost by instinct: for example, the consumer who does her grocery shopping after dinner. Weather has a significant effect on the purchase of clothing. Some items of apparel will not sell on certain days even though the season is right.

Although it may not be possible to determine the exact motives behind impulse buying, certain items can be identified as highly susceptible to impulse buying, such as convenience and shopping goods. Specialty goods, however, are seldom bought on impulse, mainly because of their higher price.

Comparison Selection

Comparison selection is most frequently associated with shopping goods, but it is by no means restricted to them. The potential purchaser of specialty goods may compare several makes of cars and actually purchase a model other than his original favorite brand. The tendency to make comparison selections appears to be considerably influenced by the amount of time available as opposed to the value of the product, as, for example, in the case of the consumer who finds his "dream home" after shopping only a day or two but takes several weeks to decide what color to paint it.

Advance Selection

In many cases a consumer will have a strong preference for a particular brand, based perhaps on habit, high recommendations, effective advertising, or some other factor. This preference may be flexible or it may be unalterable. Most cases of advance selection are susceptible to some modification based upon product availability and the existence of close substitutes. For example, if the store is temporarily out of a smoker's favorite brand of cigarette, he may select another, whereas another smoker may refuse any substitute and go instead to another store.

Advance selection is not necessarily limited to brands or even to particular categories of items. For example, a consumer shopping for a chocolate cake may discover that the chocolate cakes are not fresh that day and decide to buy ice cream instead.

Buying patterns are a matter of fact. They can be observed, measured, and objectively analyzed. However, buying motives are not easily observed and measured and therefore cannot be easily analyzed. Studies of human behavior patterns by psychologists and sociologists indicate that they are complex systems influenced by many motives. Yet knowledge of some of the principal motives of behavior can help determine the most effective marketing procedures and techniques. Buying motives are generally divided into two categories: rational and emotional.

Rational motives. Rational buying motives are those which influence a consumer to buy a product after he has compared its significant characteristics with those he is looking for. For example, if a consumer analyzes a product in terms of some established standard, such as usefulness, price, durability, cost of maintenance, probable depreciation, or other objective criterion, and then bases his purchase on the results of this analysis, he is considered to have bought for rational motives.

Emotional motives. Emotional buying motives are those that influence a consumer to purchase a product for purely subjective reasons. When she purchases a product for emotional motives, the customer frequently will state that the particular item makes her "feel good," or that she "just likes it." On occasion the consumer may give an apparently rational reason, which in fact merely conceals the true emotional reason.

Consumer Needs

Regardless of whether the consumer purchases a product because of rational or emotional motives, his decision will be influenced by a number of "needs" over which he has little or no control and about which he may be entirely unaware. These needs are based on the consumer's past experiences, his present status, and his vision of the future.

Basic needs. Every individual has certain basic needs which he must satisfy in order to survive. These include such items as food, shelter, and clothing. In our modern world these needs are generally taken for granted and therefore have little influence on our purchasing motives, except, of course, in those areas of extreme poverty where income is insufficient to meet even these basic requirements of life. In such circumstances buying decisions will almost without exception be based on rational motives, since limited income does not permit the extravagance of emotional purchasing. The consumer with an adequate income, however, buying food, clothing, or a home, tends to be considerably influenced by emotion.

Culturally imposed needs. Each culture imposes a pattern of living upon its people. In the United States our pattern consists of families that reside in private dwellings or apartments, possess refrigerators, stoves, and televisions, commute to and from work by automobile or mass transit systems, read daily newspapers, and so on. It is this pattern that creates what we call the "necessities of life." For most of us, this phrase implies, not merely food, clothing, and shelter, but a balanced and abundant diet, a house with a well-mowed lawn and attractive shrubs, and clothes that are in style. In addition, our pattern of living specifies that an automobile, possibly two, is a necessity of life, as are a television set, radio, and newspaper.

Social needs. Just as our cultural pattern requires these "necessities of life," so does our social position or status require that they be in a certain price range, of a specified quality, or on a given prestige level. For example, it would hardly be "acceptable" for the president of a bank to drive a 1940 Chevrolet, live in a low-rent district, and own a small-screen television set. Social needs are determined by a composite picture of all aspects of an individual's life, including race, color, creed, education, personality, friends, relatives, occupation, hobbies, etc. Social needs do not make consumer choice automatic, but they do establish limits within which to express individual taste and initiative.

Self-realization needs. Opposed to all this there is another intangible need that compels an individual to be different or unlike the other members of the group or groups to which he belongs. The need for self-realization motivates the individual to distinguish himself from the other members of his group, and to behave and act as an individual. One way he can satisfy this is through the things he buys.

A person of relatively low income may seek to distinguish himself by buying a flashy car or "loud" clothes, the intellectual by creating a work of art or writing a book. Between these two extremes are countless ways in which an individual may seek to set himself apart from his fellow men. Even limited insight into this particular need will prove of immense value in analyzing consumer buying motives and establishing effective marketing techniques for certain products.

SALES MANAGEMENT

The sales manager's responsibilities in the over-all marketing function are many and greatly varied. We will discuss some of them briefly.

Policies, Planning, Analysis, and Control

Not the least important function of the sales manager is that of supervising and controlling the performance of the sales force. Adequate supervision may reveal the necessity for changes in the product or in product advertising, or it may reveal the necessity for redirecting the sales force into other areas and markets, and, finally, it will reveal weaknesses in the force and areas that require further training. The individual salesman is normally exposed to only a small portion of the total product market and in most circumstances has had limited training in marketing concepts. It is the function of the sales manager to bring perspective and broad knowledge to the sales situation so that the efforts of the sales force are not wasted in useless pursuits. He must also recommend to higher management those changes that will increase product sales but which are not within his control.[1]

Sales Training

A salesman may know his territory and have all the equipment required to sell the product, but if he is not acquainted with the proper techniques of selling and the marketable characteristics of his product, then his selling efforts will be highly inefficient.

The type of sales training a man should have will depend to a great extent on the nature of the product he sells and on his prior experience as a salesman. Some companies prefer to select salesmen with no prior experience in selling their product, on the assumption that the individual will not have to unlearn previously acquired, improper selling habits. Such salesmen will generally require an extended period of training before starting to work. At the other extreme are those companies that prefer experienced sales personnel who require a minimum of additional training. The training program will vary widely from company to company, some placing great emphasis on classroom training, with lectures, technical courses, visual aids, and practical exercises; others emphasizing on-the-job training, possibly with sales meetings, conventions, and correspondence courses conducted concurrently.

Salesmanship

Historically, business has tended to be production-oriented, in part because product demand far exceeded production capacity. Consequently, the sales force was merely a "tool" for taking customers' orders rather than an organization responsible for "selling" the product. As production capabilities gradually caught up with customer demand and as competition became more keen, the era of the true salesman arrived. This occurred during the 1930s and continued into the 1950s. With the growth of mass communications and volume buying (stimulated by television and chain stores), the role of the salesman was further modified and his status upgraded so that he now has a strong voice in the operation of the business.

In the past the sales manager was the shining example of the man who started at the bottom of the sales force and worked his way to the top as the result of his personal selling achievements. The secret of his success as sales manager was his driving ambition, his extroverted personality, and his skill at "driving" the sales force on to higher achievements. These qualities may still be found in the modern-day sales manager. In most cases, however, they have taken a back seat to the managing aspect of the selling function. With the recent sophistication of the selling process, the sales manager is now responsible for selecting, maintaining, and operating a highly skilled organization capable of applying modern techniques to complex and highly technical products. Gone are the days of hand-shaking and back-slapping selling. The sales manager must now perform a manager's functions.[2]

Salesmen's Compensation and Expenses

There is no hard and fast rule as to how much or in what way a salesman should be compensated for his work. All compensation programs should insure at least minimum satisfaction.

Amount. There is significant evidence that in the past too much emphasis has been placed on the amount of compensation. All too often it was assumed that an increase in pay would compensate for any dissatisfaction the salesman might feel about his job or working conditions. It now appears that the actual amount of compensation is really not a significant factor in retaining an effective and satisfied sales force. However, compensation must at least afford a comfortable standard of living, and if it drops below this acceptable minimum, dissatisfaction will be pronounced.

Relative income. Above this minimum, the relative value of income becomes important. A salesman who knows that a man in another department of the company is receiving greater monetary compensation may be relatively unconcerned about this inequality if he prefers the work he is doing or realizes that he is unqualified to perform the other job. The same salesman, however, is not unconcerned when he learns that another salesman, doing his type of work, with approximately the same effectiveness, is being paid more for his services. This holds true even for salesmen working for different companies. Extreme spreads in compensation can result in openly expressed dissatisfaction and high turnover.

Method of compensation. Even if his compensation compares favorably with that paid his occupational peers, the salesman may still be dissatisfied. One possible explanation is that he considers the method of compensation unfair. For example, if his compensation is based on a salary plus commission, the salesman may be highly dissatisfied when he is unable to make any money on commission because of a "slump" in the market, which is beyond his control. He may also believe that the amount of effort he puts forth has no bearing on his commission earnings.

The exact method of compensation will vary from company to company. Generally, when the salesman has little or no control over sales volume, compensation should be based principally on salary, whereas where sales volume is a direct result of the salesman's efforts, compensation should be based more on commission.

There are other compensations to a job besides monetary ones, although most of these are intangible and difficult to evaluate. "Fringe benefits" may be of considerable appeal, such as an unlimited expense account, unrestricted use of a company automobile, or expense-paid vacations. Still other forms of compensation include the social atmosphere or attitude of fellow workers and supervisors or the nature of the work itself, especially when the salesman believes that he is performing a valuable service to society.

Selecting and Testing Salesmen

Salesmen are generally an important factor in product success. Their selection should therefore be given the time and consideration it deserves.

The selection of salesmen does not differ greatly from the selection of other company personnel. Qualified men should be obtained from those sources which in the past have proved to furnish the type of salesman desired. However, new sources should continually be explored. A consistent selection procedure should be followed in filling all vacancies; otherwise there is a tendency to select an individual on the basis of one strong characteristic to the possible exclusion of several weak ones. The applicant's experience and performance should, as a matter of course, be carefully evaluated in terms of the specific requirements of the job and according to the company's future plans.

SALES PROMOTION

Sales promotion includes those functions that supplement advertising and selling in creating consumer demand, generally those of a nonrecurring nature, such as introducing a new or changed product, stimulating sales in an area where competition is particularly strong, providing dealers and distributors with a preview of "things to come" in the way of product developments, advertising, and other marketing procedures. Sales promotion also includes miscellaneous functions designed to stimulate consumer demand by appealing to buying motives not directly related to the product.[3] The following are some of the more common methods of sales promotion:

Sampling. This technique is usually based on the assumption that if given the opportunity the product will sell itself.

Premiums. Today's most popular premiums are the trading stamps furnished with almost every type of purchase, which can be redeemed for household goods. Other premium offers include discounts on items upon the presentation of a label or box top.[4]

Contests. Contests are designed to attract consumer interest in a product by appealing to the desire to get something for nothing, such as an automobile, an all-expenses-paid vacation, or some other item of value. The consumer is required to purchase the product being promoted in order to enter the contest.

Special events. Special events stimulate interest and curiosity. The assumption is that if a product is associated with a special event, consumer demand will be stimulated. Special events include world fairs, personal appearances by celebrities, stunts, etc.

Displays and demonstrations. Product displays placed in strategic locations tend to attract people's attention and interest.

Window displays that involve moving objects attract greater attention than static displays.

Brands and trade-marks. Brand names and trade-marks are employed to associate products of the same manufacturer, under the assumption that if a consumer likes one product, he will be inclined to purchase another by the same manufacturer.

ADVERTISING

In its simplest form the purpose of advertising is to inform the potential consumer that a product is available for purchase. Its most common form is the newspaper ad in which the seller gives a description of the product, indicating its outstanding qualities and possibly its price. Advertising of this type is almost exclusively rational as opposed to emotional. At the other end of the advertising spectrum are the advertisements that actually attempt to create a need or desire for a product where no such need or desire exists. This type of advertising is used principally for items generally categorized as luxury goods or those beyond the more basic requirements of life. It usually appeals to those desires that tend to enhance prestige and status. Advertising of this type tends to be highly emotional and may even, on occasion, fail to make any appeal whatsoever to logical reasoning. Between these two extremes are various combinations of the rational and the emotional approach.

The style of advertising selected for a particular product will depend on the product's characteristics, the advertising style employed by the competition, the moral and social responsibilities of the advertiser, assumptions as to what motivates people, and, last but not least, the long-term effects of various advertising styles.[5]

Advertising Media

The number of ways in which advertising is accomplished is almost unlimited. We can distinguish between formal and informal ones. The formal media include those over which the producer has direct control and which he selects to accomplish a specific purpose. The informal media include all those over which the producer has little or no control and which he did not select for any specific purpose. The formal advertising media consist of the normal channels of mass communication, and include newspapers, magazines, radio, television, and billboards. The informal media include consumer recommendations to other consumers, display of a product while it is being utilized or consumed, and other unsponsored references to the product. This chapter will consider only the formal media of advertising.[6]

Newspapers. Newspapers are a widely used and highly effective medium of advertising. They have a wide range of circulation which includes people of all occupations, races, religions, and social status. Those products with broad appeal find newspaper advertising highly effective. At the same time, newspapers permit the advertiser a great deal of flexibility since he can usually publish an advertisement on whatever day he desires and change the copy at almost any time up to the publication deadline. Newspapers are not subject to the limitations of television and radio. If additional space is required, another page can be added, whereas radio and television cannot expand the time devoted to advertising without seriously interrupting their program schedule. Newspapers also permit the producer to regionalize his advertising by geographical area or appeal to consumers with specific interests via "trade" publications.

Magazines. Magazines do not have the wide circulation enjoyed by newspapers. They do have a large circulation among middle- and high-income levels; therefore the producers of luxury or nonnecessity-type items may find them especially suitable for their particular requirements. Magazines do not have the degree of flexibility offered by newspapers since the ad usually must be prepared several weeks prior to publication and last-minute changes are not possible. Magazines have limited facilities for regionalizing circulation so that an ad may appear in only a portion of the total circulation area, precluding, for example, advertising snow tires in Florida. Magazines also permit the categorization of ads by consumer interest, such as hunting, fishing, baseball, cooking, sewing, and so on.

Radio. Unlike newspapers and magazines, radio is capable of bringing a product to the attention of the consumer with little or no effort on his part. Whereas the potential consumer must suspend other activities in order to read a newspaper or magazine, radio permits him to proceed with his normal activities while listening to a program and the accompanying commercials. Radio permits the producer to regionalize his advertising through the selection of particular stations or achieve nationwide coverage by utilizing network facilities. Radio also permits the producer to select the time of day in which his advertising will be the most effective, whereas he has little or no control over the time at which a newspaper or magazine ad is read.

Television. The effectiveness of television advertising is highly dependent on two principal factors: (1) the time of day and (2) the drawing power of the program sponsored. If these key factors are properly utilized, television provides an almost unsurpassed means of appealing to the greatest possible number of potential consumers. The price the advertiser must pay for this vast audience, however, is not small, and the decision to employ it must be made only after a careful evaluation of its potential advantages.

Outdoor advertising. Outdoor advertising is an extremely effective way of constantly reminding the potential consumer of a product. Unlike the other principal media, its services extend over a period of time, usually at least a month. Its repetitive impact appeals to the subconscious since the individual may become entirely unaware of the advertisement after a period of time, yet when he goes to purchase a particular product, the brand advertised on the billboard will seem quite familiar to him.

Miscellaneous media. There are a number of other methods for stimulating the consumer to buy a product. These include direct mail, window and counter displays, handouts, posters, demonstrations, free samples, etc. They are considered under the subject of sales promotion.

Social Aspects of Advertising

In accomplishing its basic objective of informing and motivating the consumer, advertising exerts a considerable influence on our habits, morals, standards of living, styles, employment, and production. Numerous arguments can be developed both in favor of and against advertising, but its precise effects are difficult to determine. We can, however, glance at some of the claims made about it.

Stimulates competition. It is frequently argued that since advertising promotes competition, and competition stimulates efficiency, it therefore serves a useful purpose. However, opponents of this argument claim that this is accomplished only at the sacrifice of something else, such as quality or price. Both views are generalities and as such are subject to many exceptions. There are cases in which advertising has eliminated a competing producer who could not afford its expense. Likewise, there are cases where advertising has stimulated competition so that quality was improved and prices lowered.

Stimulates the business cycle. As the argument goes, our economy is based on the production of nonessential goods for which no need exists other than the consumers' desire; consequently, if this desire did not exist, there would be a sharp decline in production and employment. It is generally agreed that advertising does create consumer demand for certain products, but it is not agreed that its withdrawal would result in a disastrous decline in production and severe unemployment.

Stimulates volume business. This in turn makes possible lower prices. Criticism of this position involves the distribution of the savings generated by greater production. The consumer or worker may claim that the producer retains the savings and does not pass them on to him. However, the consumer does have the choice of selecting another product, and the worker can make his demands known at the bargaining table.

Increases product cost. It goes without saying that advertising costs money and that eventually this is reflected in the price of the product paid by consumers. What is not so obvious is the extent to which the cost-reducing factors of advertising counterbalance or outweigh its cost. This is another of the unmeasurable effects of advertising that remain open to discussion.

Degrades moral standards. This criticism is more commonly directed at the programs which advertisers sponsor. The problem is how to control programs which may influence the morals of society in a negative way. In many cases advertisers have themselves established codes of ethics governing what should and should not be included in advertisements. Other groups feel that this is not adequate and that some type of government control is necessary. Possibly, the most effective control is public reaction, and the only direct means the public has of expressing its feelings is by writing letters to the advertising media or the sponsor.

Advertising Budgets

Advertising is no small expenditure in an organization's budget. In 1945 the total volume of advertising in the United States amounted to three billion dollars; in 1962 it had risen to over twelve billion dollars. This significant increase is attributable to the greater emphasis placed on advertising in general to the expansion of advertising media, television in particular.

Why is so much emphasis placed on advertising today? Until the early 1950s demand often exceeded production capabilities; therefore no real purpose was to be served by large expenditures designed to increase demand even more. But as technology and mass production methods improved, production was able not only to meet but to exceed demand. The key to increasing profits became the ability to stimulate consumers to buy, and this meant appealing to mass markets through the mass media of communications.[7]

RETAIL MANAGEMENT

Since 1900 the field of retailing has developed at an extremely rapid rate. From the days of the country peddler and the community store, retailing has expanded to include an almost endless number of privately owned businesses, shopping centers, department and chain stores, and even vending machines. The retail organization plays the vital role of presenting the product to the end user, the consumer. The retailing process is the culmination of all the efforts of the manufacturing-distribution system, including production, sales, shipping, etc. The efficiency and effectiveness with which retailing is accomplished has a direct bearing on all other areas of business.

In order to engage in successful retailing, it is necessary to (1) determine what the consumer wants or will buy and (2) present the desired products in the most favorable terms, as to price, availability, and service. In certain fields the determination of consumer buying patterns is a fairly routine matter, based on past experience, customer requests, competitors' performance, trade publications, or some other source. In other fields, especially when an unusual product is being introduced, an accurate determination of consumer wants must be based on trial-and-error methods.

When the retailer has determined to his satisfaction the anticipated consumer demand, he must then turn his attention to obtaining the desired product.[8] The buying process will vary in complexity depending on the product. A retail car dealer, for example, has no problem obtaining cars from the automobile manufacturer. Usually there is only one source of supply, an established price, and specific procedures for each and every purchase. A department store buyer, however, must give careful attention to inventory size, style, price, arrangements for the return of unsold merchandise, and other important considerations. For many products, buying guides are available which indicate relative demand by size, color, style, etc., so that inventories may be adjusted accordingly.

When the retailer has obtained a product from a supplier,

he must then offer it for sale in such a manner that consumers will be encouraged to buy. This means giving consideration to (1) local advertising, merchandising, and sales promotion, to inform potential consumers that the product is available and to encourage them to purchase it at his store; (2) product availability and attractiveness, including store location, appearance, accessibility, and parking space; and (3) service functions, including attitude of sales personnel, policy with respect to merchandise returns, guarantee, product maintenance, and credit arrangements.[9]

WHOLESALE MANAGEMENT

A wholesaler may be defined as an intermediate marketer who performs various services in distributing goods after they are released by the manufacturer but before they reach the eventual consumer. The wholesaler does not normally come into contact with the end user of the product, but he offers certain benefits to both manufacturers and retailers.

The manufacturer who utilizes a wholesaler is freed of many distribution functions which he would otherwise have to perform. The only sales personnel he will require will be those that sell to the wholesaler. He can also reduce his shipping and handling costs since he can make a few large shipments in place of many small ones going to different places. Savings are realized not only through less physical handling but also by obtaining bulk shipping rates from carriers.[10]

The wholesaler also provides many valuable services to retailers. Since the wholesaler maintains stocks of several different products, one salesman can frequently provide all or most of the products a retailer requires. Also, since most wholesalers are located in close proximity to retailers, they provide a fast and convenient back-up supply, thereby permitting the retailer to maintain smaller inventories. Since most wholesalers are well acquainted with retailers in the area, they can frequently extend credit to retailers which manufacturers might not be willing to risk.

Recently manufacturers have started to sell directly to retailers. Such arrangements, however, usually result in the loss of some benefit.[11]

DIRECT-MAIL AND MAIL-ORDER SELLING

In "mail-order selling" the buyer orders and receives merchandise through the mails. "Direct mail," on the other hand, is a form of advertising and sales promotion whereby the seller appeals directly to a particular consumer by mail. Direct-mail promotion may or may not result in mail-order selling, and mail-order selling may or may not be the result of direct-mail techniques.

Direct Mail

The use of direct-mail sales promotion has certain definite advantages to many marketers. Direct-mail advertising is capable of reaching all areas that receive mail service, thus penetrating areas other forms of advertising cannot reach. This is true not only of domestic markets, but of foreign markets, where television, newspaper, and magazine facilities are not available. By direct mail it is also possible to aim advertising at a specific market. For example, television would be an extremely expensive form of advertising to reach a relatively small market. Direct-mail advertising, however, reaches those individuals most likely to have an interest in the product being marketed.[12]

Mail-Order Selling

The most outstanding examples of successful mail-order selling are Sears, Roebuck and Company and Montgomery Ward & Company. Both of these organizations owe much of their success to the effectiveness of mail-order selling, though each has now expanded into the retail store system. Mail-order selling has many significant advantages: (1) Overhead is normally considerably lower than with normal retailing since large display stores are not necessary. (2) Expensive advertising is replaced by relatively inexpensive catalogues. (3) Part of the distribution cost is absorbed by the consumer. However, mail-order selling also has certain disadvantages: (1) Customer service is limited since the only contact between buyer and seller is usually through the mail. (2) The cost of packing and handling merchandise adds to operating costs. (3) Mass markets can be reached only by catalogues at great expense, since many who receive catalogues do not order merchandise.

DISTRIBUTION COSTS

The principal consideration when selecting a channel of distribution for a product is normally "How can profit be maximized?" For example, at one extreme a manufacturer may decide to perform all distribution functions himself. All middlemen and intermediate handling are eliminated, the result being either lower prices for the consumer or higher profits for the manufacturer. The main drawback for the manufacturer who performs his own distribution is that he may be excluding a vast market which he would be able to reach through outside distribution channels.

The selection of a channel of distribution should normally be based on a thorough evaluation of two factors: (1) the cost of distributing through each channel and (2) the relative advantages and degree of profit that can reasonably be expected from each. The principal channels of distribution include (1) manufacturer to consumer, (2) manufacturer to retailer to consumer, (3) manufacturer to wholesaler to retailer to consumer, and (4) manufacturer to special distribution agent(s) to consumer.[13]

The first type (manufacturer to consumer) requires the greatest expenditure, for a sales force and physical facilities. The fourth type (manufacturer to special distribution agent to consumer) usually requires the least investment in sales personnel and distribution facilities, since the manufacturer may turn all his production over to an agent or several agents, who will, in turn, perform all the distribution functions. Such agents may be known as manufacturers' agents, sales agents, or brokers.

A manufacturer should be thoroughly acquainted with the type of consumer who will purchase his product, their probable number and location. This information can normally be obtained by the use of market surveys. Once it has been determined, he can then select the channel of distribution that will be most effective in reaching his market.

MARKETING RESEARCH AND STATISTICS

To set up an effective marketing program, these things should be known:

1. Will consumers buy the product?
2. How many potential consumers are there for a particular item?
3. What percent of the market is supplied by competitors?
4. What influences the market (climate, season, fads, etc.) and to what extent?
5. What is the probable rate of market growth and development?
6. What determines consumer buying motives for the product (style, price, availability, etc.) and to what extent?
7. What advertising media would be most effective in stimulating sales?
8. What additional increase in sales can be expected for each additional dollar spent on advertising?

It is physically and financially impossible to base the answers to marketing questions on a complete survey of all potential consumers. Instead, the market survey utilizes statistical techniques. In other words, answers to questions about an entire market are based on an analysis of a relative sample of the entire market.[14] Generally, the larger the sample, the greater the accuracy. However, many factors can be accurately analyzed from a relatively small sample if it is highly representative of the whole market.[15]

There are three primary methods by which such information and data may be obtained: (1) by going directly to the source and conducting basic research and investigation; (2) by utilizing raw data already available; and (3) by utilizing analyzed and interpreted data that is readily available. Information may be gathered directly from the source by casually asking consumers questions during regular contacts or it may be done formally by utilizing telephone surveys, questionnaires, and door-to-door canvasses. The formal methods are carried out almost exclusively by market survey organizations who have personnel trained and experienced in such work.

Various types of raw data can be obtained from a number of sources, grouped in a desired form, and analyzed to answer specfiic questions—from company records, trade journals, and government publications. Publications by the Departments of Commerce and Labor and the Federal Trade Commission are valuable sources of such information. Many government publications go beyond the mere compiling of data and include a detailed analysis, indicating trends and estimated future development. Such preanalyzed data often provides ready answers to important marketing questions.

QUESTIONS AND PROBLEMS

1. How is the value of advertising measured?
2. Why wouldn't mail-order selling be an effective method for selling convenience goods?
3. What factors must be considered when selecting channels of distribution?
4. What questions should market surveys answer?
5. What circumstances might cause retail sales to be low when market surveys indicate that a definite consumer demand exists?
6. What are the principal functions of a sales manager?
7. How does sales promotion differ from advertising?
8. What benefits does a retailer receive when he purchases from a wholesaler instead of directly from a manufacturer?

9. Why is personal selling still necessary when mass media advertising is utilized?
10. What is the "marketing process"?

REFERENCE NOTES

[1] Willard M. Thompson, *Salesmanship: Concepts, Management, and Strategy*, Wiley, 1963.

[2] Carlton A. Pederson and Milburn D. Wright, *Salesmanship: Principles and Methods*, 3rd ed., Irwin, 1961.

[3] Alfred Gross, *Sales Promotion: Principles and Methods for Intensifying Marketing Effort*, 2nd ed., Ronald, 1961.

[4] George Meredith, *Effective Merchandising with Premiums*, McGraw-Hill, 1962.

[5] Charles J. Dirksen and Arthur Kroeger, *Advertising Principles and Problems*, Irwin, 1960.

[6] S. Watson Dunn, *Advertising, Its Role in Modern Marketing*, Holt, Rinehart and Winston, 1961.

[7] Frank H. Eby and Myron S. Heidingsfield, *Marketing and Business Research*, Holt, Rinehart and Winston, 1962.

[8] Delbert J. Duncan and Charles F. Phillips, *Retailing: Principles and Methods*, Irwin, 1963.

[9] Ferdinand F. Mauser, *Modern Marketing Management, an Integrated Approach*, McGraw-Hill, 1961.

[10] Richard M. Hill, *Wholesaling Management*, Irwin, 1963.

[11] David Revzan, *Wholesaling in Marketing Organization*, Wiley, 1961.

[12] John T. Maguire and John D. Yeck, *Planning and Creating Better Direct Mail*, McGraw-Hill, 1961.

[13] Kenneth R. Davis, *Marketing Management*, Ronald Press, 1961.

[14] Charles F. Phillips and Delbert J. Duncan, *Marketing: Principles and Methods*, Irwin, 1964.

[15] Louis Cheskin, *Business Without Gambling, How Successful Marketers Use Scientific Methods*, Quadrangle Books, 1963.

READING REFERENCES

Brink, Edward L., and William T. Kelley, *The Management of Promotion—Consumer Behavior and Demand Stimulation*, Prentice-Hall, 1963.

Lebhar, Godfrey M., *Chain Stores in America, 1859-1962*, 3rd ed., Chain Store Publishing Corp., 1963.

Messner, Frederick R., *Industrial Advertising*, McGraw-Hill, 1963.

Richert, G. Henry, Warren G. Meyer, and Peter G. Haynes, *Retailing, Principles and Practices*, McGraw-Hill, 1962.

Sandage, C. H., and Vernon Fryburger, *Advertising Theory and Practice*, 6th ed., Irwin, 1963.

Shields, L. Daniel, *The Magic of Creative Selling*, Prentice-Hall, 1961.

Taplin, Walter, *Advertising: A New Approach*, Little, Brown, 1963.

Wedding, Nugent, and Richard S. Lessler, *Advertising Management*, Ronald, 1962.

Wright, John S., and Daniel S. Warner, *Speaking of Advertising*, McGraw-Hill, 1963.

Yeck, John D., and John T. McQuire, *Planning and Creating Better Mail*, McGraw-Hill, 1961.

14

PURCHASING AND WAREHOUSE MANAGEMENT

Unfortunately, there is a void of information pertaining to this area of management, conveying the impression that it is not an interesting field to enter. Such is not the case, for managers in the field find it a source of great personal satisfaction.

PUBLIC PURCHASING

Only recently has purchasing developed into a separate and distinct function of business. Prior to World War I, purchasing was almost always an integral part of production and therefore under control of the production manager. In the years following World War II, purchasing evolved into a separate staff organization in most companies for two primary reasons: (1) The variety of materials needed requires that personnel be thoroughly acquainted with purchasing procedures and sources of supply. (2) Increased competition requires that maximum quality be obtained at minimum price.

The purchasing officer, or procurement officer, as he is frequently called, does not determine what is to be purchased, but is responsible for obtaining the materials the operating departments require at the most favorable price. To do this, he must evaluate several factors:

Quantity. Most items can normally be obtained at a favorable price when bought in large quantities. The purchasing officer must determine the quantity to be purchased based on the item's rate of consumption; anticipated future requirements; available storage space and its cost; the possibility that it will become obsolete, contaminated, or spoil while in storage; and, last but not least, its anticipated availability and cost in the future. He has no hard and fast rules to follow, but must decide on the basis of past experience and the best information currently available.

Timing. Many items have no stable selling price, which fluctuates with demand and/or availability. Price fluctuation for some items follows a predictable pattern; for others it does not. Purchasing officers with an understanding of the factors that influence the selling price of an item capitalize on their knowledge to obtain it at the most opportune time and price.

Substitution. Frequently a production department will request the purchasing officer to obtain an item of specific brand or quality. The purchasing officer, consulting a catalogue or source of supply, may find that a similar item of different brand or quality is available at a significantly lower price. Before ordering the less expensive item, he should obtain the approval of the requesting department. In this way an alert purchasing officer can save a company considerable money.

Source of Supply. Consistent with sound principles of economy, the purchasing officer selects a supplier with a reputation for furnishing material of good quality and providing good service. If the purchasing officer establishes himself as a good customer, he will more than likely benefit by improved service. Therefore the purchaser-supplier relationship is a "two-way street" based on mutual trust and understanding.

Purchasing involves more than merely obtaining a requested item at the lowest price. A skilled and conscientious purchasing officer can contribute significantly toward increasing the profit margin of the business.

PUBLIC WAREHOUSING

Many business organizations do not possess storage facilities for the raw materials to be used in production or for storing the completed product. A company-owned warehouse may not be economically feasible if the volume of material to be stored is too great or fluctuates unpredictably. Whatever the reason, most manufacturing organizations, at some time or another, require the services of public warehousing.

Public warehouses may be classified as (1) general-merchandise warehouses and (2) special-commodity warehouses.

General-merchandise warehouses. General-merchandise warehouses are intended for the temporary or long-term storage of supplies or goods that do not require special facilities or handling. They serve principally as distribution links between producer and consumer. Incoming goods may be received in one large shipment and distributed in several smaller shipments, the warehouse thereby serving as a "breakdown" center. Or a manufacturer might ship his daily production to a general-merchandise warehouse for temporary storage until a sufficient quantity had accumulated to fill a customer's order. Or the producer or consumer may wish to take advantage of favorable price by purchasing in large quantities or when the market price is low. Care must be exercised, however, to insure that the advantage is not offset by the cost of storage.

Special-commodity warehouses. Special-commodity warehouses are intended for the temporary or long-term storage of supplies or goods for which special facilities or handling devices are required. Cold-storage warehouses are an example, since the item stored must be kept chilled or frozen to avoid spoilage. Certain agricultural warehouses may be classified as special-commodity warehouses if special facilities or handling devices (such as grain elevators) are required. Bonded warehouses do not normally require special facilities, but they do require special handling in that a tax or duty must be paid on all merchandise before it can be released. Such warehouses may be required for the storage of items from other countries or for such domestic products as alcoholic beverages, which are closely controlled by various government agencies.

In addition to storage space, public warehouses also furnish a number of services to their customers, such as assembling orders, marking packages, repacking, shipping and delivery, and record keeping. These functions are normally performed without additional charge. For some additional services not directly concerned with storage, an additional charge may be made. Such services include collection on delivery of cost of goods, credit checks on customers receiving goods on credit, and special reports on the status of goods in storage or being delivered. In some circumstances the public warehouse may act as a sales representative for the company that has goods in storage.[1]

RECEIVING AND MARKING

The receiving function in traffic management includes: (1) taking delivery from commercial carriers of supplies and material needed in the production process or for the general operation of the business; (2) inspecting incoming shipments to insure that they are in good condition and in the quantity and quality ordered; (3) identifying shipments and notifying the necessary departments of their arrival or taking action to have them added to the normal inventory; (4) providing temporary storage for incoming supplies and material until final disposition can be accomplished; and (5) maintaining adequate records of incoming shipments.

The receiving department in most organizations is under the supervision of a foreman or receiving clerk, who, in turn, is under the supervision of the traffic manager or transportation officer. The size and complexity of the receiving department will depend primarily on the nature of the product and the volume received. A large organization, for example, may have a sizable receiving department consisting of several sections of personnel who perform specialized duties. At the other extreme, the receiving department for a small firm may be nothing more than a one- or two-man operation in which each must be thoroughly acquainted with all aspects of the receiving process. The way in which the receiving department is organized will also depend on the mode of transportation, though certain functions are basically the same for all receiving departments regardless of how they receive shipments. Shipment by rail will be the basis of discussion in the paragraphs that follow.

Normally, the first indication the receiving department gets of an incoming shipment is notification by the purchasing department. This notification serves two principal functions: (1) as an alert so that adequate equipment and space can be made available to unload and store the incoming shipment and (2) as an authorization to accept delivery. It also makes it possible for the receiving department to initiate tracer action on a shipment that does not arrive by the specified date. An incoming rail shipment may be delivered to the wrong railroad siding, where it will sit for several days before being properly identified. An alert receiving department staff, meanwhile, will have started tracer action to locate the car.

If for some reason an incoming shipment is to be handled differently from established procedures, the receiving department must be so notified, along with detailed instructions on the new disposal.

An important consideration in rail shipments is the penalty often incurred when a car is held for an excessive period of time. Most railroads allow consignees to retain rail cars for unloading for approximately forty-eight hours, since excessive delay keeps needed equipment unavailable. The most frequent reasons for such delays are the consignee's lack of storage space or lack of personnel and unloading equipment. Most of these delays could be eliminated by advance planning. The penalty which a railroad assesses against late shippers or receivers is known as "demurrage." In order to avoid demurrage charges, the receiving department should see that prompt action is taken on all incoming shipments and that adequate records are maintained on the dates shipments are received and the dates and times demurrage charges will be assessed.

As a general rule, only carload-lot rail shipments are made directly to the consignee. Goods shipped in less than carload lots will normally be unloaded at the railroad's freight house by their own personnel, and a shipment arrival notice sent to the consignee. Upon receipt of the arrival notice, the consignee's receiving department will dispatch a truck or make other arrangements to pick up the shipment. The driver who makes the pick-up must complete the necessary inspection and fill out the required documents, which normally are processed in the receiving department at the plant.

A prompt and thorough inspection should be made of all incoming shipments. Any loss, damage, or destruction should be carefully noted and described on the appropriate documents. The carrier is liable only for certain types of damage; any other damage is normally covered by insurance.

To facilitate handling and future identification, every shipment should be marked so that it can be easily recognized and warehousing personnel can determine whether it is to be stored temporarily, added to existing stocks, or delivered directly to a department in the organization.[2]

SHIPPING AND TRANSPORTATION

Included in the cost of raw materials and supplies is the cost of transporting them from their source to the point of manufacture. The question as to who pays the cost of transporting the finished product—supplier, producer, or consumer—is not really significant since when the consumer does not pay it openly, it is included in the price of the merchandise.

Companies that either ship or receive a substantial volume of goods normally have a separate department to handle all matters pertaining to transportation, headed by a traffic manager or transportation officer. Depending on the size of the company, his job will vary from supervising a small staff of assistants to running a large department composed of several sections staffed by specialists in the various areas of transportation. The traffic manager must insure that routine operations are performed in the most efficient manner and that special problems are expeditiously handled. He must insure that the proper carriers are employed and that carriers which have given consistently inferior service in the past are not patronized. He must have available current information on tariff rates as well as on laws which regulate shipments.

Other than routine functions include studies to determine possible improvements, including investigating cases of excessive damage in shipments. On some occasions it may be necessary to work with other department heads to solve problems not exclusively limited to traffic management. The traffic manager also advises top management on special problems and indicates present and future requirements with respect to personnel, equipment, and facilities.

One of the principal functions of all traffic departments is the selection of the shipping route and the carrier to be used. This selection is usually based on (1) cost, (2) speed, and (3) convenience of delivery. These three factors are not of equal importance in all situations. There may be occasions when a producer requires certain materials with the least possible delay so that expensive production time is not lost. In other cases supplies may be needed at a particular location regardless of cost or time. When convenience and time are not overriding, the primary determinant in the selection of route and carrier will usually be cost.

The principal modes of transportation are rail, truck, water, and air. Each has certain advantages for certain shipments. Transportation personnel must select the form of transportation that provides the type of handling a product requires.[3]

Rail shipments. The vast majority of goods transported annually in the United States are shipped by rail. Railroads are capable of handling large quantities of merchandise over long distances at very reasonable rates. They also offer a great deal of flexibility since a vast network of tracks permits delivery to every part of the country. There are agreements between railroads whereby one shipment may be handled by several roads on one bill of lading. Most large companies are in close proximity to main railroad lines, and many even have sidings for loading and unloading beside or even in the plant. The principal disadvantage of rail shipments is that they do take time, especially in covering relatively short distances, since cars may sit in a switching yard for a considerable period before being put in actual transit. There also are a few areas where access by rail is not possible because of the terrain or some other consideration. Rail shipment, however, still offers the average manufacturer the most efficient mode of transportation at the least expense.

One of the main reasons rail shipments are so economical is their ability to haul vast quantities of material in one shipment (train), utilizing a minmium amount of labor. To achieve greater efficiency in the use of facilities, railroads have two categories of shipments: (1) carload lots and (2) LCL (less than carload lots). A higher rate is usually charged for LCL shipments; therefore manufacturers that do not have sufficient volume to warrant a carload-lot shipment may make arrangements with other manufacturers to share a car for merchandise going to the same consignee. Such a shipment is called a "mixed car" and enables the shipper to obtain carload-lot rates. If a manufacturer has merchandise going to several consignees in the same area, he may include all the orders in one car and make arrangements for proper distribution at the destination point. Such a shipment is known as a "pooled car" and also enables the shipper to get carload-lot rates.

Truck shipments. Shipments by truck also account for a substantial portion of the goods transported annually in the United States. Trucks permit a relatively rapid means of shipping with a great deal of flexibility. There is little delay in switching, as in the case of many rail shipments. Therefore merchandise may be transported from coast to coast without standing idle for long periods of time. There are few geographical areas that cannot be reached by a truck. Wherever there is a road, a truck can usually go. For short hauls in particular, trucks usually provide the most efficient means of shipment. Their only disadvantage is that truck traffic may have to be curtailed because of climatic conditions (snow, ice, fog, flood), which do not affect most rail shipments. Nor can trucks achieve the degree of efficiency of operation of the railroads. For this reason railroads normally furnish lower rates than trucking firms. The savings in cost, however, must be balanced against the advantages of time and flexibility.

Water shipments. The most important advantage of shipping by water is its extremely low cost, an important consideration for those manufacturers handling large volumes of bulky materials. Water transportation is well suited for shipping such items as coal, cement, iron ore, grain, and similar products. However, any producer can enjoy substantial savings if water shipment facilities are available. Therefore careful consideration should be given to the availability of water routes when selecting plant locations. With the opening of the St. Lawrence Seaway, the Great Lakes have become important terminals for manufacturers shipping goods to United States seaports, as well as other countries. The primary disadvantage of water shipping is its slowness and lack of flexibility. If time is an important factor, water routes will almost always be excluded. Also, many areas of the country have no access to water routes, while in others water travel is impossible during seasons when rivers and lakes are frozen or of insufficient depth to permit travel.

Air shipments. Shipping by air presents one outstanding advantage and one outstanding disadvantage. The advantage is the time factor. Air is by far the fastest method of shipment. Goods shipped from the United States in the morning can often be at their destination in a foreign country, thousands of miles away, by evening. The cost for such a shipment is considerable, but when time is of paramount importance, the shipper may be willing to pay the additional expense. Air, however, still accounts for a very minor portion of goods shipped annually in the United States.

It is also possible to combine modes of shipment in order to achieve the advantages of each. For example, a development which is gaining in popularity is to ship truckloads of goods, trailer and all, by rail. From the railroad destination point the truck can make delivery to a location not accessible by rail. Water-rail shipping offers similar flexibility since railroad cars are transported by barge to principal ports.

STOCK CONTROL

The function of the company storeroom is to obtain, stock, protect, and issue the materials required for production. As with all functions in an organization, every effort should be made to perform the storeroom one as effectively and as economically as possible.[4]

In order to provide fast and efficient service, the storeroom should be laid out in such a manner that all items can be quickly located and easily reached. Materials and supplies should be stocked in alphabetic or numerical order and appropriately recorded in a master index. A number of suitable stockage systems are available for use depending on the size and nature of the product stocked. Some items may be classed as expendables and therefore do not require the same control as supplies which should be returned after use. Regardless of their nature or use, all materials and supplies should be controlled to some extent in order to: (1) determine when reordering should be done; (2) determine who has supplies and materials that should be returned after use; (3) insure that proper and authorized use is made of all materials; and (4) establish a basis for evaluating the use of supplies and materials. Storeroom personnel should make sure that all requests for material are supported by valid authorizations which specify the item and quantity to be used. The control system should not be so complicated that it creates unnecessary delay in obtaining supplies.

The storeroom should be located in a safe and secure area where the possibility of loss due to deterioration, fire, and theft is at a minimum. Combustible materials should be stored in suitable containers, and adequate fire protection equipment should be readily available. To avoid loss of supplies through deterioration, temperature and humidity control should be utilized where required. Current stocks should be placed in front of new shipments so that the older items are used first, before they have a chance to deteriorate.

INVENTORY CONTROL

Shortage of production materials and supplies can result in long and costly delays and the cancellation of late orders. To preclude such shortages and at the same time avoid overstockage and unnecessary capital investment in inventories, with the related dangers of spoilage, obsolescence, and deterioration in quality, it is necessary to maintain an effective system of inventory control.[5] Such a system requires constant coordination between several departments in the company. The sales department must indicate the anticipated product demand and any planned programs or sales actions that could cause significant deviation from it. The production department must specify the quantity and quality of material required, making allowance for bad material and spoilage during production. Warehousing personnel must determine the amount of space available for the storage of raw materials, taking into consideration the rate at which distribution will be accomplished. The purchasing department must determine the sources of supply available for the materials required, the most opportune time to purchase them, taking into consideration seasonal price fluctuations, market conditions, and the most economical amount to purchase in view of storage limitations. It should be quite clear that far from being an independent function, inventory control must be integrated into the entire manufacturing-distribution system.

The formula. A great deal of time could be expended determining when and how much to buy. To simplify the inventory control process, most organizations have reduced the analysis procedure to a formula that proves adequate for their particular needs. The complexity of the formula will depend on the number of factors that influence the inventory, the number of variables, and the degree of accuracy required. An example of a basic formula for inventory control is described in detail in Chapter 33.

RECORDS AND PROCEDURES

The efficient and economical handling of materials required for production necessitates the use of an effective control system. A well-written set of procedures should indicate what functions are to be performed, when they are to be performed, and who is responsible for performing them. In this way unnecessary delays, frequently experienced with verbal orders, are eliminated and verbal instructions can be confined to exceptions to procedure. All operations are performed automatically, important steps are not eliminated, and personnel do not feel overly supervised.

The purchasing department should have a complete set of procedures for each major category of material that it procures. Such procedures should include instructions for processing requisitions, preparing necessary documents, and coordinating with the ordering departments. The receiving department should have a set of procedures for receiving shipments from each type of carrier. Since documents will vary depending on the type of carrier (rail, truck, air, or water), written procedures should be established indicating all steps that must be taken to receive each type of shipment so that important actions are not overlooked.[7] Receiving and warehouse personnel should know what disposition is to be made of each shipment received, such as (1) temporary storage,

(2) addition to inventory, or (3) immediate use by an operating department.

Some of the principal information control records convey is:

1. When material should be ordered (inventory records)
2. When material was actually ordered and when receipt can be expected (procurement records)
3. When material is received, the condition of the shipment, and whether it corresponds to what was actually ordered (receiving records)
4. What disposition was made of the material upon receipt and what reimbursement action was performed (warehouse records)
5. What material is actually on hand and available for use (stockroom records)

In addition to providing a ready source of information as to what materials are available and where they are located, control records play an important part in studies and evaluations of methods and procedures.

INTERIOR LAYOUT AND HANDLING

The problem of interior layout and handling of production material is usually one of determining the most efficient arrangement of equipment within a given facility. This is contingent on the type of product, frequency and extent of product change, and anticipated production volume. Frequent fluctuations in product change or demand will generally require a highly flexible arrangement of equipment and facilities. Stable protection operations require less flexibility and therefore normally permit more efficient utilization of available space.[8]

The objective in plant layout should be to keep materials handling to a minimum and to avoid congestion and bottlenecks at all areas of the production process, thereby permitting a steady flow of materials. Consideration must be given to the location of supply rooms, storage areas, work control centers, and other functions that are closely related to production. This is true of both line and functional equipment arrangements.

QUESTIONS AND PROBLEMS

1. Why should materials handling receive careful consideration when determining plant layout?

2. Why is it uneconomical to maintain large inventories of all items, regardless of use?
3. What factors must a purchasing department consider when deciding between quality and price?
4. What are the advantages of public warehousing as compared to private warehousing?
5. What is demurrage?
6. Why should incoming shipments be properly identified and marked at time of receipt?
7. How can purchase records assist a receiving department?
8. What three basic considerations must be made when selecting shipping routes and carriers?
9. Why must strict control measures be exercised over the issuing of supplies and materials from a storeroom?
10. What advantages are gained by shipping loaded trailer trucks by rail?

REFERENCE NOTES

[1] Henry G. Hodges, *Procurement: The Modern Science of Purchasing,* Harper & Row, 1961.

[2] E. H. Niece, *Production Forecasting, Planning and Control,* Wiley, 1961.

[3] Charles A. Taff, *Traffic Management: Principles and Practices,* rev. ed., Irwin, 1959.

[4] Dean S. Ammer, *Materials Management,* Irwin, 1962.

[5] Charles H. Bliss, "Are Inventories Really Too High?," *Harvard Business Review,* September, 1960, p. 53.

[6] Elwood S. Buffa, *Modern Production Management,* Wiley, 1961, chap. 16.

[7] John H. Frederick, *Traffic Department Organization,* Chilton, 1956.

[8] James M. Apple, *Plant Layout and Material Handling,* 2nd ed., Ronald, 1963.

READING REFERENCES

Anyon, G. Jay, *Managing an Integrated Purchasing Process,* Holt, Rinehart and Winston, 1963.

Avery, M. F., *Methods Engineering,* MacDonald, 1962.

Flood, Kenneth U., *Traffic Management,* William C. Brown, 1963.

Frederick, John H., *Commercial Air Transportation,* Irwin, 1961.

Hodges, Henry G., and Raymond J. Ziegler, *Managing the Industrial Concern,* Houghton Mifflin, 1963.

Moore, James M., *Plant Layout and Design,* Macmillan, 1962.

Wagner, Harvey M., *Statistical Management of Inventory Systems,* Wiley, 1962.

15

BUILDING AND SPACE MANAGEMENT

The efficient functioning of a modern business organization today depends largely upon the building(s) and grounds where its operations are physically housed. Not only do these facilities need to be adequate for the purpose, i.e., manufacturing, assembling, distributing, servicing, etc., but their physical condition should be attractive and conducive to the high morale of the employees. People want to be proud of where they work.

Top management of many organizations have responded to these needs by providing new, well-planned, attractive physical facilities. Almost every community in America has at least one such modern plant or business building, and many more are either in the planning stages or are being built.

REAL ESTATE MANAGEMENT

The function that includes the evaluation, purchasing, development, and disposal of a company's land and real property facilities is known as real estate management. Its two basic objectives are (1) the purchase of the land and facilities necessary for immediate and future use and (2) the disposal of land and property which is not required for immediate or future use.

In the selection of industrial property primary consideration should be given to initial cost, services and necessary support facilities, and future development. Selecting a geographical area for industrial operations is discussed under "Location." Real estate management begins with the selection of a particular property in the chosen location.

Land cost will normally be the prime consideration, though this may be modified by management preference for a particular property because of its prestige value or its proximity to customers or related industries. Frequently, undesirable land or property in a remote area can be purchased at a modest price, and its value substantially increased through improvement and development of the area.

Many companies, especially research organizations, prefer to locate away from congested areas, frequently selecting suburban property of a semiresidential nature where the environment is more conducive to creativity.

With the increase in the standard of living, the rise in the educational level of employees, and more prosperous business conditions, more and more companies are being judged by their outward appearance by both potential employees and customers, so the area in which a company locates will frequently have a marked influence on the success of its entire operation.

WORKING CONDITIONS

A company has the moral obligation to eliminate as many undesirable working conditions as possible. The term "undesirable," however, is relative. For example, by modern standards an office temperature of 90 degrees would be considered an undesirable working condition. However, in a steel mill a temperature in excess of 100 degrees would not be so considered. Consequently, no absolute standards can be established that apply equally in all work situations. Since many employers, however, once failed to provide even minimum desirable working conditions, it was necessary for state and Federal governments to take legislative action to eliminate many undesirable ones. Labor-management contracts frequently include provisions specifically describing the working conditions which are to be maintained.

In addition to their moral and legal obligations to maintain good working conditions, many companies recognize that there is a relationship between working conditions and employee performance.[1] Extensive studies have been conducted to determine how the work environment may be modified to improve employee morale, attitudes, and performance. Some of these improvements include painting walls a particular color, playing background music in the plant, providing frequent rest periods and comfortable lounges, and air-conditioning the work area. Sanitation and cleanliness are now considered minimum requirements in any work area.

LOCATION

The decision to locate a business or plant in a particular area requires a detailed analysis of many complex and interrelated factors. All factors are not of equal importance; therefore values should be assigned to those considered.[2] They may be divided into four general types: (1) distance, (2) natural characteristics, (3) social characteristics, and (4) cost considerations.

Distance

The distance that supplies and materials must be shipped should be carefully evaluated because transportation will involve significant costs, depending on the type of facilities required. In addition, the shipment of supplies requires time, so it is necessary to determine how long it will take to get material to the plant. Careful consideration must also be given to the proximity of markets for the product being manufactured. In the case of perishables or items for which style changes are frequent, a lengthy shipping time could result in a damaged or obsolete product.

Distance must also be considered in terms of available labor supply. If a plant is located too far from the source of labor, it will be difficult to find personnel with the requisite skills. The analysis should include not only distance but accessibility as well. For example, in the Midwest it is not uncommon for an employee to drive forty and even sixty miles to work, whereas in the city of Chicago a worker may have considerable objection to driving across town.

In the past the distance of a business from the heart of the city was of significant concern since access to shopping facilities was important for workers; however, with the development of suburban shopping communities and the almost universal use of the automobile, nearness to the "downtown" area is no longer important.

Natural Characteristics

The climate and terrain may greatly influence the decision to locate in a particular area, including temperature, humidity, earthquakes, tornadoes, hurricanes, soil condition, drainage, elevation, and other factors. Artificial climate controls permit some flexibility in plant location, but usually involve considerable cost. A mining company may decide to pass up an area possessing desired raw material because soil conditions make its extraction too costly, or a plant requiring an abundant supply of clean water may have to pass up location near a lake which contains impurities.

Social Characteristics

In many circumstances the social characteristics of an area will have significant bearing on a company's choice of location. Many companies prefer to locate in an area where their employees will have access to social and cultural attractions, such as schools, churches, museums, libraries, theaters, and recreational facilities. The company should also determine whether it is likely to meet with community resistance to the noise or dirt it may generate, river water it may pollute, and its racial employment policy. In particular, it should ascertain the local attitude of organized labor so as to determine whether it might run into extensive labor problems.

Cost Considerations

All the factors discussed above will have some bearing on the cost required to operate at a particular location; however, the dollar value of these factors is not readily ascertained. However, there are several factors for which the dollar value can be easily calculated, such as labor, utilities, taxes, facility lease and rental rates, real estate values, and local transportation costs. In many areas labor costs will depend on collective bargaining; however, a general idea of the prevailing rates can usually be obtained. Utility and tax rates are normally stable, and some communities may offer a special low tax rate to a company as an inducement to locate there. Real estate values can fluctuate as a result of land speculation; long-term leases can fix the cost in advance.

DESIGN AND CONSTRUCTION

The primary consideration in designing and constructing a facility is the intended use to which it will be put. A careful analysis must be made of the nature and type of space that will be required, including such special considerations as height of ceilings, strength of floors, utilities, flow of work, etc. In many cases it will be necessary to construct a new building in order to incorporate all special design requirements. However, for standard-type operations an existing facility may be effectively modified. Care should be taken to insure that space is available so that the facility can be economically enlarged.[3]

A principal consideration in designing and constructing a building is whether to construct a single- or multistory facility. A single-story facility is generally preferred because it makes for easier materials handling and more efficient work flow; however, the multistory facility has the advantage of compactness and can utilize gravity-flow methods of materials handling. The multistory facility also furnishes a more economical utilization of land area where land values are high.

The design and materials used in construction should conform to the recommended standards for the area, and should be as attractive as possible within reasonable cost limitations.[4]

Recent trends in building design tend to favor one-level, square or rectangular shapes. With modern efficient and economical lighting, natural outside lighting is no longer a requirement and therefore maximum exposure to windows is no longer a consideration. In fact, many modern plants are entirely windowless. The absence of windows also permits better control over heating, air conditioning, outside noise, and dirt.

Floors should be strong enough to support all anticipated load requirements. They should also be as smooth and as level as possible so that materials handling equipment can function easily. Ceilings should provide complete protection from the elements and should be relatively maintenance-free. Ceiling supports are of primary consideration from the standpoint of efficient space utilization. If supports are placed close together, layout flexibility is reduced. However, construction cost normally increases as supports are placed farther apart. A careful analysis should be made to determine the exact requirements with respect to equipment arrangement and the supports placed accordingly.

PLANT CAPACITY

Newly established organizations with little or no prior experience in the industry cannot always accurately predict the degree of their success. Consequently, when estimating future plant capacity, many organizations make conservative estimates, at the same time providing facilities which can be expanded later if required.

Plant size is not a function of sales volume alone. The possibility of adding further products at a future date must be considered since dual utilization of existing equipment would help to reduce overhead cost and increase productive efficiency. The adding of a new product would necessitate, as a minimum, additional space for handling and temporary storage of production materials and the finished product.

The key factors influencing plant size for most companies are (1) production volume and (2) relative operating costs. In order to insure its investment, a company should build a plant no larger than a reasonable sales estimate will justify. In certain rare cases, when a substantial increase in sales is anticipated, a plant may operate below the break-even point. If the anticipated sales increase does not materialize, business failure may result unless suitable corrective action is taken to achieve better utilization of facilities.

In determining plant size, consideration should also be given to the production work schedule. There are normally two alternatives: (1) low-output equipment may be utilized for many hours a day, or (2) high-output equipment may be utilized for relatively few hours a day. For example, two different companies producing the same type of product desire a daily output of 1,500 units. Company A achieves this by utilizing equipment which can produce the required units in twenty-four hours (three shifts). Company B achieves it by utilizing more costly but more efficient equipment which can produce the required units in eight hours (one shift). A determination of which is the best method will depend upon an analysis of labor costs, equipment costs, general operating expenses, and anticipated increases in sales. If labor costs are extremely low and the cost of the high-output equipment extremely high, then company A may be operating more efficiently. However, if company B requires considerably fewer personnel than company A, as well as two less shifts, then it may be operating more efficiently. Furthermore, company A is operating at full capacity, whereas company B is operating at only one-third capacity since it could add two additional shifts, and would therefore be in a more favorable position to benefit from increased product demand.

This brief analysis illustrates that many variables must be considered in determining plant size. Highly trained and experienced personnel are normally required properly to analyze all relevant factors.

LAYOUT

In order to derive maximum benefit from a particular facility, a careful analysis of the production process should be made to determine the most efficient method of operation and utilization of available space. For some production operations there is only one logical way to arrange the flow of work and location of equipment, but for most manufacturing processes several possibilities exist. In selecting the equipment arrangement, full consideration should be given to the stability of the product being manufactured (i.e., frequency of changes in design or type) and to fluctuations in volume (i.e., seasonal production, for example, Christmas toys).

The first factor for consideration is where to locate the various processes and departments within the plant, taking into account the total space required by each department as well as any special requirements. An assembly department, for example, may combine the finished parts from all other departments, and require a considerable area for ease of maneuverability. Other departments may have unique operations that require special conditions, such as access to outside walls, special utility services, or high ceilings. Such considerations must be thoroughly analyzed before a final location can be selected for any department.

One very important consideration is the flow of material between departments and the requirements for parts and supplies. It certainly would not be wise planning to locate closely related functions a considerable distance apart unless no other arrangement is possible. A company may be forced into just such a situation by future changes in production unless careful consideration is given to anticipated as well as present needs.

When a general location for each department has been selected, it is then necessary to plan in more detail.[5] Such planning requires detailed knowledge of production operations as well as basic materials-handling and space utilization principles. Equipment must be placed so that adequate space is available for processing without interruption from adjoining operations. Main aisles and feeder aisles must be sufficiently wide to avoid bottlenecks in materials handling. Such detailed planning is normally accomplished by the use of "templates" and "flow process charts," both of which are discussed under "Space Utilization."

There are an almost unlimited number of possible layouts for a plant, each possessing certain advantages and disadvantages.

The ideal solution, of course, is to select the layout that provides the greatest number of advantages in terms of efficient and effective operation, and the least number of disadvantages. The limitations on time and money that may be spent on planning do not permit a detailed analysis of all possible layouts. Therefore, the layout finally selected is the best only of those that were considered. For this reason, many companies, before making a considerable investment in a plant, will construct a pilot plant (small-scale operating test plant) to determine the feasibility of various layouts. Such a method is expensive and is generally undertaken when prior experience is not available.

SPACE UTILIZATION

There are several arrangements that can be used in solving problems involving space utilization.

Line Arrangement

In this type of arrangement a piece of equipment is placed at the particular stage of the production line where it is required, as in the case of an automobile assembly plant. If the same equipment is required at various points on the line, there will be duplication of equipment. Considerable space can be saved by this arrangement since materials handling and storage space are greatly reduced, but production volume should be significantly high since all the machines and equipment operators must be utilized each time the line is operated.

Functional Arrangement

The functional method of equipment arrangement consists of grouping all machines and equipment performing the same function in one location and then moving the product through the various functional areas for processing. This arrangement reduces the duplication of equipment and operators usually found in the line method. One operator may be qualified to operate several machines of the same type, thus permitting maximum flexibility of manpower. The functional arrangement, however, requires greater materials handling and storage facilities since the product must be transferred from one functional area to another and stored at each before and after processing. For low-volume or continually changing production requirements, the functional method is considerably more efficient and economical than the line method. In addition, it precludes the complete production shutdown that occurs when a piece of equipment in a line arrangement needs repair or replacement.

Space Requirements and Work Flow

In order to determine accurately the space requirements for a particular operation, it is necessary to know the amount, type, and size of equipment that will be needed. In addition, it is necessary to determine the flow of work through the plant so that conflicts and bottlenecks can be eliminated, and so that some machines and workers do not stand idle while others are overworked. It is also necessary to determine how much space will be required for storage operations, administration, maintenance, and recreational activities and the most suitable location for each. To facilitate the analysis of space requirements and work flow, production planners frequently employ two invaluable devices: templates and flow process charts.

Templates. A template is a flat piece of cardboard or plastic material cut to scale to represent plant equipment. The templates are superimposed on a chart of the plant drawn to the same scale, enabling the planner to determine the approximate area occupied by each, and the space required to operate it.[6] The template also enables the planner to experiment with various arrangements without moving the actual equipment. Larger templates can be prepared to represent entire areas, such as supply rooms, offices, rest rooms, etc.

Flow process charts. A flow chart is a graphic representation of a motion study of a product as it goes through the various stages of the manufacturing process, from its entrance into production to its preparation for shipment from the plant. The flow chart indicates the machines that process a product, necessary storage and delays, and includes tests and quality control inspections. Its chief function is to uncover areas of possible conflict in the production process before they actually occur.

Administration and Maintenance Area

Every plant requires space to accommodate functions not directly concerned with production but which play a significant role in support of production. These support functions may be divided into two general areas: administration and maintenance.

Administration. Plant administration includes the nonproductive functions in operation that are necessary to insure that proper control, supervision, security, and personnel services are furnished so that production can proceed efficiently without incident. The plant administrative office may be a small one-man operation or a large specialized staff, which normally includes a plant manager, production manager, personnel manager, and several assistants. Administrative areas also cover those facilities required for the health, safety and well-being of the employees, including a dispensary, rest rooms, lounge, and refreshment facilities. Some operations require a plant laboratory in which quality control tests and experiments can be conducted. Almost all plants require inspection stations throughout the production system. And last but not least, the plant administrative staff includes the security personnel and guards necessary to safeguard company property.

The administrative offices should be located where effective control and supervision can be maintained over the entire production operation and within easy access of supervisors and foremen without wasting their valuable time. Those facilities intended for employee use should also be conveniently located so as to preclude excessive loss of production time. Product analysis and inspection facilities should be as decentralized as possible to reduce materials handling.

Maintenance. Maintenance includes those functions performed for the purpose of keeping the building and equipment in efficient operating condition. Maintenance is of two kinds: (1) preventive maintenance, or those routine functions performed to forestall possible failure or breakdown,[7] and (2) repair maintenance, or the correction of breakdowns or failures which have already occurred.[8]

Preventive maintenance is normally conducted in accordance with an established schedule. Some common preventive maintenance measures include lubrication of equipment, replacement of worn parts, and minor adjustments. If there isn't enough work to warrant a full-time preventive maintenance crew, then the equipment operator is normally held responsible.

Even with an excellent preventive maintenance program there will be equipment failures and breakdowns. If the failure is obvious and minor in nature, it frequently can be repaired by the operator or the preventive maintenance crew; however, if the equipment is complicated, it will usually be necessary to call in specially trained personnel. If a plant has no maintenance crew capable of performing extensive repairs on all production equipment, help from outside the plant may be necessary.

BUILDING SERVICES

When a company moves into an existing building, the principal consideration is whether the available services are adequate for the intended operation or whether they can be easily modified to meet requirements. When constructing a new facility, however, it must consider additional factors, such as the ability of the services to meet future requirements and the anticipated cost of maintenance. By spending additional money on high-quality materials during construction, it may be possible to achieve substantial future savings through reduced maintenance expenses.

If frequent changes in layout and production processes are anticipated, then building services should be made as flexible as possible to avoid excessive modification costs in the future.[9] If building expansion is anticipated in the near future, it might be advantageous to install services capable of handling the anticipated requirements.

Building services may be divided into two categories: (1) basic utilities (electricity, heat, and water) and (2) special requirements (chemicals, gases, and other services required for production).

Electric service. Electricity is required for both normal building use and as a source of power for production operations. The cost of obtaining it from commercial sources should be compared with the cost of generating power locally.

Heat and air conditioning service. Before selecting a heating and air conditioning system, a careful analysis must be made of climate, building insulation, heat generated by production equipment and other factors which influence building temperature or humidity.

Water service. An adequate supply of water is necessary for both building facilities (rest rooms, maintenance, cafeterias, etc.) and many production processes. Some plants require an abundant supply of water for production operations, and if commercial sources are inadequate, suitable storage facilities may have to be constructed. If the water does not have to be pure, then sources of raw water (rivers, lakes, streams, etc.) may be utilized or suitable equipment installed to reuse waste water. An adequate water supply must also be available for fire protection. Since the regular water supply may be inadequate, an independent source should be utilized where possible.

Special services. Many production operations require the installation of special services. Where possible such requirements should be made a part of the regular building service system. Those services of a toxic or combustible nature may require special handling.

PROTECTION AND SAFETY

Minimum standards of construction specified by local building codes normally insure that a facility will prove safe for its intended use. In addition, insurance companies require that certain protective measures be taken before they will insure the facility.

During the construction of a new facility certain features are closely inspected to insure compliance with established standards:

Building strength. The building is inspected to insure that the materials utilized will provide sufficient structural support. Floors, for example, must be strong enough to support both installed equipment and material being transported or stored.

Installed facilities. Exits, fire escapes, sprinkler units, warning alarms, and fire walls must be strategically placed in order to furnish adequate protection of the entire facility.

Utilities. Electrical wiring must conform to established electrical standards for the type of machinery to be used. An alternate power source should provide sufficient light to enable all personnel to locate an exit in the event of a power failure.

Special-purpose items. Safety shields, combustible-material receptacles, and emergency showers should be available where toxic or volatile materials are used.

Each time a significant change in the production process occurs, a careful analysis should determine whether the change warrants a corresponding modification in safety facilities. Changes in equipment, materials, and number of personnel all have a direct bearing on protective facilities.

Safety cannot be achieved, however, unless all personnel are fully aware of its need and of the facilities available to insure it. Periodic training sessions should include a discussion of available safety equipment and its use. The best safety facilities available will serve no real purpose unless they are properly used.[10]

REPLACEMENT

Few organizations can operate for very long without undergoing changes that affect production requirements. The change may be gradual or sudden; it may be a change in market location, product design, consumer demand, production cost, or management. It may be due to normal wear and tear on plant equipment or facilities, or to competition and the need for more effective methods of production. Companies must plan for change so that they will not be caught unprepared when it comes.

To anticipate necessary changes, complete records of all phases of production should be maintained and periodically analyzed. Some of the factors to be analyzed are (1) methods of production, (2) volume of production, (3) efficiency and condition of equipment and facilities, and (4) production cost.

Production methods should be analyzed to determine if the most efficient procedures are being used in line with new developments. Analysis of production volume will determine whether the plant is operating at or near capacity and whether, consequently, possible expansion should be considered, or if volume is declining whether thought should be given to eliminating an operation. The efficiency, state of repair, and cost of maintenance of present equipment should be compared with the production capabilities and cost of new equipment. Likewise, the plant building should be inspected to determine if it is structurally sound, in a good state of repair, and provides for efficient plant operation.

To determine whether present facilities adequately meet requirements, consideration is given to the following factors:

1. Changes in product design, style, or model
2. Requirement for new products
3. Changes in labor cost
4. Changes in product demand
5. Changes in product markets and sources of supply for raw materials
6. Equipment obsolescence
7. Extent of competition

If, after the analysis, it appears that present equipment and facilities will not be adequate, plans should be made for new equipment, expansion of present facilities, or relocation to new facilities.[11]

The decision whether to remain at the present location, expand the existing facility, and obtain new equipment or to relocate in a new area and a new facility is a difficult one. In most cases a company has a sizable investment in its equipment and facilities which it may not be able to recover when it relocates. For example, the American steel industry is being confronted with foreign competition able to produce steel more efficiently in modern plants employing the latest techniques. In many cases American companies are utilizing obsolete equipment and facilities that make production costs excessively high and uncompetitive.[12] The dilemma is that no buyer can be found for the obsolete equipment, yet it is too costly to abandon.

A secondary problem involved in plant removal is what to do about the unemployed workers who will be left behind. Some companies feel this is not their problem and ignore the issue; others fear that the resultant bad publicity would adversely affect their business; and still others, feeling a genuine moral obligation to their employees, avoid relocation or make extensive preparations for it in advance.

RENTALS

When a company requires additional administrative or operation space for only a limited period of time, new construction or long-term leasing is not an economical solution. On the other hand, rental of the desired space can be terminated at any time (subject to appropriate advance notice) without incurring any penalty.

Renting also has certain disadvantages. Since the rental period may be indefinite, many property owners are hesitant to rent (as opposed to leasing), especially in the case of choice property for which there is a big demand. Renting also usually places some limitation on the property modifications the company can make to meet its needs, especially when such modifications might render the property unacceptable to future renters.

LEASING

Leasing of facilities offers the advantages of low capital investment (as in renting) and long-term security (as in private ownership). If the company does not require the use of the facility for the full term of the lease, it may sublease it to another organization, or, as specified in some leases, continue to make payments until the leasor can find another lessee.

Since a lease is prepared for a specified period of time, a company must analyze its requirements to insure that the lease will adequately accommodate anticipated future development.[13] The lease, however, should not cover an excessive period of time, for this might prove to be a burden if requirements changed.

QUESTIONS AND PROBLEMS

1. What factors should determine the capacity and flexibility of building services?
2. What future considerations should be included in building design and construction?
3. What are the principal handicaps in selecting a suitable plant layout?
4. What are the disadvantages of a long-term building lease?
5. What are the advantages of a preventive maintenance program?
6. Why is sales volume not the only consideration in determining plant capacity?
7. What factors other than cost influence companies to select suburban areas for plant and office construction?
8. Why is it not always more suitable to construct a new facility when the existing facility is inadequate?
9. Why is a flow process chart a valuable tool in efficient utilization of space?
10. Why should standards be used to determine suitable working conditions?

REFERENCE NOTES

[1] Guy C. Close, Jr., *Work Improvement*, Wiley, 1960.

[2] "Selecting Your New Plant Site," *Factory Management*, May, 1958, pp. 137-140.

[3] L. Lerner and M. Saphier, "Why Space Planning and Design Are Vital to a Company's Growth," *Office Management,* July, 1958, pp. 30-31.

[4] C. C. Rozenhard, "How to Cut Cost When You Build a Building," *Business Management*, August, 1961, pp. 48-50.

[5] James M. Apple, *Plant Layout and Materials Handling*, 2nd ed., Ronald, 1963.

[6] James M. Moore, *Plant Layout and Design*, Macmillan, 1962.

[7] V. H. Byrer, "How to Start a Preventative Maintenance Program," *Factory*, October, 1961, pp. 236-240.

[8] A. M. Robinson, "Planned Repair Jobs Hold Down Costs," *Factory*, July, 1961, pp. 132-136.

[9] Ruddell Reed, Jr., *Plant Layout Factors: Principles and Techniques*, Irwin, 1961.

[10] L. J. Bibri, "Incentive Plan for Safety," *Supervision*, March, 1959, p. 9.

[11] J. A. Rosenthal, "Build a New Plant or Expand the Old?," *Factory*, April, 1961, pp. 226-227.

[12] J. J. Jaeger, "Obsolescence Has Created Crisis," *Steel*, Februray 20, 1961, pp. 36-37.

[13] R. Sheridan, "Look Before You Lease; Nine Areas to Check," *Business Management*, February, 1962, pp. 47-51.

READING REFERENCES

Clark, Bill, *Professional Cleaning and Building Maintenance*, Exposition Press, 1960.

Hutchinson, John G., *Managing a Fair Day's Work*, University of Michigan, 1963.

Kay, Brian R., and Stewart Palmer, *The Challenge of Supervision*, McGraw-Hill, 1961.

Lewis, Bernard T., *Maintenance Management*, Rider, 1963.

McGregor, Douglas, *The Human Side of Enterprise*, McGraw-Hill, 1960.

McKaig, Thomas H., *Building Failures: Case Studies in Construction and Design*, McGraw-Hill, 1962.

Miller, Elmo J., and Jerome W. Blood, *Modern Maintenance Management*, American Management Association, 1963.

16

PERSONNEL MANAGEMENT

Dealing with the human element of an organization is of major concern to management at all levels. Discussed in this chapter are some of the major problems handled by the personnel manager.

THE PERSONNEL MANAGER'S ROLE

The role of the personnel manager has changed significantly during the past half-century. Prior to 1900 most personnel administration functions were performed by the owners of the business or by operating officials. Personnel administration at that time amounted to little more than entering an employee's name on a record card and paying him for hours worked. Recruiting was not a problem since most businesses were local in nature and the supply of labor adequate. Selection was not a problem since most jobs were of the laboring type and required little or no special education, skill, or personality characteristics.

Labor unions, although in existence as early as 1886, did not achieve significant influence until the 1920s. Then, in an attempt to resist their growing power, many companies instituted programs designed to pacify the workers and divert their interest from the unions. It was the threat of unionism that was largely responsible for the growth of company-sponsored athletic teams, the now famous coffee break, the shortened work week, additional paid holidays, attractive incentive and bonus plans, and improved working conditions. With this multiplicity of employee-centered programs, the evolution of scientific management, and the increasing demand for skilled employees, the role of the personnel manager began to extend beyond hiring, firing, and record keeping.

Today the personnel manager is vital to the success of any enterprise, for without qualified personnel business failure is assured. It is he who must advise top management on the personnel principles, policies, and procedures necessary to achieve profitable production and distribution of goods and services. In particular, the personnel manager must:

1. Be fully informed on the latest developments in the personnel field and the current status of the labor market.
2. Develop an evaluation system whereby he can determine the current personnel strength of the company and predict future requirements.
3. Assure that effective channels of communications are established and properly used so that the workers do not misinterpret management's actions, and vice versa.
4. Assure a social environment in which relations among members of the organization and between the organization and the community are characterized by mutual confidence and respect.
5. Develop a competent and efficient staff to perform the normal personnel functions of recruiting, selecting, wage and salary administration, record keeping, and job analysis.

In the large company the personnel manager may spend all his time analyzing policies and procedures and advising top management, leaving the job of recruiting, selecting, training, counseling, and record keeping to specialists in these fields. In the smaller firm the personnel manager may perform all these functions with only limited assistance. The nature of his role, therefore, depends considerably upon the type of firm for which he is working. The type of problems faced by a personnel manager for a bank, for example, will vary greatly from the problems faced by his counterpart in an electronics or chemical company.

SELECTION METHODS

The selection and placement of new employees involves attracting qualified applicants, choosing those most qualified, and placing them on the job.

The first decision to be made is whether to hire from within the company or to seek personnel from outside. This problem is frequently solved by a firmly established policy of selection from within. Other companies attempt to get the individual most qualified for the job regardless of the source. In a highly competitive industry where success or failure depends on having the most capable employees possible, their source is not an important consideration. In less competitive industries, such as public utilities and banking, a policy of selection from within is critical to the morale and well-being of the company.

Several sources may be used to locate personnel outside the firm. The company may utilize newspaper advertising, private and public placement services, and colleges, and it may occasionally rely on referrals from trade and management associations or other company employees. The recruiting method selected will depend to a great extent on the type of position to be filled. It would not be economically feasible to recruit clerical help on a college campus when such help may be obtained through a relatively inexpensive newspaper advertisement. Likewise, the college campus would not prove a fruitful source of employees for positions requiring several years of business experience.

In recent years there has been a significant increase in the use of professional recruiting firms. A company merely has to express its requirements to the professional recruiter and sit back and wait. The recruiter may be able to find the right man by sifting through potential applicants in his files. Or, as is frequently the case in obtaining executive personnel, he will launch an extensive recruiting campaign of his own, not hesitating to approach individuals already happily employed if he has something better to offer them.

When a company has accumulated a pool of applicants from which to choose, the problem then becomes one of selecting the applicant "best" for the job and for the company.[1] "Best" for the company may not be the same thing as "best" on some standardized scale of measurement, such as intelligence, personality, aptitude, etc. Each company has its own scale of values in selecting its employees. Thus some place more emphasis on intelligence and personality, while others have a definite dislike of intellectuals and will flatly turn away any applicant who exhibits such characteristics. Regardless of what characteristics a company may value, it has at least some general image of the type of person it is looking for. How, then, does it go about selecting the person that fits this image?

Interviewing

The interview is normally an applicant's first face-to-face encounter with an official of the company. It serves the dual purpose of allowing the applicant to learn more about the company and the job and giving the company representative the opportunity to "size up" the applicant, observe his ability to express himself, and investigate in depth information on the application questionnaire. The ability and skill of the interviewer are quite important since he must encourage the applicant to do most of the talking, analyze what he says, and attempt to determine his motivations. The interviewer must evaluate not only the applicant's present qualifications but also his ability to grow in the job and advance in the company.

The job application or questionnaire provides sufficient basic information to eliminate obviously unqualified applicants. For those jobs requiring a high degree of skill or training, the application form can indicate whether an applicant has had sufficient education or experience. It also furnishes the interviewer with a list of the applicant's former employers, who may be contacted as references.

Testing

Companies use tests to varying degrees. Some base their whole selection process on test results, dropping from further consideration applicants who do not achieve a certain minimum score. Others use testing only as a supplement to the interview as a source of additional information with which to evaluate an applicant. Some companies use outside testing firms, who give the applicant a battery of tests and evaluate the results. Other firms maintain professionals on their personnel staff to administer and evaluate the tests. Regardless of the extent and method of testing, the general purpose is the same: to arrive at an objective measurement of the applicant's intelligence, aptitude, and personality.

Determining the factors that lead to success in a particular job is not an easy matter. How much ability to do a job is dependent on intelligence or personality and how much on pure experience is a question. Unless this question can be answered, we cannot even begin to look for a test to measure these qualities. Likewise, if we know what qualities are necessary for success but use a test that is not "valid," that is, a test which does not measure what we intend it to measure, then we are no better off.

One significant weakness in testing to date is its inability accurately to measure motivation and creativity. A person may have all the necessary intelligence, experience, and personality for the job, but if he lacks the motivation to do it, he will be of little value to a company. For jobs that require creativity and originality, tests are of little assistance. In addition, tests are frequently costly and time-consuming, and a company cannot jump into a testing program unprepared.

ORIENTATION

Many new employees know very little about the company for which they are about to work. To insure that each employee has the necessary information about company policies and procedures, an orientation interview or briefing is desirable. A brief orientation interview immediately after he has been hired will inform him of those general aspects of the company which will be important to him initially. A more complete supplementary orientation can be conducted after he has become established in his new assignment and the tension of starting a new job has subsided. The initial orientation should be conducted in private, preferably by a member of the personnel department. The supplementary orientation may be conducted in small groups, with assistance from personnel from several departments of the company. Both the initial and the supplemental orientation meetings should be informal and permit the employee to ask questions freely.

COUNSELING

As a follow-up to selection and placement interviewing, many companies have counseling programs. The more formal programs employ a professional counselor, either full or part time, who makes himself available to the employees to discuss personal as well as company matters. The theory behind the formal program is that if a worker is troubled by problems, even personal problems that have nothing to do with the company, he will not do an effective day's work. If he is given the opportunity to discuss his problems, in confidence, with a willing listener who is removed from the immediate work situation, the company will presumably benefit in the long run.

Counseling became of interest to management in the late 1920s as a result of the experiments at the Hawthorne plant of the Western Electric Company. Quite by accident it was discovered that the interviewing connected with the experiment resulted in an improvement both in the mental attitude of the employees and in their output. Many companies attempted to apply some of the Hawthorne techniques. More recently companies are placing greater emphasis on counseling in their supervisory training programs.

In addition to formal counseling programs, every supervisor should periodically counsel the personnel under his supervision. This should not be a formal or sophisticated procedure, but rather should evolve out of daily contact. It accomplishes two primary objectives: (1) employees are given added confidence and a feeling that they know where they stand; and (2) employees who need further development can be given guidance as to what they can do to better themselves.[2]

TRAINING

Practically all new employees require training to one degree or another. The training may vary from learning "on the job" to formalized schooling of several months' duration. It may consist of lectures, conferences, discussions, or work projects. It may be conducted in the employee's working area, in a conference room, in a special room equipped with sophisticated training aids, or it may be conducted entirely outside the company, i.e., at a college, university, or business school. It may be concerned strictly with the employee's present job or it may prepare him for more responsible positions.[3]

There are three primary factors to analyze before initiating any training program: (1) the employee's background, including formal education and previous training and experience; (2) the requirements of the job; and (3) anticipated future developments, including increasing technological requirements and company growth. The more responsible the position, the greater should be the analysis of training requirements.

SALARY AND WAGE ADMINISTRATION

How important are salaries and wages? To a company they are normally the largest single operating expense. Money will also influence how hard employees work and how good a job they do. It appears, however, that it is not the absolute but the relative amount of money that is of most concern to employees. For example, prior to entering their profession, teachers generally accept the fact that they will not be highly paid. But they do not so readily accept the fact that they are being paid less than another teacher with the same, or less, education and experience. The same is true of business executives and industrial workers. Consequently, it is imperative for companies to (1) establish a fair and equitable program of salary and wage administration and (2) insure that the employees are acquainted with, understand, and consider it to be fair.[4]

A wage and salary administrator must evaluate each job, determine the degree of skill, training, and experience it requires, and then place it in one of several wage classes previously determined. The following is a wage classification system frequently used:

Class 1. Routine operation under close supervision. Worker not responsible for results or performance of others.

Class 2. Routine operation with some nonrepetitive work with little supervision. Worker is responsible for results but does not supervise others.

Class 3. Original, nonrepetitive operations with little supervision. Worker is responsible for results but does not supervise others.

Class 4. Highly creative and original work with little supervision. Worker is responsible for results and supervises the work of others.

Base wage rates or wage ranges are usually assigned to each job class. The rate is determined by the "going rate" (average rate paid for similar jobs) in the community. Since the "going rate" is an average, the beginning employee would be paid an amount somewhat less than the average, and the more skilled and experienced employee an amount greater than the average. The various rates paid within a particular class are known as "steps." The following is an example of a typical wage and salary structure:

TABLE 3.   Wage Scale Schedule

	Wage Class			
	I	II	III	IV
"Going Rate"	$1.00	$1.75	$2.50	$3.50
Step 1	.80	1.35	2.00	2.80
Step 2	.90	1.55	2.25	3.15
Step 3	1.00	1.75	2.50	3.50
Step 4	1.10	1.95	2.75	3.85
Step 5	1.20	2.15	3.50	4.20

Some companies have "profit-sharing" wage programs in which the employee not only receives an established wage or salary but also shares in company profits. In the past such plans have frequently been used for executive compensation, but it is only recently that they have come into general use for all employees in an organization.

Of the many compensation plans in existence today, relatively few apply to executives. Since an executive's performance is difficult to measure, most companies have no systematic program for executive compensation, but make subjective determinations influenced by the availability of executive personnel that possess desired skills. Bonus, profit-sharing, and stock option plans are common methods of executive compensation, along with fringe benefits designed to increase real income while keeping taxable income at a minimum.[5]

Incentives

The underlying assumption of incentive plans is that people will work harder and produce more for more money, whether they are unskilled workers or highly paid executives.[6] However, as the standard of living steadily increases, the attractiveness of higher wages begins to dim, throwing some doubt on the value of incentive programs.

In addition to the mounting unattractiveness of higher wages, companies are faced with labor union resistance to incentive programs. This resistance is based on the belief that they lead to greater output per worker and therefore fewer jobs for other union members.

EFFICIENCY AND MERIT RATING

Efficiency and merit rating is an attempt systematically to determine the worth of an individual in a particular job or class of work. Merit rating itself is not new; on the contrary it has been present as long as there has been an employer-employee relationship, for it is merely the act of determining how well the employee is performing. Systematic efficiency and merit rating is a fairly recent development and is intended to provide a more objective evaluation of an employee's performance than is normally possible by subjective judgment.[7] In addition to serving as a tool to reward the more efficient or more productive employee, systematic efficiency and merit rating assists the employer in determining which employees should be offered more advanced assignments and training and which employees need further assistance to perform their present job adequately.

Efficiency and merit rating evaluates the employee, not the

job. Most rating programs include five to ten individual characteristics and factors, and the rater is asked to determine to what degree the person being rated possesses each. In order to be valid, the characteristics and factors should have a direct bearing on the job. For example, leadership ability would not be an appropriate factor to include in a rating program for house painters; however, it would be extremely important in a rating program for officers in the military. Other factors frequently included in rating programs are integrity, attitude, output, and quality of work. A certain value or weight is assigned to each factor, and upon completion of the rating these values are totaled. The total score may then be used to determine whether an employee's level of performance is sufficient to warrant a step increase in his particular wage class or whether he is prepared to progress to a job in a higher classification.

JOB ANALYSIS

The personnel department analyzes jobs for the purpose of preparing written descriptions of the job content, including the tasks, duties, and work operations performed and the relation of the job to other jobs in the organization. The information obtained through job analysis serves as the basis for preparing specifications and standards, necessary tools in hiring, performance evaluation and merit rating programs, and wage and salary administration.[8]

Job analysis may involve nothing more than a casual observation of an employee at work or it may consist of a very complex and intensive study using the most sophisticated tools and procedures of time and motion analysis. The nature of the analysis will depend largely on the extent to which measurement is possible. Normally a production line job will permit a high degree of analysis; however, an executive position, which involves so many intangible features, will be evaluated on more subjective terms.

ABSENTEEISM AND TURNOVER

A certain amount of absenteeism is acceptable if it is necessary to take care of urgent business that cannot be accomplished after working hours. However, when absenteeism takes the form of chronic tardiness or absence without advance arrangement, the morale and efficiency of the whole work group can be adversely affected and costly delays in work load result. If permitted to continue uncorrected, a general feeling of laxness and disregard of company rules and procedures may develop which would be difficult to correct.

Turnover refers to the number of persons hired during a period of time to replace those leaving or dropped from the work force. High turnover due to employees being dropped may indicate that effective selection procedures are not being used. More commonly, however, it is due to employees leaving, of their own volition, to take other jobs or, as in the case of women, to return to family duties.

The turnover rate is only significant when related to the labor market, the particular industry, and the geographical location. When jobs are plentiful and the economy is expanding, people are less hesitant about changing jobs to improve their income, status, or working environment. When jobs are not so plentiful, the turnover rate can be expected to be lower. In certain industries, such as agriculture and construction, a high turnover rate is normal. Some geographic areas are completely unattractive to personnel regardless of the state of the labor market.

When it has been established that absenteeism or turnover is excessive, what should be done? If the cause is not readily apparent, a diligent analysis must be made of the entire organization.[9]

The exit interview is the principal method used today to get an insight into the reasons why employees are leaving the company; in particular, why good employees are leaving. However, it has not proved completely successful because employees are somewhat less than frank for fear of hurting feelings or of earning a bad reference from the company. Some organizations send a questionnaire to employees who have resigned, under the assumption that they will give more honest answers after they are settled in new jobs.

In the final analysis, however, it may be necessary to alter rules or procedures, change selection methods, or possibly do nothing more than simply accept an irreparable situation.

LABOR RELATIONS

Since labor unions are now firmly established in most production and clerical operations, harmonious relations between labor and management must be encouraged if production is to be accomplished as efficiently as possible. Experience has demonstrated that severe problems can develop when the necessary mechanics have not been established to handle labor grievances as they develop.[10]

Most labor relations programs consist of three parts: (1) periodic contract negotiations to establish, renew, or amend the written labor-managament contract; (2) a grievance procedure for processing employee complaints and problems of contract interpretation; and (3) provision for arbitration or mediation of those problems which cannot be handled through labor-management discussions.

LABOR LEGISLATION AND REGULATIONS

One of today's most controversial issues is that of government control versus free enterprise; more specifically, what type and how much control should government exercise over private business? Prior to 1900 little could be done to curb ruthless practices of unrestrained free enterprise because the workers had no strong organization to stand up against management, fight lengthy legal battles, and go without income for any period of time. Business fought the early attempts of workers to organize by employing lockouts, black lists, and strikebreakers; all with little or no intervention by government.

The first major step to stop the exploitation of labor was taken in 1935 with the passage of the Wagner Act, which granted labor the right to organize, bargain collectively, and strike. The Act maintained the free flow of goods in interstate commerce by removing the impediments to collective bargaining and establishing the machinery to prevent unfair labor practices which obstruct collective bargaining. As an enforcement agency, the Act established a judicial body, known as the National Labor Relations Board, to hear cases concerning unfair labor practices. If the Board found an employer guilty, it would issue a cease-and-desist order, and if the employer did not comply with the order, the Board petitioned the Circuit Court of Appeals to enforce it. It was this last step that gave the Act its enforcement authority.

The Wagner Act marked two significant milestones in the history of American business: (1) the beginning of governmental control over the operation of business enterprises, with a corresponding reduction of management prerogatives, and (2) the beginning of powerful labor unions. During the period 1935 to 1947 the balance of power between labor and business shifted so that by 1947 labor was guilty of many of the practices business had been guilty of in 1935.[11] The Wagner Act did not make the same requirements of labor that it did of business. In order to place business on an equal footing with labor, in 1947 Congress passed the Taft-Hartley Act. Because it reduced their power considerably, the Act displeased many labor leaders.

Then in 1959 Congress passed still another Act which many labor leaders considered a step backward for organized labor. The intent of the Labor-Management Reporting and Disclosure Act of 1959 was to eliminate corruption in organized labor and stop the irregular practices of dictatorial union bosses who utilized union funds for personal gain. Viewed in perspective, the Act has not proved to be a step backward; though it has not eliminated all corruption among union leaders. Current relations between labor and mangement suffer from no major conflict, and the theory of balanced collective bargaining appears to be a reality at long last.

SENIORITY

Seniority is determined by the length of time an employee has worked on a job, in a department, or with the organization, in comparison with other employees. Seniority serves as a basis for (1) promotion, (2) determining eligibility for special benefits, (3) laying off employees during a period of reduced production, and (4) periodic increases in compensation.

Unions are strong supporters of seniority as the primary basis for promotion, whereas management has strived to retain the prerogative to promote the man they believe to be the best qualified for the job regardless of his seniority.[12] Most organizations have resolved this conflict by selecting the best qualified from among the employees with the greatest seniority.

COMMUNICATIONS AND NEWSLETTERS

It is essential to the efficient operation of a business that employees know what is expected of them, where they stand with the company, and where the company is going. It is equally essential that management be informed about the employees, their problems, and how they interpret established rules, procedures, and policies.[13] The larger the company, the more difficult becomes this two-way flow of information, unless management establishes media of communication and the necessary environment for the free flow of information.

Communication can vary from an informal chat between an employee and his supervisor to the formal statements of policy published in the "house organ" (the company newspaper). According to Elliot Jaques, communication is "the sum total of directly and indirectly, consciously and unconsciously transmitted feelings, attitudes, and wishes."[14] Communication is an integral part of the process of change. Viewed in this light communication is continually taking place throughout the working day regardless of whether anything is said or written. Communication is accomplished by a nod of the head or by one's presence at a meeting or absence from work.

What, then, should be management's goal in attempting to establish channels of communication and an environment in which it can take place? According to Dalton McFarland, "In spite of large staffs of experts in communication techniques, and the willingness to invest large sums of money, mass communication programs have for the most part failed."[15] It appears that management has too frequently placed emphasis on communications for its own sake and without thoroughly understanding the group it was attempting to communicate with. Likewise, management has too often failed to realize that information involves emotion, sentiment, and perception. A policy that has one connotation to the people at the top of the management pyramid may have an entirely different one to the workers at the bottom. This all indicates that emphasis should be placed not on communicating information but, rather, on communicating understanding. Man perceives his environment in terms of his total experiences, and regardless of how diligently we may try, we will not find two people with identical experiences; therefore perceptions will naturally differ.[16]

Company newspapers, newsletters, magazines, and publications of various types all serve to promote better communications if used properly.

Company newspapers. Newspapers provide individual employees with the big picture or what the company is doing as a total organization. Statements about company plans for future development tend to give employees a feeling of pride in "their" organization. The newspaper may also serve as a medium for recognizing employee accomplishments.

Newsletters. Company newsletters are generally shorter than newspapers and cover a more limited range of material. Newsletters are frequently prepared for units within an organization and can thereby give greater attention to activities of interest to individual employees.

Company magazines. Magazines tend to serve the same objectives as newspapers and newsletters. Many, however, go beyond the discussion of personal and organizational events, in an attempt to contribute to the general development of employees.

COMMUNITY SERVICES

Business has a great interest in the community in which it is located, and vice versa, for the two are interdependent. The very survival of a business is frequently contingent upon the community, for it is in the community that business finds its labor force, pays its taxes, obtains utility services, and markets its products. Many a company has been forced into relocating its plants and offices in another geographical area because of strained labor relations, excessive taxes, or the unavailability of certain community-furnished services, such as adequate housing for company employees and police and fire protection for company facilities.

In many such instances, there are indications of a lack of interaction between the business organization and the community; that, in fact, business had attempted to operate as an entity separate and distinct from the community. Such a policy is certainly not conducive to the efficient operation of a business. For it is only when business exposes itself to the community that it is able to break down unrealistic images that may portray the company as a cold, ruthless machine, unsympathetic to human needs and feelings, capable only of rendering employees jobless during slack periods in production or creating an eyesore that detracts from the natural beauty of the landscape.[17]

What can business do to present a favorable image to the community? First, top management must be fully aware of the mutual relationship of the company and the community, so that it will not enunciate policies and take actions which have a negative effect on the community. Where possible, decisions which will have a major impact on the community should be discussed with the appropriate public officials well in advance. It is difficult to establish mutual trust and goodwill in a matter of days.

A second step is to cultivate the "right atmosphere" within the company, for at the end of each working day each employee carries home the observations and opinions he has formulated while at work. These are transmitted, usually unintentionally, to the other members of the community through normal day-to-day interactions, and over a period of time they form their own opinion of the company. As to what the "right atmosphere" is and how it can be created, there is no hard and fast answer. If management strives to keep its employees well informed, the result will be a secure working force that takes pride in the organization and communicates this pride to the community.

As a third step, a company may decide to institute a formal community relations program. Such a program may take the form of a speakers bureau which provides lecturers to address community organizations or it may sponsor such community projects as athletic teams. Whatever the program, its purpose is to expose the company to the community in the best possible light.

PERSONNEL RECORDS

Complete records on each employee are normally maintained by the personnel department. This record normally contains information regarding his personal characteristics, education, prior experience, present assignment, training, jobs for which he may be qualified, and any other information the company cares to include.

Such data are invaluable in the search for personnel qualified for promotion, additional training, or transfer to another job. They are also useful to official investigators seeking background information on employees being considered for sensitive positions.[18]

EMPLOYEE SERVICES

Employee services include the numerous benefits which a company extends to employees above and beyond the payment of wages and salaries. Many are provided free; however, for some the employee shares the cost. Employee services may be divided into three categories: (1) financial, (2) recreational, and (3) convenience.

Financial services include the many programs which are considered an extension of wages and salaries and have definite economic value. These are assigned monetary values and treated the same as wages and salaries during labor-management contract negotiations.

Recreational programs include company-sponsored sports teams, such as bowling and baseball. In many cases the company will furnish all facilities and equipment and pay any fees or service charges required. Their general objective is to promote employee morale and create a favorable attitude toward the company.[19]

Fifty years ago, when companies would establish operations in remote areas, it was not uncommon for "company towns" to develop. Due to the lack of adequate facilities, companies would build the houses and stores required to attract employees to these remote areas. Through the years convenience services have evolved into such present-day facilities as employee cafeterias, restaurants, and shopping facilities in close proximity to work areas.

HOURS OF WORK

The majority of business employees today work what are commonly known as "regular hours," generally from eight o'clock in the morning until five o'clock in the afternoon, for a total of about forty hours a week. Continuing pressure has been exercised by a number of labor unions and employee groups to reduce this figure. In industries where productivity has increased, the work week has already been reduced.

Though many businesses are strongly opposed to any such reduction, studies have revealed that a decrease in the number of hours worked results in an increase in hourly and weekly production. Other studies have revealed a corresponding reduction in absenteeism, turnover, sickness, and injury.[20] In view of these studies and others still to be made, significant changes may well occur in the number of hours worked.

HEALTH, SAFETY, AND WELFARE

Employee health, safety, and welfare is an area of concern to most organizations. There are several reasons for this: (1) The company has a moral obligation to insure the health, safety, and welfare of its employees. (2) Labor is a valuable resource to a business and any loss of that resource directly affects its economic status. (3) The health, safety, and welfare of employees has a bearing on morale and working attitudes.

Many organizations conduct extensive programs with specific goals. Periodic safety drives may be conducted, complete with slogans and posters. Annual health check-ups may be made to insure that all personnel are physically able to perform their job properly. Various welfare services may be extended to employees who find themselves in need of assistance.

A safety program may be given "lip service," or it can be effectively administered.[21] If its basic objectives are to be accomplished, emphasis and support must come from the top of the organization.

VACATIONS

Employee vacations are of concern to both employees and the organization. They give employees time to fulfill personal desires and get a change of pace from the working routine. They are important to the organization since the employee returning from a vacation is more relaxed and has gained a new perspective on his work, usually resulting in better performance on the job. However, several problems are created by employee vacations. A company cannot usually afford to have several personnel from one department on vacation at the same time. Advance scheduling is required to insure that certain basic functions are accomplished.[22] In some organizations where employee vacations would cause substantial inefficiency, no matter when they were taken, a set period is established during which all operations are shut down and all employees go on vacation.

A recent development that is affecting vacations is the technological advances which have made possible large-scale production with the use of relatively few workers. As a consequence, it is necessary either to (1) increase the amount of leisure time (including vacations), (2) create new jobs for displaced workers, or (3) face increased unemployment. Several plans have been made to grant extended vacations (three to twelve months) with pay to employees who have completed a specified number of years' service.

LEAVES OF ABSENCE

If it becomes necessary for a worker to leave his job for a period in excess of his authorized vacation allowance, most companies make some provision for him to be absent without pay, and later return to the same or similiar position. The length of the absence usually depends on the type of job, the length of the worker's employment with the company, and the nature of the absence. Federal law now makes provision for certain employees to be reinstated in their former or similar position upon completion of compulsory military service.

RETIREMENT AND PENSION PLANS

The new employee, and in particular the young employee, does not usually show much interest in company retirement and pension programs. Therefore the retirement program does not appear to be a strong selling point in recruiting. It is, however, useful in holding employees who might be inclined to seek work elsewhere if they did not dislike losing their accrued retirement benefits. So retirement programs are not strictly for the benefit of the employee.

There are many types of retirement programs, some to which the employee contributes and some in which the employer pays the full amount. Some companies use a simple formula for computing retirement pay, others resort to complicated calculations employing tables and many variable factors. The majority of retirement programs, however, are based mainly upon two factors: (1) the employee's years of service, and (2) the amount of his earnings.

Many retirement programs offer employees a choice, within certain limits, as to when they will retire.[23] "Early retirement" programs may permit an employee to retire at an age when he may begin another career or devote time to a project he has long desired to accomplish. One consequence of such programs is that they permit younger men to fill more top-level positions in management.

HUMAN RELATIONS, ATTITUDES, AND MORALE

Though much progress has been made in analyzing the factors that influence employee attitudes and morale, much more research is necessary before management can act with any degree of certainty in this area. Some organizations have made substantial investments in attitude surveys, human relations training, and morale measurement.[24] It is generally believed, however, that no amount of emphasis on human relations as such can compensate for significant weaknesses in organization and management. However, there is a close relationship between human relations factors and management.[25] Negative attitudes and low morale frequently serve as indicators of more basic problems; therefore instead of being considered problems to be corrected, they should be treated as symptoms requiring further analysis.

SPECIAL GROUP PROBLEMS

Not all personnel problems fall within the framework of established procedure and therefore must be handled individually. In particular, there are four special groups among whom problems can develop if appropriate action is not taken. These groups include: (1) handicapped workers, (2) older workers, (3) racial minority groups, and (4) women employees.

1. A handicapped worker is limited in performance only to the extent of his handicap. With minor adjustments of a working area, a handicapped worker can usually perform as effectively as a regular employee. Many companies have found that a handicapped worker will frequently do outstanding work in order to compensate for his handicap.

2. With increasing age there is normally a gradual reduction in the amount of physical work a man can accomplish and possibly some reduction in mental alertness and motivation. However, older employees usually more than compensate for this by their experience, dedication, and wisdom.

3. Problems with respect to racial minority groups are usually deeply rooted in social and emotional history and therefore will not be easily eliminated by any magic formula. However, constant effort by management to eliminate circumstances in the work environment that contribute to racial tension will facilitate harmonious relations and create an environment more conducive to effective production.

4. Industry's biggest problem with respect to women employees is the high turnover rate, due to marriage and pregnancies. This in turn increases the expense involved in training and the time required to gain experience in a particular job. Once again, this is a problem for which there is no magic formula, but which must be dealt with on an individual basis.

Unfortunately, many group problems are permitted to go too far before corrective action is taken. For this reason it is gradually being realized that all levels of management must be sensitive to their existence and possess sufficient knowledge to handle them at an early stage.[26]

QUESTIONS AND PROBLEMS

1. What is the first step in a program designed to correct excessive absenteeism or turnover?

2. Why are business and community interdependent?
3. What are the principal objectives of employee service programs?
4. Why shouldn't negative employee attitudes and low morale be treated as problems?
5. What are the principal reasons for conducting a job analysis?
6. What was the major difference between the Wagner Act and the Taft-Hartley Act?
7. What are the three principal parts of a labor relations program?
8. What advantage does a company receive from an efficient retirement and pension program?
9. Why is the amount of money paid not always the most important consideration in a salary and wage administration program?
10. What factors must be considered when determining selection criteria to be used in a hiring program?

REFERENCE NOTES

[1] Robert N. McMurry, "Here's a Better Way to Size Up Men," *Nation's Business,* August, 1960, p. 68.

[2] R. J. Obrochta, "The Interview Report—A Human Relations Training Aid," *Personnel,* American Management Association, May-June, 1961, p. 73.

[3] Raymond L. Randall, "Get More From Your Training," *Nation's Business,* June, 1960, p. 42.

[4] David W. Belcher, *Wage and Salary Administration,* Prentice-Hall, 1962.

[5] Arch Patton, "Trends in Executive Compensation," *Harvard Business Review,* September, 1960, p. 144.

[6] David W. Ewing and Dan H. Fenn, Jr., *Incentives for Executives,* McGraw-Hill, 1962.

[7] Harold Mayfield, "In Defense of Performance Appraisal," *Harvard Business Review,* March, 1960, p. 81.

[8] Gerald Nadler, *Work Design,* Irwin, 1963.

[9] John B. Miner, *The Management of Ineffective Performance,* McGraw-Hill, 1963.

[10] Jules Backman, "First Steps Toward Fair Work Rules," *Nation's Business,* June, 1960, p. 196.

[11] Emily Clark Brown and Harry A. Millis, *From the Wagner Act to Taft-Hartley,* University of Chicago Press, 1950.

[12] Morris Stone, "If You Were the Arbitrator: Seniority vs. Ability," *Supervisory Management,* American Management Association, April, 1962, pp. 13–31.

[13] Willard V. Merrihue, *Managing by Communications,* McGraw-Hill, 1960.

[14] Elliot Jaques, *The Changing Culture of a Factory,* Tavistock Publications, 1951, p. 301.

[15] Dalton McFarland, *Management Principles and Practices,* Macmillan, 1958.

[16] Robert Newcomb and Margaret Sammons, *Employee Communications in Action,* Harper & Row, 1961.

[17] Wayne Hodges, *Company and Community,* Harper & Row, 1958.

[18] Charles Munro, "Simplifying a Personnel Records Operation," *Personnel,* American Management Association, July-August, 1962, p. 72.

[19] Frank X. White, "New Emphasis on Recreation in Employee Relations," *Personnel Journal,* Swarthmore, Pa., January, 1963, p. 38.

[20] Joseph Tiffin and Ernest J. McCormick, *Industrial Psychology,* 4th ed., Prentice-Hall, 1961.

[21] "Supervisors Steer Safety Program," *Iron Age,* March 8, 1962, p. 43.

[22] Peter C. Reid, "What Happens While They're on Vacation," *Supervisory Management,* American Management Association, March, 1962, p. 2.

[23] Peter D. Couch and Earl F. Lundgren, "Making Voluntary Retirement Programs Work," *Personnel Journal,* March, 1963, p. 135.

[24] Owens Glennon and Albright Smith, "New Dimension in Measuring Morale," *Harvard Business Review,* January, 1960, p. 106.

[25] Keith Davis, *Human Relations at Work,* McGraw-Hill, 1962.

[26] Burleigh B. Gardner and David G. Moore, *Human Relations in Industry,* 4th ed., Irwin, 1964.

READING REFERENCES

Albright, Lewis E., J. R. Glennon, and Wallace J. Smith, *The Use of Psychological Tests in Industry,* Howard Allen, 1963.

Granick, David, *The European Executive,* Doubleday, 1962.

Haire, Mason, *Psychology in Management,* 2nd ed., McGraw-Hill, 1964.

Heyel, Carl, *Management for Modern Supervisors,* American Management Association, 1962.

Jennings, Eugene Emerson, *The Executive: Autocrat, Bureaucrat, Democrat,* Harper & Row, 1962.

Kay, Brian R., and Stuart Palmer, *The Challenge of Supervision,* McGraw-Hill, 1961.

Livingston, Robert Teviot, and William W. Waite, *The Manager's Job,* Columbia University Press, 1960.

McGehee, William, and Paul W. Thayer, *Training in Business and Industry,* Wiley, 1961.

Siegel, Laurence, *Industrial Psychology,* Irwin, 1962.

Sutermeister, Robert A., *People and Productivity,* McGraw-Hill, 1963.

17

OFFICE MANAGEMENT

Due to the great mass of information required in present-day business and managerial operations, the work of the office manager has taken on new and greater importance. It rates a vice presidency in the Ford organization and in several smaller corporations.

Costs of operating this function have risen markedly during the past decade, and every indication points toward even higher costs in the future. Consequently, administrative management is taking another look at the office area as a possible place for cost savings. This has given it new emphasis and drawn the attention of top management to it.

THE OFFICE MANAGER'S ROLE

An office manager is responsible for planning, organizing, and controlling the clerical aspects of the organization, including the preparation, communication, coordination, and storage of data that support production and operations. Since the office manager exercises responsibilities over several elements of the organization, he must be given the status that this responsibility demands. In order to promote economy and efficiency, he must be in a position to make recommendations to top management. And since he must gain acceptance of new ideas and improved methods, he must possess a high degree of tact, emotional control, reasoning capacity, and sense of humor.[1]

He must thoroughly understand the varied requirements of the organizational elements, including their need for communication, clerical equipment and supplies, data and information processing and storage. He also must appreciate the relationship between the various elements and the need for coordination.

PLANNING AND SCHEDULING

Indicators of insufficient planning and scheduling include: (1) more than casual employee complaints about excessive work loads; (2) an increase in the number of errors in work performed; and (3) obvious disorganization in which a few employees do most of the work while others do little or nothing. Poor planning results in a waste of time and resources and a consequent decline in the efficiency and productivity of an organization.

To avoid this, it is necessary to (1) determine future needs and the time and resources required to meet them; (2) evaluate the potential of existing methods, procedures, and personnel and determine what action will insure that they will meet future requirements; and (3) prepare a plan and schedule that will eliminate wasted or inefficient effort.[2]

Knowledge is the basis of all sound planning and scheduling, and the more information that can be obtained about future developments, the better actual performance will be. If it is known that personnel will be absent during a certain period, plans should be made well in advance to ensure that trained replacements will be available. Likewise, when additional equipment will be necessary, the requirement should be made known in time to allow for order and delivery.

CENTRALIZATION AND SPECIALIZATION

Centralization and specialization of office management functions are a matter of primary consideration when establishing a new office or reorganizing an existing one. A choice may be made between centralized and decentralized office management.[3] However, most organizations are partially centralized and partially decentralized. There are three principal types of centralization: (1) physical centralization, in which all office functions are performed at one central location; (2) limited or functional centralization, in which only certain related functions and activities are centralized; and (3) supervisory centralization, in which office functions and activities are decentralized, but control and supervision are centralized under an office manager.

With centralization full-time personnel are assigned to office functions, whereas decentralized operations normally require only part-time personnel. When personnel are utilized full time, they may be more thoroughly trained and more proficient. Centralization usually requires several trained and experienced employees, providing flexibility in the event that one is absent. However, in a decentralized organization only one employee may perform office functions, which in his absence may be performed inadequately. Centralization also tends to consolidate functions into one physical area, allowing more efficient supervision.[4]

Although centralization is generally highly efficient, it does have certain limitations. Since material is removed from the actual point of use, some delay may be experienced in work handling, especially when volume is high. Also, since personnel are trained primarily in office procedure, they may lack sufficient knowledge about specific procedures in functional areas. However, this problem is frequently avoided by selecting personnel who have had previous experience in the functional areas of the organization.

OFFICE MACHINES AND DEVICES

Electronic machines and devices for office use do not approach anywhere near the scope and cost of machines utilized for production purposes. Nevertheless, consideration must be given to their use since modern office machines provide an opportunity to achieve greater output with far less effort.[5] It is usually up to the office manager to determine where some form of mechanization would be of value in increasing the efficiency of office functions. Occasionally, he may conduct a special study to determine the feasibility of obtaining a particular type of equipment, such as automatic data processing machines. In any case, a careful analysis of requirements is necessary to insure that all investments in equipment bring maximum benefit to the organization.[6]

Much is to be gained by purchasing machines of the same brand. If the number required is large, a substantial discount may be obtained by purchasing in volume. Also, the training of operators is facilitated and the machines may be used interchangeably. In addition, the maintenance function is simplified since one repairman can service several machines on a single visit. Standardization also permits spare parts and supplies to be procured in volume at discount prices and an adequate stock maintained to preclude shortages.

When the equipment is received, a decision must be made as to whether it should be centralized in one location or distributed throughout the organization. This question is usually determined by the nature of the equipment, what elements of the organization will use it, and the extent of its use. Some equipment must be closely supervised to insure efficient utilization. All equipment should receive some degree of supervision and control to see that it is maintained in proper working order and that waste of supplies and materials is kept to a minimum.

FURNITURE AND FIXTURES

In the selection of office furniture and fixtures, consideration must be given to two factors: (1) their function and (2) their aesthetic values. A receptionist does not require the same equipment as a clerk-typist and an executive does not require the same as an administrative assistant. Jobs also vary with respect to status in the organization and extent of public contact, considerations which influence the condition, style, and appearance of furniture and fixtures selected.[7] Office furnishings have also been found to influence employee morale, attitude, and motivation, which in turn influence work output and efficiency.

Office furniture consists primarily of desks, chairs, tables, and storage facilities. A primary consideration in all is size. Each item must be large enough to permit the efficient performance of the job, but it should not be so large as to limit working space and aisles, creating bottlenecks and a cluttered appearance. Clerical desks will require ample storage facilities, whereas an executive's desk will require a minimum of storage space but must appear commensurate with his organizational status. Again, a typist's chair must serve a different purpose from an executive's chair.

Based on his knowledge of organizational needs, the office manager must procure (rent, lease, or buy) that equipment which will contribute most to the over-all functioning of the organization.[8] As equipment becomes worn, obsolete, or is no longer required, it should be turned in or replaced.

SUPPLIES

The supplies required to operate a clerical or administrative organization usually represent a sizable dollar investment. In order to control costs and promote over-all efficiency, they should be obtained and utilized in accordance with sound management principles.

The office supply function may be divided into two areas: (1) procurement and (2) utilization. Procurement consists of determining requirements with respect to type, quantity, and quality and then obtaining the required supplies at the most favorable price. Care must be taken that items of a higher quality than required are not obtained and that only a reasonable quantity is purchased, to avoid taking up too much storage space.[9] Large-quantity purchasing may also result in obsolescence if organizational requirements change. However, sufficient quantities should be purchased to gain volume discounts. Supplies should also be ordered in time for delivery before shortages occur and cause a delay in work.

Improper use of supplies, such as wastage and appropriation for personal use, can result in a substantial loss to the company. Supplies should be stored in a secure area, with one person responsible for issuing them on the basis of authorized requisitions. Supervisors should periodically remind employees of the principles of supply economy.

DUPLICATING

Most business organizations require a considerable amount of reproduction or duplication of correspondence, reports, and forms of various types. Possibly the most basic method of duplicating is the use of common, everyday, carbon paper. At the other extreme are the various photographic and electronic devices in common use.[10]

Because of equipment cost and complexity, and the need for trained operators, duplicating processes are frequently centralized in one location. This also facilitates supervision and control of equipment use. It is usually the responsibility of the office manager to (1) insure that suitable equipment is available for making the type of copies needed and in the quantities required; (2) see that trained personnel are available to operate the equipment; (3) inform interested personnel of the equipment's availability and capabilities; and (4) supervise and control the material duplicated.

CORRESPONDENCE AND REPORTS

The accuracy and clarity of the enormous volume of paper work that is prepared and distributed each business day has a direct bearing on the effectiveness of the entire organization. A principal responsibility of office management is the establishment, operation, and maintenance of correspondence and reporting procedures.[11]

Correspondence

Letters comprise the bulk of written business communication. Correspondence is required for both the internal and external functioning of the organization. Internal correspondence consists of notes, memos, and disposition forms that relay information from one department, division, or section to another. External correspondence serves a number of purposes concerned with the exchange of information, such as: (1) answering inquiries pertaining to employment and products; (2) seeking information pertaining to the procurement of the resources required for production (labor, money, and material); and (3) special circumstances or events, including invitations, deaths, birthdays, meeting notices, and payment collections.

To maintain efficient correspondence procedures, the office manager must: (1) develop standardized procedures which meet the needs of the organization; (2) make sure that all elements of the organization understand and follow them; and (3) continually review them to eliminate what is no longer applicable and implement what is required.

Reports

With a few exceptions, reports are limited to the internal functioning of the business. They serve as a routine channel of communication by which information is relayed regularly from one level of the organization to another. They are intended to inform management of the success, status, and progress of the various functions necessary to achieve the basic business objectives. In most cases it is the responsibility of the office manager to establish, operate, and maintain efficient and effective reporting channels. It is his job to see that reports are as clear as possible, that unnecessary ones are eliminated, and that new reports are established when required.[12]

DICTATION AND TRANSCRIBING

The great demand placed on the modern businessman's time requires that he function as efficiently as possible. This applies to the enormous amount of correspondence necessary in the modern business organization. To assist him in this area, he usually has either a stenographer (transcriber) or a dictating machine, or both. Each has its advantages.

Dictating machines. Unlike a stenographer, a dictating machine operates only when material is being dictated. If the executive is interrupted with a telephone call or visitor, dictation may be stopped and resumed at will without distracting a stenographer from another assignment. The machine also gives the executive a degree of mobility since many are now portable and can be operated under almost any circumstance, including in an automobile or airplane. The dictating machine permits maximum flexibility in the rate of dictation. An executive may dictate rapidly, with assurance that everything will be transcribed, or slowly, allowing time for careful analysis, with no waste of a stenographer's time.[10]

The stenographer. In spite of the economy and convenience that a dictating machine provides, many executives have a definite preference for a stenographer. A stenographer usually possesses a thorough knowledge of the functional aspects of the business and understands how a particular executive operates. For this reason, she can also function as an administrative assistant or secretary and prepare replies to much correspondence with little or no instruction.

FORMS AND CONTROLS

Anything which initiates, guides, limits, or restricts action in an organization is said to be a control. Some of the commonly recognized controls are policies, rules, procedures, standards, schedules, and budgets. However, one of the most basic but seldom recognized controls in an organization are the forms which are established to achieve particular objectives. A form is actually a communications medium in that it is frequently a request for information which, when supplied, will serve to initiate, guide, limit, or restrict action. However, it is also a control in the sense that the requested action may or may not be granted or may be modified to conform to established policy or to work-load limitations.

The completion of a form may be likened to the preparation of a plan before action is initiated. Basic information must be analyzed, sorted, and arranged in a definite order indicating action to be performed and the time and sources required for performance. In this way the person who is to take action can schedule accomplishment based on established priorities and the existing work load. It is normally the responsibility of the office manager to maintain control over the number and type of forms in use. Since a substantial amount of time is required daily to complete all the forms used in a modern business organization, any forms control program should include (1) centralized approval for requests for new forms to eliminate duplication and promote standardization; and (2) periodic review of existing forms to determine whether they should be eliminated, modified, or reordered.[13]

OFFICE MANUALS

Office manuals serve to instruct employees how to perform their assignments in line with the objectives and standards established by management. Therefore manuals should be prepared to cover each of the major functions performed in the office. Each employee should receive a copy of all manuals which relate to his assigned job. Additional manuals should be available at some convenient location so that they may be consulted on any problems that arise.[14]

Correspondence manuals are intended to furnish employees with information as to correspondence form, style, and type to be used. They generally contain statements of policy and procedure as well as examples and suggestions for preparing effective letters.

Filing manuals serve to acquaint employees with the established filing system. The manual may include a list of frequently processed documents, indicating where they should be filed. It may also give the frequency with which files are deactivated or retired and the procedure to be followed. (See Chapter 18, "Records Management.")

Equipment manuals are frequently furnished by the supplier of office equipment to describe its proper operation. Supplementary manuals may be prepared by the company to limit or otherwise control the use of office machines and equipment.

SYSTEMS AND PROCEDURES

The manner in which a function is performed, including the sequence of steps and method of operation, is known as a procedure. Several related functions which achieve a common objective are referred to as a system. For example, a system for selecting new employees may include: (1) recruiting and preliminary screening by the personnel department; (2) interviewing by interested divisions in the company; (3) psychological testing by a consulting firm; (4) a physical examination by the company doctor; and (5) final selection and orientation by an immediate supervisor. Similar systems and procedures may be established for accomplishing an unlimited number of functions and for coordinating them to achieve desired objectives.

When sufficient information is available, written procedures may be prepared for each function, which will indicate the various steps to be accomplished.[15] The system of operation thereby established will result in work being performed in a routine, orderly, and uniform manner, permitting more time to be spent on unique situations.

QUALITY CONTROL

Frequently, the only way an organization is judged by outsiders is by the manner in which it performs, which includes the quality of correspondence, reports, and forms it issues. Material lacking in clarity and neatness will most certainly create an unfavorable impression, to say nothing of the possibility of its relaying incorrect information. The same also holds true of material used entirely for internal operation. If it is improperly filed, vague in organization, or difficult to read, then internal communications will be impaired and the over-all efficiency of the organization affected.

The need to maintain quality standards will vary with the material being processed. Payroll checks must be completely accurate; on the other hand, an occasional error in the typing of an interoffice memo will normally be tolerated. The office manager establishes the degree of quality that must be maintained in various office functions and then takes action to see that it is achieved. Materials purchased must comply with desired standards, including the quality of paper, equipment, and supplies required for clerical functions. To insure good workmanship, personnel must be selected and trained to perform assignments in accordance with established policies, procedures, and standards of quality.[16]

STANDARDS AND STANDARDIZATION

Standards serve two general purposes: (1) as goals to be accomplished and (2) as tools to evaluate efficiency and performance.[17] Standards tend to direct an organization toward specific goals with a minimum of communication. For example, the fairly routine matter of typing a letter may be a cause of great concern to a new typist unacquainted with company policy and procedure. However, a sample letter in the company's organization manual may answer puzzling questions with respect to margins and spacing. In addition to what is stated in the correspondence manual, a supervisor may indicate that erasures on correspondence are not permitted. This serves as a standard of quality which the typist should achieve (an objective) and as a basis on which she will be judged (an evaluation tool).

If the various elements within an organization do not have a common method of exchanging information and data, misinterpretations and confusion will result. One of the principal reasons for using forms is to group information and data in a standardized manner so that it is readily available to all elements of the organization concerned. It is the responsibility of office management to strive continually to promote procedures standardization wherever the efficiency and effectiveness of the organization can be improved.

MEASUREMENT

Office work, like production, must be supervised and controlled to insure that maximum benefit is derived from investment. To facilitate supervision and control, it is necessary to measure the efficiency or output of an office unit so that prompt corrective action may be taken as required and so that costs may be contained within tolerable limits.

Accurate measurement of available work can greatly facilitate scheduling and serve as a basis for determining the status of projects and indicate areas where additional help will be required.

Office work does not always lend itself to easy measurement since many actions are not routine in nature and since tangible objects are not always involved. Some type of standard may be achieved, however, by grouping several functions, unmeasurable by themselves, and establishing a standard for the total process or assignment.[18]

PRODUCTION RECORDS

Records of work accomplished serve as the basis of corrective action and future planning. Production records also provide a basis for determining work standards for a particular office. Since duties vary from office to office, each office must establish internal standards of its own.

The way in which production data are collected and analyzed will depend on the nature of the work. If a tangible unit of measurement is available, it may be recorded and analyzed with ease. Examples of such data include the number of documents processed, letters typed, and telephone calls completed. Data obtained from production records may be entered on a "work distribution chart," which indicates the various activities performed by an entire office and the individuals who perfrom it. In this way the relative accomplishments of all employees in an office may be compared and analyzed for the purpose of determining where adjustments in work load or job content are indicated.

Production data may also be used to prepare "flow process charts," which indicate the sequence in which operations are performed, the personnel involved, and the time required.[19] In this way, delays in the processing work can be detected and steps taken to correct or compensate for them.

WORK SIMPLIFICATION

See Chapter 12, "Factory and Production Management."

SKILLS DEVELOPMENT

To achieve maximum efficiency in office functions, personnel must perform their assignments with a high degree of skill. However, there are many factors which tend to limit employee skills. A primary one is a high turnover rate, especially among female personnel. When highly trained employees leave an organization, every attempt must be made to achieve a period of overlap during which new personnel can work along with departing personnel and thereby learn some of the required techniques and procedures.

Another limiting factor in skill development is the amount of time that may be devoted to achieving proficiency.[20] Work-load requirements may not permit interruptions for training and practice. In jobs that require a number of different operations, there may be a tendency to emphasize one aspect of the job at the expense of another. An employee may become highly skilled in those functions to which adequate time is devoted, but develop little or no skill in less frequently performed functions.

Still another limiting factor is the lack of qualified instructors or instruction material. It is the responsibility of the supervisor to see that all employees receive the necessary instruction to develop the skills required for effective performance.

MAIL AND MESSENGER SERVICE

In the modern business organization work is frequently functionalized, with several geographically separated sections or departments each performing a distinct function. In order to accomplish a particular objective, a substantial amount of coordination and interaction between them is normally required. Since the same procedures and channels utilized for internal written communications are usually utilized for the receipt and dispatch of external written communications, it is important that maximum efficiency be maintained in order to provide efficient service to customers and other important correspondents.

Mail is normally routed through and controlled by a centralized mail room. Incoming mail is sorted into groups for messenger delivery or pick-up by the appropriate organizational element. At the time of delivery the messenger will normally collect outgoing mail and return it to the mail room for sorting and dispatch to the post office or other elements of the organization. Pick-up and delivery are normally performed according to an established schedule. In addition, the centralized mail room may perform additional functions, such as wrapping, addressing, weighing, and stamping. It is the function of good office management to insure that these functions are performed in accordance with the requirements of the organization.[21]

QUESTIONS AND PROBLEMS

1. What are the principal disadvantages of centralization of office functions?
2. Why should organization reports be reviewed periodically?
3. What factors should be considered before an office manager purchases dictating machines?
4. Why should the office manager be the person responsible for approving requests for new forms?
5. What factors should determine the frequency of mail pick-up and delivery?
6. What is an effective method of work measurement for a secretary's job?
7. When should office machines not be centralized in one location?

8. Should office manuals be used as a substitute for training?
9. What basis should be used to determine quality standards with respect to office work?
10. Who should be responsible for establishing an organization's filing system? For establishing filing procedures?

REFERENCE NOTES

[1] W. G. Cole, "Supervisory Control of Clerical Assignments," *NAA Bulletin,* February, 1961, pp. 81-88.

[2] J. A. Rhea, "Decade of Progress in Office Planning," *Office Management and American Business,* January, 1961, pp. 41-44.

[3] Ernest Dale, "Centralization Versus Decentralization," *Advanced Management,* June, 1956.

[4] E. C. Hanna, "Operation of Centralized Clerical Services," *Office Executive,* May, 1961, p. 32.

[5] L. Victor, "Efficiency and Office Machines," *Administrative Management,* January, 1962, pp. 28-31.

[6] R. Ritter, "Is This Machine Necessary?," *Management Review,* March, 1961, pp. 42-44.

[7] C. E. Lippincott and R. Margulies, "Office Must Reflect the Company," *Office Management and American Business,* January, 1961, pp. 52-55.

[8] R. L. Caleo, "Lowdown on Leasing Office Furniture," *Administrative Management,* May, 1961, p. 38.

[9] H. J. Woods, "Applying Value Analysis of Office Purchasing," *The Office,* January, 1962, p. 169.

[10] Emma K. Felter and Marie Reynolds, *Basic Clerical Practice,* 2nd ed., McGraw-Hill, 1959.

[11] J. H. Menning and C. W. Wilkinson, *Communicating Through Letters and Reports,* 3rd ed., Irwin, 1963.

[12] E. W. McNamara, "Methods of Analyzing Reports," *The Office,* March, 1958, p. 128.

[13] F. Nestle, "How to Design a Form," *Supervisory Management,* December, 1961, pp. 18-22.

[14] R. Dreyback, "How the Smaller Office Can Prepare a Procedure Manual," *The Office,* June, 1961, pp. 90-91; and E. Mezner, "Procedure Manuals Program the Work," *NAA Bulletin,* January, 1958, pp. 51-57.

[15] J. B. McMaster, "Case for Written Procedures," *Office Executive,* October, 1958, pp. 19-20.

[16] R. M. Smith, "Statistical Quality Control Based on Work Sampling Raises Office Standards," *Office Management,* December, 1958, pp. 25-27.

[17] A. E. Fain, "Time Measurement Provides Supervisory Control Standards," *The Office,* September, 1958, pp. 71-79.

[18] S. A. Birn, "Master Clerical Data; Approach to Work Measurement in the Office," *Office Executive,* April, 1961, p. 41.

[19] C. L. Littlefield and Frank Rachel, *Office and Administrative Management,* 2nd ed., Prentice-Hall, 1954.

[20] G. Paul, "How Employee Training Can Be Made More Effective," *The Office,* August, 1961, p. 16.

[21] C. E. Ginder, "Mail Room Practices," *Office Executive,* July, 1961, pp. 10-13; and "Mailroom Procedures Surveyed," *The Office,* July, 1961, p. 24.

READING REFERENCES

Barron, Allan E., and James R. Taylor, *Clerical Office Training,* Prentice-Hall, 1963.

Duchan, Simon A., *Basic Dictation,* Pitman, 1963.

Hawken, William R., *Photocopying from Bound Volumes: A Study of Machines, Methods, and Materials,* American Library Association, 1962.

Menning, J. H., and C. W. Wilkinson, *Communicating Through Letters and Reports,* 3rd ed., Irwin, 1963.

Parkhurst, Charles Chandler, *Business Communications for Better Human Relations,* Prentice-Hall, 1961.

———, *Modern Executive's Guide to Effective Communications,* Prentice-Hall, 1962.

Reynolds, Charles O., *Work Simplification for Everyone,* Pyramid Books, 1962.

Schutte, William M., and Erwin R. Steinberg, *Communication in Business and Industry,* Holt, Rinehart and Winston, 1960.

Strong, Earl P., *Increasing Office Productivity,* McGraw-Hill, 1962.

18

RECORDS MANAGEMENT

The subject of this chapter is a relatively new management area. It grew out of the field of office management and has, like offspring in the past, practically outgrown its "parents." The filing, storing, and retrieval of business records is a vital necessity to all organizations, whether they be large or small. A few of the most important subjects in this area are discussed here.

CONTROL

Normal day-to-day business operations result in the generation of a considerable volume of information, data, forms, and records.[1] Much of this material contains vital information which must be referred to periodically. Many important management decisions are based on past records of production, sales, purchasing, inventory status, labor costs, absenteeism and turnover, and many other areas of operation. Many current business problems have their origin in actions taken weeks, months, or even years past. In order to appreciate why certain actions were or were not taken, it is often necessary to review and analyze pertinent records and trace developments over a number of years. So that all important records are available when required, an effective records control system must be maintained.

Centralized control is the localization of the responsibility for recording, protecting, and filing the records of an organization. The alternative is to divide records management among the officials and department executives, such as the president, vice president, secretary, treasurer, and managers of the purchasing, personnel, advertising, production, accounting, and other departments. In this way each department is responsible for establishing and maintaining its own files and records. The disadvantages of this include: (1) inconsistent filing and difficulty in locating required records; (2) records are not retired or released for disposal according to an established schedule, so that filing space is taken up by material no longer required; (3) all the information pertaining to a particular subject is not included in each separate filing system and one department does not know what action has been taken by another department with respect to a particular matter; (4) considerable duplication of records and information is inevitable; and (5) personnel trained and experienced in effective filing procedures are not usually available in the functional departments since filing is frequently considered only a secondary, part-time duty.

Centralized control of organizational records is therefore considered an important prerequisite for sound records management. Under centralized control, responsibility for the organization and maintenance of files is usually assigned to a records administrator, who is given the authority to organize, maintain, and supervise all records of the organization regardless of the physical location of the files. His specific duties include:

1. Control and follow-up of incoming communications
2. Control of outgoing communications
3. Maintenance of a complete up-to-date record of each file, describing the class of records and method of filing
4. Separation of permanent from transitory records to facilitate disposal
5. Periodic elimination of duplicate records that are maintained for current use only
6. Maintenance at all times of a staff of trained clerks for indexing and filing
7. Maintenance of a complete schedule of records with authorized periods for retention or disposal

In organizing a records department it is necessary to study existing files and records as well as potential requirements, in particular:

1. Contents of each file in all locations
2. Uses made of the records
3. Kind of copies—original or carbon—and the number of extra copies filed

4. Period of reference requirements
5. Volume of work
6. Arrangement of contents of the files
7. Possible consolidation of the files
8. Point of greatest activity
9. Periods of retention

When the study has been completed, a detailed plan of operation is prepared and incorporated into an operating manual. The plan specifies the type of records that are to be maintained, indexing and filing procedures to be observed, and provisions for retiring and disposal of each type of record. In addition, it should cover:

1. Use to be made of the records currently, six months hence, a year hence, or longer
2. Frequency of reference
3. Records that are required at the same time
4. Value of the records
5. Cost of filing and finding
6. Overhead costs—equipment, supplies, floor and storage space

When a suitable records management plan has been incorporated into an operating manual, it is brought to the attention of all personnel generating and requiring the use of organizational records. Like all plans and methods of operation, it should be periodically reviewed.

PROTECTION

Once vital records are lost or destroyed, it is usually extremely difficult to replace them. Such a calamity could place a company at a competitive disadvantage, harm customer relationships, and severely limit an organization's ability to plan for the future. For this reason all records should be given a degree of protection commensurate with their value to the functioning of the organization.

They should be protected from accidental misplacement, unauthorized access by personnel from within and outside the company, theft, fire, or other disaster (including atomic attack). Since all records do not require the same degree of protection, a careful review will determine their relative value. Consideration must also be given to the frequency of access which each record requires and the location of its users.

Minimum Protection

Routine records not containing sensitive or important data require only minimum protection. Such records usually consist of seldom-used reference data; information in common usage or which can be easily replaced, such as government and commercial publications; routine correspondence not containing operating data or dealing with special problems; and general bulletins, memos, and other material used by many departments, which normally have their own copies.

Such materials require little or no special consideration with respect to location, filing equipment, and degree of access permitted.

Moderate Protection

Forms, reports, data, documents, and records which contain information of a slightly valuable or sensitive nature require a moderate degree of protection. Included in this category is material used in current operations which could be replaced only at great inconvenience; information which should not be available for general usage either within or outside the organization; and information pertaining to sales, production, customers, and suppliers which is required for current operations. Destruction of material of this type due to fire or other disaster, although inconvenient, would not tend to endanger the over-all operation of the business.

Such material may be protected by: (1) maintaining adequate control over access during normal working hours and (2) locking or otherwise securing it during nonworking hours. Normally, it is stored in filing equipment or rooms which may be locked when not in use, and under the charge of one person during working hours.

Maximum Protection

Records of vital importance to the successful operation of a business require maximum protection. Such records include information relative to the plans, capabilities, and financial status of the organization, are usually not in general usage throughout the organization, and frequently exist in only one copy, making replacement difficult if not impossible.

Such records must be given maximum protection against all types of loss and destruction, including theft, fire, and other disaster. Access should be limited to a few, select individuals, and their exact location known at all times. When not in use, vital records should be stored in equipment which can be securely locked and which provides adequate protection from fire. Because of the great importance of certain records, many organizations maintain microfilm or other types of photographic copies stored at some alternate location. Many private organizations, as well as the United States Government, utilize caves and other underground storage facilities, which includes protection from atomic explosion.

It is usually one of the responsibilities of the records administrator or office manager to determine the degree of protection required for various records and the equipment and facilities that should be used.[2]

RETENTION

Too many organizations have no established procedures for retaining, retiring, or destroying old records. When primary files become filled, they do one of two things: relocate old records to some remote, low-cost storage area or destroy all records of a certain age and type without distinction. Both methods have distinct disadvantages. Relocating old records in a remote storage area incurs unnecessary transportation and storage costs, and the records are no longer available for convenient use. The categorical destruction of all records of a certain age and type usually results in the destruction of some which might be of value to current or future activities.

The way to eliminate the unnecessary costs and disadvantages of records retention, retirement, and disposal is to systematically classify all records according to their value and period of usefulness.[3] This takes time, but the long-term savings and benefits make it well worth while. The disposition of records should be the joint effort of the records department and the operating departments concerned. The records administrator arranges the files according to disposition schedules submitted by the operating departments. Some organizations utilize a records committee, composed of representatives from key offices, to review the disposition schedules. In this way any unit having need of a particular record may indicate its requirement before the disposition schedule is implemented.

In preparing a records disposition schedule, the operating departments must determine the value of their records on the basis of (1) physical value, which is the cost of producing the records;

and (2) actual value, which is their value to the organization in carrying on its operations. Consideration should also be given to their (1) importance as an administrative tool or historical value, (2) accessibility for current operations, (3) reproduction possibilities and costs. (4) filing space and costs, and (5) filing equipment used. When the evaluation is completed, a responsible authority should place an appropriate symbol in the upper left corner of the record indicating the retention period required. One frequently used system of marking uses the following symbols:

Symbol	*Retention Period*
P	Permanent
PV	Permanent—vital
T	Temporary (state time and specific date)

Ideally, when the records are forwarded to the records department, they should be so organized as to provide for periodic disposal without the necessity of a reindexing or refiling operation or the costly operation of reading (weeding out) each record to determine its value when filing space is needed.

STORAGE

Attempting to arrive at a suitable balance between records accessibility and cost of storage is no easy matter. Many factors must be analyzed, such as (1) the best storage location, (2) the best type of storage, and (3) the frequency of access required. For example, if the rate of access for a particular category of records is once every ten years, then no great inconvenience will be incurred if they are stored at some remote location. However, if the rate of access is once every hour, a storage location in close proximity to the users will be necessary.

Records may be stored in their orginal form (typed letters, forms, documents, etc.) or they may be converted to another from (microfilm, photostatic copies, magnetic tape, etc.) for the sake of economy of space or safer preservation.

Original-Form Storage

For records transferred from active to inactive status in their original form, transfer cabinets are available in single units in steel, wood, pressboard, and cardboard. Reinforced corrugated-cardboard boxes are now available in drawer styles. Since inactive records may be more tightly packed, two transfer cases will usually accommodate three drawers of current material. Those which are collapsible and open at the top must be placed on shelves. The recommended type has sliding drawers, so that the cases can be stacked one upon the other, four to eight units high.

It is not necessary to keep the records for one department in one location, so long as an inventory card shows the exact location of all records.

Modified-Form Storage

Records are converted to some other form for storage to conserve storage space, protect vital records from deterioration, and permit rapid access to required information. Microfilm and other photographic processes have been the principal forms of modified-form storage, but with the growth of automatic data processing and computer applications, data cards and magnetic tape are gaining rapid acceptance.[4]

Microphotography is the process of photographing documents at high speed on narrow safety film. Negatives are read by means of a projector which produces a photographic copy on sensitized paper. Projectors are also used to flash filmed records on a small screen. The advantages of microfilming include:

1. Ninety-nine percent saving in space and equipment.
2. Better preservation and protection of records stored for long periods.
3. Microfilm records are acceptable in courts of law as primary evidence.
4. According to the National Bureau of Standards, the life of films is that of 100 percent rag-content paper, which is approximately one hundred years. At the end of fifty or one hundred years a new film can be made from the old one if desired.
5. Records on film are less costly to move from one location to another.
6. Nonreplaceable records are preserved in case the originals are accidentally destroyed.
7. Refiling of individual records is eliminated, the error factor being thereby reduced.

When electronic computer equipment is utilized, magnetic tape possesses most of the advantages of microfilm plus the added advantage of extremely rapid access (even from remote locations). The data on magnetic tape can also be integrated into an existing computer program with very little effort.

SYSTEMS

A filing system consists of the arrangement of records by indexed filing captions. Since most organizations have several different classes of records, a separate filing system should be established for each class if efficiency will be increased.[5]

There are actually only two basic types of filing systems: (1) alphabetic and (2) numerical. There are, however, several forms and variations of each type. In an alphabetic system, records may be filed by (1) names of individuals, (2) organization names, (3) location (geographic and political divisions), (4) months and days, (5) topics and things (subjects), or (6) code letters.

In an alphabetic name filing system, the surname comes first, followed by first name or initial, then middle name or initial. Other identifying items, such as date of birth, location, and occupation may be added where further distinction is required.

Organizations are alphabetized by name, followed by further identification (divisions, departments, dates).

Filing systems arranged by location may have several forms: according to cities, states, or countries, or by company locations, such as territories, divisions, regions, or other geographical areas.

Filing systems established by data will normally be grouped according to the most convenient chronological period. For example, if an organization files daily bulletins by date, it might establish file folders by month since there would be no more than thirty bulletins in any one month. However, the same company might file daily folders for sales orders which numbered fifty per day.

The number of topics under which material may be filed is unlimited. To facilitate access, material can be divided into major subjects, subsubjects, and even sub-subsubjects; e.g., personnel (subject), administrative personnel (subsubject), and finally clerical personnel (sub-subsubject). Such a division reduces the time required to locate material filed under a particular topic.

Selection of the proper subject title for a record is not always an easy matter. When filing personnel are in doubt, the material should be referred to the records administrator. He is usually well acquainted with organization functions and can easily determine the proper subject title.

Still another type of alphabetic filing system uses a code composed of letters or in some cases a combination of letters and numbers (alpha-numeric). To facilitate reading, the number of letters should be kept as few as possible. The letters may have a variety of meanings as determined by their use.

In numeric filing, records may be filed by systems known as (1) consecutive numeric, (2) duplex numeric, (3) decimal numeric, (4) code numeric, (5) skip numeric, and (6) terminal-digit numeric.

Consecutive numeric filing is merely the assigning of consecutive numbers to records, beginning at some established starting point (normally 1, but it could be any number) and continuing indefinitely.

Duplex numeric filing is arranged in strict numeric sequence, with the parts of the number separated by dash (–) signs, such as 100–1, 100–12, or 14–2–6754. The numbers are arranged (first) by the first part in numeric sequence, (second) under each of the like first parts by the secondary division in numeric sequence, and (third) by the tertiary division in numeric sequence.

A decimal numeric filing system is arranged in strict numeric sequence by the ten main group numbers 000 to 900. The main subjects are assigned the hundreds (000 to 900), the subsubjects under each main subject are assigned the tens (00 to 99), and the sub-subsubjects are assigned the units (0 to 9). If further subdivision is desired, the decimal point and additional numbers may be added.

Code numeric filing is the same as the alpha-numeric filing method. The items are arranged in strict numeric sequence or in alphabetic sequence and under each alphabetic code in numeric sequence.

A skip numeric filing system is arranged to maintain a numeric and alphabetic sequence. This arrangement is rarely attained and usually requires a supplemental index, using suffix or prefix letters, numbers, or reassigning numbers, which makes coding slow.

The terminal-digit numeric system is arranged by the final digits 0 through 9, in primary, secondary, and tertiary groups of digits reading from right to left. A typical grouping might be 04, 01 04, and 13 01 04, the primary group in each of these cases being 04, the secondary group 01, and the tertiary group 13.

SUPERVISION

For those companies large enough to warrant the establishment of a separate records department, the person placed in charge should have a prominent position in the company's organizational structure. He should be charged with responsibility for: (1) planning the files, whether centralized or under centralized control; (2) the retention and disposal of records; and (3) maintaining a manual of filing operations, which contains a description of each file and all operating procedures. The specific functions he must supervise include: (1) assigning of work and fixing of responsibility for its quality and quantity; (2) indexing, cross-referencing, sorting, and arranging records; (3) producing records when required or determining who has them; (4) disposition of records; and (5) selection of the correct subject titles for records.[6]

In order that records will be available upon demand, all records personnel must be assigned specific jobs and given the necessary instructions and training required to achieve a high degree of proficiency. They must be sure persons requesting records have authorized access to them. If they do, the name of the person and department receiving the record should be obtained so that records may be easily located if required for some other use.

Records personnel must be constantly reminded to adhere strictly to disposition schedules established by the various operating departments. It is not uncommon for personnel to postpone less urgent functions, such as records disposition, in order to complete their routine daily assignments.

QUESTIONS AND PROBLEMS

1. What should be the status of a records administrator in the organizational structure in relation to the heads of operating departments? Who has final authority with respect to records control?
2. When would it not be advisable to centralize records control?
3. How should a company determine when the cost of microfilming or other forms of reproduction is justified? What factors in addition to storage costs must be considered?
4. What possible future uses for records must be considered when preparing destruction schedules?
5. Why are both classification and preclassification necessary in preparing records destruction schedules?
6. What factors must be considered when selecting a records storage area?
7. Why is it necessary for some records to be stored in their original form rather than on microfilm or other type of reproduction?
8. To what extent should the records administrator be technically qualified in all areas of records management?
9. When records control is centralized under the responsibility of a records administrator but records storage and filing is decentralized and located in operating departments, what authority does the records administrator exercise over records personnel?
10. What are the principal disadvantages of numeric filing systems?

REFERENCE NOTES

[1] "Paper Tide," First Annual Conference on Records Management, *The New Yorker*, October, 1954, p. 27.

[2] Charles B. Hicks and Irene Place, *Office Management*, 2nd ed., Allyn and Bacon, 1962.

[3] John G. Kirk, Maurice L. Crawford, and Mark H. Quay, *General Clerical Procedures*, 3rd ed., Prentice-Hall, 1959.

[4] Tom Jaski, *Electronics in Business Machines*, Barnes, 1963.

[5] Donald G. Malcom, Alan J. Rowe, and Lorimer F. McConnell, *Management Control Systems*, Wiley, 1960.

[6] Margaret K. Odell and Earl P. Strong, *Records Management and Filing Operations*, McGraw-Hill, 1947.

READING REFERENCES

Collison, Robert L., *Modern Business Filing and Archives*, Benn, 1963.

Griffin, Mary Claire, *Records Management: A Modern Tool for Business*, Allyn and Bacon, 1964.

Kahn, Gilbert, Theodore Yerian, and Jeffrey R. Stewart, *Progressive Filing and Records Management*, McGraw-Hill, 1962.

Littlefield, C. L., and Frank Rachel, *Office and Administrative Management*, 2nd ed., Prentice-Hall, 1964.

McCracken, Daniel D., Harold Weiss, and Tasi-Hwa Lee, *Programming Business Computers*, 4th printing, Wiley, 1963.

Perry, Enos C., John C. Frakes, and Joseph J. Zabornik, *Clerical Bookkeeping*, Pitman, 1962.

Stafford, Allison R., and Billie Jean Culpepper, *The Science-Engineering Secretary*, Prentice-Hall, 1963.

Terry, George R., *Office Management and Control*, 4th ed., Irwin, 1962.

19

INTERNATIONAL MANAGEMENT

International business management is the outgrowth of export and import activities that have developed rapidly since 1950. In this new, dynamic management area, many interesting and exciting problem areas exist, some of which are discussed in this chapter.

FOREIGN MARKETS

United States exports in 1960 amounted to approximately $18.3 billion. This sizable figure indicates that a considerable volume of United States goods is being marketed in foreign countries. The list of countries to which goods were exported and from which goods were received serves to point out that the United States is not the totally independent nation many believe it to be. The resources of the world are not equally distributed among its nations. On the contrary, many countries have an abundance of particular materials, far exceeding their own needs, while many, including the United States, have extreme shortages of certain materials. This establishes the basis for world trade.

A company contemplating foreign marketing must analyze many factors that are not present in domestic marketing. To begin with, there are the physical handicaps. It is difficult to sell a product from an office located several thousands of miles from its potential market. There are economical and technical problems involved in transporting the material to that market, even when sales are assured. The political nature of a country will have a significant bearing upon the cost and convenience with which a product can be marketed. A government unfavorable to imports has many tools at its disposal to discourage them.

Most of these factors, although complicated, can usually be evaluated with a reasonable degree of accuracy. However, one factor difficult to assess is the willingness and ability of people in other countries to accept products (other than certain obvious necessities) from the United States. To date, the only accurate method of determining consumer demand in many countries has been by trial and error. If a product was marketed overseas and it sold, then there was a demand for it. If it did not sell, then it was assumed that there was no demand for it and further sales efforts were curtailed.[1]

The principal barriers to determining product demand are the differences between countries in language, culture, personal values, and all those factors that influence individual motivation. Too frequently, companies will launch an overseas marketing campaign on the assumption that people are basically the same everywhere, the only real difference being language. All people may be basically the same, but from this it does not necessarily follow that their wants and desires are.

The company interested in foreign marketing must first decide between direct exporting and indirect exporting.

In direct exporting a company establishes its own marketing and distribution system in the foreign country, normally opening a branch office there staffed with its own marketing employees. Carrying direct export one step further, some organizations establish production plants in the foreign country if a sufficiently large consumer demand is anticipated. The direct-export method of foreign marketing permits the producer to maintain a maximum degree of control over the entire marketing process. He will also have immediate feedback as to the success of marketing techniques and may place as much emphasis on advertising and sales promotion as he desires. With his own staff in direct contact with consumers, he is able to provide a degree of customer service that would not otherwise be possible. The principal disadvantage of direct export is that many companies do not have the personnel experienced and qualified to conduct the necessary marketing functions.

An effective marketing program in a foreign country requires extensive information about the buying patterns and motivations of consumers. Still another disadvantage of direct export is that it usually involves a substantial financial investment. And if a company is not certain that it will be successful, it will be hesitant about making this investment.

MARKET SURVEYS ABROAD

Marketing abroad requires answers to the same questions as domestic marketing, namely:

1. Who will buy the product?
2. What type and amount of advertising are required?
3. What is the current competition and what is it expected to be in the future?
4. What merchandising and sales promotion techniques are required?
5. What share of the market can be obtained?
6. What will it cost to market the product?

Answers to these questions are more difficult to obtain about foreign markets than about domestic ones.

In most foreign countries marketing is still in the early stages of development. Most of them have only recently achieved a state of economic development enabling their citizens to buy other than the basic necessities of life. Consequently, the development of advertising, sales promotion, and merchandising has not progressed at anywhere near the rate it has in the United States. For example, a United States manufacturer desiring to market a new product in a domestic area merely has to consult one of the many advertising or marketing firms at his disposal. Domestic market surveys are conducted by highly trained and experienced personnel who are keenly aware of human behavior patterns and the factors which motivate people to buy. However, such highly trained personnel are not readily available overseas. A few highly advanced nations have their own marketing firms, but these are still relatively few in number. Some United States companies with an interest in foreign sales have established an entire staff operation in a country. Such endeavors, however, are in the pioneering stage and limited primarily to the more developed nations.

A primary consideration for most companies planning foreign sales is whether to establish a centralized or a decentralized market research operation.[2] The centralized operation retains administration and control of market research in the home office in the United States. The decentralized operation establishes foreign market research offices or uses the other country's private market research firms. A centralized market research operation has the advantage of personnel who are highly skilled in market research techniques and procedures.

The centralized market research operation may be organized according to either product or geographical area. Organization by product places greater emphasis on the requirements of individual countries. To study the problems of a particular country or groups of countries, the market research operation may be organized according to geographical areas. The staff organized under the geographic concept is usually better acquainted with the buying patterns and motivations of the people of a country than the staff organized according to the product concept. The product-oriented organization, however, makes better utilization of personnel since a separate staff is not required for each of the areas where market research is required.

The decentralized method of market research transfers responsibility for all market research functions to the country concerned. The personnel in the decentralized office are usually thoroughly acquainted with the language of the country as well as buying patterns and other factors which influence sales. In addition, they are in a position to maintain close coordination with local advertising media representatives.

The choice between centralized and decentralized market research is determined primarily by the extent of the company's anticipated operation. If the company is just getting started in the country, the centralized procedure will generally prove sufficient to conduct preliminary surveys and establish the initial marketing and sales program. For the company whose product is firmly established in a country, a full-time local market research staff will aid in future market development, especially when competition is expected to enter the market.

TRANSPORTATION AND INSURANCE

Every practice and procedure required in domestic shipments is also required for foreign ones, along with many additional requirements. In most companies the traffic manager is responsible for foreign shipments. He must not only see that functions under his immediate supervision are properly performed, but also maintain close coordination with other departments in the organization to insure that delays and improper actions do not occur.

If the traffic manager fails to utilize the best methods and procedures in carrying out his responsibilities, then this will be reflected in the organization's profits and competitive position. Unlike other areas of a business, however, the duties concerned with transportation do not always lend themselves to easy evaluation; therefore they must be assigned to highly experienced and qualified personnel. The traffic manager is usually responsible for: (1) preparation of all forms, documents, and records necessary to enter a foreign shipment; (2) packing and crating all goods; (3) selecting the most appropriate method and route of shipment; and (4) determining that all shipments are properly insured. The preparation of shipping forms, documents, and records is discussed under "Permits and Records."

Packing and Crating

Most of the losses which occur in foreign shipments are usually the result of insufficient or improper methods of packing and crating. The principal ones are:

1. Theft and pilferage of high-value or attractive commodities shipped in containers which permit easy access. Cardboard boxes, wooden boxes constructed of rotten or green lumber, and other containers which are not properly secured present attractive challenges to even the least experienced criminal.
2. Breakage, which can usually be attributed to one of several possibilities: (a) failure to disassemble delicate items to permit more secure packing, (b) failure to bolt or brace objects, (c) insufficient use of shock-absorbing material, and (d) use of too rugged insulating material.
3. Damage resulting from the use of improper materials-handling equipment.
4. Accidental loss in transit due to inadequate markings.

To avoid such losses, the traffic manager must insure that proper packing methods and materials are utilized. An excessive amount of packing can result in increased shipping charges, difficulty in handling, and difficulty in unpacking; therefore a satisfactory balance must be achieved between too little and too much. Many insurance contracts specifically state that the exporter is responsible for seeing that all goods are properly packed and crated for shipment.

Improper packing may also have an indirect effect on future relations with importers in other countries. When goods are consistently received in damaged condition, an importer will be inclined to give careful consideration before reordering from the same manufacturer.

Exporters may fail to realize all the handling that goods

receive once they have left the country. In many cases, other countries do not have the advanced materials-handling equipment available in the United States. Consequently, complete information must be obtained regarding the type of handling that goods will receive in the destination country. Many foreign importers will request the exporter to pack all shipments according to certain specifications.

Routing and Carriers

A determination of route and carrier must be based on several factors:

1. Nature of the product (size and weight)
2. When it is required at the point of destination
3. Part of the world to which it is being shipped
4. Most convenient port of departure
5. Most convenient port of arrival at the destination area
6. Most suitable inland route in the United States
7. Most suitable inland route at destination area

The above factors will normally be thoroughly evaluated with respect to time and cost. For example, where the time consideration is of greater importance than cost, air shipment may be indicated.

Insurance

Most international shipments involve goods and commodities of considerable value. The loss of a shipment can result in a substantial hardship to importers and exporters alike. In order to avoid such loss, most international shipments are completely insured.

Insurance is necessary to cover only those losses which do not result from the failure of the carrier to take proper precautions. For example, an ocean carrier is required by law to equip, man, and provision his ship in such a manner that it will be completely seaworthy and capable of withstanding all normal hazards of sea travel. The ocean carrier cannot, however, be held liable for events entirely out of his control, such as acts of God, catastrophes at sea, and criminal actions. It is to cover these events that insurance is intended.[3] When insuring a shipment the exporter should be sure that all conceivable aspects of the shipment are included and that the entire financial investment is covered. Specifically, the total financial investment is not merely the total cost of the goods being shipped, but includes related expenses, such as duties, various fees, and contingencies. Marine insurance is especially designed to cover the shipment of commodities in both domestic and foreign areas.

CUSTOM BROKERAGE

All goods which are imported into the United States must be inspected by a collector of customs at the port of entry. Customs procedures are extremely complicated and require the services of personnel who are highly experienced. The customhouse broker is a person who is thoroughly acquainted with all the forms, documents, and records which must be completed, as well as the procedures required to transport the incoming goods from the ocean carrier to their final destination. He acts as the legal agent of the importer and, as such, usually possesses the power of attorney so that he may execute various actions for the importer.

Each port of entry for goods from other countries is included in one of the customs collection districts established by the United States Customs Bureau (a branch of the Treasury Department). A collector of customs assumes ownership of all shipments received until proof of ownership has been filed by either the importer or his authorized representative (the customhouse broker).[4] Proof of ownership is normally established by presenting (1) a properly completed ocean bill of lading signed by the shipper, (2) a shipper's invoice, (3) an entry form, and (4) a consular invoice, if required. The entry form gives a complete description of the goods and indicates that all necessary duties have been paid. The consular invoice is normally required only for those items in excess of $250 in value.

Upon presentation of the required documents, the collector of customs will classify the shipment and collect any duties that are required. The amount of duty is based on either the value of the shipment or its size (bushels, tons, etc.). It is determined by a customs appraiser who inspects all incoming goods to verify their stated quantity and value. The degree of inspection will depend on the nature of the product. Generally, low-value products are not closely inspected, and even high-value products are normally inspected on a sampling basis.

After all required documents have been submitted and found to be in order, the shipment has been properly classified, and the necessary duties have been collected, the collector of customs then completes the entry and the shipment may continue to its final destination. If for some reason the importer or his authorized representative is not in agreement with the findings of the collector of cus' ms, he may file a protest with the United States Customs Bureau, which will then review the matter and make a determination on it. If the importer is still not satisfied, the matter may be appealed to the Customs Court for a final decision.

All incoming shipments from other countries must pass through a designated customs control point, even if duty-free. If the necessary documents for proper entry are not completed within a specified period of time, the collector of customs will issue a "general order," and the shipment will be sent to a government warehouse, where it will be held until proper entry has been accomplished. In cases of goods marked for shipment to a bonded warehouse at or near the port of entry, no duty is assessed until the shipment is to be released for transfer to the domestic importer. If for some reason the shipment is not accepted by a domestic importer, it may be removed from the bonded warehouse and returned to the ocean carrier for shipment back to its port of origin or some other country. No duty is assessed against shipments not accepted by a domestic importer.

The customs laws make special provisions for the importing of certain raw materials into the country. If they are to be used in the manufacture of a product which will be exported at some later date, then the duty on the raw materials shipment may be refunded to the importer. In order to receive the refund, however, the importer must file the appropriate supporting documents with the United States Customs Bureau.

As is readily apparent, the process of clearing a shipment through customs requires a great deal of time and coordination. For this reason, a customhouse broker experienced in receiving shipments is usually of invaluable assistance to an importer.

PERMITS AND RECORDS

All the shipments into and out of the country require the preparation, handling, and processing of considerably more documents and records than are required for domestic shipments. Many of these are not standardized from country to country. Therefore the traffic departments of most United States companies engaged in exporting normally have experienced personnel to complete and process them. Following is a list of some of the forms, documents, records, licenses, and permits used in foreign shipments:

1. Bill of lading
2. Invoice
3. Export declaration
4. Delivery permit
5. Booking request
6. Export license
7. Import permit
8. Dock receipt
9. Manifest
10. Consular invoice
11. Certificate of origin

Bill of lading. All commercial shipments, including those for foreign destinations, are originated by the preparation of a bill of lading. It normally contains the following information:

1. The shipper
2. The consignee
3. The port of destination
4. Parties to be notified
5. Description and weight of the shipment
6. Number of packages in the shipment
7. Space occupied by the shipment

In some foreign shipments only one bill of lading is required, called a "through bill of lading." Most foreign shipments, however, require that separate bills of lading be prepared for each major segment of the route the shipment will take. For example, the traffic department may prepare the original bill of lading for shipment of an item from one of its plants to the port of export. There a commercial agent will normally prepare another bill of lading in exchange for the domestic one received from the inland commercial carrier. Many steamship companies also issue bills of lading to acknowledge receipt of merchandise for shipment.[5]

Invoice. An invoice is a statement of the total cost or value of the goods being shipped. It is normally prepared by a sales department and then forwarded to the traffic department. From it the traffic department can determine how much insurance is required on the shipment. A copy of the invoice may then be attached to the bill of lading to act as a supporting document in calculating customs duties.

Export declaration. The United States Department of Commerce requires that each exporter prepare an export declaration which is used to classify shipments for customs purposes. The export declaration will usually contain information with respect to the shipper, the consignee, and the carrier, in addition to a complete description of the shipment, its size and value. An approved export declaration may then be used to obtain a delivery permit from a shipping company.

Delivery permit. Upon presentation of an approved export declaration, an exporter may obtain a delivery permit from the commercial (ocean or air) carrier that will perform the shipping. At the same time the exporter may make detailed shipping arrangements, including the date and time of shipment, port of shipment, pier number, and the name of the ship or air carrier. This information will be recorded on the exporting company's booking request form.

Booking request. When a plant or other manufacturing unit in a company desires to make a foreign shipment, it normally prepares a booking request form. This form authorizes the traffic department to make preliminary arrangements for the shipment. The traffic department will enter all the necessary shipping instructions on the booking request and return it to the plant or manufacturing unit, which will then release the goods for shipment.

Export license. If the goods being shipped are one of the commodities controlled by the United States Department of Commerce, then an export license will be required.

Import permit. Certain countries may require that the importer secure an import permit from his government. He must send this to the exporting company in the United States, who must in turn present it to the appropriate authorities at the port of shipment before the goods may be released.

Dock receipt. A dock receipt is a document issued by an agent of the ocean shipping company as evidence of receipt of goods. The dock receipt also serves to verify that the goods were received at the port of shipment in apparently good condition.

Consular invoice. Several importing countries require that a sworn statement be presented to their consulate in the United States, bearing certain information about shipments on which customs duties are based. The consular invoice will normally be presented in conjunction with the import permit obtained by the consignee.

Certificate of origin. A certificate of origin is merely a statement, prepared by an authorized agent, that a particular shipment originated in the United States and not some third country.

DRAFTS AND EXCHANGE

Reimbursement for sales in the United States is fairly routine. The buyer writes a check in payment for his purchase and gives it to the seller, who presents it at his bank for payment or deposit to his account. The check will then be processed through the Federal Reserve System so that the buyer's bank account will be decreased by the amount of the check. If the buyer's account has insufficient funds to cover the purchase, it is usually due to an oversight and can normally be corrected through informal channels. If the buyer had knowingly written a bad check, the seller has recourse to legal action. This is seldom necessary since a seller usually determines the credit rating of the buyer before merchandise is shipped.

International transactions, on the other hand, are characterized by:

1. Absence of a system for adjusting bank balances of all banks, domestic and foreign
2. Differences in currency among countries, both in form and value
3. Language barriers, which tend to complicate routine transactions
4. Lack of an accurate method of checking a foreign buyer's financial status and credit rating
5. Considerable expense and inconvenience in correcting discrepancies through informal channels
6. Complexity of legal recourse in processing alleged criminal actions

In foreign trade reimbursement may be accomplished in a number of ways:

1. The importer may "pay in advance," thereby eliminating any credit risk on the part of the exporter.
2. The exporter may extend credit to the importer by the use of an "open account." In this case the exporter is usually assured that the importer is a good credit risk.
3. The importer may have his bank issue a "letter of credit" by which the bank secures the transaction.
4. The exporter may be reimbursed by the use of drafts or bills of exchange. Since these have a substantial impact on international transactions, they will be discussed in detail.[6]

The use of bills of exchange for international transactions eliminates practically all the disadvantages mentioned above. For example, if a Japanese firm wishes to import a particular United States product, it may obtain a bill of exchange at its bank in Japan and send it to the United States exporter. The United States exporter will take the bill of exchange to his bank to be discounted (exchanged for the United States currency). This is made possible by the fact that foreign banks maintain accounts in United States banks (and vice versa). When the United States bank discounts the bill of exchange, it merely withdraws the appropriate amount from the account of the Japanese bank that issued the bill of exchange.

Bills of exchange also affect the economic status of the countries involved. For example, their price (known as the "rate of exchange") depends on their availability. If they are readily available in foreign exchange markets, they can be obtained at a relatively low cost. If, however, they are in short supply, then their price will be considerably higher. Their availability is determined by the demand for them.

The question arises as to what factors influence the demand for bills of exchange. The answer is that their demand is determined by the balance of trade that exists between various countries. If a country has a favorable balance of trade (exports exceed imports), then the flow of bills of exhange into that country will be greater than the flow out of the country. Thus the country enjoying the favorable balance of trade will have a surplus of bills of exchange (relative demand being low—and their price as well). Therefore, as a general rule, if a country enjoys a favorable balance of trade, the rate of exchange will be low; if it does not have a favorable balance of trade, the rate of exchange will tend to be high. When a country's rate of exchange is high, then exporters in that country tend to benefit (at the expense of importers who desire to purchase the bills of exchange). When a country's rate of exchange is low, then importers tend to benefit (at the expense of exporters). The most satisfactory condition, it would appear, is to have an even balance of trade (exports equal to imports) and therefore an even rate of exchange.

The goal of a country's foreign exchange program should be to strive for the maximum development of its resources. Such a program places emphasis on exporting those commodities which can be produced most efficiently and importing those which can be more efficiently produced by other nations. For example, the United States has the raw materials, skilled personnel, and effective production methods required to produce certain electronic devices. Most other countries do not have the resources to produce these devices as efficiently. Brazil, on the other hand, is ideally suited by climate, land, and labor for the production of coffee, a commodity which the United States cannot produce efficiently. It would not be logical for Brazil to spend substantial sums of money on the production of electronic instruments, which it can purchase from the United States for less, or for the United States to spend large sums of money raising coffee. By maintaining an even balance of trade all countries can experience an efficient rate of development and achieve the highest possible standard of living. Therefore, rather than striving for a favorable balance of trade, each nation should attempt to keep the import-export balance at an even level. If the favorable balance continues for too long a time, the country that experiences it may find that debtor countries are unable to redeem the bills of exchange which it issued.

QUESTIONS AND PROBLEMS

1. What services does a customhouse broker perform for importers? Why don't most importers prefer to perform these services themselves?
2. On what basis are duty charges assessed?
3. Why are some exporters hesitant about being reimbursed by im-importers on an "open account" basis?
4. Why is a favorable balance of trade not necessarily a desirable situation?
5. What are the principal limitations in conducting market surveys in foreign countries?
6. What is direct exporting?
7. What are the advantages of a centralized market research operation?
8. What is an "export declaration" used for?
9. What are the principal considerations in selecting the mode of transportation for overseas shipments?
10. What factors must be considered in packing a product for overseas shipment?

REFERENCE NOTES

[1] Alexander O. Stanley, "How to Make a Profit Overseas," *Nation's Business,* January, 1960, p. 36.

[2] S. Watson Dunn, *International Handbook of Advertising,* McGraw-Hill, 1964.

[3] Charles A. Taff, *Management of Traffic and Physical Distribution,* 3rd ed., Irwin, 1964.

[4] Richard C. Colton and Edmund S. Ward, *Industrial Traffic Management,* Traffic Service Corp., New York, 1959.

[5] Kenneth V. Flood, *Advanced Traffic Management,* William C. Brown, 1959.

[6] Charles A. Taff, *op. cit.*

READING REFERENCES

Baker, Robert L., *Business Leadership in a Changing World,* McGraw-Hill, 1962.

Bartels, Robert, *Comparative Marketing: Wholesaling in Fifteen Countries,* Irwin, 1963.

Bryson, George D., *American Management Abroad: Business Executive Overseas,* Harper & Row, 1961.

Fayerweather, John, *Management of International Operations,* McGraw-Hill, 1960.

Jefferys, James B., and Derek Knee, *Retailing in Europe,* Macmillan, 1962.

Miller, E. Willard, *A Geography of Manufacturing,* Prentice-Hall, 1962.

Payne, Bruce, *Planning for Company Growth,* McGraw-Hill, 1963.

Robinson, Richard D., *Cases in International Business,* Holt, Rinehart and Winston, 1962.

PART IV

ANALYSIS OF THE ADMINISTRATIVE
SKILLS OF MANAGEMENT

The administrative skills of planning, organizing, motivating, directing, and controlling make up the "guide wheel" of management. While the problems in an organization arise in the technical area (the bicycle's rear wheel), the solutions to those problems come about through the application of administrative skills. A basic understanding of them and their application is vital to the successful operation of an organization, whether it be small, medium, or large in size.

The administrative skills should not be isolated from the other parts in our bicycle analogy; they do not stand alone but operate in relation to the technical parts of the organization, and they are practiced by each individual manager, whether he be a section head, department manager, division manager, plant superintendent, or member of top management. Here the word "skills" is used purposely to communicate the idea that practice of these functions will improve them. They must be used, practiced, and applied constantly by the individual manager; he must be constantly aware of his planning, his directing, his controlling, etc. These skills are so fundamental that a manager will automatically use them even though he has never formally heard of or studied them, but when they are used consciously and purposefully, they become far more effective. Understanding them is therefore of prime importance to the person aspiring to manage or who is managing.

In the pages that follow, a more detailed treatment of the administrative skills reviews and builds upon their introduction in Chapter 4 of Part I.

20

THE SKILL OF PLANNING

Planning is the first logical step in the solution of a management problem. A manager's effectiveness will be measured largely by his ability to solve the problems that come his way. To do this, he must know how to plan and how to motivate others to follow his plan.

THE NATURE AND SCOPE OF PLANNING[1]

Planning is anticipating. It is done by everyone in the organization. The sweeping out of an office is planned. The work of a maintenance crew is planned. Corporate growth is planned. Some planning involves minutes; some years. Some involves one man; some hundreds. There are long- and short-range plans, administrative and operative plans, one-time plans and "five-year rolling plans." But the biggest difference between plans is this: As the level of responsibility *increases,* the facts available *decrease.*

A fact is something on which a number of experts agree. Facts can involve numbers, dates, and places. They can relate to physical things: desks, buildings, lines. They can concern actions, trends, or processes: people are moving to the suburbs; leisure time is increasing; water boils at 212° Fahrenheit at sea level.

In planning, the higher one is in an organization, the more information he has, but facts that relate to the decisions he must make are few.

For example, when the floor is to be swept, there are an

abundance of time-place, physical, and action facts. Everything needed to plan the work can be seen at a glance.

By contrast, what are the facts on which corporate growth is planned? What are the facts about state and national economies five or ten years from now? What are the facts regarding changes in laws and regulations? What facts have we concerning processes or trends that might compete with our product? What about materials, labor, financing? What facts have we about population shifts and customer location. Who will our market be? Where will they be? What will they want from us? The facts are few, the risks are great, and the assumptions naggingly many.

Fig. 2 pictures the general relationship of planning to the other managerial functions, and to nonmanagerial work (e.g., selling, observing, making external contacts, doing operative work, etc.), at two key levels of management. The basic proposition is that planning increases in significance at higher levels.

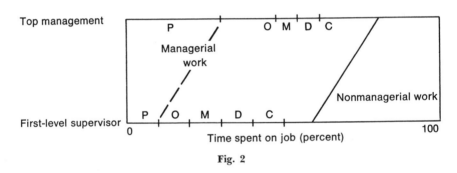

Fig. 2

The length of time covered by planning varies with the level of management. In general, the higher the managerial level, the longer the time period covered by the planning. The lowest-level supervisor is usually planning the immediate future: Who is immediately available to handle that emergency call? The president and the board of directors are involved in long-range planning: What will be the primary source of energy in 1990? The supervisory level, of course, is expected to concentrate on the managerial skills required to assure that the plan will be achieved, i.e., motivating, directing, and controlling. A rough guide to the emphasis, time-wise, on planning at various levels follows:

Level of Management	*Time Span Emphasized*
Top management	Long-run (ten to twenty years)
Middle management	Intermediate (one to ten years)
Lowest-level management	Immediate (now to one year)

Managers plan objectives, policies, plans and programs, organization structure and job content, and standards of quantity, quality, time, and expense. Planning will be briefly related to each of these.

Objectives. The starting point for all planning, organizing, motivating, directing, and controlling activity is the objectives of the firm. Objectives identify perimeters of allowable action. Thus they "manage" the broadest activities of managerial and operative personnel. An example of their use in managing follows:

Company X has, as one of its over-all objectives, leadership in its industry. In 1958 it had 20 percent of the total annual sales of its industry. Three other firms had higher percentages. Company X sets 50 percent of industry sales as the quantitative measure of leadership.

Company X established the following company-wide sales objectives:

Year	Sales Expected Percentage of Industry
1962	25
1963	30
1964	35
1965	40
1966	45
1967	48
1968	50

The president of the company directs the vice president in charge of sales to implement these sales objectives with quantitative goals by product line for each year. He observes, further, that these objectives will be his major test of sales effectiveness.

Policies. Policies are especially useful in providing guidelines for managerial subordinates. Lower-level managers will find in established policies guidance for their planning activities. As an example, a personnel policy prohibiting the hiring of relatives of current employees limits the hiring plans of subordinate managers.

The use of a policy manual provides an effective perimeter of planning action for all managers. Requiring them to check the manual to make certain that a contemplated action is allowable establishes reliable control over individual managers in the more important areas of their decision-making.

Participation in policy-making also has important supervisory results. If a manager's opinions have at least been requested prior to the formulation of a policy at a higher echelon, he is more likely to abide by the policy than if it were handed down to him as an accomplished fact. Such participation usually generates in managers a willingness to sell their subordinates on the value of the policy. The absence of such participation encourages "copping out" by such bland statements as "Don't argue with me, I'm not on the policy-making level." The wholehearted support of company policies by subordinate managers insures their success.

Plans and programs. Plans and programs may be in considerable detail or broad outline. They may be intended only as general, over-all guides to subordinate planning action, or they may be considered detailed, rigid instructions for such action.

Organization charts, organization manuals, and job descriptions. The absence of an organization chart and/or manual virtually insures some overlapping and duplicating of authority and responsibility by subordinate managers. To obtain the maximum utilization of all personnel, the relationships of work to work, people to work, and people to people must be planned. In this way duplication of effort is minimized and each employee can be held accountable for results. Since a part of that accountability involves his supplying data to and/or using the end products of others, each subordinate must be furnished with information regarding his cooperation with others.

Planning obligations can best be portrayed by a job description setting forth the objectives, duties, and responsibilities of a particular work assignment. It may be a relatively simple listing of duties or an elaborate, involved delineation of all aspects of the assignment. In either event, the job description, by telling the worker what we want him to do, helps management control his output.

The three tools mentioned above—chart, manual, and job description—establish a perimeter of activity and pattern of relationships for each position in the enterprise. Even with the use of all three tools, however, it is difficult to plan and control the degree of responsibility and authority (i.e., degree of activity) intended.

Standards. Another product of planning effort is standards of quantity, quality, time, and expense. Standards are essentially short-run objectives. In general, managerial standards are broader than those for operative personnel. Thus for managers we establish broad standards for the return on sales or investment, departmental or divisional expense ratios, ethical conduct, and other matters. Specific standards for individual managers will vary depending upon the activity for which each is responsible. We might set a standard of X man-days per thousand man-days as an allowable loss through work stoppages for the Personnel Group. The Power Group might be judged on a standard of Y cents per kilowatt-hour of generation costs.

Qualitative *and* quantitative standards must generally be established for each segment of the business. These will include standards of service and conduct, physical standards, personnel standards, and performance standards.

Whatever the nature and kind of managerial standards established, they should be:

1. Reasonably stable. They should be expected to be in use, without substantial change, for some time in the future.
2. Capable of fairly precise definition. It should be possible to state them in written form so that their users can understand what is intended.
3. Capable of measurement. They should be subject to measurement under all conditions and situations in which they will be used.

FACTORS AFFECTING PLANNING

The managerial environment within which planning takes place is very important. A manager may work for a superior who does not appreciate planning. The problem in that case is to avoid being "caught" planning, for the superior is apt to mistake it for idleness. Consequently, with some superiors we run the risk of being discredited for planning.

The physical environment may not be conducive to planning. The manager may have to plan in an office completely lacking in privacy. The distraction may be noise and traffic or subordinates and superiors who stop in to check with the manager.

Along with a variety of internal considerations which affect planning, many external factors must be considered. These include such questions as:

What is the proper role of the Federal Government in producing and distributing energy? What is the government's attitude toward business in general, and the utility industry specifically? To what extent is this attitude shared by the state and local governmental units which are involved in activities directly affecting the company? To what extent should the company give consideration to a change in influence within one or another political party? What effect will the continuation of present governmental fiscal policy have on the company's financial planning?

What are the population trends and its composition by age, income level, educational level, etc.? What is happening to population in the company's operating territory? How will population trends affect personnel requirements for the company?

What are the probable business trends in general in the United States? Which of these trends, if any, will be beneficial to the company? Which, if any, will be harmful to the company? How will the operation of other businesses affect the internal operations of the company?

These are but a small sample of the considerations which must be given to external factors in planning. Good planning requires close attention to events outside as well as those within the firm.

CONTROLLING THE PLAN

In planning, our needs, forecasts, decisions, and schedules all relate to our appraisal of where we are and where we want to be when the plan is completed. Fig. 3 provides a rough check list to

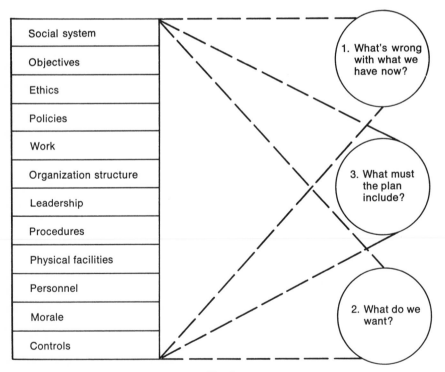

Fig. 3

help us be sure that our appraisal is complete. If used with judgment, the check list can be the backbone of the planning function. Each category on the list is a broad one. Altogether, they can explore a business from end to end. The first three items on the list would be in the same sequence for any plan. The order of the remaining items is typical but not ironclad.

The check list helps us look more carefully at the questions we ask ourselves, whatever our level in the organization, as we anticipate or plan by:

Desiring to change things
Determining what we want to change
Inventorying our present position and our planned position
Locating the knowns and unknowns, facing the risks,
    weighing alternatives, getting more facts
Deciding and firmly setting our objective
Establishing our schedule
Preparing to act on the schedule

Once we have analyzed our plan against the check list, we must establish a time limit for the activity covered by the plan, together with check points along the way by which we can measure progress. Sometimes the check points can be set out in time periods —e.g.: "Sam, check with me on this at the end of each month." Sometimes the check points must be keyed to events—e.g.: "Sam, check with me when the foundation is ready for the turbines." No plan is complete until certain points are established where progress can be appraised and corrective action taken if required.

APPROACH TO PLANNING

The basic planning concepts are limited in number. They run from the least formalized, trial and error, to the most formal, the scientific concept. Most managers use all of them at one time or another, but each manager will exhibit a tendency to use one concept most often.

Trial and error. This is simply trying whatever solution to the problem comes to mind, and continuing to try other solutions until the problem has been solved. One objection to this approach is obvious. It is most expensive. Yet in good times the momentum of prosperity may carry a company over much trial-and-error planning. Subordinates will find that they must be constantly prepared for changes if this method is used.

Imitative. In this method the planner copies the procedures others have used to solve the same or similar problems. Sometimes it is possible to find the solution for your problem in another company's solution, though the other company's methods were developed in a different environment, and perhaps even for a basically different problem. Usually so much information, development, analysis, and modification are involved that it proves to be very expensive and time-consuming as contrasted with the scientific method.

Scientific. The most advanced of the planning concepts is the scientific approach. Here the manager adopts the technique proven effective through scientific research. He becomes scientific in his approach to planning. Thus he asks himself, "What is the real problem here? Do elderly workers really want wage increases, as they say, or are they actually searching for recognition?" He then goes on to develop as much information as he can on the problem, tests each possible approach, and selects the most likely one from his tests.

Thought Processes

Since thinking is a primary tool in planning, a glance at three ways of thinking might be helpful.

"Trial and error" characterizes research thinking. It is poking into the unknown, trying a hundred or a thousand experiments to find the one that works. An illustration is Edison's search for a light bulb filament. In its simplest form, it is random effort; a more sophisticated version would isolate the "riper" areas rather than probing at random. The formal description of this would be "formulating an hypothesis."

"Step-by-step" reasoning is characterized by four distinct phases. The first involves "cramming"—gathering all possible information and ideas about a subject. The second phase is "frustration." You have all the facts, but they just don't add up. Phase three introduces "insight." The facts suddenly, almost magically, fall into place. The final phase is "testing," in which the solution is given good stiff tests to make sure it works.

The third type of thought process, "emotional" thinking, hardly deserves to be dignified as thought. This is thinking based on what we would like to believe rather than what is true. It is the sort of thinking that causes a grown man to believe that he can actually take that curve at sixty miles an hour. Although not a constructive mental process, it is an extremely popular one.

PLANNING TECHNIQUES

Creative Thinking

This is the discovery of fresh alternatives to meet new or recurring situations. In planning, it would be the original determination of an effective, economical basis of action for the achievement of specified objectives. One of the principal tools of creative thinking is brainstorming.

Brainstorming is an idea-stimulating, creative conference in which all participants are encouraged to put forward any ideas on the selected subject that come to mind. A time limit is set, and no evaluation of ideas is made; the only aim is to generate as many as possible. Brainstorming is a technique applied and refined by Alex Osborn, a New York advertising executive.

Countless business situations offer opportunities for the modified use of brainstorming. Developing solutions to problems, approaches to new standards, or policies that may be needed in the future are illustrations. The process itself increases tolerance and respect for the ideas of others and encourages more constructive group thinking.

There are four rules to be followed: (1) Don't prejudge ideas. (2) Free-wheel; don't fence your thinking in. (3) Go for volume; the more ideas, the better. (4) Hitchhike; add on to the ideas of others.

If there is a secret to brainstorming, it is withholding judgment until last. Free-wheeling means jumping all over the map. As to volume, you'll be doing well if 10 percent of the ideas generated are worth pursuing. But without brainstorming, that 10 percent might never have come to the surface. Hitchhiking is speaking up promptly when the idea someone else contributes gives you a thought. These thoughts seem the most perishable and the most productive of all. So the "hitchhiker" is usually given priority; if he snaps his fingers, he is called on next.

Osborn tells of a hitchhike that occurred in the Navy. A destroyer was at anchor when the lookout noticed the current carrying a mine toward the side of the ship. A typical Navy wit suggested that all hands line up amidship and blow the mine away. The officer of the desk hitchhiked from this idea to the use of fire hoses. The jets of water held the mine off until the ship could move into position to destroy it by gunfire.

Certain phrases denoting prejudgment are not allowed in a brainstorming session. Here are samples:

"But that didn't work in 1955."
"We can't afford it."
"It's against policy."
"The boss won't like it."
"We've never done it before."
"It won't work because . . ."

Such so-called "killer phrases" are so common in business that none of us can prevent an occasional one from popping out. Try to keep new killers from slipping out, but don't feel like a wet blanket if it happens to you.

Who is to judge the ideas is usually determined before the session starts—a committee, the boss, or a staff member, whatever appears to fit your situation.

Here are some pointers that may help if you are chosen to lead a brainstorming session:

1. Open the meeting in the shortest possible time. Tell your group what is wanted, how brainstorming works, and how their ideas will be used.

2. Start out with some random subject just to get the group in the mood. Spend five minutes brainstorming the uses for a brick around the house or some other light, "warm-up" subject.

3. Before the session is called, judge the scope of your questions. There are "spade" and "steam-shovel" questions. One is narrow, the other broad. A steam-shovel question is, "How can we improve morale?" A spade question is, "How can we get more people to come to the Friday evening dance?"

4. Use "who, what, why, where, when, how" questions. They stimulate brainstorms. "Do or don't" questions stimulate judgment.

Creativity seems to increase when several people work face to face in a judgment-free atmosphere. Use it to develop new angles, product names, new shapes, sizes, colors, new uses for tools or equipment. A power company in Washington state, facing the problem of ice breaking mountain power lines with its weight, brainstormed a new use for equipment. They flew a helicopter low over the lines, and the downdraft blew the ice off before it got too thick.

One parting idea on brainstorming. Don't prejudge it; *try* it sometime.

Critical Thinking

The "logic" in popular use for hundreds of years was founded almost entirely on the "all-or-none" concept. Recently, people have come to believe that life's problems are not solved on the "all-or-none" basis. Problems are not "black or white"; they are shades of gray.

Following are some mental habits and tricks about which we should "think critically" when we are faced with them:

Charged words. This is the use of "loaded," usually highly colorful language. "The tiny hands of these frail little infants reach out for your contribution to maintain the immortal spark of life in their fragile little bodies."

The selected instance. This is taking one example and making a Federal case out of it. "Jane's cigarette caused a fire in the waste basket; therefore women should not be allowed to smoke."

Extension. You say "some." Your listener implies that you said "all." You may say, "There was a complaint about the four-way stop streets in Centerville." Your listener may then say, "I see, the people in Centerville do not like the four-way stop streets."

Compromise. In some cases, this is a matter of your giving up some of what you believe in and my giving up some of what I believe in so that both of us can agree on something that neither of us believes in.

Repetition. This is the standard advertising device. It is merely "grinding it into them." It is saying over and over again, "Joe deserves a raise," "LSMFT," or "Ford sells more cars than anyone."

Confidence. When you have no logical argument, when none of the facts are on your side, there is only one thing to do. Get to your feet, beat on the table, and use confidence as a substitute for ignorance.

Authority. This is using your own authority or that of someone in charge to gain your point. "I know how you feel, but I had lunch with the boss yesterday, and his feelings are different from yours. Would you care to reconsider?"

Analogy. This is merely saying that one thing is like something else. "A good business is run like a good football team." Analogies are wonderful devices to convey a general idea, but beware of them when attempting to solve a detailed problem.

Either or. This is an "all-or-none" device. "Either you give me a raise or I quit." The maker of this statement is putting himself in a precarious position. He might have done better by using a degree rather than the extremes.

The bandwagon. This is the idea that fifty million Frenchmen are *always* correct. Recognize that every good idea the world has ever had came from the mind of one lonesome soul. He was definitely in the minority. Also, the answer that is right for fifty million Frenchmen may not be right for you.

Prestige. This is an effort to sway you by saying that others who have prestige are doing it. "We should do it in Riverton because the people in Cincinnati do it, and they were written up in *Life* magazine."

Geometry. This is an analogy that appeals to the eye, a picture or drawing that "is like" the subject under discussion. For example, if you have three good points and one rather weak one, represent them as the four corners of a square. People commonly accept the proposition that each of the four points is of equal value.

There are four points to consider in improving our thought processes:

1. Do I understand the question and do I understand exactly what I am to do about it?
2. Is my decision consistent with my usual methods of deciding or is it something that I have chosen merely because I happen to have wet feet today?
3. Is this Cloud Eighteen thinking or is it something that I can use? If it is useful, prove it by showing me where I can swing into action immediately on it.
4. If I am faced with four alternatives, the one that is simplest to me— the one that I can best understand and explain—is probably the one that will work best for me.

Operations Research

During World War II a new aproach to planning was devised. A task force of "thinkers" from a variety of disciplines was assembled to bring the systems of their diverse areas of specialization to bear upon the problem at hand. Thus a medical specialist in a team investigating the problem of German submarine wolf packs preying on Allied shipping is credited with suggesting a system of depth bombing based upon one of the systems of the human anatomy. It proved highly successful.

In the post World War II period business firms have utilized the technique of operations research to solve such diverse problems as distribution patterns for products, warehousing systems, determination of advertising appropriations, and the scheduling of flights by commercial airlines. The use of the brainstorming technique within an operations research group is fairly common.

Simulation

Simulation, including model-building or simulation in miniature, is being increasingly used in business. One of the most highly publicized is the use of mock-up cockpits of jet airliners to train pilots to fly new types of jet aircraft. The pilot is exposed, in the form of data changes on his instruments, physical reorientation of the cockpit itself, and terrain changes on a motion picture screen in front of the cockpit, to a close approximation of landing, take-off, loss of power in one or all engines, loss of braking action in touchdown, etc. If he fails to react as he should, the company does not lose lives and a $5.5-million airliner.

Similar applications are being made to managerial business problems. Sales managers, for example, are asked to "role-play," before a group of peers, the presentations they will be making to their subordinates on new products, new promotional programs, etc. Constructive criticism from his peers should make the actual presentation more effective.

For many business problems, the best approach is to construct a model of the problem. The familiar weather map is really a mathematical model. From the information available, we can "put in" to the model certain alternatives and "get out" rather precise answers. That is the basic use of models: they enable us to work with "inputs and outputs" that are accurate representations of situations our plans may call for in the future. The model lets us "put our toe in the water" without the risk of getting in over our heads.

The future in planning and forecasting seems paved with simulations. The Army can now fight "model" tank battles, down to trees and bushes on the terrain, without moving from their computing machines.

The use of certain kinds of models, primarily mathematical ones, has been referred to as "gaming." One form of gaming is the waiting-line theory, which is a mathematical way of solving problems involving a situation in which people or things are arrayed. Thus determining the number of lines a commercial cafeteria should have at various times of the day can be handled by this form of gaming.

PLANNING RESPONSIBILITIES

From the very definition of management it is obvious that every executive at every level is responsible for planning. Top executives must formulate broad plans for the whole enterprise. Those at lower levels have to develop plans for their departments or units to carry out their share of the plans handed to them from above.

Yet troublesome questions arise about planning responsibility. One of these concerns the degree to which staff departments should plan for the line organization. For example, if a staff marketing department is given complete authority to develop marketing programs which must be carried out by a sales force which is part of a line division, then the line is asked to assume responsibility for something over which it lacks authority. On the other hand, if the staff authority is merely advisory, the staff may have to beg for the acceptance of its plans. There is no single answer as to the best relationship in all cases. In each case the issue must be faced squarely, and all involved must clearly understand the degree of responsibility that is to be distributed between staff and line.

In recent years there has been much discussion in management literature about the desirability of delegating planning responsibility to lower levels. This view is supported by four arguments: first, that it is a means of strengthening or developing stronger junior executives; second, that it reduces the planning burden of higher executives; third, that it results in better planning, because lower-level executives are more familiar with the problems and conditions that will be encountered in carrying out the plans; and, fourth, that it results in higher morale, since people tend to believe more strongly in, and will work harder to attain, goals they have set for themselves.

These arguments are persuasive, but it must be remembered that the only way that top executives can be assured that lower-level planners are not running off in many different directions at once is to place greater emphasis on control. Thus relatively more planning at lower levels implies relatively more controlling at higher levels.

ALTERNATIVES

Two specific planning approaches are of special interest. One is the production of alternate plans. The other is segmenting —cutting the big parts into smaller, more precise ones.

Alternatives give us a safer feeling when we are flying. If we can't land at our destination, we know alternate courses have been *planned* in advance.

The Arabian American Oil Company is in a business that demands a great number of precise, well-understood, alternate plans. It must (and does) plan for 100 percent evacuation in three months, in two weeks, *and* immediately. Plans for routing oil to its customers are based on the possibility of one or several countries prohibiting the transportation of oil across their land. Lease arrangements call for "turning back" certain land each year and developing new fields. This necessitates plans for homes, schools, sanitation, water supplies *if* the company is allowed to develop certain areas or *if* other areas must be turned back unexpectedly. Because of the numerous variables in this business, alternate plans are almost as essential as the oil itself.

SEGMENTS

Segmentation breaks the major problems into more specific parts. It appears that the survival of American Motors automobiles is due to their appeal not to "the public," but to a specific segment with specific automotive requirements. The sales increases in recent years of such diverse automobiles as the Jaguar, Renault Dauphine, and the tiny "perambulating phone booth," the Isetta, illustrate the appeal to segmented markets.

The Air Force uses the segmentation idea in planning purchases. It is not enough to know how many hydraulic pumps are on the aircraft and how many are in stock. By segmenting, it gets a much more precise picture: How many are at the bases now? How many are up for repair? Of that number, how many will be scrapped? How long does it take to repair the pumps? How many does this indicate must be purchased to fill the "pipeline" from the aircraft to the maintenance shop and back again to the bases?

These questions are but a very few of the segments that aid in planning a precise, long-range purchase.

ROLLING PLANS

"Five-year plans" have been common in government and business for generations. Their main drawback is their lack of flexibility. This has been overcome to a degree by "rolling plans." The rolling plan is a five-year plan that is analyzed carefully, and modified as needed, annually. After the analysis, it is pushed one additional year into the future. At all times, the plan is no more than five years, and no less than four, ahead of the daily running of the business.

The need for long-range planning which incorporates social and moral responsibilities within its framework is the subject of the following comment by Peter Drucker, one of the best-known authors and consultants in the field of management:

Two important trends in American management in the last generation have been (1) the emphasis on long-range planning and systematic organization to achieve formulated objectives, and (2) the steady recognition of the social and moral responsibilities of management, calling for broader skills and higher performance standards.

While the effect of these two developments together has been to transform the theory and practice of management in this country, for the most part they have occurred independently of each other. They have been sponsored by different people speaking different languages, and have been pointed to different ends. An outside observer might well be justified in believing that the two are entirely disconnected phenomena.

But of course both developments pertain to the same activity: the management of the business enterprise. Both are carried out by the same managers at the same time. The manager is not an "economic" man making practical decisions from 9 to 10, and a "social" or "moral" man discharging broad responsibilities from 10 to 11.

The need to integrate the two trends of modern management into one managerial theme has therefore been felt by thoughtful managers for a long time. Every year it becomes more imperative. Increasingly the business objectives of the manager will become unattainable unless the long-range planning includes, built right into it, the managing of men and the realization of basic ethical and spiritual values. And increasingly the social and moral needs of the business enterprise can only be satisfied by and through rational, systematic, and long-range business planning.[2]

PROGRAMS

According to one classification, the kinds of plans used by business may be divided into two categories: (1) single-use plans, applicable in a specific situation, and (2) standing plans, which are designed to be used over and over again.

Programs are single-use plans which plot a course of action to fit the needs of a situation, and which are "used up" when the goal is reached. Such programs may be general or special.

General Programs

A general or major program is one that plots the principal steps to be taken to accomplish a business objective of broad scope. Professor William H. Newman of the Graduate School of Business at Columbia University gives the following illustration:

The character of a general program is illustrated by the over-all planning for a vegetable cannery that was recently purchased from the former owner-manager by an investment group, which installed a new man as president. Three members of the investment group also had interests in grocery wholesaling companies, and part of the general scheme was that the cannery would serve as a significant source of supply for these wholesale houses. The new president proceeded to map out a general program. The types of vegetables to be canned were decided first, and then a sales forecast was prepared showing estimated sales of each product to the associated grocery houses and to the general trade for the next three years. On the basis of these figures it was possible to ascertain the capacity of plant and equipment that would be needed and to make general plans for additions to the facilities. Another feature of the cannery program was deciding what key, full-time personnel should be maintained, and a plan was devised for additions and for dropping some of those already on the payroll. Inasmuch as canning is highly seasonal, it was also necessary to make estimates of fluctuations in the inventory that would be kept. And finally, on the basis of the foregoing decisions and estimates of cost and selling prices, the financial requirements were determined and a plan for financing the cannery was set up. By developing this comprehensive program, each part of which dovetailed into the other parts, the president was able to anticipate possible trouble or bottlenecks and arrange to meet these difficulties. Moreover, a basis was provided to guide the more detailed planning for several phases of the cannery operations.[3]

Special Programs

Special programs are single-use plans that deal with one phase of a company's operations.

This may be illustrated by the planning that a motor truck transportation company did to change its marketing and personnel-shifting arrangements.

The company, which operated eighteen terminals in key cities, was administered by a staff of corporate executives, including a president, marketing manager, highway operations manager, traffic manager, controller, and terminal operations manager. All these men operated in a staff capacity except the president, to whom the others reported, and the terminal operations manager, to whom the eighteen terminal managers reported.

Terminal managers were responsible for sales and for local customer service. For various reasons, it was decided to separate the sales function from the terminal operations function, and to make sales a line function within the marketing department. This involved establishing a new pattern of supervision, with three new posts of regional sales managers created to supervise the sixty-three salesmen in the company.

Some of the major steps involved:

1. Defining the enlarged responsibilities of the marketing manager
2. Defining the more limited responsibilities of the terminal operations manager
3. Defining the job of the new regional sales manager
4. Defining the more limited responsibilities of the local terminal managers
5. Deciding upon the evaluative criteria to be used in judging performance of the above positions
6. Selecting personnel from among the sales-oriented terminal managers to fill the posts of regional sales managers, and arranging for their training for a new work assignment
7. Selecting personnel within the organization to be promoted to the three terminal manager posts being vacated, and arranging for their training
8. Planning all other relocations of personnel involved in the accomplishment of Step 7
9. Communicating the reasons for and the nature of the change to all company personnel affected by it

There were other ramifications, but the point is that all foreseeable steps were plotted in advance, a timetable was established for the accomplishment of each, and the responsibility for each phase was clearly defined. The change was, therefore, brought about in an orderly manner, with a minimum amount of friction and unanticipated problems.

POLICIES

Policies are a form of plan designed to be used over and over again. Other types of continuing or standing plans, such as systems, procedures, and methods, are discussed later in this chapter.

Nature of Policies

Policies are guides to objectives. They are our position on how and why we act in certain ways. The "how" outlines the general action to be taken; the "why" gives the reason for the action. Here is a policy statement on personnel that is used by the Nationwide Insurance Companies of Columbus, Ohio:

The payment of higher wages when consistent with lowered unit costs is a sound economic principle. Furthermore, the predominant wage policy of a free society is to compensate according to contribution.

It is a general personnel policy, accordingly, to provide the highest possible financial incentives to employees consistent with the ability of the Companies to pay, and to compensate according to the individuals occupying the various jobs, to the attainment of the Companies' objectives.

If the *reason* for the policy is not included, "the right thing" may be done in the wrong way. For example, if the policy is "buy locally," it would be applied one way if the reason were "to speed delivery" and another way if the reason were "to create maximum local goodwill."

Second, the reason is a built-in way of keeping policies current. Reasons sometimes become outdated; prohibiting smoking on the job because the public feels smoking is wrong is an example. Policies can easily be changed when they are no longer in tune with our times.

A third reason for stating the principle which is the basis of a policy is the tendency of people to make up their own motives for policy. For example, most firms have a policy of supporting community welfare projects. This is not because they are anxious to get business from that governmental unit, but because they believe the company should act the way any good citizen of the community is expected to act.

To avoid misinterpretation, policies should be written clearly and simply. Writing a clear and simple policy takes time, talent, and hard work. Their number ought to be held to a minimum. Keep in mind a commanding officer's comment during World War II: "If the good Lord can run the universe with Ten Commandments, we don't need forty policies for this division."

A few quality policies for each part of the organization is the goal. Those policies should be built to last. This means that they should be broad enough to ride out the typical bumps and jolts of a business year.

A side issue here is the difference between a rule and policy. A rule does *not* allow judgment ("No smoking"); policy *does*.

Formulating Policy

In formulating policy, there are several things to be done:

Determining need. Is it a repetitive situation? Is it important enough to warrant a policy on it?

Preparing policy. The guide to action and principle is prepared in rough draft form. The draft is checked to see that it is compatible with existing policies. It is tested and retested until it is clear to those who will use it. Then final draft is prepared and presented to the level accountable for it for their study, adjustments, and acceptance.

Introducing policy. The policy is published so that it will get into the hands of the people who will use it. It is then impressed upon their minds by meetings and discussions; if need be, it is reworded to get the idea across. The goal here is to "sell" the new policy in such a way that it will be used, and used *as intended*.

Use of Policies

Routine use. After proper introduction, 95 percent of a policy's life should consist of its calm, consistent, routine application to the daily work situation. The policy should guide the manager in his decision-making.

Interpretations. There is a rough similarity between policy and law. Both run into unusual situations. Both call for interpretations. The one sin is to say, "Do it because it's policy." If it doesn't seem to fit, check with the man above you. Re-examine the reasons for the policy; check the intentions of the men who formulated it as they apply to your current problem. Policy is not written for blind acceptance. Managers are not hired as "blind accepters." Policy is good reason; search for it, find it, apply it.

Follow-up. Keep the few policies pertinent, fresh, and useful. Review them once each year to be sure that none are obsolete, and that there are no gaps that really require policy. Check to see that the policies are being applied on the job; if not, why not? Consider the number of interpretations. Should the policy be rewritten?

There is a much broader policy-making level in most businesses than we normally assume. Top management makes general policies that govern the entire company. But middle management also makes policy. In fact, every manager who is faced with important repetitive situations should prepare a few sound policies to communicate his thinking to the people he directs.

In summary, policies help keep work in line with objectives. All managers must support company policies in order that they may operate throughout the organization.

PLANNING OF SYSTEMS, PROCEDURES, METHODS

Systems, procedures, and methods are forms of standing plans that link tasks together into a "flow" of work. Organization structure runs from top to bottom, but procedures, in contrast, usually run from side to side. At the higher echelons of the structure, systems, procedures, and methods are naturally broader in scope and fewer in number.

A system is a complex of procedures and methods required to accomplish some major element of operation, e.g., the accounting system, the quality control system, the safety system, etc.

A procedure is *the* approved or standard way of doing some task requiring the sequential action of people in two or more positions in the organization; it may even involve the action of outsiders.

A method is the approved or standard way of doing a specific operation which can be accomplished entirely within a single position.

Business firms must improve their systems and procedures in order to survive competition. In setting up a plan of long-run improvement in operations, management is most apt to minimize the resistance of employees and managers to change. However, changes in operations designed to create more product or service values at the same cost to the customer, changes which reduce costs and thus increase profits without imparing customer values, and changes which create a greater assurance of company growth are necessary. The firm that fails to improve its operations because of worry about what its employees will think or do increases the actual insecurity of everyone connected with it.

ACTIVITY ANALYSIS

Planning systems, procedures, and methods begin with activity analysis. Activity analysis, however, has other purposes and uses.

One is to review periodically the organization structure in

terms of particular jobs to see if the structure and/or the jobs are doing what management wants them to do. Another is to increase the effectiveness of the organization by identifying areas which require strengthening. Further, activity analysis provides a medium for establishing a sequence of training and developing situations from the standpoint of the organization as a whole.

Activity Analysis Environment

If we bear in mind our exchange with an auto mechanic when our car needs a tune-up, we are off to a good start in understanding activity analysis. Certain tangible indicators have pointed to the car's need of a tune-up: the passage of time, sluggishness, the number of miles on our plugs and points, and the like. At any rate, *we know* what the car needs.

When we talk with the mechanic, we outline the items we want checked or replaced, or we simply ask for a major or minor tune-up. The mechanic makes a rough estimate of parts and labor in order to give some indication of the cost and time involved. We then accept, reject, or modify our original request and arrive at a mutual agreement.

Leaving the analogy, here are the points it makes that have a place in our discussion:

The leadership comes from the driver or boss. He says what is to be done. It is not a "from the bottom up" arrangement. But the mechanic knows the detail of the work and his opinion is respected. The final arrangement is a mutual understanding on the major points: what is to be done, when, and what is "within bounds" ("new plugs, if needed") and what is "out of bounds" ("If it gets up to forty dollars, call me before you go any further.").

Activity analysis is based on this sort of relationship. Just as there are professional managers, so there are professional employees. The manager is an authority on the needs of the company, the employee on the doing of the work. Each has a contribution to make to the analysis.

Methods of Analysis

There are a number of ways to analyze the activities involved in a position, including those at the managerial and executive levels. The technique of job evaluation is one. In job evaluation the responsibilities of each position are analyzed and described in a word picture called a "job description." Each position is also related to others by depicting its coordinating and reporting functions.

A second way to analyze an activity is to make a time and duty analysis. Essentially, this consists of listing the array of tasks involved in the job and estimating the percentage of total time spent on each task. The time and duty analysis may be made by a staff analyst from industrial engineering or personnel or by the position incumbent himself.

The latter is the method generally used with managerial positions. A form is developed upon which, over a period of time, the individual notes the different things that he does on his job, together with the time spent on each. At the end of the survey period, the results are summarized. The individual then adds any other tasks that he does which did not occur during the survey period. From the total array of tasks and estimates of time, a profile of the job is developed. This profile can serve as the basic tool for analyzing the position and appraising the individual on it.

A third method of analyzing activity is by informal observation. Over a period of time, usually longer than the study period of the time and duty analysis, the superior observes his subordinate in his job. The observation may be somewhat formalized by establishing a set of items or duties which the superior wishes to check out. The informal appraisal may be supplemented by comparison with the requirements set forth in the job description, or by a recording of so-called "critical incidents" during the interval between appraisals.

A fourth way to analyze activity is by work sampling. The incumbent on a position or a staff observer will make observations of the work, either at random or at fixed time intervals. A record of what is happening is made. Several hundred observations, each of short duration, may be made over a period of two or three months. An estimate of the time spent on each duty is made by developing a ratio of the number of times a particular duty was observed to the total number of observations. For example, if the manager was observed in staff conference on 125 occasions out of 1,250 observations, it is assumed that 10 percent of his time is spent in staff conferences. The activities and times developed in the work sample form the basis for an appraisal of activity and of the performance of the person on the position.

A fifth method of analyzing activity is by means of a staff conference of all persons in the organizational element under review. This involves the active participation of subordinates and thus reduces the work burden which the other methods impose. For this reason, it promises a greater measure of success than the more autocratic methods described earlier. Consequently, a more extended discussion of it follows.

Analysis by Conference

You begin by calling a conference of your subordinates. On a blackboard or chart, outline for them the goals set for your organization. Then ask them to tell you the activities they must perform if these goals are to be reached. Write out the question: "Our tasks as managers are to do *what?*" Let them know that they have the ball and that you will write down what they say, no more and no less. If two men disagree on tasks, write down what both feel. If you have five or six men reporting to you, this process will take several hours. But it is time well spent. The process is more important than the words that appear on the board. It is the "hashing over," "getting the feel of," their activities that is important. Learning is discovering. Employees can be *told,* but they don't get the full feeling for an idea until they discover it.

After all ideas are out on the board, you may choose to adjourn for a week or two and send them each a typed copy of what they discovered. Or you may choose to move immediately on to the next step, which is to combine, adjust, and eliminate items on the list in order to come up with a list of common activities, those *each* manager must perform. Here you will probably have to take a more dominant role, separating the activities needed from those to be dropped or de-emphasized. Be realistic. Don't ask for the moon. Better a few jobs done well than many vague activities.

After another breather, begin searching for a way to measure whether or not each activity is being satisfactorily performed. This evidence must be tangible. You might start with the question, "What are tangible evidences of satisfactory performance of [a sample activity]?"

Again, let *them* tell you the evidences of satisfactory performance. Here you may need to challenge their thinking through questions to keep the length of the session within bounds.

After agreement has been reached on the duties your managers have in common, the next step is isolating their separate duties. Two-man interviews replace the conference at this point.

Let each of your men know well in advance what you are doing. They may want to prepare a list of their specific activities.

If you wish, you may prepare a list too. They can be swapped at the start of the interview and discussed. At any rate, the specific duties are talked over, described, explored, evaluated, and probably changed by mutual consent before both parties agree to them. Again, this is followed by the collection of evidence of satisfactory performance.

When the common activities, the specific activities, and the measures of both have been put in writing, you and each of your men have an unofficial contract or charter under which to operate. Usually, these are reviewed at least once each year to keep them up to date. Like any other contract, they are not made to be violated or broken. But they can be changed, and should be in order to reflect accurately current activities and performance standards.

DEVELOPING SYSTEMS, PROCEDURES, AND METHODS

The results of activity analysis will be the basic methods, procedures, and systems by which work will be accomplished.

Although countless procedures exist in a company, all of them are not worth writing down. There are three kinds of situations in which written systems, procedures, or methods are essential: (1) when exceptional situations are easily identified and separated from the great majority (normally more than 90 percent), which can be handled in routine fashion; (2) when the system must comply with external laws or regulations; and (3) when the company has entered into an agreement with a third party to do something a certain way, such as a contract with a labor union which specifies the use of certain standard procedures or methods.

If the work is a maze of exceptions, it will be run by the application of judgment and special decisions. It should not be considered a procedure to be put into written form. When the work is routine, see that it is written down, step by step. A step is anything that changes or advances the work. Each step should start with a verb—an *action* word. Here are illustrations:

1. Match payment and bill with stub.
2. Stamp stub "paid [date]."
3. File stub in "paid" file.
4. Drop payment and bill in your "accounting" out basket.

The written steps may tell who, what, where, when, or how. They do not tell why the step is taken. The "why" of each step is often obvious; it would take forever to write it out, and in the case of a new employee it can better be supplied by the supervisor.

Systems and procedures are not written in the office. The reason is accuracy. If we don't go out and follow the work, there is a good chance we will omit a number of its steps.

"Otis"

"Otis" tests procedures of work methods. "Otis" stands for "operate, transport, inspect, and store." Any procedure can be divided into these four classes of work:

Operating is adding to or changing a product: typing or signing a letter, shoveling coal, fixing a machine.

Transporting is moving the product from desk to desk or from city to city.

Inspecting is measuring against a standard. It is nothing more than that. If the inspector adjusts the product, that is a new "operating" step.

Storing is putting the product down for a minute or a year. It can be stockpiling an item before or after working on it, putting a letter in an "in" or "out" box, or filing a record, perhaps for years.

The operating step is the core activity of the procedure. It is generally assumed that it is the core activity that creates value, and that the others—transporting, inspecting, and storing—are costs that must be minimized. Can some of them be combined or rearranged? Can some be cut out altogether? For example, if two separate inspections can be combined, the steps leading up to and going away from one of them can be eliminated.

Making Procedures Work

Two more steps are required to make systems and procedures work. One is double approval. The other is constant follow-up. Double approval means that they must be acceptable to both the person accountable for the work and to the people doing the work. Systems and procedures work only when people *want* them to work.

Finally, there is the matter of keeping the system or procedure current. This means constantly watching every factor that affects it. These factors are:

New people	New organization
New forms or materials	New training methods
New machinery	New laws or regulations
New end products	New customer needs
New floor layout	

Changes in any of these factors can create opportunities for rearranging, combining, or eliminating steps that are no longer necessary.

Systems and procedures that are well designed and well cared for produce more end product with less effort by smarter, not harder, work.

QUESTIONS AND PROBLEMS

1. What are plans and how do you use them daily?
2. Why are we often reluctant to set up plans and then follow them through?
3. What are two types of plans? Give illustrations of each.
4. What function does communication have in planning?
5. What is the relationship between planning and objectives? Explain.
6. What are policies and what relationship exists between planning and policies?
7. What factors affect planning? Make a list and explain them.
8. What controls do we have on plans?
9. What is the place of creative thinking in planning?
10. Hold a brainstorming session with ten people on a subject of your choice. List all the ideas you get from the group. How many can you use?
11. Who is responsible for planning? For setting policy? For carrying out policies?
12. Write out a plan on a topic of your own choosing.
13. Write out a policy on a topic of your own choosing.
14. How would you go about implementing your plan? Your policy?
15. What is the relationship of systems, procedures, and methods to planning?
16. Make and write a short-range plan on a problem of your own choosing.
17. Make and write a long-range plan on a problem of your own choosing.

REFERENCE NOTES

[1] William R. Davidson and James H. Healey, *Power Management*, Allegheny Power System and Its Subsidiaries, 1962.

[2] Peter Drucker, "Integration of People and Planning," *Harvard Business Review*, November-December, 1955, pp. 35-40.

[3] William H. Newman, *Administrative Action: The Techniques of Organization and Management*, Second Edition, © 1961, 1963, by permission of Prentice Hall, p. 31.

READING REFERENCES

Alderson, Wroe, and Paul E. Green, *Planning and Problem Solving in Marketing and Management,* Irwin, 1962.

Bellows, Roger, Thomas Q. Gilson, and George S. Odiorne, *Executive Skills,* Prentice-Hall, 1962.

Bowman, Donald M., and Francis M. Fillerup, *Management: Organization and Planning,* McGraw-Hill, 1963.

Branch, Melville O., *The Corporate Planning Process,* American Management Association, 1962.

Davis, Ralph Currier, *Industrial Organization and Management,* rev. ed., Harper & Row, 1940.

——, *The Fundamentals of Top Management,* Harper & Row, 1951.

Fayol, Henri, *General and Industrial Management,* Pitman, 1949.

LeBreton, Preston P., and Dale A. Henning, *Planning Theory,* Prentice-Hall, 1961.

Newman, William H., *Administrative Action,* 2nd ed., Prentice-Hall, 1963.

Newman, William H., and James P. Logan, *Management of Expanding Enterprises,* Columbia University Press, 1955.

Newman, William H., and Charles E. Summer, Jr., *The Process of Management,* Prentice-Hall, 1961.

Richards, Max D., and William A. Nielander, *Readings in Management,* 2nd ed., South-Western Publishing Company, 1963.

Schleh, Edward C., *Management by Results,* McGraw-Hill, 1961.

Steiner, George A., *Managerial Long-Range Planning,* McGraw-Hill, 1963.

Taylor, Jack W., *How to Create New Ideas,* Prentice-Hall, 1961.

Terry, George R., *Principles of Management,* rev. ed., Irwin, 1960.

Thompson, Stewart, *How Companies Plan,* Research Study No. 54, American Management Association, 1962.

21

THE SKILL OF ORGANIZING

The second logical step in the solution of a problem is organizing the plan that has been chosen. A problem that is thoroughly planned and organized is well on its way to solution. Organizing blends into planning on the one hand and into directing and motivating on the other. It links "thinking about" with "doing."

PHASES OF ORGANIZING

There are three major phases to the organizing function: (1) establishing the pattern of relationships between activities required in the accomplishment of objectives in terms of positions in the organization structure; (2) developing standards of mental and physical talents required to discharge the responsibilities of each position, and staffing the positions with persons having the required qualities; and (3) providing each position with all the other resources—materials, machinery, money, and authority—needed to get the job done.

ORGANIZING THE ENTIRE ENTERPRISE

Revamping organization charts is one of the more popular indoor sports of American management. Among the common reasons for this are company growth and increasingly complex technical and managerial problems. Some other reasons include internal politics, desire for change or excitement, the needs and clashes of personalities, tradition, lack of firm corporate goals, and lack of understanding of organization principles.

Business is organized in order to minimize waste and achieve maximum operating efficiency. The difference between the real purpose of organization and what we actually observe in the typical company is due to the fact that firms are staffed by very human humans. And while there are broad guides to working together, as well as specific rules, there still is not enough information or experience available to chart the best structure for a specific company at any given time.

Developing the Structure

Nevertheless, it is possible to establish the steps involved in developing an organization structure. These are:

1. Determine the direct responsibilities of the enterprise. The objectives of an enterprise must be carefully analyzed to determine what functions will be required to accomplish them. Those of predominant importance Professor Ralph C. Davis has referred to as organic functions, "so vital that business activity will cease unless they are performed somehow, somewhere, and by someone."

2. Determine the indirect responsibilities of the enterprise. Certain activities are required in support of, or as a part of, the direct functions of an organization. These include the providing and maintaining of funds, the securing, training, and maintaining of an adequate work force, the providing of material and equipment resources essential to the discharge of the direct functions, and similar activities.

3. Integrate or segment responsibilities. The next step is to combine responsibilities wherever possible and to separate them where necessary. Integration and segmentation are normally determined by the expected volume of operations. If the volume of a particular activity appears to be sufficient to warrant the full-time attention of two people, it must be manned by two people. If it appears to warrant only the half-time attention of one person, that activity must be combined with another, or others, with similar characteristics.

4. Create organizational elements. Once specific positions have been created, they must be combined into organizational elements. These elements may be sections, departments, districts, divisions, offices, or groups. The more common bases for grouping positions into elements are:

Functional. In an electric power company, for example, a direct function is called a "group." Engineering is a group. Its derivative functions include civil engineering, electrical engineering, communications engineering, and planning engineering.

Territory. The entire service area of the enterprise is broken up into territories and positions grouped by the territory served. Further territorial separation can occur within divisions; e.g., divisions separated into districts.

Product. Sometimes positions are grouped on a product basis. A common example is the department store, where the departments are set up on the basis of the kinds of merchandise each handles.

Customer. For some types of businesses, the basis for slotting positions into organizational elements is the customer. For example, the marketing group of a public utility is organized largely on a customer basis. Its principal components are the commercial sales, industrial sales, residential and farm sales departments, together with the area development, advertising and promotion, and market research departments.

Process or equipment. The grouping of positions about a process or type of equipment is most often employed in the lower levels of manfacturing organizations.

Frequently, a combination of bases is used.

5. Combine the organizational elements to create the over-all structure.

Types of Structures

The types of over-all structure are generally classified as (1) line, (2) line and staff, (3) line and functional staff, and (4) functional.

Line. This is numerically the most common form, for almost all small enterprises use it. It is a simple form of structure in which authority and responsibility flow downward in a direct pattern from top management to the lowest employee. It may be diagrammed as in Fig. 4.

Under such a structure, each line manager would select and train his own people, maintain stocks of needed materials and supplies, acquire and maintain required equipment, and account for all proceedings in records kept by him, or under his direct supervision.

Line and staff. In larger firms, indirect functions are "spun-off" the direct functions, to be established as separate organiza-

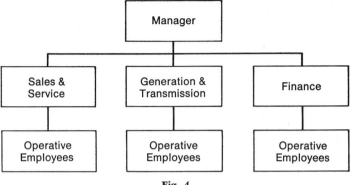

Fig. 4

tional elements, and are usually referred to as staff units. In the resulting line-and-staff structure, while authority appears to flow directly downward as before, it flows to the lowest organizational level only within the line parts of the structure. Staff elements have authority only over people within their own activity or specialization.

The simplified structure of a centralized company organized on a line-and-staff basis might appear as in Fig. 5.

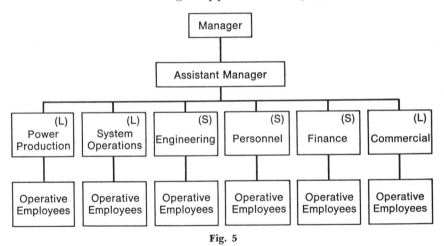

Fig. 5

Line and functional staff. The line-and-functional-staff type of structure takes the same diagram form, but it differs in operation. The specialized staff units have authority over other staff units and over line units *for matters within their field of specialization.* As an example, if a personnel problem arises in the power production area, the personnel manager has authority to settle the matter. In the line-and-staff structure, the staff merely advises the line and other staff department; it cannot order or direct them to do anything.

Functional. This form of structure is chiefly of historical interest. F. W. Taylor conceived it in an attempt to compensate for the limited knowledge of production supervisors. He set up four first-line supervisors and four clerks over each production unit. Each had specialized supervisory responsibilities. The eight positions and their responsibilities were:

1. Gang boss—preparation for production
2. Speed boss—instructing men and getting desired production
3. Inspector—quality of work
4. Repair boss—repairs to equipment and tools
5. Order-of-work clerk—planning, routing, and scheduling orders
6. Instruction card clerk—determining best way to do work
7. Time-and-cost clerk—maintaining information on cost and production
8. Shop disciplinarian—handling personnel activities

The major disadvantage of the functional organization was that it divided command, so that the workers could not so clearly determine where one supervisor's authority stopped and another's began. But it contained the prototypes of modern quality control, maintenance, personnel, cost accounting, methods, and production control departments. It illustrated Taylor's deep conviction that efficiency was the product of detailed, scientific analysis of every phase of a man's work, together with an over-all system of coordination and control of individual effort.

Combinations. There can be blends or combinations of the line, line-and-staff, and line-and-functional-staff structures within a single enterprise.

Line-and-Staff Relationships

To minimize potential conflicts between line and staffs, it is common to spell out their responsibilities in writing.

Two aspects of staff organization which affect line-and-staff relationships may be expressed in the form of the following organizing principles:

Principle of the limitation of staff economy. *In order that line or organizational units be provided with the assistance needed to perform their assigned missions, it is probable that the staff units will operate with some degree of inefficiency.*

A fire department, measured by any of the tools of scientific management, is an inefficient organization. It could operate with much less equipment, personnel, fireplugs, and other fire-fighting resources than it now does. Society has decreed, however, that when we want fire-fighting equipment, we want enough of it to do the job, and we want it as quickly as possible.

Staff units in any business firm are in a similar position. Take maintenance as an example. If the department were operated so as to provide the lowest possible maintenance costs, the primary activities associated with the generation, transmission, and distribution of power to customers would be subject to periodic and prolonged interruptions. This would be true because we would be scheduling these activities to minimize idle maintenance resources rather than to minimize idle power resources. From this and similar examples, it can be concluded that staff units must operate for the purpose of making line units efficient, not to make their own units efficient.

This does not mean that a firm is not interested in efficient staff operations. It merely sets up a priority of efficiencies in which line unit efficiency is ranked above staff unit efficiency. In practice, since staff units produce no direct customer values, it is more difficult to measure their efficiency. Their output is not readily measurable, for it is essentially an output of ideas.

As a consequence of these two facts—staff service to line and the difficulty of measuring staff values—management may have to give more attention to staff organizing and organizations than to comparable line activities. Particularly, it must make certain that there is no "empire building" within staff units. With a lack of objective criteria to measure staff performance, management must essentially trust the judgment of its staff managers.

Principle of compulsory staff advice. *In the absence of policy guidance, before making a decision or initiating action on a problem which lies within an area of staff specialization, the manager must obtain the advice and counsel of that staff.* It is not required that the staff specialist's advice be adopted; the principle indicates only that the specialist's advice must be obtained. This differs from a functional staff concept in which the staff's advice, in its own field of specialization, is binding upon the manager.

An example of the operation of this principle is a situation in which a manager has a problem with obvious personnel ramifications. If no existing personnel policies provide guidance, the manager must contact personnel and obtain their advice.

After he reviews that advice, he may elect to ignore it. The relationship between the manager and staff will probably play a major role in determining how often the manager will elect not to follow staff advice.

Many companies place the burden on staff people to make certain that line units receive their counsel; they also require that line personnel consult with and advise staff personnel on the technical aspects of line activities. The aim of this dual approach is to weld line-and-staff units and their respective personnel into an organizational team.

Organizing Tools—Tests of a Good Organization

The effectiveness of an organization structure can be evaluated by applying the following standards:

1. Is the leadership effective?
2. Is it related to basic objectives and policies in such an integral fashion that these objectives are assured of accomplishment?
3. Are the objectives assured of effective and economical accomplishment by the adequate provision of resources to each position?
4. Is there a good complement of abilities throughout the structure to handle probable business problems economically and effectively?
5. Is there organization stability, i.e., will the organization be capable of absorbing personnel losses without substantially reducing its effectiveness?
6. Is there organizational flexibility, i.e., can the organization adjust to temporary changes in business conditions without serious loss of efficiency?
7. Does the organization have capacity for growth, and are its people being prepared for advancement?
8. Does the organization have good morale?

Each manager is encouraged to apply these tests to his area of organizational responsibility and determine where and what weaknesses exist. Immediate steps should be taken to improve weak areas.

ORGANIZING THE DIVISION, DEPARTMENT, OR DISTRICT

Organization structure is a means to an end. A good structure is the most efficient harness a company can build to keep each division, department, or district pulling its allotted load. Good structure is constantly questioned, constantly subject to judgment, constantly readapting to meet changing circumstances.

In addition, it is subject to long-range planning. It is not unusual to find a company that has planned its organization structure ten years in advance. The organization then evolves from what it is now to what the management wants it to be. Well-planned, evolving structures avoid the losses of corporate momentum and wounds to company morale that unplanned, wrenching shifts in structure evoke.

Every manager of any element within the company, be it division, department, district, or section, has an interest in developing the best structure of relationships between the positions in his element. Attention here is focused on those organizational principles and/or topics most appropriate to the unit. Principles which are appropriate to individual positions will be discussed later.

Basic Principles

Principle of functionalization. *The unit organization structure must be built upon the needs of the enterprise and not around the qualities of the individuals who will man (or are manning) the unit.* The supervisor, proceeding from the statement of objectives of the firm, asks himself:

What are the major functions of my unit required to achieve these objectives?

What other functions are needed to support these major functions?

Are there still other functions, which do not fall into the categories of major or supporting functions, but which must be provided for, because law or custom dictates that they be done?

What activities make up the functions in these three categories?

Which of these activities can be combined?

Which of these activities support or implement what other ones?

In answering these questions, the supervisor must also make assumptions as to the volume of each activity in order to determine the total number of positions required in the unit. He searches for the simplest way to provide for each activity as well as for patterns of complementary and supplementary activities.

Several structures may be developed to indicate the various combinations of activities into positions within the unit. The one selected would be that which is considered best in terms of the criteria which are most pertinent to the company's interest.

Principle of unity of direction. *Any group of activities having similar characteristics and the same objective should be placed under the same manager and be governed by the same plan.* The basic idea of this principle is that the program or plan for an activity, wherever it may occur in the organization, should emanate from the same source. The use of planning staffs is an application of this principle. With the development of objectives, policies, and programs relating to a particular activity centered in a single staff group, inconsistencies and differences in actions and programs for this activity should be minimized, if not totally eliminated.

Principle of span of control. *The number of subordinate positions directly accountable to a position should be that number which best balances the essential subordinate activities, the spans of personality, energy, knowledge, and attention of the superior, and the communications and expense problems associated with additional levels of organization.* There are two fundamentally opposed groups of opinion on span of control. One group holds that the manager's span should be limited to a small number of people, variously reported as from six to nine subordinates. (A study of over 600 manufacturing organizations by J. H. Healey indicated that commonly chief executives have from three to eight subordinates.) This group is supported by mathematical calculations made by a French management consultant, A. V. Graicunas. Graicunas demonstrated that as the number of subordinates increased arithmetically, the number of relationships among them increased geometrically. A simple demonstration of this follows:

I. Relationships with a group of three—a superior (A) and two subordinates (B and C):

A to B	B to A and C (as a group)
A to C	C to A
A to B and C (as a group)	C to B
B to A	C to A and B (as a group)
B to C	Total relationships: 9

II. Relationships with a group of four—a superior (A) and three subordinates (B, C, D):

A to B	B to D
A to C	B to A and C (as a group)
A to D	B to C and D (as a group)
A to B and C (as a group)	B to A and D (as a group)
A to C and D (as a group)	B to A, C, and D (as a group)
A to B and D (as a group)	C to A
A to B, C, and D (as a group)	C to B
B to A	C to D
B to C	C to A and B (as a group)

C to B and D (as a group)

C to A and D (as a group)

C to A, B, and D (as a group)

D to A

D to B

D to C

D to A and B (as a group)

D to B and C (as a group)

D to A and C (as a group)

D to A, B, and C (as a group)

Total relationships: 28

Another group, which is devoted to the concept of a "flat" organization, i.e., one with few levels, holds that the manager's span of control has no empiric limits. This group counsels that as you restrict your span, you increase the number of levels in the structure, and develop what is called "layering." This generates a communication problem by increasing the number of levels directives, policies, and other communications must pass through to get from the top to the bottom of the structure.

Further, this group favors as much delegation of authority as possible. Some advocate giving a manager so many subordinates that he must delegate because of the pressure of numbers upon him. A counterpoint to this concept is that there is a limit to the number of important activities at a subordinate level which automatically limits the number of reporting positions. To hold otherwise would be to create Vice Presidents of Broom Closets and other less important functions.

Essentially, the two viewpoints may be combined by determining the span of control on the basis of the important activities at the next lower level of the structure, the personal qualities of the executives filling the superior and subordinate positions, and the development of efficient communications within and between the levels.

Assistants for Managers

Some managers organize their work by utilizing the services of some type of an "assistant." These services may be of either staff or line nature.

Staff assistants. A staff assistant usually represents his boss in matters of administrative detail; he observes but he does not supervise subordinates. Such assistants may vary from inexperienced trainees, recently recruited from universities, to executives of vice-presidential rank, operating in a personal staff capacity for the principal executive officer.

Various titles are given such positions. "Assistant to" commonly designates an assistant who is not restricted to any particular portion of his boss's work. "Executive assistant" commonly indicates an assistant to a chief executive officer of the company. "Special assistant" provides specialized advice or service in a particular area, such as economic forecasting, speech writing, or legal matters. An "Administrative assistant" is limited to work of a minor administrative nature, such as answering inquiries, assembling records, planning meetings, etc.

Line assistants. A line assistant is distinguished from a staff assistant in that he assumes authority and responsibility for his superior and acts in his place when he is absent. Line assistants are used in a variety of ways. In some companies a line assistant may take over specified portions of his boss's job even when the boss is on the scene. In other instances, a manager and his line assistant may act as a team, the manager remaining accountable for the entirety of his job, but delegating parts of it to his assistant manager. Or the assistant may be delegated a separate package of responsibility and authority. For example, a "director of marketing" may have an assistant director of marketing to whom he has delegated responsibility for sales promotion and advertising.

Dangers in the use of personal staff. Opinions on the use of personal staff vary. Many companies utilize assistants at all levels, while, at the other extreme, some companies have a firm policy against the use of any personal staff assistants. There are four possible dangers or pitfalls in the liberal use of personal staff:

1. Excessive administrative expense. When no restrictions are placed on management with regard to the utilization of personal staff, their use can get out of hand. The number of assistants reporting to a given manager may be interpreted as a mark of prestige, encouraging competition among managers to see who can accumulate the most assistants.

2. Failure to delegate. A manager with a personal staff may be tempted to reserve for his own office routine administrative details which should be delegated to levels lower in the organization. Examples include handling of correspondence, relaying of messages, making travel arrangements, all which might better be handled in most cases by a secretary.

3. Neglect of line subordinates. When a manager depends on and confides in a personal staff assistant, there is risk that he will neglect appropriate communication with his line subordinates.

4. Use as a crutch. A personal assistant is sometimes used to overcome a deficiency in organization structure, or to strengthen

a position which is filled by a manager who lacks appropriate skill and ability.

Justification for the use of personal staff. The use of personal assistants seems especially justified in two circumstances. First, when a manager is constantly absent from his job, because of extensive travel or a heavy burden of meetings or conferences, a line assistant may be needed to cover some aspects of his job for him. Second, the discriminate use of assistants may be part of a management development program, providing people eligible for promotion with the opportunity to broaden themselves and gain understanding in the problems confronting their managers.

Committees and Conferences

A committee is a formally organized or chartered group of individuals who meet repeatedly to consider some problem or problem area. Conferences of managers may serve similar purposes, but would ordinarily be called to consider a specific, immediate problem rather than to function on a continuing basis.

Both committees and conferences have tended to increase in importance in recent years. Committees, in particular, have come to be recognized as a formal part of the organizational structure and are to be found at all levels of the management hierarchy in large companies.

While some committees have decision-making powers (for example, the executive committee of the board of directors of a large corporation), most committees operate in an advisory capacity to executives with major responsibilities in the area of coordination and communication. Most committees are essentially horizontal in that they are composed of representatives from the various functional departments concerned. For example, a "new product committee" might consist of the director of marketing, the director of engineering, the director of manufacturing, and the controller, with the general division manager serving as committee chairman.

There is, however, an increasing tendency for committees to exist within functional departments, e.g., a "marketing strategy committee," consisting, say, of the director of marketing, serving as chairman, the sales manager, the advertising manager, and the marketing research manager.

Approaches to group management, via committees and conferences have been severely criticized by many students of management. They also prove very unpopular with many operating executives, who regard them as time-consuming and inefficient methods of accomplishing anything. This is suggested by a slogan that developed among certain managerial personnel in one large company: "Let's have fewer committee meetings—they are interfering with our conferences."

In spite of a rather common tendency to malign committee activities, committees and conferences can provide well-balanced, competent advice for the line executive. They can:

Save time in the communication of essential information.
Provide for an integration of the ideas of various parties.
Deter hasty action.
Stop unilateral action by a single executive which might have dangerous consequences.
Promote voluntary acceptance and interested execution of plans and policies through participation.
Produce new ideas, through group interaction.

Several requirements for the successful operation of committees are recognized. These may be indicated in the form of questions:

1. Does the work of the committee justify its costs? The best way to arrive at the cost of a committee or conference activity is to ascertain the number of man-hours involved and project these on the basis of the salary of each participant. The total can be balanced against the committee's contributions to the organization.

2. Is the committee organized to operate effectively? This involves consideration of such questions as effective committee size, the selection of a proper chairman and suitable secretary, the advance preparation and dissemination of agenda and reports, and the advance scheduling of meetings to facilitate attendance.

3. Are the subjects assigned to the committees suitable for committee discussion? Special studies indicate that committees are superior to individual action in settling questions which may give rise to jurisdictional disputes among various departments or other subgroups of an organization. On the other hand, individual managerial action appears to be superior in providing leadership, executing ideas, and decision-making. Committee action has been judged as approximately equal to individual action in the areas of control, technical innovation, and advisory activities.

ORGANIZING THE INDIVIDUAL POSITION

Basic to the organizing of the individual position is an understanding of responsibility, accountability, and authority.

Responsibility—"that which an employee is required to

do." Each position carries with it an obligation for the employee on it to perform the responsibilities, i.e., duties, that are an integral part of that position. To be effective in his employment, he must know what these responsibilities are. These are set out for him in the position description, with which he should be thoroughly familiar.

Accountability—"the obligation of an employee to answer to his supervisor for fulfillment of his assigned responsibilities and authorities." Periodically, each employee should render an accounting, orally or in writing, to his superior on how well or poorly he has accomplished the duties assigned to him. Each employee should then be judged fairly on this record. A supervisor may delegate responsibility and authority for one or more of his own duties to subordinates, but he remains accountable to his superior for his total job performance, including the performance of those job elements he has delegated.

Authority—"the right of an employee to carry out his assigned responsibilities." While the placing of a responsibility in a position might appear automatically to give the person in that position the right to decide and/or act to discharge that responsibility, it is usually necessary to provide additional evidences of authority—the manpower, materials, machinery, and money essential to carry out the responsibility. These become evidences or symbols of authority.

Principle of equality of authority and responsibility. *The authority assigned to a position should be commensurate with the integral responsibilities of the position.* It is commonly held that one cannot be properly charged with accountability for the performance of all the duties, i.e., the responsibilities, of a position if one is not given the necessary authority to carry them out. Perhaps it might be appropriate to coin a new word—"authoritability"—which would mean both authority and responsibility. In this way we might reduce the number of situations in which we give boy-size authority to man-size responsibilities, or vice versa.

In implementing this principle in specific instances, however, realistic difficulties appear in spelling out the precise limits of authority. The authority of any position is a product of the organization structure, as represented on the organization chart; the job description; policies and procedures appropriate to the discharge of the position responsibilities; the budget for the organizational unit and/or position; and the initiative displayed by the incumbent of the position.

Principle of fixed accountability. *The accountability of a subordinate to his supervisor is never delegated away or abdicated.* This principle holds that a subordinate cannot relieve himself of the "accounting of his stewardship" by delegating portions of his responsibilities to his subordinates. Thus, the president of a firm must answer to his board of directors for the success of all its operations. He cannot escape his accountability by blaming his subordinates. The board holds him accountable for the work of these subordinates. If it is ineffective, the board correctly expects the president to take remedial action.

It must be understood, also, that the way in which a superior appraises his subordinates will vary from one to another. One manager may hold subordinates strictly accountable for all the details of all their subordinates' jobs. Another manager may only appraise subordinates on the over-all accomplishments of their departments. If these are acceptable, he leaves to his subordinates the matter of the acceptability of their subordinates' work.

Principle of delegation of authority and responsibility. *Authority and responsibility should be delegated to the lowest level of the organization at which the particular responsibility can be efficiently discharged.* For some things, this lowest level may be the presidential level; for others it may be the clerical level.

Decentralization is often considered to be synonymous with delegation. Decentralization of authority is the same as delegation of authority, but decentralization may refer to the geographic decentralization of the maintenance function, authority for which might remain at a comparatively high organizational level. Conflicts occasionally arise from a misunderstanding of this point. Managers occasionally confuse geographic decentralization of activities with delegation of authority and infer or presume an authority not intended. In all circumstances, the degree of delegation of authority practiced by a company is more clearly inferred by the kind of policies, procedures, systems, methods, and controls it uses than by the philosophy of delegation it may indicate in its communications.

Principle of unity of command. *Each subordinate should have but one superior.* In plain terms, this means that an employee should have only one "boss"—at least at work; otherwise the employee might take orders from any one of several people he believes to be his superiors. Conflicting directions are certainly possible when the line of command is obscure.

Occasionally, the presence of staff units in an organization structure makes for some confusion of this sort. Thus the personnel man in an operating division of the company usually has a line of policy guidance from the headquarters personnel staff to himself. He also has a direct line of command from the division manager to himself. While the company's concept of staff gives him considerable guidance in separating the two lines, there will always be "gray areas" of command. On the one hand, his division manager is clearly identified as his immediate superior; indeed, he is appraised by him. On the other hand, the specialists in his profession are in the headquarters personnel unit. In the case of conflicting opinion between his chief and the headquarters unit, authority concepts guide him to follow his division manager, but technical considerations lead him to favor the opinion of those at higher organizational levels in his chosen profession.

The scalar principle. *The degree of responsibility and corresponding authority decreases in relation to the levels of organization structure, from relatively complete responsibility and authority at the top to relatively little responsibility and authority at the lowest level.* This principle refers to the process by which authority is transmitted from the highest level, the owners of the business, to the lowest level. The owners have almost complete authority and responsibility, subject mainly to the laws and customs of the society in which the enterprise operates.

The process by which this authority and responsibility are transferred has been termed "the scalar process." Essentially, since scale denotes steps, it means a graduated release of responsibility and authority from the owners to the lowest ranks of employees. The closer to the ownership group, the greater the authority and responsibility vested in an individual position; the farther away, the lesser the authority and responsibility assigned to a specific position. In any event, a chain of command is created which must be followed in matters of responsibility and authority, but may be departed from to seek or offer information.

The principle of delegation is not inconsistent with the scalar principle. No matter what the degree of delegation, the scalar process will result in the highest positions still having greater responsibility and authority than the lowest ones. Managers who delegate very liberally merely reduce the difference in authority and responsibility between levels; they do not eliminate the difference.

The exception principle. *To the degree permitted by delegated authority, each manager should make all the decisions he can. Only those matters not covered by his assigned responsibility* *and authority should be referred to his superior.* This principle is an implementation of preceding principles, especially the principle of delegation.

Regardless of the degree of delegation advocated by management, the exception principle still applies. For within the amount of authority delegated—much or little—the subordinate is directed to exercise initiative in decision-making.

The exception principle has very wide application in management. A common application in control is the use of two time card racks at time clocks. One is labeled "In," the other "Out." As employees come to work, each takes his card from the "Out" rack, punches the time on it, and places it in the "In" rack. A little after starting time, the supervisor can quickly check the rack and readily determine who is absent. Other examples of the widespread use of the exception principle will occur to you.

Linear responsibility chart. In applying the above principles to the organization of positions within any organizational element, a comparatively new type of work sheet has been increasingly used in business. A Dutch engineer, Ernest Hijmans, is usually credited with creating a chart in which data are organized so that not only the chief executive but also the individual manager can get a much more complete picture of organizational relationships at a glance. A recent issue of *California Management Review* described a form of Hijmans' chart used by the Lockheed Missile Systems Division.

Hijmans' "Linear Responsibility Chart" relates the work done, the people involved, the roles of those people in each type of work.

To contrast an organization chart with the "Linear Responsibility Chart," let's look at both charts as they describe a Philadelphia consulting firm.

The top of their organization chart looks like [that in Fig. 6]:

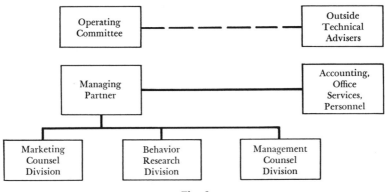

Fig. 6

From this chart, which is typical of most organization charts, it would be difficult to draw enough information for administrative controlling.

By contrast, notice the facts available from a "Linear Responsibility Chart."

SEQUENCE OF RESPONSIBILITY FOR RESEARCH OPERATIONS

Key to Symbols:

X. Work is done
1. Direct supervision of work done
2. General supervision
3. Must approve
4. Must be consulted
5. Must be notified
6. May be called in for consultation
→ Possible routes of delegation

Project Functions:

	Managing Partner	Assistant Coordinator	Negotiating Partner	Senior Partner	Project Director	Analyst	Research Assistant	Director of Planning	Technical Services Department	Typing and Reproduction	Accounting Department	Fiscal Officer
1. Inquiry processing	5	5	X	X				6	6			5
2. Proposal development and presentation	4	4	X	X	6			4	6	X		5
3. Planning and budgeting	3	3	3	X	X	6		X	4	6	5	5
4. Situation analysis			5	4	1	X→	X→	X	6	X		
5. Review of plan and budget	3	3	3	X	X			X	6	6	5	5

Specific job titles are listed across the top of the chart. Functions are listed in sequence down the side. The symbols clearly show the relationships that exist for each function. Where two titles have the same symbol—as the two "5's" under Managing Partner and Assistant Coordinator, it means that the men operate as a team.

The chart here is a "sample"; only a few of the functions of the firm are shown to illustrate the idea of the "Linear Responsibility Chart."

It serves both as an administrative coordinating and control tool—and, in addition, it can be used to locate gaps and overlaps in the job relationships.[1]

Managerial Position Descriptions

In the 1920s job descriptions for operative employees were a controversial matter. Today they are widely used because they have proved useful in organizing work, selecting and training new workers, and administering compensation programs.

More recently, it has become well recognized that such descriptions for managerial employees can be valuable in delineating the functions, responsibilities, authorities, and organizational relationships involved in the various individual positions in an organizational structure. The nature of activity analysis, and its role in the development of position descriptions, has already been discussed. An end product of such analysis is illustrated by the description of the position, "Vice President of Public Relations" in the American Radiator and Standard Sanitary Corporation, as follows:

I. Basic Function

The Vice President of Public Relations is responsible for developing, establishing, and promoting the use of public relations policies, procedures, plans, and programs which will develop and maintain favorable attitudes by general and specific publics toward the Corporation and its operating divisions; and for advising and making recommendations to the President of the Corporation in the determination of Corporation objectives, policies, and plans insofar as they affect or are affected by public relations considerations.

II. Responsibilities and Authority

Within the limits of authorized Corporation policies, procedures, programs, and budgets, he is responsible for and has commensurate authority to accomplish the duties set forth below:

1. Directs the development of and recommends short- and long-range public relations objectives, plans, and programs for the Corporation.

2. Directs the development of and recommends such Corporation public relations policies and procedures as are necessary to assure the effective and consistent handling of these activities throughout the Corporation.

3. Advises and assists the heads of operating divisions in the development and establishment of short- and long-range divisional public relations objectives, plans, and programs consistent with over-all Corporation policies and objectives.

4. Advises and guides the President and the heads of the operating and other service divisions in the proper interpretation and use of the foregoing objectives, plans, programs, policies, and procedures.

5. Sees that authorized public relations plans and programs are properly executed at the Corporation level; and encourages, guides, and advises the operating division heads in the execution of divisional public relations plans or divisional aspects of Corporation plans.

6. Plans and directs such public relations research as is necessary to realistically evaluate the degree and nature of the understanding and

acceptance by various publics of the Corporation and its operating divisions; keeps the President and operating division heads informed with respect to the findings; recommends and, as directed, takes such action as the findings indicate may be required to achieve more effectively the public relations objectives of the Corporation.

7. Advises the President and the heads of the operating and other service divisions on the public relations effects of proposed policies, plans, and activities.

8. Sees that favorable relations are maintained with all news media, particularly in communities where the Corporation has plants or other major installations; and acts as Corporation spokesman to all news media unless otherwise directed.

9. Advises the President and the heads of the operating and other service divisions on all phases of Corporation and division identification, including organizational names, trade-marks and trade-names, in order to promote consistent and effective recognition of the Corporation, its operating divisions, and the relationship between them.

10. Sees that all divisions are advised and, where necessary, assisted in the creation, release, and distribution to the public of information about their activities through such means as news releases, booklets, pictures, speeches, and film, radio, and TV scripts; reviewing and authorizing such material when so required by governing policy or procedure.

11. Provides assistance in the assembly and preparation of the Annual Report and other stockholder communications.

12. Sees that all non-product mass communications material of the Corporation or the operating divisions is reviewed for consistency with governing policy or procedure; and authorizes, or approves, and recommends release in accordance with governing policy and procedure.

13. Represents the Corporation before public groups and organizations.

14. Sees that all public addresses and articles involving the affairs of more than one division or basic Corporation policy are reviewed for consistency with governing policy and procedure.

15. Provides advice and assistance in the preparation and execution of programs to promote better understanding and acceptance of the Corporation and its operating divisions in plant communities.

16. Sees that periodic audits of public relations activities are conducted throughout the Corporation; and recommends such additions or revisions in authorized public relations objectives, policies, practices, plans, and programs as may be required.

17. As a member of the Contributions Committee, participates in the development, revision, and administration of policies and procedures governing the handling of contributions by the Corporation and its divisions.

18. Participates in the development and administration of policies and procedures governing membership of the Corporation and its components in organization and associations; and reviews these policies and procedures regularly, recommending changes as necessary or desirable in the public relations interest of the Corporation.

19. Executes the general responsibilities common to all executives and supervisory positions.

III. Relationships

He will observe and conduct the following relationships:

1. The President of the Corporation

He is accountable to this executive for proper interpretation and fulfillment of his function, his specific and general responsibilities and related authority, and his relationships.

2. Other Division Heads

He will coordinate his efforts and cooperate on matters of mutual concern with the heads of the operating and the other service divisions, particularly the Director of Personnel Administration on plant community relations.

3. Personnel Conducting Public Relations in Other Divisions

Through the division heads, he will exercise functional guidance over these executives in all matters for which he has functional responsibility throughout the Corporation.

4. Industry, Trade, and Professional Associations, Government Agencies, Customers, Suppliers, Business Organizations, Religious and Educational Institutions, and the General Public

He will conduct such relationships with organizations in these and related categories as are necessary to the accomplishment of his function.

5. Others

He will conduct such other relationships as the President of the Corporation may from time to time specify.[2]

In the late 1950s the American Management Association made a large-scale study of the use of managerial position descriptions in industry. The role of such descriptions in organizing individual positions, and various uses and misuses of such descriptions, are indicated by the following comments from the study:

Many firms do not consider it worthwhile to go into managerial position descriptions when the organization is small (say, under 200 employees); has a closely knit, highly personal top management group; and has little prospect for expansion. In such a situation, duties and responsibilities are fairly well understood, and carefully written delineations of them may be superfluous. Of course, small companies may wish to change managerial relationships and job content; in such a case, position descriptions can be a useful tool.

Descriptions written during a period of spasmodic and unplanned expansion are often wasted, since they are soon outmoded and bear no visible relationship to the actual work being done. However, a company that wishes to undertake an expansion program of an organized, *planned* nature can use descriptions advantageously as an adjunct to organization planning. For example, a complete set of descriptions can be written before a new department or division is set up and, if well conceived, can form a fairly satisfactory outline of the new unit when combined with a well-drawn organization chart. Needless to say, descriptions written in this circumstance are invaluable as induction and training aids.

Descriptions are, in a sense, a mirror—a means whereby a company may take a candid look at itself. Often, when the first set of descriptions for the managerial group is written, anyone studying them comes to the conclusion that there are considerable overlaps in authority and responsibility, ambiguities in the chain of command, even duplications of work by whole departments. Well-formulated descriptions bring this out as nothing else can, provided someone in authority takes the time and effort needed to study all of them. If, at this point, immovable unwillingness to make any changes in basic organization structure is encountered, the descriptions lose much of their value. More simply stated, descriptions can uncover organizational ills, but if the doctor (or the patient) is not courageous enough to attempt a cure, much effort has been wasted. . . .

Managerial position descriptions are probably not worthwhile if they are to be used on one occasion only. The effort that goes into preparing them is too time-consuming and expensive. If, for instance, an entire set of managerial descriptions is prepared merely to give a new president an over-all look at his organization, they may be somewhat out of date by the time he receives them or he may have gained the requisite information through personal observation before they are ready. This situation is unlikely, however, simply because most descriptions are soon used for a multiplicity of purposes, even though only one purpose may have been in mind at the outset.

A well-considered description project is not a brief matter. It is likely to take a minimum of three months to organize and initiate. It takes several more months before any sizable number of descriptions are complete (written, compared, adjusted, approved, and distributed). Another three months may elapse before all the "bugs" are eliminated and the program is really part of continuing operations, so that descriptions are revised regularly. It takes approximately an entire year from the starting point to a program which operates almost automatically. This is understandable when it is remembered that a top management description sometimes determines the nature of an entire department or division employing thousands of people. Actually, a well-formulated description at the executive level is very important, and considerable judgment must be used, especially because the description constitutes a sort of "charter of authority" to an individual manager. It is wise to go slowly; the damage resulting from poor descriptions can be enormous.

Do not plan to use managerial position descriptions for salary comparison and adjustment purposes only. This is rather a luxury. Descriptions are useful for organization planning and clarification purposes, once written, and it is perhaps best to keep this in mind even if the primary purpose at the beginning is salary adjustment. The survey shows that quite a few companies started their programs with salary purposes exclusively in mind. Almost all of them later used the descriptions for other purposes. It is almost inevitable, and therefore it would perhaps be better to formulate the descriptions from the beginning with the knowledge that they may be used in much broader areas. Needless to say, this often affects the content of the descriptions in a very marked way.

Managerial position descriptions are not a panacea. Many of the respondents stated that the process of working out the description is very beneficial to both the incumbent executive and the company. Relationships, overlaps, and sensitive areas are dragged out into the open and discussed, with resulting stimulus toward betterment. This is the "training aspect" of position descriptions. It is very real, yet descriptions are worth more if they are kept in good condition and used regularly once they are formulated. Accurate revision must be made whenever job content changes significantly. Descriptions which are put away in a confidential file because the necessary work involved in keeping them up to date seems onerous are not doing their full duty.

Can your company afford them? A good program needs the full-time (or nearly full-time) effort of at least one person. It also absorbs considerable work time among the executives whose positions are being described. The out-of-pocket expense increases if an outside specialist is called in. . . . Again, it amounts to deciding whether the requisite time and money are well spent in a description program. At least, the remarks of the survey respondents reported in this study offer some hints on previous experience.[3]

PARKINSON'S LAW

Professor C. Northcote Parkinson, Professor of History, the University of Malaya, and world traveler, author, and lecturer, has written a very provocative book, *Parkinson's Law,* which is a satire on the ways in which organizations grow. The general thesis is that a natural increase in the number of administrative or managerial positions occurs with or without any increase in the amount of work to be done. Four of the "principles" of organizational growth illustrated in the book follow:

The principle of triviality. In meetings the time spent on any item of the agenda will vary an inverse proportion to the amount of money involved. Discussion of a multimillion-dollar power station will take ten minutes. Discussion of a new snack bar in a power station will consume several hours.

The principle of the coefficient of inefficiency. As committees grow in size, they lose a proportionate or greater amount of effectiveness. Committees of over twenty-one members are completely ineffective.

Administrators create work for one another. The very existence of administrators creates work which requires additional administrative personnel to carry out. Professor Parkinson notes that while the British Navy decreased a third in manpower, and two-thirds in ships, from 1914 to 1928, there was a 78 percent increase in civil servants in the Naval establishment. His conclusion is that officials would have multiplied at the same rate had there been no seamen at all.

The principle of the administration block. The ultimate in planned layout and in physical facilities is only reached by organizations on the point of collapse. Everyone is so busy during other stages of growth that there is no time to plan and organize such layouts and structures. An example of this principle is the old United Nations building in Switzerland.[4]

ORGANIZING THE INFORMAL ORGANIZATION

The formal organization is a power structure designed to accomplish the company's goals. It is based on delegated authority. It is designed in advance. It takes into account, but is not based on, the personality of the individual. It can bind together vast numbers of people.

By contrast, the informal organization is a *social* structure designed to meet personal needs. Authority is based on personal acceptance. It arises spontaneously. It depends for its existence on the personalities involved. It is limited in number to individuals who want to communicate with each other and who have a good opportunity to do so. Wherever people gather for a common purpose, their natural gregariousness generates an informal organization.

Activities of the Informal Organization

The informal organization is engaged in many activities. Among the things it can do are the following:

It *can* threaten the formal chain of command.
It *can* start rumors.
It *can* create attitudes.
It *can* develop and point out the natural leaders in an organization.
It *can* carry true and false information with almost unbelievable speed.
It *does* shape morale.

The "goodness" or "badness" of the informal organization depends not on the organization, but on the feelings of the people involved. It *will* exist. It cannot be "ordered" or stamped out; in fact, that makes it grow. Our feelings toward the informal organization, then, must center around the question of its use. To use it constructively, we should understand its origins and purposes.

Origins and Purposes

It is based not, on vested authority, but on *accepted* authority. This can be the authority of age, seniority, job knowledge, information, personality, strength, or skill.

Cliques inevitably grow around the hub of accepted informal authority if this authority can (1) help employees determine what they want and (2) show them how to get it. What they want may be relaxation, variety, play, adventure; a strengthening of background ties, cultural, religious, or racial; strength to meet a threat or problem; a feeling of belonging, of being "one of the boys"; information, often about their work or company; or ego support: "We *are* important."

Informal cliques are strengthened by their feeling of uniqueness (each group feels it is "different"); the feeling of threat or challenge; their common environment—their working ties; the satisfactions the informal organization offers its members; and the tradition, customs, and common experience of the group.

The informal organization has a point in common with our PTA's, unions, and political parties. They can be dormant for long periods of time, kept alive only by the efforts of a few dedicated people. They are unused social muscles until a need arises. In time of need, we rally and strengthen these "muscles" to cope with our need. And then, when the time of need has passed, the "muscles" are returned to the custody of the few, to lie dormant again until we face another need.

All of this is a way of saying that the informal structure helps people meet needs not covered by the formal organization. This is nothing to bemoan. The formal structure is not intended to meet all of people's needs. The company's goal should not be to uproot the informal structure or to compete with it. The goal should be harmony, based on sound face-to-face supervision.

Uses

Harmony calls for understanding the clique, the grapevine, the informal organization. It calls for purposeful action by the manager to bring the goals of the informal and the formal organization into line. He should know the informal leaders, see that they get straight information and get it fast, and not overlook them when appointing leaders for civic, social, welfare, or sports functions. They can be a ready-made help or hindrance depending on how they are viewed and worked with.

Relationship Between the Formal and Informal Organization

Some of the relationships that may exist between informal organizations and the formal organization structure were ascertained in comprehensive studies carried on at the Hawthorne Works of the Western Electric Company. An interesting contrast is provided by F. J. Roethlisberger and William J. Dickson:

> It is well to recognize that informal organizations are not "bad," as they are sometimes assumed to be. Informal social organization exists in every plant, and can be said to be a necessary prerequisite for effective collaboration. Much collaboration exists at an informal level, and it sometimes facilitates the functioning of the formal organization. On the other hand, sometimes the informal organization develops in opposition to the formal organization. The important consideration is, therefore, the relation that exists between formal and informal organizations.
>
> To illustrate, let us consider the Relay Assembly Test Room and the Bank Wiring Observation Room. These two studies offered an interesting contrast between two formal working groups; one situation could be characterized in almost completely opposite terms from the other. In the Relay Assembly Test Room, on the one hand, the five operators changed continuously in their rate of output up and down over the duration of the test, and yet in a curious fashion their variations in output were insensitive to many significant changes introduced during the experiment. On the other hand, in the Bank Wiring Observation Room output was being held relatively constant and there existed a hypersensitivity to change on the part of the worker—in fact, what could almost be described as an organized opposition to it.

It is interesting to note that management could draw from these studies two opposite conclusions. From the Relay Assembly Test Room experiment they could argue that the company can do almost anything it wants in the nature of technical changes without any perceptible effect on the output of the workers. From the Bank Wiring Observation Room they could argue equally convincingly that the company can introduce hardly any changes without meeting a pronounced opposition to them from the workers. To make this dilemma even more striking, it is only necessary to recall that the sensitivity to change in the one case occurred in the room where no experimental changes had been introduced whereas the insensitivity to change in the other case occurred in the room where the operators had been submitted to considerable experimentation. To settle this question by saying that in one case the situation was typical and in the other case atypical of ordinary shop conditions would be to beg the question, for the essential difference between the two situations would again be missed. It would ignore the social setting in which the changes occurred and the meaning which the workers themselves assigned to the changes.

Although in both cases there were certain informal arrangements not identical with the formal setup, the informal organization in one room was quite different from that in the other room, especially in its relation to the formal organization. In the case of the Relay Assembly Test Room there was a group, or informal organization, which could be characterized as a network of personal relations which had been developed in and through a particular way of working together; it was an organization which not only satisfied the wishes of its members but also worked in harmony with the aims of management. In one case the relation between the formal and informal organization was one of compatibility; in the other case it was one of opposition. Or to put it in another way, collaboration in the Relay Assembly Test Room was at a much higher level than in the Bank Wiring Observation Room.

The difference between these two groups can be understood only by comparing the functions which their informal organizations performed for their members. The chief function of the informal group in the Bank Wiring Observation Room was to resist changes in their established routines of work or personal interrelations. This resistance to change, however, was not the chief function of the informal group in the Relay Assembly Test Room. It is true that at first the introduction of the planned changes in the test room, whether or not these changes were logically in the direction of improvement, was met with apprehension and feelings of uneasiness on the part of the operators. The girls in the beginning were never quite sure that they might not be victims of the changes.

In setting up the Relay Assembly Test Room with the object of studying the factors determining the efficiencies of the worker, many of the methods and rules by means of which management tends to promote and maintain efficiency—the "bogey," not talking too much at work, etc.—were, in effect, abrogated. With the removal of this source of constraint and in a setting of heightened social significance (because many of the changes had differentiated the test room girls from the regular department and as a result had elevated the social status within the plant of each of the five girls) a new type of spontaneous social organization developed. Social conditions had been established which allowed the operators to develop their own values and objectives. The experimental conditions allowed the operators to develop openly social codes and these codes, unhampered by interference, gave a sustained meaning to their work. It was as if the experimenters had acted as a bugger for the operators and held their work situation steady while they developed a new type of social organization. With this change in the type of social organization there also developed a new attitude toward changes in their working environment. Toward many changes, which constitute an unspecified threat in the regular work situation, the operators became immune. What the Relay Assembly Test Room experiment showed was that when innovations are introduced carefully and with regard to the actual sentiments of the workers, the workers are likely to develop a spontaneous type of informal organization which will not only express more adequately their own values and significances but also is more likely to be in harmony with the aims of management.

Although all the studies of informal organization at the Hawthorne Plant were made at the employee level, it would be incorrect to assume that this phenomenon occurs only at that level. Informal organization appears at all levels, from the very bottom to the very top of the organization. Informal organization at the executive level, just as at the work level, may either facilitate or impede purposive cooperation and communication. In either case, at all levels of the organization informal organizations exist as a necessary condition for collaboration. Without them formal organization could not survive for long. Formal and informal organizations are inter-dependent aspects of social interaction.[5]

QUESTIONS AND PROBLEMS

1. What are the three phases of organizing?
2. What are the steps involved in developing an organization structure?
3. Distinguish between line and staff structures. Give examples.
4. What is the purpose of staff in an organization?
5. Why is there so much confusion about line-and-staff organization?
6. Select one of your local business organizations or an organization with which you are familiar. Apply to it the tests of a good organization given in this chapter. Note the items that are found to be

in agreement and those in disagreement. Use your findings as a basis for discussion in class.

7. Explain why organization is so important to all parts of the activity.
8. Explain the principle of span of control. Why is it so important?
9. Explain how you would use staff if you were the manager in charge of a company. A department. A division.
10. What is the difference between responsibility, accountability, and authority?
11. How would you apply the principles of organizing as they apply to the individual?
12. What are the advantages of using a linear responsibility chart?
13. What is your version of Parkinson's Law?
14. Why is the informal organization so important to the formal organization? Explain.
15. How can harmony be established within the informal organization?

REFERENCE NOTES

[1] George A. Steiner and L. Eugene Rott, "Linear Organization Charts." Reprinted from the *California Management Review,* Volume I, No. 2 Winter 1959, pp. 11-19. Copyright 1959 by the Regents of the University of California.

[2] Used by permission of American Radiator and Standard Sanitary Corporation.

[3] *Defining the Manager's Job,* Research Study No. 33, American Management Association, 1958, pp. 32-40.

[4] C. Northcote Parkinson, *Parkinson's Law,* Houghton Mifflin, 1957.

[5] F. J. Roethlisberger and William J. Dickson, *Management and the Worker,* Harvard University Press, 1939, pp. 559-561.

READING REFERENCES

Allen, Louis A., *Management and Organization,* McGraw-Hill, 1958.

Argyris, Chris, *Interpersonal Competence and Organizational Effectiveness,* Dorsey Press, 1962.

Dale, Ernest, and Lyndall F. Urwick, *Staff in Organization,* McGraw-Hill, 1960.

Drucker, Peter F., *The Practice of Management,* Harper & Row, 1954.

Haire, Mason, ed., *Organization Theory in Industrial Practice,* Wiley, 1962.

Healey, James H., *Executive Coordination and Control,* Bureau of Business Research, Ohio State University, 1956.

Holden, Paul E., Lounsbury S. Fish, and Humbert L. Smith, *Top-Management Organization and Control,* McGraw-Hill, 1951.

Jennings, Eugene E., *The Executive: Autocrat, Bureaucrat, Democrat,* Harper & Row, 1962.

Johnson, Richard A., Fremond E. Kast, and James E. Rosenzweig, *The Theory and Management of Systems*, McGraw-Hill, 1963.

Koontz, Harold, and Cyril O'Donnell, *Principles of Mannagement*, 3rd ed., McGraw-Hill, 1964.

Leavitt, Harold J., *Managerial Psychology*, University of Chicago Press, 1958.

Newman, William H., *Administrative Action*, 2nd ed., Prentice-Hall, 1958.

Pfiffner, John M., and Frank P. Sherwood, *Administrative Organization*, Prentice-Hall, 1960.

Whyte, William H., Jr., *The Organization Man*, Simon and Schuster, 1956.

22

THE SKILL OF MOTIVATING

Motivating the efforts of other people is one of the skills most sought after by managers. The skills of planning and organizing are of great importance in the managing of an activity, but the skill of motivating involves working with people—the lifeblood of an organization. It is important, therefore, that we understand people, what makes them "tick," and how to handle them.

MOTIVATION AND PRODUCTIVITY

Let us start first with morale. The morale of an employee is his attitude toward the organization that employs him. Motivating is creating and maintaining employee attitudes that will influence them to subordinate their personal objectives to organizational objectives.

An employee cannot be expected to subordinate his interests to those of his employer unless by so doing he stands a better chance of achieving his personal interests in the long run. If he rates his chances high, his morale is good and he will, with proper direction, be productive of the organization's aims. If he rates his chances low, his productivity will fall with his morale.

At this point we are interested in morale from the viewpoint of the supervisor and his motivating responsibility.

Employees, as a group and individually, strive to meet certain physical and psychological needs. Drs. Harry A. and Bonaro Overstreet have identified these as follows:

1. The need to be affirmed as a person, appreciated as a person, to be hoped about as a person.
2. The need for a number of basic skills:
    Skill with materials (not a fumbler)
    Skill with his own body (swimming, skating)
    Skill in some field of work
    Skill with tools of communication (not a bottled-up person)
3. The need for responsible sharing-contributing.
4. The need for imagination about others. Empathy—the ability to put ourselves within the point of view of the other person.
5. The need for imagination about the possible, about the "what may be." To be inventive, creative.
6. The need for perspective on the human situation. A "big picture" look at his job, his company, his world.
7. The need for the experience of contact with that which is immeasurably greater than himself. To sense and to build the kind of above-mediocre quality that makes a great individual.[1]

The Overstreets mention that satisfaction of these needs makes a person move away from egocentricity, hostility, and apathy toward "that surplus of productiveness that comes from being on good terms with himself, and good terms with his situation."

Another list of motivating factors was supplied by Professor Douglas McGregor of the Massachusetts Institute of Technology. He puts them in "first-things-first" order:

1. Physiological or biochemical needs (food, shelter)
2. Safety needs (protection against danger, threat, or deprivation)
3. Social needs (belonging, acceptance, love)
4. Egoistic needs (self-confidence, independence, status, deserved respect)
5. Striving for self-fulfillment (self-development and the sense of having fulfilled one's mission in life)

McGregor makes two very important additional points: (1) Once a need has been satisfied, it ceases to motivate. (2) The satisfaction of some needs cannot be "given" or bargained for (social, egoistic, and self-fulfilling needs). Their achievement is up to the individual. Most of the needs that can be "given" (food, shelter, safety) have already been given. The new goal in motivation is helping people help themselves.

THE ROLE OF THE ORGANIZATION IN MOTIVATING

Dr. O. A. Ohmann of Standard Oil of Ohio presented a paper, "Work and Authority," to the Philosophical Club of Cleveland on November 26, 1957, suggesting several major areas in which a company can help people help themselves on the job:

1. Redefinition of the manager's role by the top officers of the company, making clear the source and nature of his authority and how he is expected to exercise it. It is important to stress that the manager has authority over *work* which is to be shared with his associates, and not personal power over *subordinates*.

2. Enlarging narrowly specialized, segmented jobs to include participation in setting objectives, planning, and evaluating as well as doing the work.

3. Sharing the managerial function through greater use of participation in setting goals and solving problems. This requires careful differentiation at every organizational level between problems which should be solved by experts and communicated to the group and problems which require prompt executive decision.

4. Maximum decentralization and delegation to overcome the disadvantages of size and to make participative management genuine.

5. Definition of the purposes of the enterprise in terms of its multiple social functions, terms that will capture the loyalty and imagination of all who must contribute to its successful operation —customers, owners, employees, suppliers, distributors, governmental officials, and the public. This assumes, contrary to the union view, that partisan interests are not only harmonious but interdependent.

6. Dealing with the union as a legitimate and worthy representative of one partisan interest, among a number of countervailing forces with which the manager must negotiate and operate. This should be viewed, not as a reluctant concession of managerial authority, but as a right which, in fact, was always vested in the worker. But because some of the more important satisfactions in work do not lend themselves to being bargained for and established by contract, and because the power apparatus of the union naturally tends toward large-scale industry bargaining, it would be a great mistake for the manager to look to the union to solve all the problems of work satisfaction and creative productivity. The manager should therefore press for the type of legislation recently suggested by Roscoe Pound to curb the monopolistic power of unions. And

if that power can be limited, a company should then explore the possibilities of broader, more creative, and genuine participation on the part of the workers.

THE MANAGER'S ROLE IN MOTIVATING

On the job, the factors essential to morale are:

Security	Understanding
Fair pay	Advice on "outside" problems
Credit for work done	Interesting work
Safe, clean work place	Being in on things
Good supervision	Tactful discipline
Promotion on merit	

You may ask, "What is the best order of the items on this list?" The answer to that depends on the situation. After an accident, safety is first in people's minds. When new machinery has been acquired, security and interesting work might appear at the top of the list. The point is that morale and motivation are not altered by *one* management action at any *one* time. They are changed by each manager's action *all* the time.

Everything the manager does has a response in the morale of his people. The fact that the response is usually delayed, and is usually the result of a number of things, makes the man who says he can "play his people like a piano" appear either naïve or a dangerous optimist.

To improve a manager's motivating behavior, these points might be considered:

1. Every general rule for working with people has exceptions. No two people are identical. No man is "the same man" yesterday, today, and tomorrow.
2. Do we use empathy? Seeing the work as Joe sees it does not mean we are soft and does not necessarily mean we agree with Joe.
3. What are our plans for next year, next month, next week, tomorrow?
4. Can we base our plans on the SOS pattern? Can we plan a tangible *Series of Successes*, a series of attainable steps toward each of our goals?
5. Does our plan allow time for play, loafing, relaxing? Rest supplies the energy that backs up motivation.
6. Do we keep in tiptop physical shape? Will we be in good health to enjoy what we planned and to start ahead on the next plan?
7. Can we learn from our setbacks?

8. Do we know what we *don't* want? Have we eliminated the energy waste of keeping up with all the Joneses?

9. Are our goals broad enough and high enough?

The way in which a worker may be motivated by his relationships with his group is illustrated in the following report of a situation at the Hawthorne Works of the Western Electric Company:

. . . the belief that the behavior of an individual within the factory can be predicted before employment upon the basis of a laborious and minute examination by tests of his technical and other capacities is mainly, if not wholly, mistaken. Examination of his developed social skills and his general adaptability might give better results. The usual situation is that after employment his relation to "the team" will go far to determine the use he makes of such capacities as he has developed. Operator No. 2 in the Hawthorne test room was the most accomplished worker; No. 4 was remarkable for the number of unnecessary movements she made in the assembly of telephone relays. Yet the latter at many points in the years of experiment almost rivaled the former. She probably accomplished her output at high cost to herself, but the incentive was the experimentally arranged proximity of the best worker and her desire to stand well with the team.[2]

The "desire to be in on things" as a motivating factor is discussed by F. J. Roethlisberger in the following statement:

In very broad outline—tentatively and approximately formulated—the failure on the part of top management, in mass production industries in particular, to understand the social implications of its way of doing "business" has resulted in the development of certain rigidities which do not make for cooperation in the industrial structure.

1. At the bottom of the organization there are people called em-employees who are in general merely supposed to conform to changes which they do not originate. Too often the attitude is that employees are merely supposed to do what they are told and get paid for it. Directing them there is . . .

2. A group of supervisors who again are merely supposed to uphold —"administer" is the popular word—the standards of performance and policies determined by other groups, one of which is . . .

3. A group of technical specialists who are supposed to originate better ways and better standards through which the economic purpose of the organization can be better secured and more effectively controlled by . . .

4. A group of top management men who in their evaluation of the worker's behavior assume that the major inducement they can offer to people to cooperate is financial (i.e., that they are merely providing

a livelihood, rather than a way of life); that informal organization is either "bad" or not "present"; and that authority comes from the top, so that no attention has to be given to that authority which is a matter of individual decision and comes from the bottom. This group's whole explicit theory of human cooperation—but not necessarily the practice of it— dates back to the eighteenth century: (a) society is composed of a rabble of unorganized individuals; (b) these individuals are only interested in the pursuit of profit and pleasure; and (c) in the pursuit of these ends the individual is essentially logical.

These rigidities in operation make people in one group feel that they are excluded from the activities of other groups and prevent the wholehearted participation of all groups in a full attainment of the organization's objectives.

These rigidities in the industrial structure also have serious consequences for the satisfactions of individuals. Man's desire to belong, to be a part of a group, is constantly being frustrated. Things that are important to him seem to be disregarded. Opportunities for personal and social satisfaction seem to be denied. Yet, contrary to the assumptions made by management, all of the evidence of modern investigaions shows: (a) society is composed of people related to each other in terms of group associations; (b) the desire to belong, to be a part, the desire for continuous and intimate association at work with other human beings, remains a strong, possibly the strongest, desire of man; and (c) in the pursuit of these ends man is essentially nonlogical and at time irrational, i.e., willing to die or, as management should know only too well, to "cut off his nose to spite his face."[3]

An interesting viewpoint on the nonfinancial aspects of motivation has been expressed by Alexander R. Heron in one of the concluding chapters of his book, *Why Men Work:*

No research is needed to demonstrate that material rewards or promises of security and future benefits are not in themselves the factors which induce us to work willingly and well. The failures of plans of organizations, systems of pay, and mechanisms to enlist worker interest, outweigh the successes. No one of these material or mechanical inducements has proved to be a fundamental answer that can be generally applied.

In all the diversity of methods which accompany the examples of good teamwork, we must depend on further research to find the greatest common denominator. The proposal in these pages may be the hypothesis against which the scientific observer can tabulate his findings of fact. . . .

Here is a modest offer of the framework of such a working hypothesis:

1. There is a common denominator in all the situations in business and industry where teamwork has been achieved; here the answer has been found, whether identified or not, to the question of why men work.
2. The devices of compensation, security, and organized consultation which consistently accompany good working relations are those which can give expression to this common denominator.
3. The presence of one or all of these devices does not prove the presence of the common denominator.
4. Where the devices are used without the ingredient of the common denominator, they do not succeed, except temporarily, in achieving teamwork.
5. The common denominator can operate successfully in the absence of any one or all of the conventional devices for enlisting worker cooperation.
6. The common denominator is the opportunity for the average worker to share in the task of thinking.[4]

NONFINANCIAL MOTIVATING FACTORS

One can conceive of motivating factors as a series of concentric environments, with the "self" at the center as the most powerful motivational force. Other motivational environments are shown in Fig. 7.

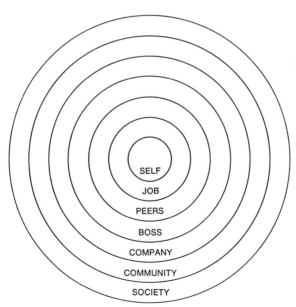

SELF
JOB
PEERS
BOSS
COMPANY
COMMUNITY
SOCIETY

Fig. 7

According to this conception, a person is most motivated by self-interest, somewhat less by his job, less by his fellow workers, less by his boss, less by the company, still less by the community, and least by society in general. It takes an extremely attractive set of fringe benefits and personnel policies to overcome a job one detests.

The Job Environment

Perhaps basic to a person's motivating force is the way he got into his work. If he consciously trained for it and had a succession of early experiences leading to his present employment, he would appear to be in a "choice" situation. He is probably getting more enjoyment out of his work than if he got into it by pure "chance." Yet many people are working at jobs for which they made no preparation, but which are virtually the result of accident.

Everyone recognizes the joy that comes from doing something you really enjoy. Two recent surveys, one of Chrysler technicians and another of retail employees, indicate the strong appeal of "interesting work." Further, if one's superior respects this interest and adopts a permissive attitude, it is even more likely that the job can itself be motivational.

Another motivating factor is what others think about one's work. This has at least two dimensions: an internal company one and an external societal one. In other words, there is a company work-significance system and a status work system in society in general. In some companies, the engineering work appears to be the most important; in other firms, it is the financial work; in others, sales.

In society at large, the job of janitor is usually considered one of the lowest in social significance, and that of the Supreme Court Judge among the highest.

Employees with less significant work in either category present a challenge to their supervisors to overcome the depressing effect of the work itself. On the other hand, the person in work considered highly professional, such as the law, may also present a challenge, that of getting him to see the relationship of his position to the company's needs rather than as an end in itself.

An important aspect of the job is its actual physical environment. In surveys of employee interests, this item is apt to rank well down on the list. This may be explained by the fact that working conditions in most American business firms are of a high order.

For many positions, the status symbols that are associated with it are important. Thus a private office is desirable not primarily because one's work requires privacy, but because only certain echelons of the firm are "allowed" private offices. The company car, the right to use a company plane, expense account privileges, attendance at industry conventions are all "badges" of status within a firm. Many purchase with their own money the status symbols to which their positions do not entitle them, such as office draperies, water bottles, briefcases, etc.

The Group Environment

A common cartoon depicts a businessman complaining to his secretary about how "lonely" it is at the top. Only those who must work alone know how difficult it can be to cope alone with all the challenges of a job. There is a considerable comfort in being able to call upon one's fellow workers for aid, recognition, and information, and to share one's gripes.

Working with others can be extremely rewarding if they are people you respect, or extremely frustrating if they are people who reject you or for whom you feel little respect. Virtually everyone wants to be accepted by the group with whom he works. It is especially important, indeed necessary, for women to be accepted by their co-workers.

Because of this need, an employee's co-workers usually affect his motivation more than his boss. Even in managerial ranks it is generally unwise to get too far ahead of one's peers, for there are many ways life can be made difficult for the man who does. We can cut off his source of materials or data; we can choose not to invite him to our social affairs, or even talk with him; we may begin a campaign with our mutual superior to decrease his stature.

The old gang. Another influence on motivational values is the "clique." In some units, the boss regularly golfs, plays tennis or bridge, or socializes with certain of his subordinates only. Special status is attached to these men, and frustration, disappointment, resentment (and somewhat lowered morale) is felt by all other subordinates.

The informal leader. Of special significance to the motivation of groups is the informal leader mentioned earlier. This kind of leader can create a spirit of teamwork or wreck the morale of the group, depending upon his attitude toward the organization and the formal leader. If his attitude toward either is bad, he will contaminate the attitude of all the members of his group.

Formal leaders make use of the informal leader in their motivational activities. A new personnel policy may be "sounded out" on the informal leader, or it may be "sold" to him in advance of public announcement so that he can assist in putting it across with his group. In many instances, the informal approach can circumvent the morale difficulties that could be encountered in the formal method of correcting a specific problem.

As an example, suppose a manager notices that his group has extended the morning coffee break from the permissible fifteen minutes to twenty. He can approach the problem in a formal manner by posting a notice calling attention to the violation and indicating that disciplinary action will be taken if it is not discontinued. This notice becomes, in a sense, a test of his leadership in the over-all operation of the unit. If his people resent the tone of the message, or the way he communicates it, they may rebel and force his hand.

The informal approach would be to work into a casual conversation with the group's informal leader your concern about the coffee break breach and how it should be handled. Because of his greater rapport with the group, the informal leader may suggest an approach that will avoid morale difficulties; or, without saying anything, may next day lead the group back to work at the end of fifteen minutes.

Using informal leaders motivationally is a tricky business. It should always be done subtly and *infrequently.* Any evidence the group gets that the informal leader is being so used will cause him to lose his leadership status.

The Supervisory Environment

Virtually every phase of company direction is translated to the individual employee through his supervisor. Personnel policies are good or bad depending on their interpretation by that supervisor.

His type of leadership adds to, or subtracts from, his motivating effectiveness. If it is basically that of a supreme autocrat (or "oracle"), the effect upon the subordinate will be to suggest that his value to the organization is low and his abilities not very great. For the oracle has *all* the answers—a situation totally destructive to the human dignity of any thinking person.

The free-rein leader may be just as bad if he is the type of abdicator who calls his staff together and says, "Gentlemen, our next project is to boil the Pacific. Unfortunately, I am about to begin my vacation and, due to the fact that the CEI conference begins upon my return, I shall be away about six weeks. I have full confidence in your ability to do the job!"

Six weeks later, he is back and calls another conference at which the subordinates proudly announce the completion of the project. They have indeed boiled the Pacific. But what does the boss say? "But, gentlemen, *at what a cost!*" He had failed to mention, as one of the criteria, the necessity of doing the job cheaply.

This is probably the worst kind of superior—the kind who changes signals in midstream.

So extremes of leadership of both types are bad for morale.

The most effective leader from a motivational standpoint is the consultative type, who seeks his subordinates' advice and counsel, but only on problems for which he has no solution. He listens to all they have to say. He may agree with no one or with the majority. He accepts the obligation of making a decision, but gives his subordinates a feeling of worthwhileness by involving them in his preaction planning. He will always lead in a manner that respects the human dignity of his subordinates.

Everyone wants direction of some sort from his supervisor, and he wants that direction to be consistent, based on a set of standards of what is expected of him. Providing this type of direction goes a long way in properly motivating others.

Personal Skills

Motivating involves a high degree of communication, and communication is built on the personal skills of reading, writing, speaking, and listening. Probably the skill of greatest impact is listening, for it is a key to empathy, and without empathy there can be no real motivating.

Most of us listen poorly, however. Think for a moment of a typical return home at the end of a long workday:

MANAGER: "Evening, dear. Is the paper here?"

HOUSE MANAGER: "Yes, but first let me tell you what Johnny did today. That little tyke almost got hit by a car. He was playing on his new skates—the ones mother sent him—and he started down the driveway, and, etc., etc., etc. . . . And so, you are really going to have to do something about him, Sam."

MANAGER: "Hmm; yes, I suppose so—now where did you say the paper was?"

The manager did not really want to talk to his wife. He wanted to settle down with the evening paper and let some of the cares of the day ebb away. His wife, however, had been waiting all afternoon to tell him about Johnny, and she was really worried and anxious for her husband to do something.

This is illustrative of the listening situations we often find with supervisors. The subordinate has a problem and wants the supervisor's help. The supervisor may be engrossed in another problem—one of his own with his boss—or on his way to lunch or have a hundred and one other things on his mind. However, he invites the subordinate to speak. He turns his ears in the latter's direction. He nods periodically, he smiles sympathetically. *But he is not listening!*

If, on the other hand, he is that rare breed of manager who really concentrates on listening, it will pay dividends in a better understanding of both the subordinate and his problem. And the better a manager knows and understands his subordinates and their problems, the more effectively can he motivate them.

The Company's Image

Every company has a personality, which is a composite of its managerial philosophy, history, moral tone, objectives, and the place it has set for itself in the industry and in society. Often an outsider can detect the "tone" of a company after a brief visit. He may be appalled at the griping from managerial personnel he has heard almost immediately upon his arrival. He may be vastly impressed by the orderliness with which business is conducted and the good manners everywhere evident.

The employee is even more sensitive to these things. The "tone" of the firm is amplified by the "tweeters" of his associates and the "woofers" of his bosses. It may reach him sweet and clear and beautiful or loud and discordant and disorganized. If the tone is sweet and clear, it will add to the motivation he gets from his job, his peers, his boss. If it is rough and jumbled, it will detract from whatever values he derives from what he does and whom he works with.

Benjamin M. Hines of General Foods has suggested that "since compensation, the prime motivating factor, has become a magnet of uniform strength for almost all companies," it is necessary to look to other motivating factors to inspire top managerial performance. He suggests that executives are properly motivated when:

1. They are convinced that they are performing useful and challenging work.
2. They share a feeling of enthusiasm and optimism about the aims and capability of company management.
3. They respect the ability and understanding of their immediate supervisor.
4. They know the objectives, responsibilities, and standards of acceptable performance connected with their jobs.
5. They have a chance to take part in formulating goals, policies, organization, and procedures related to their own areas of activity.
6. They are free from fear of whimsical or capricious actions that will end their jobs.
7. They are provided with the possibility of advancement in salary and position, if deserved.

FINANCIAL MOTIVATION

Morale is essentially getting the employee to work for what *his employer wants*. An employee usually is motivated to do this because he believes it is the best way to get what *he wants*.

It is generally easier to get employees to see that their incomes and working conditions can be improved through the general improvement of the company's financial condition than to get them to work directly for company growth, better community relations, or other organizational objectives.

Employees do not normally want wages or salaries as such, but for what the wages or salaries will obtain for them: food, clothing, shelter, and other basic necessities. Each employee's wants differ, and his consequent needs for money differ. In its Columbus, Ohio, plant the North American Aviation Company has had many employees who worked only until they had sufficient funds for some specific need, say, a motorcycle or automobile. Having made what they considered their fortunes, they returned to their simple, uncomplicated life in the Kentucky and Tennessee hill country.

Other individuals seem to be endowed with an insatiable hunger for the "good things" of life. Some are willing to work extremely hard and long to achieve extraordinary wants. Others are too lazy or indifferent to work for what they want, and become daydreamers waiting for their "ship" to come in. Management's interest lies in the first group—those who have the ability and the will to work for riches. They are self-motivated, but their motivation can be channeled, through incentives, into working toward company objectives.

Because of the wide differences in individual patterns of material wants, there can never be a compensation system that will equally motivate all employees. There are some basic principles, however, which have general validity and form the foundation for all good compensation systems.

Compensation Principles

Principle of economics. To the company, compensation is payment to an employee for service rendered; to the employee, it is a means of satisfying basic needs and establishing a place in society. Before any compensation can be paid, various tax bodies and the owners of the business must receive their share of every revenue dollar. Therefore, any proposed compensation plan must first bear a reasonable relationship to the over-all financial structure of the company.

Principle of a living wage. The individual's compensation should be substantial enough that he can maintain a reasonable standard of living. Theoretically, the minimum wage authorized by law provides a reasonable standard of living for incumbents of lower or basic levels of work. If this minimum wage is not sufficient to attract competent employees, one must be established that is.

Principle of competition. Compensation should provide employees with the means to live reasonably well among people in the community who work on a comparable level of employment. It must be competitive. It must compare favorably with pay for similar work in both the area and the industry. A company cannot attract, hold, and motivate competent employees if compensation is not reasonably competitive.

Principle of significant differences. Compensation (among other factors) can tell an individual how well he is appreciated. Some pay differential for differences in job status is evidence that his job is of more value than others. Therefore a compensation plan should recognize significant differences in responsibility, authority, accountability, and level of employment within the organization.

Principle of contribution. Among the basic human needs are belonging, opportunity, security, and recognition. It is through the fulfillment of these that an individual improves his work performance and qualifies for greater responsibility within the organization. Therefore compensation should be based upon the individual's contribution to the objectives of the company, and reward him for improved performance and the acceptance of greater responsibilities.

Principle of change. A compensation plan cannot attract, hold, and motivate competent employees if it cannot change in response to changes in organization, economics, technology, and improvements in people. Therefore, compensation plans should be capable of revision to meet changing conditions.

Principle of status symbolism. Earnings provide the individual with a yardstick to measure his place in society. He can compare what he gets with what he believes his neighbors receive and mark his progress in life accordingly.

Compensation Procedure

Essentially, compensation administration consists of these steps:

1. Determining the relative value of positions. Even among managerial positions, there is usually a considerable difference in salaries. The relative importance of positions can be established in several ways: by trial and error, the pooled judgment of principal executives, following the example of similar firms or the findings of professional association surveys, or using a formal system of standards. In a job evaluation system, factors common to all positions—or to all managerial or other broad groupings of positions—are identified. Each position is then analyzed in terms of these factors, either collectively or individually. The result is a ranking of all positions, from the lowest to the highest, in terms of its value to the company.

2. Grouping positions into classes or grades. Once the positions have been analyzed, they can be grouped into grades or classes. The criteria for doing this may vary, but it is quite common to separate all positions into two broad groups: managerial and nonmanagerial. The latter group is often further separated into those classes exempt from the Fair Labor Standards Act or union contract and those covered by the Act or contract.

3. Deciding upon general compensation levels. Many factors enter into the determination of the general pay level. Obviously, if the firm is unionized, those classes of positions covered by the union contract will be subject to collective bargaining on such matters as wages and working conditions. Underlying the company's position in the bargaining, and setting boundary lines to it, are factors which apply equally to nonunion positions. Included in

these is the need to attract and hold an efficient work force at wages or salaries paid to comparable jobs in the area and industry. For, unless the company meets the more important of these two levels (for some firms it is industry levels; for others, area levels), it will lose its employees to its competitors for the labor supply.

The company's relative ability to pay can influence its decision on general levels of compensation. Usually this becomes a factor at the economic extremes: in companies operating at a deficit or near the break-even point and in those which are the most profitable. The former cannot always meet area and industry competition and must temper these groups' compensation levels with their own relative inability to pay. The latter companies may deliberately set their pay levels above area and/or industry levels in order to attract the best people available.

The general compensation level may also be influenced upward by pressures of impending unionism coupled with a desire to remain nonunion. An upward influence, also, is the anticipation of a rising cost of living and the desire to protect employees against a consequent loss in morale. The level may also be influenced upward by the paternalistic—"Dutch Uncle"—attitude of management. On the other hand, the firm may elect to establish a lower general level of compensation because it is the only major employer in the community or because it uses principally women and other industries employ predominantly men, thus creating a reservoir of idle females. The firm might elect to set its compensation below the area levels because its jobs are not so highly skilled as others in the area, or it is in an industry characterized by lower wage levels, such as a laundry, a library, or a social service organization.

Managerial positions will normally reflect somewhat different patterns of compensation than nonmanagerial positions.

4. Devising the range of compensation for the class. It is fairly common to set up ranges of compensation in which the lowest point of the range is one-half its highest point. As an example, if grade IV pays a minimum of $6,000, it might have a maximum pay of $12,000. There is, however, no absolute rule on how wide the range should be, or the differential between position grades, or whether one grade should overlap another. The "science" of wage and salary administration has much to learn on these counts.

5. Establishing criteria for advancement through the range. As an individual gains experience in a position, his work normally improves and there should be recognition of this by increasing his

salary or wage. The fundamental criterion for movement within the compensation range is individual productivity or ability.

6. Evaluating the individual. The specific salary or wage John Jones is to receive is the product of the preceding steps plus the firm's evaluation of John, which may be based on many factors which we have considered elsewhere.

What should not be overlooked in the above analysis is that it is not the procedure but its effect upon morale that is most important.

QUESTIONS AND PROBLEMS

1. Why is morale so basic to the success of an individual?
2. Why do people not more readily recognize the morale of others?
3. How can you build your own morale?
4. What is the relationship between the morale and climate of an organization?
5. What is the role of the organization in motivating?
6. What is the role of the manager in motivating?
7. How can we improve the morale of others? The morale of our boss?
8. Name some nonfinancial motivating factors in addition to those listed in the text.
9. What are status symbols? Why are they so important?
10. Name the three environments in which each person works? Give examples of each from your own experience or from the experience of someone you know.
11. What has the company's image to do with morale? Why is this so?
12. What have finances to do with the morale of an individual? Why?
13. Select one of the compensation principles and write a 500-word paper about it.
14. Assume you are a manager and must revise the compensation plan. What procedure would you follow?

REFERENCE NOTES

[1] Drs. Harry A. and Bonaro Overstreet, *Journal of Industrial Training,* May-June, 1953.

[2] Elton Mayo, *The Social Problems of an Industrial Civilization,* Division of Research, Harvard Graduate School of Business Administration, 1945.

[3] F. J. Roethlisberger, "The Foreman: Master and Victim of Double Talk," *Harvard Business Review,* Spring, 1945.

[4] Alexander R. Heron, *Why Men Work,* Stanford University Press, 1948, pp. 171-172.

READING REFERENCES

Davis, Keith, *Human Relations in Business*, McGraw-Hill, 1957.

Gellerman, Saul W., *Motivation and Productivity*, American Management Association, 1963.

Leonard, William P., *The Management Audit*, Prentice-Hall, 1962.

Roethlisberger, F. J., *Management and Morale*, Harvard University Press, 1941.

23

THE SKILL OF DIRECTING AND DELEGATING

A manager's prime function is to direct the efforts of others. In a large organization, he may escape some of the planning and organizing, but he cannot escape his responsibility to direct the efforts of the people under his supervision. His effectiveness as a manager is closely bound up with how well he practices this skill.

In its broadest sense, directing is providing all the guidance that an individual needs to carry out his assigned responsibilities. Its scope is broad enough to include ethical guidance, yet narrow enough to include specific instructions on minute aspects of a responsibility.

ELEMENTS OF DIRECTING

The managerial function of directing consists of three major phases or elements, as follows:

1. Orientation in the general philosophy, policies, and rules of the company and of the unit within the company to which the employee is assigned.
2. Training the subordinate to bring the highest possible proficiency to his present assignment, as well as to prepare him for promotion to higher-level responsibilities.
3. Prescribing, which is the issuing of detailed instructions to guide

the employee's daily work. Normally, the lower the level of the organization, the more frequently will such instructions be issued.

In a typical large company the manager will receive considerable staff assistance from the personnel department in handling the first two phases. The issuing of work intructions (prescribing), however, is usually his responsibility alone.

LEADERSHIP AS AN ASPECT OF DIRECTING

Leadership requires authority, and authority comes ultimately from those being led. As managers it is sometimes difficult for us to face the fact that only the *seed* of authority is planted from above. It is *nourished* from below. It increases as we issue orders that "make sense." It decreases when those orders—in the eyes of the people receiving them—are "nonsense."

Mary Parker Follett was one of the early students of good management. She pointed out the fact that "edicts" are not required in all directing situations. Adults who are treated as adults can quite often see for themselves what needs to be done, and frequently go ahead and do it without the necessity of a command.

We can sum up by saying that authority comes from giving job satisfaction to those who are led, and that the cornerstone of satisfaction is self-respect. This does not mean no edicts are ever issued. It means that directives are given in such a way as to maintain or increase self-respect. To understand this, we should consider some of the damage a manager may inflict on a man's self-respect when he issues a directive.

Overdirecting. This is squeezing all creativity out of a job by thinking through every tiny detail and then decreeing that it be done "by the numbers." Every job has enough restrictions without the boss adding more that are uncalled for.

Taking authority personally. This has been the downfall of many a manager. He wasn't born with authority. He gives orders not because he "feels like it," but because the situation requires it. Orders issued merely at the whim of the boss tend to reduce a worker's self-respect.

Withholding information. The manager who forgets to keep his aides informed or who withholds information "because it might worry them" is not treating them as adults. People want to know the facts, good as well as bad, about their jobs. If you want to issue man-sized orders, then day in and day out treat your people like man-sized men!

Power over and power through. The manager who wants power over people should be replaced. He has confused means with ends. The manager needs power *through* people in order to get power *over* results. The good manager recognizes this and encourages each of his men to make the most of himself and to respect himself. With that kind of men, he can achieve far better results.

The man and his deeds. Executives, giving orders or disciplining, are learning to separate the man from the deed. It is proper to criticize the work, but think twice before criticizing the man. For example, why say, "You are lazy," when you mean "Your production is down 5 percent this month"? Production records are matters of fact that need to be communicated. "Laziness" is an assumption that we would do well to keep to ourselves.

The fallacy of giving raises. No good manager ever *gave* a raise. They aren't given; they are earned. Therefore don't expect gratitude beyond the normal "thank you." A raise doesn't make a man "beholden" to his boss. It is no time for him to grovel on the carpet. Quite the reverse; when an earned raise is received, a man should be proud that his worth has been recognized, and the good manager will respect him for this.

Know yourself. Ever oversleep, bolt soggy toast and scalding coffee, see your lawnmower in your neighbor's yard covered with snow, and get to the office and decide to clear the air by giving a good bawling out? Sure you have; it's happened to all of us at one time or another.

But don't. Don't deliver the bawling out until you have taken stock of the situation. Who needs the air cleared, you or the work? Before clearing the air, examine yourself; it pays needed dividends in respect. Through his actions, the leader builds the climate of his part of the organization. The kind of leadership he exerts will depend on the degree of followership he develops among his subordinates.

The Leader, the Led, and the Situation

Authority is the ability to "make up a man's mind for him." Influence is the ability to help him make his mind up—your way. Generally speaking, authority is compulsive and influence is impulsive. Each is a way of directing or getting work done. Why can't it be said that one is "good" or "right" and the other is "bad" or "wrong"?

Here are some of the reasons: (1) A particular pattern may not fit you as a manager. It may be a "mask" that doesn't fit. (2) It may not "wear well" with your people. They may be new and need a firm lead, or they may be seasoned and resent it. (3) It may not fit the situation. A reluctant leader would be out of step if the building were burning down, or with teen-agers, or in any situation calling for firm leadership and quick response.

This can be summed up in the words, "the leader, the led, and the situation." The pattern of leading that we select should be one that fits our own personality, works well with the people we lead, and suits the situation at a particular time and place.

Does this call for us constantly to change directing patterns? No, it doesn't. It means that we use a particular blend of attitudes that fit our normal situation, but that we *can* change pace if the people we lead or the situation calls for a change of direction.

The Delegation Process

In all organizations, large or small, delegation occurs when the responsibilities of an individual become so great that he has to get someone to help him get his job done. Those portions of his job that he assigns to this assistant are the scope of his delegation. Delegating is sharing know-how, responsibility, authority, budget, materials, and equipment to the degree necessary to do the work. It is not a blank check, nor is it a bad check. It is a check for the *right* amount.

And, although the work has been shared, the person delegating it is still accountable for the results achieved. When the boss asks him about the status of a certain job, it is not an acceptable answer to say, "I delegated it."

Does one have to be able to do the work better than anyone else before he can be accountable for what he delegates? It certainly helps, but the answer definitely is "no." An illustration is working with specialists, such as scientists or professionals. The specialist's work is *doing the job.* The manager's work is seeing that it is done as the company needs it done.

With accountability as the reference point, let's consider three basic questions: (1) when to delegate, (2) what to delegate, and (3) how to delegate.

When Do You Delegate?

You delegate if you are a manager and more than half your job is routine. You are paid to look ahead, to be where the trouble is, to help men grow in their work, to assure results. These are not routine tasks. Another point: What has become routine to you may be a challenge, a developing agent, to one of your people.

You delegate, of course, when your people are better qualified to do a job than you are.

You delegate when it costs too much, in money or time, for you to do the work yourself.

You delegate when you need additional time to plan, develop men, or do work that has been delegated to you. If the executive function were limited to but one resource, that resource would be the process of delegation.

On the other hand, there are times not to delegate: when no one else can do the work (but what does this imply about the manager as a man builder?); when you must maintain *absolute* control; and when you want to learn the work yourself. Finally, the problems of the people who report *directly* to you cannot be delegated.

What Do You Delegate?

You delegate responsibility for specific results. You delegate ends desired, not means. Here is the difference between "ends" and "means" delegation. In an "end result" delegation, a manager might be asked to revamp the distribution system for a certain town in consideration of certain growth factors. By contrast, a delegation of "means" would take him step by little step through the "how" of revamping. The first method develops managers. The second develops messengers.

You can delegate broad end results that are long-range or permanent, or you can delegate specific short-range tasks that will be done in the next half-hour.

How Do You Delegate?

First of all, delegation comes easy if you believe in it. If your attitude is one of "coaching" rather than that of a "prima donna," you are on your way to good delegation.

Second, you plan and organize for it by knowing your people, what they are doing now, what must be done next, and what it will take (motivation, manpower, equipment) to do it.

Third and last, you control. This starts the minute you ask for a result and continues until the result has been evaluated. You let a subordinate know what is wanted and how you will measure results. Your criteria will have a lot to do with his progress. Are you measuring speed, quality, quantity, cost? What will your yardstick be when he brings you the final result?

Next, you must be sure that both of you have the same understanding of the mission. After he has had a chance to think about the job, ask him how he plans to proceed. Listen till you are sure the job is "under control" by being what you intend it to be. Many jobs are done wrong because this "initial feedback" step was short-circuited.

After this, arrange *in advance* for additional feedback—for progress reports. "Let's get together on this at least three times before the deadline. What dates would work well with you?"

Finally, after the job is done, hold at least a brief "post-mortem." Look the job over from beginning to end with him. Let him tell you what was well done and what wasn't. Slip in your own opinions and feelings. This "builds in" control standards that will be useful to him in the future. Just as important, it sets up a milepost of accomplishment that is good for both your morale and his.

Benefits of Delegation

First, it allows you to practice your profession—management. Second, it gives you time to plan and helps your people develop themselves on the job. Delegation offers everyone additional peace of mind. It is a way to accomplish more with less worry, less tension, less risk of health through being a "one-man show." Finally, it builds a reserve of additional executive talent by allowing others to become managers rather than mere messengers.

Directing and Orders

Direction may be given by *express orders,* but it also takes place when a subordinate anticipates orders before they are given. The contrast is the key point of this quotation from the writings of a noted writer on management, Herbert A. Simon:

A final complication must be added to the notion of authority. If authority were evidenced entirely in the acceptance of explicit orders, or in the resolution of disagreements, its presence or absence in any relationship could be sought in the presence or absence of these tangible concomitants. But it is equally possible for obedience to anticipate orders. The subordinate may, and is expected to, ask himself, "How would my superior wish me to behave under these circumstances?" Under such circumstances, authority is implemented by a subsequent review of completed actions, rather than a prior order. Further, the more obedient the subordinate, the less tangible will be the evidences of authority. For authority will need to be exercised only to reverse an incorrect decision.

This phenomenon has been pointed out by Friedrich, who calls it a "rule of anticipated reactions." It affords a striking example of the manner in which expectations and anticipations govern human behavior, and the difficulties which result from this for the analysis of human institutions. The difficulty in determining authority relations because of the operation of the rule of anticipated reactions is common to all "power" situations. Any study, for instance, of a governor's veto power must take into consideration what bills failed of passage in the legislature because of the anticipation of veto, and what bills were passed for the very same reason.[1]

Fear in Delegation

The manner in which fear may interfere with proper delegation of responsibilities is highlighted in the following quotation:

One major psychological hurdle confronts every manager . . . the *fear* of delegation. The manager may be frightened to let go. He may fear that his subordinate will not perform his assignment properly and, as a result, reflect discredit on his superior. On the other hand, he may be afraid that his subordinate will perform only too well. This fear has the greatest traumatic possibilities. The boss may feel he is outshone by his junior. Or, worse still, he may feel that his job is threatened and that outstanding performance on the part of this subordinate will mean his own displacement. Either attitude is fatal to effective delegation and coaching. Sometimes the manager himself is at fault. In other instances, the trouble may be due to poor promotion practices within the company. If the latter is the case, personnel policies should be reviewed and improved.[2]

TECHNIQUES OF DIRECTING

The managerial function of directing is handled in a wide variety of ways by different kinds of leaders. Without going into detail about each type at this point, it may be pointed out that the way that a manager directs will be related to the assumptions he makes about human behavior.

An autocratic manager will likely employ the "carrot-and-stick" theory in directing his subordinates. That is, he will reward those who comply in a satisfactory manner and punish those who do not, perhaps directly or by withholding expected rewards.

This is consistent with what Professor Douglas McGregor of MIT describes as "Theory X," which, he claims, is based upon the following assumptions about human behavior:

1. The average human being has an inherent dislike of work and will avoid it if he can.
2. Because of this human characteristic, most people must be coerced, controlled, directed, or threatened with punishment, to get them to put forth adequate effort to achieve organization objectives.
3. The average human being prefers to be directed, wishes to avoid responsibility, has relatively little ambition, wants security above all.

Professor McGregor contrast these assumptions with those underlying what he describes as "Theory Y":

1. The expenditure of physical and mental effort in work is as natural as play or rest.
2. External control and the threat of punishment are not the only means for stimulating effort toward organizational objectives. Man will exercise self-direction and self-control in the service of objectives to which he is committed.
3. Commitment to objectives is a function of the rewards associated with their achievement.
4. The average human being learns, under proper conditions, not only to accept but to seek responsibility.
5. The capacity to exercise a relatively high degree of imagination, ingenuity, and creativity in the solution of organizational problems is widely, not narrowly, distributed in the population.
6. Under the conditions of modern industrial life, the intellectual potentialities of the average human being are only partially utilized.[3]

When a manager's views about human nature and behavior corresponds with the "Theory Y" assumptions, he is likely to direct in a much different manner than an "X" believer. He will be less judicial, and will spend time and effort helping his subordinates achieve their own as well as the company's goals. He will work on the principle of integration, that is, the creation of conditions wherein members of the organization can achieve their own goals best by directing their efforts toward the success of the enterprise.

The "Y" advocate, then, will be more of a coach and counselor, less of a commander and judge.

APPRAISAL AND DEVELOPMENT AS TOOLS OF DIRECTING

The purpose of management appraisal and development is improved results on the job. The function of appraisal is measurement of results. The function of development is improvement of results. There is no clean break between the two. Recognizing this, let's look at some of the distinguishing points of each, and then we will look at the two together.

APPRAISAL

To appraise is to measure and compare. We may weigh the processes a man uses against the processes he should use. How does he plan, organize, and control? Farther along on the job, we may measure his results against his plans or against his responsibilities. Did he meet quota?

These measurements may be made through check lists, through lists plus short descriptive statements, or by descriptive essays alone. They may be done by the man being evaluated, his boss, a staff person, an outside specialist, or some combination of these. The measuring may be done at fixed time intervals, ranging from weekly to annually and beyond, or it may be done "when needed."

Generally speaking, these are the "what's," "how's," "who's" and "when's" of appraisal. They may be used in infinite combinations and variations to meet different situations.

There are limiting factors, too. Seneca was once asked if he had given the people "the best laws." He replied that he had not; had given them the best laws *they could accept*. Some of the factors that limit appraisal are:

What will the employee accept as being right and fair?
When does an appraisal overstep the bounds of the relationship between the company and the individual?
When does it "stop managing and start meddling"?
What will the boss (or company) accept as timesaving rather than timewasting? What will he accept as the best things to measure? What will he accept as his role in the process?

Only through the employee's honest acceptance of the appraisal can there be any assurance of real understanding and measurement.

What Should We Measure?

We should measure what we need most. The boss cannot be everywhere at once. If he needs honesty, he should invest some time in measuring it. If he needs improved planning, he should measure it. The same is true for results. Companies frequently measure both results and the ways they were obtained.

How Should We Measure?

We should measure with standards that are appropriate to the situation, that is, the position, the man on it, and his superior.

Some firms rate their people against a list of common criteria, i.e, factors common to all positions. Different factors are generally used for managerial than for nonmanagerial positions. An appraisal can include the common denominators of management: planning, organizing, motivating, directing, and controlling; or it can start with a blank sheet of paper and evaluate *anything* that the boss and the man agreed earlier to use as yardsticks, from "honesty" to "planning" to "end results." The more tangible the area measured, the more likely is acceptance to be assured. It is more difficult to agree on "honesty" than on "results."

A criterion of measurement no longer much used, except perhaps at executive levels, is the "after the fact" yardstick. This involves not saying what will be measured or considered an acceptable level of accomplishment until *after* the event has taken place. The anguish caused by this "system" is only exceeded by its futility. From it, we certainly have learned to *get agreement in advance* about what and how we will measure.

Finally, how many yardsticks need we set up? The less we use, the easier the task. By measuring things in the order of their importance, we can use three or four, possibly as many as twelve, yardsticks. The appraisal is not intended to cover *all* of a person's responsibilities, only to direct attention to a few points that will most improve his performance on a specific job.

Who Should Measure?

The man who measures should be the man most involved: the person being appraised. If the purpose of appraisal is development rather than setting levels of pay, the man is much more apt to be honest with himself, and his boss, in his appraisal. The points being appraised should, of course, be clear and the yardsticks precise. The boss should also measure from time to time so that both he and the man clearly understand how things are progressing.

In addition to the two men most directly concerned, the boss's boss needs to know his assets in manpower. He should initiate requests for information at least annually. At times staff personnel may help write appraisals, or they may desire copies as an indicator of training needs.

The primary goal of appraisal is to provide, through development of individuals now in the company employ, an adequate pool of managerial talent to meet the company's needs, present and future. Additional goals of managerial appraisal are: providing the information necessary to formulate a methodical development program; forming a basis for deciding courses of action to achieve improved performance from managerial employees; and preparing individuals for advancement.

Another basic goal in appraising is strengthening the working relationship between the man and his boss. Ideally, the man should be able to see for himself where he stands, while the boss should be able to stimulate his thinking about new goals or ways to improve progress toward present ones.

When Do We Measure?

We measure when necessary. In some situations it could be daily, but six to twelve months is the normal span between appraisals. Rarely should the period be extended beyond twelve months.

"Formal" appraisals do not replace the informal ones that are needed more frequently. Don't store things up till appraisal time; tell the man while it's hot. Then, if it seems appropriate, tell him again when the formal appraisal is due. Think of formal appraisals as "annual inventories," of the others as part of the day-to-day job of "running the store."

MANAGEMENT DEVELOPMENT

There are different levels of development. In some cases, all that is sought is a general idea of the work (a job in the next department, for example). You may want to know how to actually *do* a job (a job immediately above or below yours). You may want a high level of skill (on your own job).

The step and key-point system used in job instruction training courses is still hard to beat in learning about or how to do a job. A simple example from the program is the check list for those preparing to instruct. The steps are: (1) Have a timetable. (2) Break down the job. (3) Have everything ready. (4) Have the work place or demonstration properly arranged.

But when we go beyond the "learning about" and "how to do" stages, when we approach a job demanding a high level of skill, we face a totally different situation. Skill isn't taught; it is learned.

Ideas are understood in the classroom or through reading or discussion. Ideas are *learned* in the situation—on the job through thinking, trying out, rethinking, redoing.

But there is still a role for the boss in building his subordinate's skills. It consists of:

Letting the man work with live ammunition: a real job.
Assigning end results and yardsticks.
Considering the value of different approaches. Will *his* way work?
Listening. Let *him* solve his problems.
Asking questions. Get feedback.
Challenging. Raise alternatives for him to consider.
Providing the freedom to fail, the right to fall on one's face and rise unaided.
Scheduling follow-up meetings with him to discuss progress. And schedule them ahead of time—don't "surprise" him.
Holding post-mortems. After each assignment, let him talk it over with you. What would he change? What did he learn?
Sharing credit as well as work. Skill is impelled, not compelled.

To this point, we have discussed those aspects of development that are accomplished as part of the job. There is another area, not part of the work-centered man-boss relationship, which is useful for picking up new concepts of management. Reading this book is a supplementary form of development. So are:

Training courses, within or outside the company
College or evening courses
Job rotation
Buddy system (each one teach one)
Vacation replacements
Junior cabinets
Committee assignments

Trade and professional associations
Outside activities (Scouts, PTA)
Visits to other organizations

Management appraisal and development can be a fad, a practical science, or an art depending on the people using it. There are varieties of appraisal and development techniques. In any case, the methods must be based on acceptance rather than edict.

Both appraisal and development work better if they are job-centered (getting results rather than building men "in our image"). Both flow through and can strengthen the relationship between a man and his immediate superior. Each has a direct responsibility for management development, with the larger share resting on the individual rather than on the boss or the company.

Some things can be taught, others must be learned. Development involves both.

Staff and outside agencies can help the process along in many ways, but the core ingredients are (1) a job to be done; (2) a way to measure progress; (3) a close supporting "man-boss" relationship; and (4) impulsion to improve.

The very frank appraisal made by President Lincoln of a general who had just been assigned new responsibilities is contained in the following letter. Note the early statement of dissatisfaction, the complimentary statements which immediately follow, and then the detailed reservations.

EXECUTIVE MANSION
WASHINGTON
January 26, 1863

MAJOR GENERAL HOOKER:
GENERAL:

I have placed you at the head of the Army of the Potomac. Of course, I have done this upon what appear to me to be sufficient reasons. And yet I think it best for you to know that there are some things in regard to which, I am not quite satisfied with you. I believe you to be a brave and skillful soldier, which, of course, I like. I also believe you do not mix politics with your profession, in which you are right. You have confidence in yourself, which is a valuable, if not an indispensable quality. You are ambitious, which, within reasonable bounds, does good rather than harm. But I think that during Gen. Burnside's command of the Army, you have taken counsel of your ambition, and thwarted him as much as you could, in which you did a great wrong to the country, and to a most meritorious and honorable brother officer. I have heard, in such a way as to believe it, of your recently saying that both the Army and the Government needed a Dictator. Of course, it was not for this, but in spite of it, that I have given you the command. Only those generals who gain success, can set up dictators. What I now ask of you is military success, and I will risk the dictatorship. The government will support you to the utmost of its ability, which is neither more nor less than it has done and will do for all commanders. I much fear that the spirit which you have aided to infuse into the Army, of criticizing their Commander, and withholding confidence from him, will now turn upon you. I shall assist you as far as I can, to put it down. Neither you, nor Napoleon, if he were alive again, could get any good out of an army, while such a spirit prevails in it.

And now, beware of rashness. Beware of rashness, but with energy, and sleepless vigilance, go forward, and give us victories.

Yours very truly,

A. LINCOLN

Can a management development program succeed in accomplishing its objectives without constant application of the knowledge acquired by managers during the program? Pertinent observation is contained in the following quotation:

Hundreds of millions of dollars are spent in business and industry every year to develop management talent. The results of this effort are many and often plainly visible to the naked eye, such as the periodic enrollment of executives at conferences and seminars to upgrade their management skills. Rare, in fact, is the up-and-coming manager who does not bear service stripes on his family escutcheon to mark two or more forcible uprootings and transfers from one plant or office location to another. Cumulatively, the time and effort spent by managers on company courses devoted to leadership, human relations, and related subjects would undoubtedly be sufficient to run an enterprise of great size.

Despite this wholehearted devotion to a vitally important objective, many companies are beginning to ask: *Is management development actually developing managers?* The answer, of course, will vary with the company. But in a large number of cases, it can only be a decided *No.*

There are many reasons why. One is programitis—a blind faith in a set of procedures which purports to turn out well-machined, perfectly integrated management talent. The assumption here is that if people are appraised, counseled, and coached, required to attend their quota of conferences, and are shown in colors on a management replacement chart, they will inevitably develop as managers. The reason this assumption is so frequently unfounded is that it fails, at the very outset, to answer the key question: *For what are these managers being developed?*

Consider also the common endeavor to develop managers to fit some theoretical "ideal type." Here every effort is focused on producing individuals who are dynamic, aggressive, decisive, stable, cooperative, tactful, and adaptable. Where do such paragons exist? Dynamic, aggressive, decisive, "entrepreneurial" men are, from their very nature, anything but patterns of conformity and stability. Managers are people first. Outstanding managers show many different characteristics of temperament. It is a variety of personalities which makes the most effective team, not one stereotype, endlessly repeated. The conclusion: Management development must come to focus on the work a manager performs, not on an illusory set of personal characteristics he is supposed to possess. . . .

There are two key reasons why management development programs so often fall short. First is the failure to identify, *from the beginning,* what a manager must do in managing, and to develop and train managers to perform this kind of work. Second is the assumption that managers can be trained to manage away from the job. While courses, seminars, and conferences are an indispensable part of the training process, the most they can accomplish is to provide the right attitudes, to fill gaps in knowledge and provide a certain amount of practice in management techniques. In the final analysis, managers can learn to manage only through the direct application of this acquired managerial knowledge, attitudes, and skills to the responsibilities of their jobs.[4]

QUESTIONS AND PROBLEMS

1. Is "directing the efforts of others" a *doing* skill or a thinking process? Explain.
2. Summarize the three elements of directing in a few terse statements. Do you know what they mean?
3. Why is leadership described in the text as an aspect of directing?
4. What is delegation? Why is it so important in the management process?
5. When is delegation necessary in the management process?
6. Why does delegation seem to be so difficult a skill to develop?
7. What are the major blocks to delegating to others the work of management?
8. How do you go about delegating a task? Describe carefully.
9. What are the benefits of delegation?
10. Write a summary of the statement quoted from Herbert A. Simon in the text.
11. Why should there be *fear* in delegating to others?
12. What is the basis for this fear? Explain.
13. Explain what is meant by "Theory X" and "Theory Y." Which type are you?

14. Why is appraisal necessary in an organization? Of what value is it?
15. Is it possible to train someone to become a manager, or must he train himself? Explain.

REFERENCE NOTES

[1] Herbert A. Simon, *Administrative Behavior,* Macmillan, 1947.

[2] Louis A. Allen, "Does Management Development Develop Managers?," *Personnel* (American Management Association), September-October, 1957, p. 24.

[3] Douglas McGregor, *The Human Side of Enterprise,* McGraw-Hill, 1960, pp. 33-34, 47-48.

[4] Louis A. Allen, *op. cit.,* pp. 18-19.

READING REFERENCES

Haire, Mason, *Psychology in Management,* 2nd ed., McGraw-Hill, 1964.

McGregor, Douglas, *The Human Side of Enterprise,* McGraw-Hill, 1960.

Pfiffner, John M., and Frank P. Sherwood, *Administrative Organization,* Prentice-Hall, 1960.

24

THE SKILL OF CONTROLLING

As the fifth and last skill in management, controlling gives us an idea of accomplishment and results. The manager takes stock of the plan he set up to solve his problem and determines whether it was a success or a failure. By such successes and failures, he gets his bearings for future actions.

CONTROLLING OPERATIONAL ACTIVITIES

Controlling (1) measures the results against objectives, plans, programs, and standards; (2) decides if any deviation is significant; (3) takes actions designed to prevent future unfavorable deviations; and (4) assures the continuation of above-standard results.

In this chapter we will consider the general nature of the control function, particularly in its application to operational activities. Later in the chapter, attention will be directed to some of the special problems involved in controlling support or staff activities.

The Control Process

Control starts with the first impulse of management to "do something" and continues until that "something" is done and has been evaluated. It combines management tools (controls) and actions (controlling).

The controls are instruments or gauges that offer a "playback" or "feedback" of information, which can be measured against yardsticks or criteria.

To illustrate, the speedometer in your car is a control. With it you measure the speed of the car against the yardsticks of state laws, road signs, and highway conditions. If the car speed exceeds the yardsticks, you make decisions and take corrective action. This is "controlling."

Let's examine the process from the beginning to discover the principles that apply to all control situations.

First comes the idea to "do something." The plan for doing includes precise dates, people, materials, amounts of money, which are determined to be reasonable and realistic. Then, as

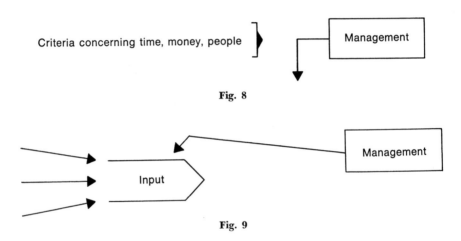

Criteria concerning time, money, people

Management

Fig. 8

Management

Input

Fig. 9

action on the plan gets under way, these elements become yardsticks or controls (deadlines and budgets) against which the action is measured. Deviation from them is a danger signal to management that controlling is indicated.

Next, an organization of men and machines is established to repeat the process in order to get the same results. Control of the process involves the same points as control of the initial plan.

In diagram form, management's plan to "do something" is shown in Fig. 8. The organizing step involves an actual "input" of people, buildings, machines, and materials to carry out the plan, as shown in Fig. 9.

The process planned is then physically set up, and management "directs" it to swing into action. The process produces certain results or output, shown in Fig. 10.

To be sure that the results obtained conform to those origin-

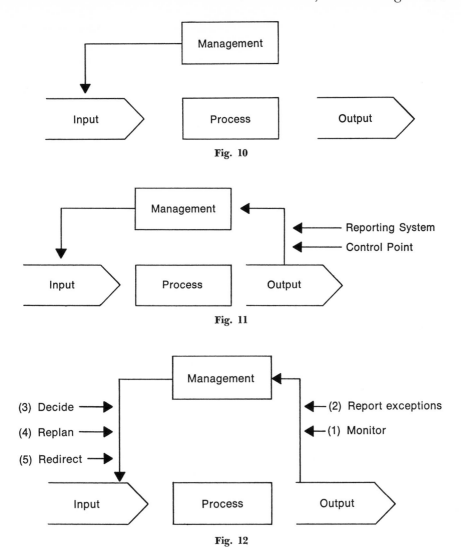

Fig. 10

Fig. 11

Fig. 12

ally planned, the output is monitored, sampled, or measured. This becomes the first permanent control (see Fig. 11). The control point is equipped with yardsticks to measure the output and with a reporting system to pass exceptional findings along to management for action. Based on the control data, management changes or modifies the original plan, replanning and redirecting to get the desired result (see Fig. 12). This takes us through one crude but complete control-controlling cycle. Two obvious modifications should be mentioned before we go away further. First, the cycle would probably be monitored at several points to control each key

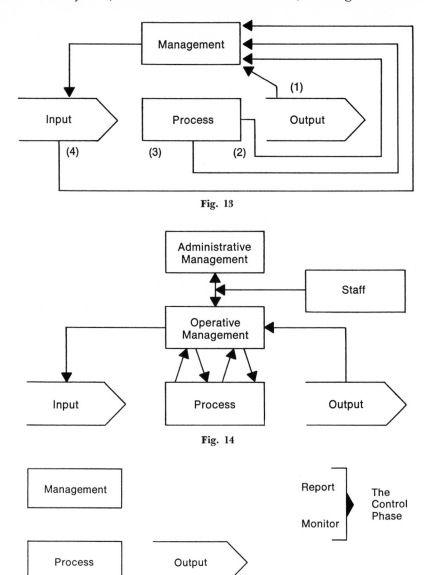

Fig. 13

Fig. 14

Fig. 15

step from input to final result (see Fig. 13). Second, management would be broken down into separate parts with reporting systems leading into them as shown in Fig. 14.

The Control Phase

Now we will look at one part of the control-controlling cycle: the monitoring and reporting of information. This is the control phase (see Fig. 15).

The steps in the control phase are: (1) specifically determining what we want to control; (2) selection of a control unit; (3) establishment of yardsticks or criteria against which we measure the control units; (4) establishment of reporting systems both to and from the monitoring point; and (5) the actual comparison of control units with yardsticks.

Let's look at these steps one at a time.

1. Specifically determining what we want to control. The more specific our control objective, the more exact our information and action can be. Our goal, then, is to establish specific control points to monitor specific data. To do this, we narrow down from district to local level, from office to individual job, from job to task. Once we are satisfied that we are at the area to be monitored, we must decide exactly what it is that is to be controlled. Do we want information on quality? quantity? time? expense? some combination of these? When we have narrowed down the field, as to location and data needed, we are ready to move on to the second step.

2. Selection of a control unit. Here we are looking for something that can accurately measure what we want to control. The control unit may be one of the following:

Kilowatts	Inches, feet, miles
Hours	Poles, meters
Dollars	Bills issued
Pounds	Payments made
Gallons	

Other questions about the control unit are: Can it be counted? Is it representative of the work being done? Is its quality consistent? Is it in language that is familiar to all people concerned?

3. Establishment of criteria. These are the schedules, quotas, goals against which we will be measuring our control units. Yardsticks are built around the word "per." They can be kilowatt-hours per customer, dollars per customer, cents per kilowatt-hour, or billings per typist per hour. Like all parts of the control phase, they vary in type and scope from level to level in the organization. They can be established in several ways. They can be engineering standards that were established while the work was being planned. They can be standards based on past performance, or they can be negotiated standards set through discussion.

4. Establishment of reporting systems. Under ideal conditions, the monitoring point would be right where the work is done so that immediate adjustments are possible. But since the

ideal situation usually doesn't exist, we need *two* reporting systems, one from the work to the monitor (who measures and compares) and a second from the monitor to the manager (who decides and acts). As an alternative, the undigested information can be passed directly to the manager from the work. In any case, there are two points to consider, one involving expense, the other speed.

Controls require desks, floor space, office supplies, people. In other words, they cost money. To keep these costs down, control should "live off the existing systems." It should be as much as possible a by-product of the actual work being done. Rather than developing special control forms, the production figures, sales slips, and lists of payments now required by the operative departments can furnish the facts needed.

Working against this is the need for speed. Control speed is based on (*a*) Assembly time—how long does it take to get all data to the monitor and to spot exceptions? (*b*) Transmission time—how many bottlenecks exist between the monitor and the manager responsible for action? (*c*) Reaction time—how long does it take the manager to get to the message, make his decision to take new action, and see that the action has been successfully taken? Reducing one or more of these three time spans may call for a separate and independent control system. Each organization calls for its own custom-tailored answer to the proper balance of economy with speed.

To this point, we have been talking primarily about the flow of information from the work to the monitor. There is the second flow to be considered—from the monitor to the manager. Here the message is filtered and put into formalized language. We change "Joe Smith was out two days with flu" to "Number of man-hours lost due to illness." Here we strive for balance between over- and undercommunication. The prime questions in this flow are: What data, in what form, are necessary to the manager to make his decisions? What reporting system furnishes the shortest distance, the straightest line, the best balance of speed and economy between monitor and decider? What coordinating advantages can the reporting system supply? In addition to the deciding manager, who else needs to know?

The reporting system can be no better than its terminal points, the monitor and the deciding manager. We should not assume that all decisions must be made "at the top." Often, they are made better and more quickly at a level nearer the work. In overlooking this, a control system can develop "intercepted feedback" by feeding control data to a level *above* the manager immediately concerned. As the data continue to *rise* from that point, lack of control increases because the information gets farther and farther away from the manager involved and is put into terms less and less useful to him.

5. Comparison of control units with yardsticks or criteria. First of all, it is not uncommon for the language of figures to be much more precise than the systems those figures represent. Many control systems are not accurate within a 10 percent range. This means that figures 5 percent above or 5 percent below the yardstick may be *system* errors rather than accurate reflections of the current work process. Because of this, managers are inclined to use a *range* rather than a specific figure as a control yardstick. Rather than saying, "Notify me when we vary from 75," he may say, "Notify me if we go under 70 or above 80."

In addition to control system error, the work may fluctuate without being out of control. So long as the work is "under control" there is little need for the manager to involve himself in the control process. His talents come into use when abnormal signs show up in the control data. He should *determine in advance* that they are to be called to his attention. Without advance determination, there is no "exception method."

Some reports are needed daily, others weekly, monthly, or annually. Some may be needed only when there are "exceptions" regardless of the time intervals. Some reports are informal oral controls; others are permanent records. The language of the permanent records may be a combination of figures, charts, and written matter. Some of the writing may be "weak-link reports" giving the progress of a particular part of the process that is temporarily in difficulty.

In summary, the manager's duties in the comparison step are establishing ranges and reporting times and methods. The monitor's duties are obtaining the data, posting them, comparing them with the yardsticks and ranges, and submitting them when and as requested. In some cases, the manager may do the work of the monitor.

Testing the control phase. Are there yardsticks against which the control themselves can be measured? Yes, controls can be evaluated. Some of the key questions to ask about a control are:

1. What is its purpose? Does the control exist because of tradition, or is it a necessary finger on a necessary pulse?

2. Are the monitoring and deciding points as close to the work as possible? This is the accountability test. Are the roadblocks to decentralized control real or artificial? How far down the line can accountability go without loss of control?
3. Is it worth what it costs? Is its "output" worth its "input" in dollars, hours, floor space?
4. Is it fast enough? Does it furnish facts we can do something about or "post-mortem" information?
5. Is it precise enough? Is it sensitive without being wild, specific without breeding gaps or overlaps?
6. Is it brief enough? In the most readable, understandable form?
7. Is it adaptable? Is it in a form that allows it to be related to other control information?
8. Is it used? How often do we actually make decisions based on this control? Is it frequent enough; too frequent?

This section looked at the steps in building a control. The next section will consider when and how it should be used.

The redirecting phase. Returning to our diagram, the control phase involves deciding, replanning, and adjusting the input or redirecting as shown in Fig. 16. The purpose of controlling is to

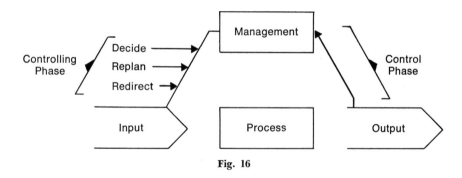

Fig. 16

assure corporate survival by (1) searching for gain and (2) avoiding loss. To do this, the manager must do the following:

Predict—to prevent as well as cure, to aid the "search for gain" by pointing out areas of opportunity as well as problems.
Compare—to evaluate, to help in deciding.
Locate trouble—to know where the trouble is, its kind, degree, and trend (improving or getting worse).
Provide limits—to outline objectives, responsibilities, and resources; to let each person reporting to him know what is expected of him and what his assets and liabilities are; in other words, to set up yardsticks.

Decentralized Control

Operating control, control over work being done, was one of the first elements of control successfully decentralized within large companies. To more limited degrees, financial and budgetary control has been decentralized in some of the larger organizations. The following paragraphs are concerned with operational rather than financial control.

Decentralization is primarily a matter of organizational rather than physical distance. Control data age as they cross *either* physical or organizational distance, so the nearer the control point to the work, the better.

Decentralized controlling can locate and correct problems while they are small, thus bringing us a step nearer to self-correcting controls.

Self-Controlling

This is the theoretical goal. Under it, each individual would "self-control" his own work. Where it has worked, it has been the result of the careful training, sound judgment, and the all-round maturity of everyone involved.

For successful self-controlling the individual must receive simple control data fast. The data must relate to his work and his work goals, and show where he stands and the direction in which he is moving. This means that he must plan his work, compare his progress with the plan, and have ready answers to questions about his plans and progress.

What Is Controlled?

In its broadest terms, the answer is: "The efforts of people are controlled." These can be broken down into three areas or stages: input, process, and output.

In the input stage, we are concerned with control of money, manpower, machinery, materials, and physical facilities—buildings and the like.

In the second or process stage, we compare progress against budgets. We measure the completion of products, their transportation, storage, and inspection, and the qualities, quantities, times, and expenses involved.

In the third stage, output, we look at the goods and services produced and the marketing costs—advertising, dispatching, and distribution—of getting them to consumers.

Integrating these three control areas are the master controls of any business, which account for income and expenses in running the over-all structure. With guidance from these master controls plus information supplied by his own unit, the manager is able to keep his part of the business coordinated with others, moving along according to plan. These actions are "controlling."

An exposition of the basic framework for control used by American Enka Corporation is contained in the following remarks of John E. Bassill, its President:

The control function embraces all those activities by which our company's operations are guided and motivated to the attainment of a desirable end. It is the final step in the performance of a completed job. It involves objectives, planning, and appraisal.

Very often when the word "control" is mentioned some people shy away from it. It's because they think of it as something restrictive, whereas, it is really the means by which management can, with confidence and safety, delegate authority and responsibility broadly.

The control process follows a regular cycle:

1. Control begins with planning—in the determination of objectives through the medium of profit goals, work programs, procedures, quality standards, and the like.
2. Once decisions have been made and the job is being done, these management tools and objectives permit the individual to better accomplish the task at hand and to gain the inner satisfaction which comes with a performance that meets the objective.
3. The process of control includes the appraisal of performance by those who have delegated authority and are responsible for seeing that the job is done properly.
4. On the basis of appraisal, it is possible to ascertain the points at which performance has varied from planned objectives or standards and to determine the reasons for variance. Either performance has been inadequate, or our goals were incorrectly set.
5. The cycle of control is completed with the planning function again coming into play to determine how performance can be improved in those cases where it has fallen short of the objective.[1]

CONTROLLING SUPPORT ACTIVITIES

Sometimes it is said, "The staff is not controlled in terms of being accountable for results. They are just there to advise and counsel the line. Only the line can be controlled in terms of measured accomplishment."

Such an attitude is ridiculous, and probably reflects a situation where the need for staff was not clearly justified to begin with. If the expected results can be stated, then they can be measured and controlled, even if only in a crude or approximate way.

Controlling Specific Kinds of Staff

Different kinds of staff activities pose different types of control situations.

Autonomous staff. Some support activities interfere little or not at all with the work of the line, and may be regarded as autonomous in this sense. The legal department of most companies would be a good example. In such cases, the staff is expected to accomplish its results on the basis of its own efforts, and control activities are not complicated severely by problems of line-staff relationships.

Control staff. Some staff functions are established primarily to advise on trends. They compile information and report deviations to line management so that line management can take necessary action. Examples include cost-recording functions, quality-control-record functions, and sales-statistical functions. A danger is that control staffs of this kind may start giving advice on what to do, instead of interpreting the information so that the line manager can make his own decision.

Problems of controlling a control staff can be minimized if standards of performance are established with reference to the timeliness, adequacy, and accuracy of the records and information provided. Such standards should involve no implications about responsibility for action taken by the line. When this distinction is carefully drawn and rigorously applied, the control staff may be effectively kept from supervising the line.

"Assistant to." The "assistant to" type of staff, discussed in Chapter 21, often has as its basic function the extension of the scope of the superior, by interpreting to those down the line his stand on a particular problem and by feeding information back up to him.

As previously explained, a staff assignment of this nature should be so defined that it carries no authority over the superior's subordinates, each of whom should have easy access to him by going around the "assistant to."

Controlling such a position can be accomplished through performance standards that reflect (1) how well the assistant interprets the superior's position to subordinates and (2) the quality of information he provides the superior in turn.

Manipulative staff. The term "manipulative staff" is sometimes used to denote support activities that give advice or assistance to the line (e.g., on safety, wage and salary administration, advertising, plant engineering). Such advice often appears to intrude into the relationships between a line supervisor and his subordinates. It is this type of staff work that is most likely to produce organizational conflicts and pose special problems of control.

Control Implications of Staff Characteristics

Most staff activities, particularly so-called "manipulative" ones, have unique charactertistics that give rise to special control problems.

Work orientation. Three major objects of work orientation are things, people, and ideas. Orientation toward *things* is best illustrated by the factory whose environment and activities are mainly determined by principles of engineering, mechanics, physics, chemistry, etc. Orientation toward *people* is well illustrated by the sales department of a typical company, for the salesman has to adapt his approach to individual human differences. An orientation toward *ideas* is commonly the focal point of staff effort. The danger here is that an attractive idea will be pursued regardless of its effect upon people or things. For example, if a new idea about pensions appears good, it may be assumed that it is good for everyone, regardless of their individual needs.

Staff position. The staff is usually closer to top management than the line group. It can get the ear of the top boss. This can make line people very cautious about a conflict with a staff man, feeling he would lose in a showdown.

Special knowledge. Many staff people have had special training or education in their area. The line people, who must know a good deal about a wide variety of activities, may resent the staff man's air of specialized superiority.

Effect on line. When a staff man appears in a line department, the uneasy question can come up: "Wonder what they're going to change this time." The staff is supposed to bring about improvements in operations—new programs, work methods, plant arrangements, etc. These often carry with them implications about the elimination or transfer of people, which can threaten a worker's security.

2. Policies and procedures covering functions supervised are periodically reviewed and improved.
3. The workload of the department is analyzed periodically and the number and composition of staff is kept:

   a. Adequate to meet departmental performance standards.
   b. No higher than necessary.

4. Definite responsibilities are assigned to each person in the department, and sufficient authority is delegated to carry them out effectively.
5. Job assignments are made in accordance with the knowledge and skills of the individual concerned, so that:

   a. Each person is given the opportunity to use his highest skills in carrying out his assigned work.
   b. The less complex tasks are delegated to the greatest practical extent.

6. Up-to-date job descriptions exist for each position in the department.
7. Performance standards have been developed for all major measurable functions and for the activities of each individual employee.
8. A definite plan of personnel development has been established and is being carried out as follows:

   a. The individuals to be trained have been identified.
   b. The types of experience or training needed have been determined.
   c. The method of providing such training has been devised.
   d. The individuals are actively obtaining such experiences or training.
   e. Periodic checks are made of the individual's progress.
   f. There is other specific evidence of professional development of staff members as set forth in their individual performance standards.

9. Starting and completion dates have been set for all principal projects such as research reports, studies for *Management News* articles, major procedural changes.
10. A budget based on future plans has been prepared, and any variances from it can be justified.
11. Equipment and physical layout of the department are periodically restudied with a view to improving efficiency, working conditions, and appearance.

II. Doing. Performance as to execution of work is up to standard when:

   1. In reply to their inquiries, members are supplied with or guided to

the best information available from internal or external sources and:

   a. The efficiency of operations is such that visitors' inquiries are effectively handled during the time visitors are present, replies to telephone and telegraph inquiries are dispatched within an average period of seven working hours, and replies to letter inquiries are sent within an average period of 21 working hours.
   b. The resources and competence of the staff are such as to assure that useful answers are supplied to at least 95 percent of all members' inquiries which it is within policy for the Information Service to answer.
   c. The quality of replies is such as to evoke "fan mail" or complimentary acknowledgments from at least 10 percent of the persons using the Service, and replies suggestive of dissatisfaction or error from not more than 0.2 percent.
   d. The quality of service and information available to the members in the several AMA divisions is sufficiently uniform to lead to usage which is substantially proportional to the numbers of members in the divisions.
   e. Assistance from the Information Service is a directly identifiable factor in at least one new membership per month.

2. Research reports are of such quality and quantity that:
   a. At least one is produced annually in the subject area of each AMA division.
   b. They produce income at least equal to direct and prorated expense.
   c. They give tangible evidence of effort to produce "firsts" and to serve broad segments of the AMA membership.

3. At least ten two-page articles for *Management News* are submitted annually and meet the following requirements:

   a. They are acceptable to the Editor and of significance and interest to the AMA membership.
   b. They are factual in character and usually based on unpublished surveys or case studies.
   c. The surveys and writing are so scheduled as to create no emergencies by failure to meet deadlines.
   d. Subjects are fairly distributed over areas of interest to the various AMA divisions.
   e. Insofar as possible, a division is featured in a "quiet" season sometime between major conferences.

4. Bibliographies for all seminars, and for special conferences where required:

a. Are prepared by the dates scheduled.

b. Are assured of quality by being reviewed by persons familiar with their subjects.

5. Surveys conducted by the department are of such interest, and are sufficiently free of burden for the respondent, as to produce at least 40 percent returns.

6. Library materials are made speedily available to members and staff by:

   a. Starting publications on their routes on day of receipt.

   b. Providing sufficient copies and follow-up to permit route to be covered within one week for dailies, ten days for weeklies, one month for other publications.

   c. Clipping, marking, and filing of material within two weeks of availability of uncirculated copy, "clip" copy, or magazine retired from shelf use.

   d. Cataloguing new books within two weeks of receipt.

7. The working time of Information Service personnel is effectively utilized, as evidenced, for example, by applying at least 90 percent of time devoted to inquiries to handling those of business-executive members (as contrasted to nonmembers, students, international members, libraries).

8. Qualified persons are available and properly assigned for all jobs in the department.

9. Each person in the department is guided in carrying out assigned responsibilities and assisted to assume more important responsibilities.

10. Each person understands clearly the assignments for which he is responsible, including:

    a. Basic objectives

    b. Techniques or methods to be used

    c. Extent of authority

    d. Proper time for completion of work

11. The following conditions exist in the department:

    a. Employees are informed in advance of any changes which will affect them or their work.

    b. Each person in the department is currently informed of his job status, appraisal of his performance, and so forth.

12. Personnel within the department are given opportunity and encouragement, through group conferences or other means, to communicate with supervisors on matters of importance, such as possible improvements in operations and the like.

13. At least six department conferences per year are held with all

personnel for the purpose of planning the work of the department, reporting progress, discussing problems, soliciting suggestions or ideas, making assignments, and so forth.

14. Duties and responsibilities of each person in the department are carried out in accordance with their specific performance standards.

15. The director maintains a personal awareness of the current management developments by:

   a. Attendance annually at at least three AMA conferences
   b. Attendance annually at at least three major non-AMA conferences dealing with pertinent subject matter or research
   c. Reading regularly at least 50 of the most significant business periodicals
   d. Reading annually at least 25 new books on management and related fields, and scanning at least 150 more

16. The director keeps personally informed as to the methods and operations of other information services and survey or research departments by personal visits to at least three comparable organizations annually.

17. Completion dates for specific projects are met within 20 percent of time originally estimated.

18. Other departments and individuals are kept informed of matters of joint interest, such as research-report plans and progress.

19. Funds spent for books, periodicals, and business services are effectively utilized, as evidenced by circulation records or other measures of usage.

20. All AMA policies and procedures are adhered to.

   III. Appraising Results. Performance as to departmental control is up to standard when:

1. Actual performance of the functions of the department is periodically compared with standards of the individuals in the department and with the standards listed above.

2. Performance of individuals which is above standard is recognized and commended, and any laxities or breaches of discipline are corrected.

3. The department head reports accurately to his superiors on plans, progress, irregularities, or other significant factors affecting assigned responsibilities.

4. Variances from standard are analyzed for cause and corrective action is taken.[2]

FINANCIAL CONTROL: INVESTMENTS

Accounting statements are the basic working tools of the finance man. While he does not need to be able to prepare them or understand all their intricacies, he does need a knowledge of basic accounting principles and accounting terminology.

The Balance Sheet

The balance sheet is merely a statement of the company's financial position at a designated time. It lists as assets all the wealth of a business unit. This wealth may be material goods and resources or claims against others. It also lists all liabilities and owners' equity. The liabilities are legal claims of creditors which would be satisfied by a court judgment in the event of default. Owners' equity represents the claims of owners (preferred and common stockholders in a corporation) in the business and includes their initial contribution and all retained earnings.

The balance sheet always balances because owners' total equity is the difference between the value of the assets and the amounts owed creditors.

The Statement of Income

Unlike the balance sheet, the income statement explains in financial terms the transactions during a designated period of time. The statement subtracts expenses from revenues and arrives at a net income figure for the period. Since modern business does not keep records on a cash basis, items of revenue are listed when earned rather than when cash is received, and items of expense are deducted when incurred rather than when paid.

Thus the income statement is substantially different from the statement of cash receipts and disbursements. For example, payment for a new plant would involve a sizable cash disbursement, but expenses would only be affected as depreciation was charged against the plant over a number of years following the cash outlay.

Financial Analysis

From the grouping of figures in the above financial statements and others, various relationships can be established to measure the financial status of the business. Certain accounts may be compared to similar accounts in previous years, to similar accounts in other companies, or to other accounts in the same company for the same period.

Year-to-year analysis. By following one item, for example, operating expenses, for a period of years, increases or decreases in both actual amounts and percentages can be determined.

Trends for one item may be related to those of another. Sales increases become meaningful only when related to the trend of operating expenses. The two trends together indicate increasing or decreasing margins of gross revenue.

Static ratios. From the balance sheet for a given year, certain comparisons can be made that aid financial controlling. The current ratio divides total current assets by total current liabilities. There are no set "good" ratios. Generally, business considers 1 to 1 or 1.5 to 1 satisfactory.

In the case of a public utility, due to the high-funded debt, a second ratio showing net worth to *current* debt is also desirable. The net worth consists of all assets less all liabilities (excluding capital and surplus accounts).

Other ratios used in financial controlling are (1) net worth to fixed assets, (2) net worth and funded debt to fixed assets, and (3) current assets to fixed assets.

Dynamic ratios. From the income statement come ratios having to do with turnover or velocity within the business. They include (1) operating expenses divided by operating revenues, (2) net income divided by revenue, (3) net income divided by owners' equity, and (4) operating revenue divided by total assets.

As you can see, countless relationships may be established to show trends or compare business to business or year to year. The key to financial controls, however, rests not in the ratios, but in the judgment and experience of the finance man in utilizing these ratios.

Financial Management

The financial problems of business management revolve around the acquisition of capital (assets) and its control. Capital is basically obtained in one of three ways: borrowing, renting, or owner contribution.

Borrowing capital has advantages in that it can be paid back when no longer needed; it is more readily available and, generally, its long-run total cost is less than that of other types. On the other hand, borrowing involves substantial risk to the business enterprise in that interest payment must be met regardless of availability of earnings, and a maturity date will eventually arrive.

Renting assets rather than owning them offers the advantage of a much smaller total capital investment but the disadvantages of possible loss of use of the asset and the higher costs of renting.

Capital contributed by owners is the safest for a business

in that it need not be repaid and there is no interest charged for its use. It has the major disadvantage of being relatively expensive in the long run. This is true because return on owner capital has to be greater than return on other types of investments in order to attract owner-investors in the face of the greater risk involved.

Choosing sources of funds. In planning expansion of a business, all the advantages and disadvantages of each possible source of capital have to be carefully weighed in order to determine the best one. Reinvested earnings must not be overlooked as an excellent source of owner capital.

Proper ratios should be maintained between owner and borrowed capital and between long- and short-term borrowing. A new development in recent years is intermediate-term capital supplied by banks and equipment manufacturers with maturities from one to five years. Regular bank credit and credit from suppliers are sources of short-term capital, but should be used for that purpose only. It must be remembered that working capital is a permanent need of the business. Too much short-term financing ties management's hands in the use of assets and creates concern for liquidity to meet near-term maturities.

Financial planning. Not only should cash needs and sources be carefully budgeted over a period of time, but total capital requirements and sources also require planning. Any plant expansion or volume growth requires added fuel and materials, and cash for proper operation. Growth may drain working capital to a point where solvency is questioned. Sufficient new permanent investment must be available to meet permanent expansion requirements. A business firm cannot safely rely on increased earnings from expansion to provide immediately the necessary additional capital.

Cost of capital. The use of capital costs money regardless of its source. Bank credit normally involves a stated interest charge. Actual rates charged rather than quoted rates should be determined. Trade credit, even if no interest rate is quoted, involves a charge for the use of capital. Bond financing involves periodic interest payments.

There is a tax advantage to any borrowing. Interest payments are considered a business expense and are deductible from profits before Federal income taxes. Dividends or owner profits are not an expense and are not deductible. Thus the U.S. Government is really paying a part of all interest costs by levying no taxes on them.

Too many businesses overlook the fact that owner capital

also costs. While it is not deductible for tax purposes, it carries an inherent promise of some future return to the owner. Re-invested earnings also involve an inherent promise of future return or the owner would not leave them in the business.

Return on investment. Certainly the most important reason for investing in business is to make a profit. This profit should be a return on the capital turned over to the business for its use. A common measure of business profit today is return on sales. This is only one side of the picture. Return on capital must also be considered. A 5 percent return on a revenue of $100,000 may be very profitable for a business employing only $10,000 in capital but very unsatisfactory for a business employing $200,000 in capital.

All return should, of course, be considered relative to the amount of risk involved. Since it is capital that is being risked, return should be measured relative to capital and compared to similar firms' return on capital invested. No expansion should be considered unless the potential return on the additional capital required is sufficient to overcome the risk being taken. Management efforts should be judged in the light of return on capital. Business decisions should be made in relation to their effect on return on investment. Fig. 17 indicates the factors which affect operating return on investment.

A very partisan but interesting viewpoint on the role of financial management and the financial manager in industry is conveyed in the following statement by Alvin Brown, Vice President for Finance of the Johns-Manville Company.

Every man is a financial man.

A research man develops a new product. As you well know, that is not so simple a proceeding as words can make it sound. His performance is not an accident. He will not have spent his time on this development without foreseeing the result as nearly as he could. He will have foreseen as nearly as he could what it will cost to produce and market his new product and what people will be willing to pay for it. He will have satisfied himself that these figures of cost and price bear an economic relation to each other. Were he not to foresee these effects as nearly as he could, he would risk a fruitless expenditure of his effort. He is too practical a man to take that risk.

In this sense, and to this extent, he has been a financial man. He could not have done his job properly except by so being.

Of course, the research man may err in his calculations: of this it can only be said that we are all exposed to error from time to time. And, of

Relationship of Factors Affecting Return on Investment

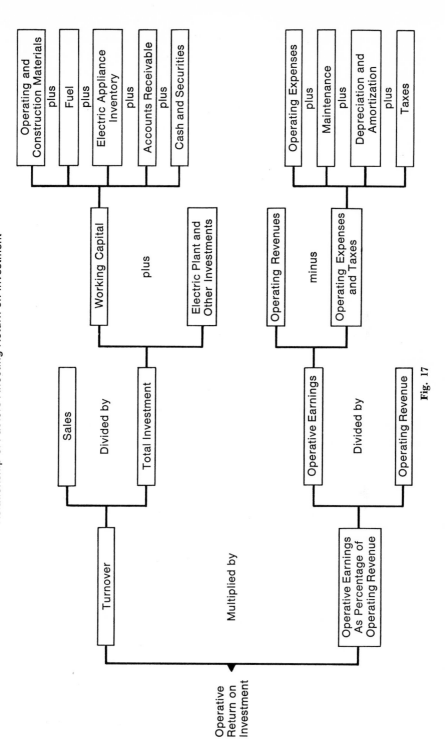

Fig. 17

course, he may neglect the prudent calculation that his job requires: of this it can only be said that he fails in his duty. Neither deviation impeaches the fact that he is a financial man in his approach to decisions.

But the research man has taken only the first step in adopting a new product. Whether and how it shall be produced and marketed remain questions to be decided. To these decisions, the engineer, the production man, the merchandiser, and perhaps others, must all contribute. What they contribute are facts—the facts that each is skilled to obtain. To the facts so contributed, moreover, someone must apply reason—intelligence —so as to give them their proper weight, evaluate them and relate them properly to each other. This is the material—the foundation—of decision. This is the financial approach.

This first example, however, is not typical. It is not every day an enterprise decides whether to market a new product. But decisions are made every day. More often the question is whether to expand the facilities for an existing product, or whether to re-equip a process so as to reduce the cost of the product. Oftener still, the production man will be making decisions about the use of labor and material, the salesman about selling and advertising, the personnel man about employment. Each of these men has a primary operating function, but each must approach that function with a financial viewpoint because his decisions will affect the earnings of the enterprise. In that sense, each is a financial man. The financial man is anxious to spend—wisely.

One sometimes hears the financial man described as a "penny-pincher" or as the "watchdog of the treasury." To the extent that this means that the financial man should try to ward off unjustified raids on the treasury, it is apt. Often, however, it is said with the implication that the financial mon abhors spending per se. In this sense, it is slander. . . .

As should be quite clear from what has been said before, the financial man should be just as anxious to spend when spending is profitable as he is reluctant to see money spent unwisely. It is just as much his duty, in other words, to promote—and, indeed, to originate—expenditures that should be made as to resist those that should not be made. His role in spending should be active as well as passive.[3]

FINANCIAL CONTROL: EXPENSE MANAGEMENT

The process of planning for future financial requirements to maintain solvency and gain profit is known as budgeting, and the formal presentation of the plan in writing is called a budget.

The budget is the product of both planning and controlling. Like the plan, it is based on forecasts and estimates of future performance. Like both the plan and the control, it is a tool which cannot rise above the skill of its user.

Budget and Budgetary Control Defined

A budget is a financial plan of the future needs of some or all of the activities of an organization for a period of time. As such, it is a very effective control tool.

Budgetary control is achieved through the establishment of standards of performance and the continuing comparison of actual with planned performance. Each subordinate is held responsible for any variance from the standard established in his area of responsibility. Where a difference exists between budget and actual figures, it does not automatically mean that the standard is right and the subordinate wrong. It may be that circumstances call for a change in the standard.

Nature of Budgetary Control

Financial statement analysis contributes to control by providing historical prospective—what has happened before—in planning future action. Budgeting, in a sense, takes up where statement analysis leaves off. Budgeting contributes to control by (1) anticipating cash needs, (2) planning for necessary financing, and (3) establishing standards by which to test current operating performance.

Advantages of Budgetary Control

Budgetary control provides management with an over-all viewpoint and an awareness of the position of many different activities, thus fostering their coordination. By anticipating requirements in advance, management substitutes a rational plan for snap decisions and thus provides for more efficient investment in assets. Arranging for financing in advance of need avoids hasty and panicky action and enables management to select that method of financing which best fits its requirements on terms which are the most satisfactory.

Budgetary control establishes standards or limits whose purpose is to see that revenues are maximized and expenses held to a minimum. Their achievement will result in the most satisfactory return on investment that can be obtained within the resources of a given business.

Budgetary control focuses attention on those items which deviate substantially from budget standards, and which can subsequently be corrected.

Budgetary control, finally, helps fix responsibility. There is less question as to who is responsible when actual results are compared to a properly prepared budget.

Limitations of Budgetary Control

Budgets are no replacement for executive accountability. They do not make up the manager's mind for him. Every effort should be made to live within the budget, but if good reasons exist for deviation from it, they should be freely expressed and understandingly accepted. Too high budgets can devastate morale. Too low ones are not conducive to maximum effort.

Budget Prerequisites

The relationship between budgetary control and other aspects of managing is clearly revealed by the following list of prerequisites to effective budgetary control:

1. Establishing and communicating definite objectives, both long- and short-run, for the organization
2. Developing a sound organization in which the responsibilities of each position are clearly and concisely defined
3. Providing a reliable cost accounting system containing comparative data of past performance to help establish standards for the future, and to provide throughout the budgetary period actual data to compare with the budget items
4. Making available forecast and research information so that the standards are more apt to be true approximations of the future rather than projections of past performance
5. Participation in the formulation of budgets by executives whose areas are subject to budgetary control to give them a greater sense of responsibility for making their budgets work
6. Provision for flexibility so that the estimates can be adjusted to reflect actual operating levels rather than those assumed in budgetary planning

Types of Budgets

Budgets can be utilized in many areas, such as purchasing budgets, production budgets, and so on. Financial budgeting falls into three main classes: (1) cash budgeting, (2) capital budgeting, (3) and operating budgeting.

Cash budgeting is a plan or forecast of future cash receipts and disbursements. It informs management in advance when excess cash will be on hand so that profitable use may be made of it. It also informs management when additional cash will be required and how much, so that sources can be arranged in advance. It is easier to obtain additional capital when it is not immediately needed than when the business is in obvious need of cash.

Capital budgeting is a plan for future investment in fixed assets. It enables management to predetermine financing techniques and encourages an advance analysis of profit possibilities from the proposed investment. Construction budgets are a type of capital budget used to control investment in a new project.

Operating budgets are the most important type for control purposes because they make for an effective pattern of expenditures.

Fixed versus Flexible Budgets

A fixed budget is one that sets a single level of expected operations and estimated costs. Thus a company or division may base its operations and expenses upon an expected sales of $40 million. If the results differ from this figure, an adjustment must be made in the budgeted figures, usually by altering the actual costs to agree with the change in sales volume. Rarely will a firm be able to estimate its exact sales.

To provide for a variety of possible results, a flexible budget may be used. A series of levels of possible production and sales are projected, and expenses estimated for each level. At the very least, two levels will be projected, a high and a low level. The actual results will probably fall somewhere in between, and the expenses at this level can be compared with a projection of the budgeted ones.

Fixed costs remain unaltered, but variable costs are projected for various possible volumes of production. Actual production and costs may then be compared against the costs of the actual volume. Differences between actual and budgeted costs may then be evaluated, and adjustments made in operations to take advantage of better-than-budgeted performance or to correct for poorer-than-budgeted performance.

The Budgeting Process

The process of budgeting is complex, but operating budgets are generally based on some kind of sales forecast. On the basis of this forecast, each divisional and departmental manager estimates the expenses necessary to meet its requirements. Top management then coordinates these estimates and molds them into an over-all budget. If the results do not meet the firm's profit objectives, a review of suggested department expenditures is required to bring composite budgeting into line with objectives.

The Controllership Foundation undertook a field study on certain human relations aspects of budgeting in order to develop more effective budgetary control. Professor Chris Argyris of Yale University, who participated in the study, developed from it the following implications for management:

. . . budgets and budgeting can be related to at least four important human relations problems:

1. Budget pressure tends to unite the employees against management, and tends to place the factory supervisor under tension. This tension may lead to inefficiency, aggression, and perhaps a complete breakdown on the part of the supervisor.

2. The finance staff can obtain feelings of success only by finding fault with factory people. These feelings of failure among factory supervisors lead to many human relations problems.

3. The use of budgets as "needlers" by top management tends to make each factory supervisor see only the problem of his own department.

4. Supervisors use budgets as a way of expressing their own patterns of leadership. When this results in people getting hurt, the budget, in itself a neutral thing, often gets blamed.

Now, in the light of these findings, what lines of action should management take? Though the problems obviously are complex, and the research into them exploratory, there do appear to be two areas in which management action may prove fruitful.

The first is in the problem of getting an acceptance of budgets. Interviews with controllers suggest that this area is a crucial one. Time and time again our research group was told that the best way to gain acceptance is to have the supervisors all participate in the making of the budgets that affect them. In particular the controllers emphasized the need for participation of all key people in instituting any changes in budgets, plus the willingness on the controllers' own part to revise their budgets whenever experience indicates it necessary.

The second area in which management action may attack these budget problems is that of training in human relations. . . .

1. The training should be focused to help the finance staff perceive the human implications of the budget system.

2. The training should help show the finance staff the effects of pressure upon people. Thorough discussions seem necessary to understand the advantages and disadvantages of applying such pressure.

3. The training should also include discussion concerning the effects of success and failure. The accounting staff should be helped to perceive

their difficult position, namely, that of placing others in failure. They should also be taught the symptoms of people who feel they have failed. Most important, the course should include practical techniques which the finance staff can use to get along better with the factory people, knowing full well that they may place these factory people in failure.

4. Again, the human relations training should include thorough discussions of the human problems related to the department-centeredness of supervisors that is caused by budgets. The finance people should be helped to perceive this department-centeredness as a defense on the part of the factory supervisors rather than as the "narrow-mindedness" which many of them seem to think it is.

5. Finally, there needs to be some instruction in the basic content of human relations as a field of study. This includes the concepts of informal and formal organizations, industrial organizations as social systems, status systems in industrial organizations, and such subjects as interviewing, counseling, and leadership.[4]

QUESTIONS AND PROBLEMS

1. Why is controlling such an important skill in the management process?
2. Could controlling lead to further planning? Explain.
3. Describe the control process.
4. How do you go about setting up controls? Give an example in some detail.
5. Why do we need to set up reporting systems as a part of the controlling skill?
6. What is the control phase? How do we test it?
7. Why is it necessary to set up controls on staff personnel?
8. Describe the principles relating to the control of staff.
9. What is the significance of the standards of performance issued by the American Management Association?
10. Why are the balance Sheet and statement of income good control devices for an organization? In what ways are they misinterpreted by employees? By management?
11. How can you control through the use of financial ratios? Why don't more managers manage through this control device?
12. Work out five sets of financial ratios that would be of assistance to management.
13. How can financial controls assist management in its long-range planning?
14. What is the basic purpose of budgeting? How does it fit in with controlling?
15. What is the relationship between budgeting control and planning? Is this relationship important to the success of the venture?

REFERENCE NOTES

[1] John E. Bassill, from an address before the Executive and Staff Departments of Algemene Kunstyzijde Unie, N. V. at Arnhem, Holland, May 19, 1951.

[2] Enell, John W., and Haas, George H., *Setting Standards for Executive Performance*, Research Study No. 42, American Management Association, 1960.

[3] Alvin Brown, *Financial Approach to Industrial Operations*, Society for Advancement of Management, 1957, pp. 7-8, 22.

[4] Chris Argyris, "Human Problems with Budgets," *Harvard Business Review*, January-February, 1953.

READING REFERENCES

Enell, John W., and George H. Haas, *Setting Standards for Executive Performance*, Research Study No. 42, American Management Association, 1960.

Goetz, Billy, *Management Planning and Control*, McGraw-Hill, 1949.

Jerome, William Travers, III, *Executive Control—The Catalyst*, Wiley, 1961.

Lemke, Bernard C., and James D. Edwards, eds., *Administrative Control and Executive Action*, Merrill, 1961.

Malcolm, Donald G., and Alan J. Rowe, eds., *Management Control Systems*, Wiley, 1960.

Rose, T. G., and Donald E. Farr, *Higher Management Control*, McGraw-Hill, 1957.

Rowland, Virgil K., *Managerial Performance Standards*, American Management Association, 1960.

Tucker, Spencer A., *Successful Managerial Control by Ratio-Analysis*, McGraw-Hill, 1961.

Welsch, Glenn A., *Budgeting, Profit-Planning and Control*, 2nd ed., Prentice-Hall, 1964.

PART V

ANALYSIS OF THE LEADERSHIP
CHARACTERISTICS OF THE MANAGER

The personal elements that make up the characteristics of the individual who manages successfully boil down to one word—leadership. Hundreds of research studies have been made to determine the nature of leadership, how it functions in a business organization, and how it can best be learned. At the present time, so many differing points of view exist about these problems that students of management and executives themselves are somewhat confused. Various theories of leadership have evolved which leave unsolved the age-old problem of the uneasy balance between individual and organizational needs, between freedom and authority.

Leadership theory has run the gamut from scientific management, through human relations, to the more recent findings of the revisionists. At this juncture in time, however, most theorists fortunately realize that leadership is the fulcrum on which the demands of the individual and the demands of the organization are balanced (as on a bicycle).

The complexity of leadership appears to stem from the fact that it is difficult to view the leader (the manager) as an individual, separate and apart from the structure and other people that make up the group (the organization). Even while granting that the manager's work is related to all these other factors, to look at him as an individual seems to be the most satisfying way to approach the problem. Consequently, the manager here has been separated from the group and will be discussed as an individual, using the theories of leadership only as they relate to the environment in which he operates.

Certain broad categories of personal elements that characterize the leader as standing out from his fellows are used in this book because they take into account a number of studies that have been made and appear to have greater practical application than many others. The three categories used are: (1) intellectual capacity, (2) emotional stability, and (3) relations with others.

Decisions must be made by individual managers, and it is probably a fair assumption that such decisions are directly related to characteristics inherent in the individual. Of course, he makes his decisions with the group and the organization in mind, based upon facts available to him, but his own intellectual capacity, his emotional stability, and his personal relations with others will undoubtedly have a bearing on what his decisions are and how they are made.

The fact that the field of leadership is cloudy does not mean that we should adopt a fatalistic attitude or that there are no guideposts to management characteristics. But we must remember that each day, each situation, each group of subordinates is unique. Each manager faces a constantly shifting pattern of relationships which must be carefully studied to determine the precise "mix" or combination of executive characteristics that will obtain desired results. All men are not leaders in *all* situations. The characteristics of one man, however, can cause him to be the most effective leader in a *specific* situation.

It was said earlier that no one can develop you as a manager; you must develop yourself. This point cannot be overstressed. In addition to increasing your technical knowledges and skills, your administrative skills, your ability to handle people and to communicate with them, your personal characteristics can, and probably should, be refined and developed. Modification of his individual personality, then, becomes one of the greatest challenges in the manager's self-development.

25

THEORIES AND CONCEPTS OF LEADERSHIP

Out of the jungle of information, research studies, theories, and concepts, emerge some broad understandings of the field as well as some specific approaches. The three broad-brush theories of leadership in its relation to organization are characterized by Warren G. Bennis as (1) scientific management theory, (2) human relations theory, and (3) revisionist theory.

Scientific Management. The first approach, really scientific management *and* bureaucracy, describes a body of theory (prevalent from 1910 to 1935) which tended to view organizations as if they existed without people. Max Weber, the German sociologist, contributed the first fully developed theory of bureaucracy. . . .

Writing about the same time as Weber (1910) was an American engineer, Frederick W. Taylor, who more than any other individual advanced the professionalization of management. Taylor, the "father of scientific management," attempted to rely on a "third force" that would mediate between man and the organization. Whereas Weber emphasized the legal domination of "role" or position in a status hierarchy, Taylor stressed the impersonal rationality of measurement.

Human Relations. The second group of theories (thriving from 1938 to 1950) appropriately is called the *human relations* approach. Here people are regarded essentially as if they existed without organizations.

What precipitated the change was the formulation of the human relations model, crystallized in the early 1930's by Fritz Roethlisberger and W. J. Dickson in *Management and the Worker.* Now, the dominant focus of organization was transformed from a rational model, free from the friction of man's emotions, to a model which appears less determined (or mechanistic) and hence more unfathomable. That is, the new look in organizational theory took cognizance of unanticipated consequences of organizations—workers' feelings, attitudes, beliefs, perceptions, ideas, sentiments.

Management—partly through the seminal work of several social scientists (names primarily associated with this pioneering work are Elton Mayo, Kurt Lewin, J. L. Moreno, and Carl Rogers)—began to take seriously not only the formal organizational chart, but also the informal and interpersonal contexts. The major assumption of the human relations model was that man could be motivated to work more productively on the basis of fulfilling certain social and psychological needs. This "new look" of organizations was no less "rational" than the earlier machine model, except that man's motivation was a trickier and more elusive concept than was the concept of the machine.

The Revisionists. Since 1950 a number of authors have attempted to reconcile and integrate classical and modern organizational theory. I will refer to these theorists as the *revisionists.* In general, they share a common concern for revising the native, unsubstantiated, and unrealistic aspects of the human relations approach without sacrificing its radical departure from traditional theory. These revisionists (Douglas M. McGregor, Robert N. McMurry, and Chris Argyris) . . . are concerned with external, economic factors—with productivity, formal status, and so on—but not to the exclusion of the human elements that the traditional theorists neglected. . . .

We have a great deal more to learn about leadership. And where the revisionists seem to require particular help is in the nature of change. Change that facilitates the motivation and skills of managers and their employees and allows them to develop more authentic human relations, more true collaboration, a more reality-centered leadership—all within the high structured organization—must always be sought.[1]

From the above reference, it can be concluded that further study of the entire subject is needed to define more sharply the role of the leader or manager.

APPROACHES TO LEADERSHIP

Gordon L. Lippitt points out that today laymen and scientists hold different views about leadership. He presents the following approaches:

TRAIT APPROACH

Hundreds of studies have been done comparing the physical, intellectual, or personality traits of leaders and followers. For example, leaders tend to be bigger and brighter, better adjusted, and have more accurate social perceptions than followers (but not so much as to be unacceptable to the group). On the whole, this approach has been disappointing. Only 5 percent of the traits in over one hundred such studies appeared in four or more studies. This trait approach has led to selection procedures by paper and pencil test and/or performance test.

SITUATIONAL APPROACH

This could best be described as an insight rather than an approach to understanding leadership. It is based upon the hypotheses that behavior of leaders in one setting may be different from those in another. Those which are needed vary from one situation to another. This is recognized by the Air Force which allows "mutinies" to occur in emergency situations, involving the lives of survivors following a crash. That is, although the pilot is in command of the flight, during a crash and struggle for survival in enemy territory, the group may select a different commanding officer whose leadership skills better meet the situation. Although there has been little research on this, these situational factors do suggest the need for flexibility in the principles of selection, training, and sensitivity of leaders.

There are a good many variables that enter into producing leaders. There are, however, two types of forces which influence how a leader arrives at a leadership position. One of these types includes personal drives and hungers—it is motivational. Probably vitality to survive pressures brought to bear on people in leadership positions is important, also. Then, there are external forces that present men and women with the opportunity to be leaders. Sometimes, in other words, people are motivated by personal drives to become leaders; sometimes they find themselves in leadership positions as the result of external forces, and they may or may not be aware of the forces influencing them. Usually both factors are at work. There are both motivational and social factors which tend to produce leaders.

BEHAVIOR APPROACH

We have seen some of the forces which bring people into positions of leadership. Now let's look at what they do when in that position. The kind of leadership position a person holds will determine the different kinds of leadership functions he performs. There are, we feel, four major ones. A leader may perform a symbolic function, such as the Queen of England performs at present, and her leadership is primarily a symbolic type of leadership. A leader may perform primarily a problem-solving type or decision-making type of leadership function. He may perform an advisory or information giving function. He may function primarily as an initiator or an advocate of some plan or proposition. Of course, no leader performs just one of these functions to the exclusion of all others. Rather, these are the jobs which are so indispensable that the people who do them attain leadership or have it thrust upon them.

The three styles of leadership are autocratic, democratic, and laissez faire leadership. These are complex terms which refer variously to leadership style or group climate. In attempting to find adequate definitions for these terms, one might try to place them on a scale representing amount of freedom. When one suggests "freedom" as a continuum along which these terms might be ranged, the autocratic leaders should placed low on the scale and the others higher. However, there is considerable disagreement as to whether democratic or laissez faire permitted more freedom, and among those who placed laissez faire leadership higher, there was disagreement as to where along the continuum democracy belonged. Freedom, then, seems to be inadequate as a criterion for defining these terms. A second possible criterion is efficiency. This, too, seems inadequate. Laissez faire leadership would be placed low on such a scale and the other two higher; we would not agree on the relative positions of autocracy and democracy. I suggest a third way of defining leadership: in terms of the location of the decision-making function. In this case, we can all agree that the decision-making function resided in the *leader* in the autocratic group, and in the *individual* in the laissez faire group, and in the *group* in the democratic group.

Three major studies have been made of leadership style and climate. The first two were done in 1938 and 1940 at the State University of Iowa; the third in 1942 at Stanford University. All were done with clubs of youths with adult leaders. The two general purposes of the clubs were achievement and recreation. The boys were engaged in activities such as building furniture, making papier-mâché masks, etc. The same club had all types of leaders, and the same leader used at least two of the styles, after extensive training. The results showed six kinds of differences:

1. Democratic leadership resulted in a more satisfying, efficient leadership than did laissez faire.
2. A democratic social climate can also be efficient.
3. An autocratic style creates hostility and aggressiveness among its members.
4. Discontentment which does not appear on the surface occurred in some of the autocratic groups. (Four of the six autocratic groups showed no overt discontent.)
5. There was more dependency and less individuality in the autocratic than in the democratic group.

6. There was more orientation to the needs of the group and more acceptance of each other in the democratic groups.

This concept of leadership seeks to discover what actions are required by groups under various conditions if they are to achieve their objectives, and how different members take part in these actions. Leadership is viewed as the performance of those acts which are required by the group. The group functions' approach to leadership takes into account the other approaches discussed. Groups differ from one another in a variety of ways. Actions vary from one group to another. The nature of leadership traits or acts will accordingly vary from group to group. Situational aspects will determine what functions are needed and who will do them (i.e., the nature of group's goals, structure of group, attitudes of members, and similar situational factors).

Many classifications of leadership functions in the group have been proposed. Administrators refer to planning, decision-making, coordinating, etc.

Basically there appear to be two main classifications of leadership functions in groups:

1. The achievement of the group goal.
2. The maintenance or strengthening of the group itself.

In this respect, it is important to note that any specific behavior may be helpful for both or favor one at the expense of the other (i.e., a group may be so intent upon maintaining good relations that it avoids friction at all costs, thereby retarding its problem-solving process). On the other hand, a wise solution may solve a problem and also help the solidarity of the group.

The distribution of leadership functions in a group occurs in several ways. Usually in a well-organized group, certain functions are assigned to certain members, or granted to them. Distribution may be centralized or spread among many members. There has been little research on the consequences of restricting or spreading distribution of leadership. In studies and experiments those who distributed functions got better results (i.e., productivity, morale, etc.).

There are many factors which determine the distribution of leadership functions:

1. Provided by members to meet a need of the group. This is group maintenance function which is, in effect, shared leadership.
2. Granted to persons who hold central positions in the communications system.
3. Granted to persons of high power or prestige by those of lower status.
4. Granted to persons of greater visibility. Members who talk a lot are

chosen for leadership positions, a decision which the group sometimes regrets.

5. Assumed by those who are hungry for power.
6. Assumed by conscientious members. An experiment by Pepitone
illustrated when members who were told that their tasks are important to the group performed with a higher quality than those told
that their tasks were not important to the group.
7. Granted to persons seen by the group as able to meet their needs.

IMPLICATIONS OF FUNCTIONAL LEADERSHIP

1. Leadership can be learned. First of all, the modern view of leadership implies quite clearly that leadership behavior can be improved; it
is not fixed by heredity or childhood experience. Learning initiative
or intelligence is difficult or even impossible. But learning, for example, to summarize at the right point the contributions of others in a
group is quite possible and is certainly easier than mastering most of
the content of a particular field, as in the situational approach. The
functional view leads, then, to an emphasis on training, on growth of
persons. A trait-centered approach—since traits are relatively fixed—
tends to encourage attempts at better selection of leaders, which is a
difficult task at best.

2. Leadership is a shared matter. This approach to leadership ex-
plicitly indicates that all members of a group may supply leadership;
that it is less a case of a leader and his followers, and more a case of
persons contributing, with different amounts of effectiveness, to the
operations of a working group. The whole range of leadership functions
needed by a group suggests that no one person can do the job alone.
Whether these functions are handled by one person or widely distributed through the group, however, the emphasis is on the fact that
the functions are needed; without needed functions, the group will fail
in its task and the members will feel frustrated.

3. Process skills are essential. This view of leadership indicates that
careful attention must be paid to the process or procedural aspects of
group behavior. Noticing what is said is not enough. The effective group
member must also be aware of how things are said, by whom, when, and
what function they serve in what group context. From this point of
view, learning to be a better contributor to groups is more a matter of
acquiring essential process skills than intensively studying the content
of topics to be discussed. Knowledge of content is essential, but it is
not sufficient for effective group work.

4. Diagnostic skill is basic. Finally, this view of leadership and group
behavior implies that a fundamental process skill is that of diagnosing
group difficulties and sensing needed, missing functions. A doctor must
learn through his training to look at symptoms, form a diagnosis, and
prescribe treatment. Just so, group members must learn to notice group

difficulties, form a careful diagnosis of what is blocking productivity, and take appropriate action in light of their diagnosis. A diagnostic focus emphasizes growth in the learner's ability to examine group situations thoughtfully and accurately. No medical school would teach a doctor to prescribe the same medicine for every ailment, and no effective program for learning about group behavior can focus on panaceas or gimmicks which promise to solve all group problems.

In summarizing the above, problems of leadership cannot be separated from problems of group functioning. If we are to understand leadership we must understand groups. In training effective members we are doing the best training for effective leadership since a leader can be no more effective than his group members.[2]

CONCEPTS OF BUSINESS LEADERSHIP

Business leadership is a composite of two concepts: (1) that of a leader and (2) that of an executive, both of which are discussed in current literature more or less independently. The two concepts, however, have three common features: (1) people must be motivated to get things done; (2) decisions made have binding power; and (3) certain outstanding personal characteristics are expected.

Many business executives should be considered as managers rather than as leaders since their activities are strictly defined and limited by rules and routines and their position requirements demand mainly technical knowledge.

In earlier times, leadership was regarded mainly as a passive status, then later as a necessary result of certain desirable personal characteristics. Now the emphasis has been shifted to the group and the situation. In the last analysis, it is the group that selects, or at least accepts, the leader. It does so if it believes that the given individual, because of his personal characteristics, will best be able to satisfy its needs in a given situation. The leader accepts the challenge because he gains satisfaction in terms of prestige or reward.

There are various ways in which a business leader gets things done: by threat of dismissal (authoritarian system); by enhanced rewards in expectation of higher performance (paternalistic system); by agreement with a representation of the followers (unions); or by establishing a common objective (participation in management). The last method gives superior performance by tapping the resources of the whole group; but it is more often claimed than attained. Many managers are unable to achieve the cooperation of their followers or are fearful of losing power. The selection among these methods is largely determined by the company's policy.[3]

TYPES OF LEADERS

Many studies have been made on types of leaders. Three types have been distinguished according to their principal ways of action: (1) the persuasion type, (2) the organization type, and (3) planning type; and each type has been identified by certain physical characteristics. The persuasive type, called endomorphic, is round, and is interested in food, comfort, and people. The organizing type, called mesomorphic, is square, and is interested in action and domination. The planning type, called ectomorphic, is linear, and is inhibited and oversensitive. In childhood these types manifested themselves as egocentric sovereigns, as altruistic pedagogues, or as goal-centered apostles, respectively.[4]

Most researchers believe that physical characteristics are not correlated with traits of character, although some persons in responsible positions still so believe.[5]

The Personnel Research Board of Ohio State University has spent over one million dollars to detect and define leadership performance. They used observation, depth interviews, opinions of associates, and rating scales by superiors, peers, and subordinates. They ended up with five basic types of business leaders:

1. The *Bureaucrat:* He sticks to routine, appeases his superiors, avoids his subordinates, and they feel apathy and some contempt for him.
2. The *Autocrat:* He is directive and expects obedience. His subordinates tend to be antagonistic and use expediency.
3. The *Diplomat:* He is opportunistic and exploits people. He is met with distrust.
4. The *Expert:* He is concerned only with his field. He treats his subordinates as co-workers. They respect him but are against any changes.
5. The *Quarterback:* He identifies himself with his subordinates, even at the risk of displeasing his superiors. But he is sought by business.[6]

Another classification distinguishes three types of leaders: directive, permissive, and participative:

1. The Directive Type: He initiates rewards and penalizes. His subordinates, feeling inferior, are passive. The morale is low; no leadership develops.

2. The Permissive Type: He initiates actions for others. He has high frustration tolerance and is sensitive to the feelings of others. He will get the job done, but will not develop leaders.

3. The Participative Type: He helps others to develop their initiative, decisions, and procedures. He gets them to recognize their own wants and their limitations. He freely expresses his feelings. If his subordinates had been accustomed to directives, he must proceed very cautiously.[7]

Still another classification includes the following types of leaders:

1. The autocratic type, who sets the goals according to his own needs, plans and decides by himself, gives piecemeal instructions and insufficient information, refrains from delegating authority, and uses threats.

2. The benevolent type, who, instead of threats, uses bribes; besides he proceeds the same way as the above.

3. The laissez-faire type, who lets his subordinates set the goals, organize, and proceed.

4. The participative type, who himself sets the goals according to work-centered objectives, confers with his subordinates before decisions, and helps them with planning.[8]

Other classifications have been made on the basis of executive skills:

1. The master of detail; he has a comprehensive knowledge.

2. The coordinator; he can organize and integrate.

3. The problem solver; he is an expert in technical matters or in human relations.

4. The people-minded; he gets people to work together.

5. The target-minded; he carries on persistently.[9]

The following types of executives are distinguished by Danhof according to their degree of independence:

1. The innovator, an imaginative planner

2. The implementer, taking care of details

3. The partial implementer, working within a small area

4. The line follower, working under detailed orders[10]

No uniform check list of personality traits of leaders can be established because of the great variation in the requirements from position to position, and also because of difficulties in determining the criteria of good leadership.[11]

Possessing the attributes of a leader is no guarantee of

effective leadership. A leader must do, and not just be. But a study of personality traits and characteristics can contribute to the self-analysis and character-building that every leader must undertake in his own way. Biological heritage and cultural influences may give one person more leadership ability than another; nonetheless, any person of intelligence can acquire some measure of this skill.[12]

SELECTION OF PROSPECTIVE LEADERS

There is at present great demand for people with managerial skills and training. High qualifications are required of the business executive by government, communities, businesses, unions, and consumers. There is increasing nationwide competition in a buyer's market. High-grade personnel is still relatively cheap.[13]

Definite procedures for screening candidates are needed, yet many problems have not been solved.[14] The normal procedure begins with the collection of data on the background and training of candidates, plus information from people who know them, e.g., members of clubs, churches, and civic organizations. Well-planned interviews are held; rating sheets and performance evaluation reports are filled out. In addition many tests have been devised; yet their effectiveness is questioned in many quarters.[8]

In general, tests are useful in measuring intelligence—as distinguished from knowledge—and special aptitudes, but not motivation. Often one sees through the "favorable" answers. Projective tests are more dependable, but they must be administered and interpreted by experts and there are not enough available. A man should not be rejected because of a test; he may simply lack the specific background the test was developed to measure.[15]

Tests and examinations are simply substitutes when there is no other basis for judgment. They do prevent favoritism, make the placement procedure more thorough and systematic, and alert management to the selection problem. Evaluation of a man is so difficult that even college seniors, for example, do a poor job in judging their classmates. A college degree is valuable, particularly if it was obtained at a sacrifice. Grades in most cases are used as a first screening device.[13]

To find the management qualities most needed in industry in 1964—to see just where the American executive stands today and where he is likely to be in the future—*Dun's Review* polled nearly three hundred of the nation's top business leaders who make up its Presidents' Panel. They were asked to assay the skills most needed by executives on the level of chairman, president, and vice president. Their answers presumably reveal the qualities top management is looking for in the men it will designate as its successors or promote to middle management:

It can be generalized that what top management seeks most desperately is the man who can handle all the complexities of business today. Not the computer specialist, but the man who understands the place of the wizard machine in the whole organization. Not the technologist, but the man who can translate the fruits of technology into products and profits.

The most ready way for a man to do that is perhaps best put in the words of the president of one of the nation's largest manufacturing companies. "Today's successful executive," he says, "must do a lot more intelligent reading than his counterpart of ten years ago did. He must obtain a working knowledge in the various scientific fields so that he can understand and direct the specialists who carry the day-to-day responsibility of the company's business."

Looking at the problem in much the same way, President W. M. Dillon of Northwestern Steel and Wire Company says: "Today's top general executive doesn't really need what I consider to be new *skills*, as compared to those his counterpart needed a decade ago. But he does need more of a well-rounded education and background if he is to keep abreast of the analytical and scientific skills that experts and specialists can bring to bear on his company's problems."

What it boils down to in the opinion of most of the presidents: today's executives need to have quicker responses to meet the ever-increasing pace of change, sharper conceptions of the goals at which they want to aim and a firmer quality of decisiveness than were required of executives in general ten years ago.

President Edward L. Steiniger of Sinclair Oil Corporation, looking to the needs of the general chief executive today as compared to the past, says: "He needs not so much new skills as broader general knowledge of people, places, languages, history—in short, the liberal arts—together with a good grounding in business, economics and commercial law. When he has such a broad view, the chief executive is able to put into perspective—worldwide—new methods, materials, and processes, and is better able to direct specialists in new fields."[16]

In writing on the selection of management personnel, Milton M. Mandell quotes Lyle Spencer, head of the Young Presidents' Organization, as follows: "Finding, training, and motivating key executives is, in several respects, the thorniest and longest-lasting problem a president faces. Mandell goes on to say:

Yet systematic selection is less common at the upper levels than down the line. In many companies where clerical, secretarial, sales, and production help are carefully chosen through batteries of tests and interviews, the top jobs are filled by guess, by gamble, and by hunch—this despite the fact that the importance of the jobs justifies greater expenditure of time and money.

One of the chief difficulties in executive selection is defining the qualities the executive needs to play his many roles. Reporting on one large-scale survey of the selection process, Robert K. Stolz wrote, "One company claims that, if the standards implied in its appraisal forms had been applied to its top management group when these men were on the way up, the strongest of them would probably have been forced out of the company." . . .

Stolz also pointed out that "most successful executives are curious combinations of great strengths and great weaknesses. . . . But they certainly are not people who have nothing wrong with them, nor are they people who always get along with others."

It is beyond human capacity to play brilliantly each of the various roles an executive must assume. How can one man have the sensitivity, maturity, and physical vigor to inspire others; the brain to analyze problems as complex as those facing the nuclear physicist; the persuasiveness to get others to accept his goals and the relaxed attitude needed to teach others; the ability to work fast on some matters and stall on others; the knowledge and talent to be a production wizard, an expert salesman, and a keen financial analyst; the courage (or stubbornness) to make decisions against the advice of "experts" and the flexibility to follow meekly at other times; the self-confidence to know that his judgment is good and the willingness to delegate to those less able and experienced than himself? Where is the man who is outstanding in all these attributes?

But just because the perfect executive cannot be found, it is not necessary to fall into the trap of accepting the mediocrity, the man who has neither outstanding merits nor defects. Realistic executive talent hunting will track down the man who is outstanding in the qualities necessary of the *particular* executive job. The executive who has the essential qualifications may be shored up with strong assistants by a realignment of duties and responsibilities, and by guidance in his weak areas. The key to sound executive selection is recognizing which qualities are vital to the job and which are expendable.[17]

TRAINING AND DEVELOPMENT OF LEADERS

Routine performance in business does not always give the opportunity for development as an executive. To acquire "breadth," special training is needed. Business consultants first called attention to this need. Now, general interest has developed in the philosophy and techniques of management and training for it. Some fifty universities have created programs for executive development. Dr. Kenneth R. Andrews of the Harvard Graduate School of Business reports his findings on these programs in his book, *The Effectiveness of University Management Development Programs.*

After a rapid spawning of university training programs, some skepticism set in. For one thing, proper evaluation of the improvement made by the students is difficult. They themselves usually make very favorable comments, but this might be attributable to courtesy. Faculty members give no examinations. Information obtained from employers is equally inconclusive. It would seem that the success of a program depends a good deal on the level and skill of the faculty members and on their informal contacts with the participants. Still more depends on the personalities of the participants. The greatest advantage seems to be derived by those with narrow experience, e.g., by specialists who become managers. What most of the participants do gain is a fresh approach to their jobs, new respect for their management, broader interest in civic affairs, and greater self-confidence.[18]

In addition to formal education, on-the-job training needs further study and organization. Such programs should include lectures, reading, orientation to one's company, work in different departments, association with leaders, guidance in report writing, public speaking, conference leadership, participation in conferences on business problems, special assignments as substitutes for executives on leave, administrative leadership in small and large groups, and coaching by a senior executive.[8,14] Coaching is recommended particularly to develop "conceptual skill," defined as the ablity to see the enterprise as a whole, the interdependence of its various functions, and its relations to the given industry, the community and the nation.[19]

In the last analysis, the training of leaders cannot be entirely accomplished by outside agencies or persons. Others in the organization can contribute knowledge of subject matter, but the leader or manager must make the effort to train himself in the knowledges and skills that he needs. He must therefore have the ability and courage to analyze his own needs (weaknesses) as well as his strengths and then proceed to fill in the gaps. He may do this in a variety of ways: by more courses in school or college, adult training courses, correspondence courses, attendance at seminars and other group meetings, reading on his own time outside of working hours, and many other ways.

Development Techniques

The techniques available for managerial training and development are many. William F. Rogers, Director of Personnel, Giant Food Department Stores, Inc., Washington, D.C., has delineated them as follows:

Individual. Development may occur with one learner or with a group of learners. Since persons learn individually, there is no clear-cut distinction. A division between some activities may be useful to indicate the usual method by which development takes place, i.e., on the initiative of the individual, or as a part of a group.

1. Coaching. Coaching is the old reliable. It stems from antiquity. Call him the learner, the disciple, the potential, the student—he learns from the master in person. Its use ranges from the poorly organized, unsympathetic "push-'em-off-the-dock" type to the "guided experience" documentation of the highly organized program.[20] It is closely related to job performance. It may involve counseling, relations with the superior, office morale, or the example of the boss. Each of these has a part. Coaching has one distinction—it is found in just about every successful management development program.

2. Understudy or apprentice. Understudy is quite like item one. It does, however, concentrate on the job of the man ahead, rather than the man in the job. And from sad experience, many programs start with one understudy and end on a "two understudies for each key job" program. The one man understudy left the firm, got too cocksure about his position, or dropped out when the going got tough.

3. Job rotation. Managerial jobs are composites of subordinate jobs plus something. Increasingly, job rotation is being used to prepare the potential manager to *be* a manager. It is useful to apply in an organization.

4. Work project. The work project is a task assigned by management to meet a realistic need, with general guidance toward a desired result.

5. Professional societies. The society associates the potential manager with people of like interests and usually leads to "broadening viewpoints."

6. Transfers within the organization. This differs from job rotation primarily because of its infrequency. Where job rotation has the learner move from place to place, this category involves primarily a single transfer or change and the period during which the learner operates in the changed situation is generally longer.

7. Special assignment. These are different from transfers primarily

because they are added to the duties of the individual in his regular job. The more important assignments will naturally interfere with the usual routine but trainees frequently devote added time in order to secure the additional experiences that are available through this device.

8. Developmental reading. Today there is a wealth of information available through books and periodicals. Management literature now occupies a respectable part of the library shelves. Professional reading in this area will aid not only in suggesting new ideas and understanding, but it will also make a learner "at home" in the professional jargon that seems inevitable.

9. Public speaking engagements. A major developmental activity is that of speaking to a group. As the world and its professions become more complex the amount of communication needed increases. It is completely inefficient to give this information on an individual basis. Of necessity much must be given to groups. Public speaking is an important method for doing so.

Group. Effective group development depends on three things: the method, the members, the degree of participation.

1. Case studies. One of the best group methods is the case study. The cases must walk the tight wire between being "a real problem" pertinent to the trainee's own type organization and not being a problem of persons he knows (which leads to emotional judgments). Cases are briefly written statements of an administrative problem. They are discussed in organized groups of potential or present managers with approximately the same "level of operation." The experience results in (a) decision-making, (b) broadened ideas, (c) appreciation of the other man's viewpoint, and (d) observation of "a mind in action."

2. Multiple management.[21] This is the McCormick plan. It is well documented. It works where management wants it to work. "Junior Boards" are set up to tackle real problems by assignment and to recommend possible answers to the boss. Be sure to read the reference noted above.

3. Conference leadership. Conference Leadership has several values: (a) it is in frequent use by managers, (b) it appeals to the "self-improvement" phase of the individual, (c) the conference is an indirect method of revealing other management needs of the leader, (d) conference leadership aids in applying most other group development methods. This, too, can be studied in many good references.

4. Role-playing.[22] Role playing is serious play-acting of management problem situations. Many bosses flinch at the word "role." Yet, they are willing to "take the part of the central figure in a case" or "show how a grievance should be handled." Talk of "roles" only when you are sure of your group.

5. Problem-solving. Here you tackle an actual management problem.

The group resembles a staff meeting on a crisis. Major hurdles: (a) Can you get real problems? (b) Can you talk about the real issues without getting fired? (c) Can you avoid an emotional solution?

6. Seminars. Seminars are periodic (usually weekly) meetings of groups with similar interests to follow a predetermined schedule desired by the group.

7. University courses. College study is a valuable adjunct to any organized program. The courses are equally acceptable for a personal development plan. The new full-time summer "Executive Development Groups" are heartening signs of additional progress. If you expect to spend money on one of these, (1) demand a biographical sketch on each instructor, and (2) demand a list of trainees by name, position, and firm (from the current or a previous group). Make your decision only in the light of these facts. College names and course titles are unimportant by comparison.

Miscellaneous. The major development categories above certainly do not exhaust all possibilities. These listed below are added because they are "smaller," and because they may be used with or without an organized program. Several have served as "entering wedges" for a program.

1. Manager absent (on vacation or field trip). Assign substitute for training purposes. Insure briefing before and reporting after the period. Get some sort of rating on his performance.

2. Substitute for manager. Have the learner (a) act for the boss on a committee, (b) do preliminary employment interviews when a new worker is under consideration, (c) write a report, or (d) speak to a group.

3. Evaluation. Send a trainee to observe and evaluate a particularly good operation relating to agency business. Ask him to recommend its usefulness in his own office.

4. Counseling. Have the learner counsel a younger worker (and evaluate him for the boss).

5. Organizing. Have the trainee propose a new organization, or a reorganization of a unit.

6. Communicating. Have the trainee study speaking to groups, conference leadership, or instructor training.

7. Committee work. Differing from being a committee member— have the learner plan and direct the activity of a committee.

8. Community activities. Many persons do not realize that serving on the Community Chest Committee or chairing the local PTA can be an excellent experience in the area of management..

9. Teaching or instructing. There are opportunities here both in educational institutions and as a part of in-service training programs. The experience will emphasize the proof of the old saw that the teacher learns more than the student.

Summary. Two final things need to be said. First, no attempt has been made to touch on "subject-matter" needs of potential managers. This is no reflection on its importance. Researchers agree that managers generally have a recognized subject-matter knowledge in some field. But the methods of achieving it are well covered in educational and professional circles. Therefore, we ignore it here. Second, each method listed above should suggest two more development methods for a particular person in a particular organization. The way is open.[23]

Organizational Needs—Inventory

There are gaps in the organization and gaps in the person. The inventory concentrates on the gaps in the organization. These can be reviewed in one of two ways. The first is the impersonal determination of the needs of staff by recording experience in turnover or shortages in classes of work. The second, and more personal, way is to use individual appraisals as a basis for establishing a position-by-position inventory. In dealing with each of these types of inventory it is important to remember that the results are true only at a point in time. They are more like snapshots from a continuing life. Therefore it is necessary to interpret them in terms of the present rather than to accept them as a frozen image from the past.

Impersonal Inventory

1. Management turnover. How many managers have been replaced in the last year—two years? Why? Can any part of this be forecast into the next year—two years? Is there a replacement for them? How many would you replace if you had good replacements? ("We would handle things differently if we had men who could . . .")

2. Shortage—by level. Is each administrative echelon "backed" by one with larger numbers? There is always attrition. For each key position there should be two "back-ups." This is a simple insurance against a single failure.

3. Shortage—by skill. Is each key skill area "backed" by lesser skills that can develop in a reasonable time? Are there gaps with no identifiable source from which replacements can be drawn?

4. Expansion needs. Do you operate from forecasts? By plan? Will you need more of any of the above types? And when?

5. Cases. Best of all (for illustration only), can you point to a case where failure to inventory resulted in a vacancy? Or assignment of a "weak sister," just because no plan had been made? Can you say the appointment was made from fright, not forecast? Cases impress management because their problems appear to them as cases.

Inventory—Personalized

In this second form of inventory a judgment has already been made through appraisal of each staff member and he is placed in one of the following general categories:

1. Promotable—could be placed in another job whenever it is available.

2. Satisfactory—doing the present assignment satisfactorily. Might be able to take a higher job with additional experience or training, but not otherwise.

3. Indefinite—unable to judge because of
   (a) Lack of knowledge of his performance
   (b) A newly assigned employee.

4. Unsatisfactory—is not performing his present job well. Also mark as unsatisfactory all vacant jobs and those where the present holder will be lost in six months, due to retirement, transfer, physical conditions, etc.

5. It is most useful to chart (on an organization chart) a "color diagram" as follows:
   (a) Promotable—blue
   (b) Satisfactory—green
   (c) Indefinite—yellow
   (d) Unsatisfactory—red[23]

Other Methods of Personal Inventory

Other methods of judging an individual's leadership qualifications include:

1. Individual interviews. Individual interviews will occur in any executive personnel action. The problem is to organize them and record them. All executives want to see a potential manager. And this is not limited to a formal interview. He will wish to "see how the man operates," or "see the fellow at his home base." He does not want to write down, "This man won't get along with the staff" or "I doubt his ability to think like a manager." But he might tell a proper person both of these things. We hesitate to commit our thoughts to writing. For results, use oral reports or ask for a general rating of "A" quality, "B" quality, or "C" quality.

2. Merit rating. Merit rating is a judgment based on the elements of the job and the characteristics desired to perform them. Its prime virtue is that a total judgment is reached by consideration of many individual judgments. Its special value is that each individual element that does not appear strong is a made-to-order part of a training plan—a gap to be filled.

3. Experience/training assessment. When you hire a new employee, you carefully review his experience and training. It is shocking to find

that many managers assume they know about present staff—without *checking*. You may find a new potential by assessing your present staff as to experience and training they received before you knew them.

4. Testing. Generally, a written test is meant. This is a very useful method of appraisal. Intelligence tests indicate learning ability levels. Administrative judgment tests indicate facility with problem situations. Personality tests are—to date—more useful in development counseling than in appraisal. This fact is not surprising. No one test can touch all management facets. And we are not yet agreed on the management traits. Tests help find out what an interview cannot. But they must be regarded as one element only in the appraisal process. (Incidentally, in most programs, a poor test result can drop a candidate for development at the junior levels; at the senior level it does not.)

5. Critical incidents. One type of appraisal that must be added is the "critical incidents technique." To state it roughly: What happened to make you (a) want to fire a manager on the spot or (b) want to promote him on the spot? Does a careful review of this incident justify a judgment? Can you tell a potential manager that careful handling of "this type of situation would make him rate high"? Better yet, does it suggest a "case study"?[23]

CONTINUITY OF LEADERSHIP

Attempting to identify leadership, its elements, traits, and characteristics, is one thing, but its continuity, once established, is quite another. This point is highlighted by Ralph J. Cordiner, Chairman of the Board, General Electric Company, when he says:

Finally, there is the responsibility for a smooth succession when the chief executive's work is done. In the modern corporation, the chief executive is generally not the owner of the business. He is a temporary steward for the shareowners. It might satisfy his secret vanity to find that his retirement produces a great jolt to the organization because there is no one qualified to take his place. But to my view, such an executive must be adjudged a failure, because one of his primary duties is to assure the continuity of leadership.

When the time comes, the chief executive will have to make the most difficult decision of all. He must sense when the new leadership is ready, and then leave the scene, gracefully and completely, so that his successors can make their own contribution in the vigor of their prime.[24]

QUESTIONS AND PROBLEMS

1. Name and describe the three theories of leadership discussed in this chapter.

2. Which concept of business leadership do you subscribe to? Why?
3. What is functional leadership?
4. Name four factors which determine the distribution of leadership functions.
5. Can leadership be learned? Discuss.
6. Can you identify which type of leader you are? Justify your choice.
7. Name and describe four techniques used in selecting leaders.
8. Which technique is most reliable?
9. Is it possible to train all leaders (managers) in school? Why or why not?
10. Name some of the development techniques used to develop executives today.
11. Write out a training program for yourself.

REFERENCE NOTES

[1] Warren G. Bennis, "Revisionist Theory of Leadership," *Harvard Business Review*, January-February, 1961, pp. 26-31.

[2] Gordon L. Lippitt, "Concepts of Leadership for Today's Executives," mimeographed paper, Leadership Resources, Inc., Washington, D.C., July, 1964.

[3] Schuyler D. Hoslett, ed., rev. ed., *Human Factors in Management*, Harper & Row, 1951.

[4] J. F. Bender, "Leadership—What Makes It?," *Sales Management*, August, 1948.

[5] G. U. Cleeton and C. W. Mason, *Executive Ability—Its Discovery and Development*, Antioch Press, 1946.

[6] R. M. Stogdill and C. L. Shartle, *Methods in the Study of Administrative Leadership*, Research Monograph 80, Bureau of Business Research, Ohio State University, 1955.

[7] Chris Argyris, "Research Trends in Executive Behavior," *Advanced Management*, March, 1956, pp. 6-9.

[8] Robert N. McMurray, "Man Hunt for Top Executives," *Harvard Business Review*, January, 1954, pp. 46-62.

[9] Auren Uris, *Developing Your Executive Skills*, McGraw-Hill, 1955.

[10] *Ibid.*, Clarence Danhof quoted, p. 126.

[11] Myles L. Mace, *The Growth and Development of Executives*, Harvard University, 1950.

[12] U.S. Air Force ROTC, *Principles of Leadership and Management*, Air University, June, 1954.

[13] Eli Ginzberg, *What Makes an Executive?*, Columbia University Press, 1955.

[14] George C. Houston, "Developing Qualities of Leadership," *General Electric Review*, November, 1953, pp. 49-51.

[15] M. L. Briggs, "How G. E. Uses Tests to Select Executives," *American Business*, April, 1956.

[16] John Maughan, "The Changing American Executive," *Dun's Review and Modern Industry*, January, 1964, pp. 38-40.

[17] Milton M. Mandell, "How to Gauge Executive Potential," *Dun's Review and Modern Industry*, March, 1957, pp. 43-44.

[18] Kenneth R. Andrews, "Is Management Training Effective?," *Harvard Business Review*, January-February, 1957.

[19] M. Brewster Smith, "Social Psychology and Group Processes," *Annual Review of Psychology*, 1952, p. 175.

[20] Earl Planty, *The Development of Executive Talent*, Ronald Press, 1954.

[21] C. P. McCormick, *The Power of People*, Harper & Row, 1949.

[22] "Role Playing," *The Journal of Industrial Training*, American Society of Training Directors, January-February, 1953.

[23] William F. Rogers, *Management Development*, mimeographed release, Air Force Resources Management Program, George Washington University, 1955.

[24] Ralph J. Cordiner, "The Nature of the Work of the Chief Executive," paper presented at the International Management Congress, New York City, September 16, 1963.

READING REFERENCES

Bellows, Roger, Thomas Q. Gilson, and George S. Odiorne, *Executive Skills*, Prentice-Hall, 1962.

Benge, Eugene J., *How to Become a Successful Executive*, Frederick Fell, 1960.

Mandell, Milton M., "The Selection of Executives" in M. J. Dooher and Elizabeth Marting, eds., *Selection of Management Personnel*, American Management Association, 1957.

Mandell, Milton M., *Selecting Executives*, NAVEXOS P-2255, Office of Industrial Relations, Department of the Navy, Washington, D.C., 1960.

Shartle, Carroll L., *Executive Performance and Leadership*, Prentice-Hall, 1956.

Simon, Herbert A., *Administrative Behavior*, 2nd ed., Macmillan, 1959.

Taylor, Jack W., *How to Select and Develop Leaders*, McGraw-Hill, 1962.

Principles and Problems of Naval Leadership, Bureau of Naval Personnel (NAVPERS 15924), Washington, D.C., 1959.

The Armed Forces Officer, U.S. Government Printing Office, 1961.

26

ELEMENTS OF LEADERSHIP
CHARACTERISTICS

Numerous articles and books have been written on the subject of
leadership traits and characteristics without a great deal of agreement being reached. Nevertheless, research studies indicate that
certain basic characteristics can be identified which may be helpful
to the individual looking for guidance in his own development as
a leader.

BEHAVIOR TERMINOLOGY

Terms descriptive of human behavior are often used so
loosely that there is confusion as to their meanings. Some general
terms found in the literature and in use in organized activities
have been identified by Carl Heyel[1] and their definitions adapted
as follows:

Ability	The power to perform
Aptitude	A latent capacity to perform
Behavior characteristic	A pattern which is set up by habitual repetition
Character	The basic code of conduct by which a man lives
Disposition	Temperament of a stable and predictable sort
Emotion	A departure from a calm state
Intelligence	The capacity for knowledge and understanding

Personality	The sum total of traits and behavior characteristics
Skill	A highly developed ability
Temperament	Proneness to certain feelings, moods, and desires

POSITIVE VIEWPOINTS

In setting up a basis for a leadership pattern, Tannenbaum and Schmidt say:

Forces in the manager. The manager's behavior in a given instance will be influenced greatly by the many forces operating within his own personality. He will, of course, perceive his leadership problems in a unique way on the basis of his background, knowledge, and experience. Among the important internal forces affecting him will be the following:

(1) His value system
(2) His confidence in his subordinates
(3) His own leadership inclinations
(4) His feelings of security in an uncertain situation

The successful leader is one who is keenly aware of those forces which are the most relevant to his behavior at any given time. He accurately understands himself, the individuals and group he is dealing with, and the company and broader social environment in which he operates. And certainly he is able to assess the present readiness for growth of his subordinates.

But this sensitivity or understanding is not enough, which brings us to the second implication. The succcessful leader is one who is able to behave appropriately in the light of these perceptions. If direction is in order, he is able to direct; if considerable participative freedom is called for, he is able to provide such freedom. Thus, the successful manager of men can be primarily characterized neither as a strong leader nor a permissive one. Rather, he is one who maintains a high batting average in accurately assessing the forces that determine what his most appropriate behavior at any given time should be and in actually being able to behave accordingly. Being both insightful and flexible, he is less likely to see the problems of leadership as a dilemma.[2]

To observe a manager from an over-all viewpoint is important. Morris Pickus gives us an excellent overview of what a manager must be:

A manager must have the desire to achieve. Managers can be classed as doers and followers. Today the first requirement is for a manager, who is constantly seeking methods for achieving greater results, to whom real achievement means more than money earned. A manager must be a well-rounded individual with a wide general knowledge, a large number of aptitudes, and he is broadly interested not only in the work with which he is directly connected but in all the affairs of the setting in which he is placed. A good manager is extremely curious minded about methods for achieving more. A manager must have a language facility. One of the most interesting research findings has to do with the ability of the manager to speak and write fluently. Virtually all studies of leadership have found a linguistic skill to be one of the principal skills of the successful manager. After all, speech is a primary medium of communication, and communication is of utmost importance to the successful leader. A manager must possess maturity. Another significant result of scientific studies on management is that the effective manager is mentally and emotionally mature. He is grown up. He is detached and objective in his thinking and actions. A good manager is relatively free from prejudices, is comparatively self-sufficient and is well adjusted to life. He thinks realistically and his judgment is sound. A manager must have achievement, motivation. Inner drive or native power is the important element which propels the successful manager. A good manager has a strong will to accomplish. He likes and gets great satisfaction from his work. He has a strong urge to excel and to move upward and onward. He has a marked inclination to be original and to use his own initiative. He controls his environment and makes things happen. A manager must have social orientation. A leader accomplishes things through others. To secure desired results he learns the secret of getting others to cooperate willingly with him. A manager has as one of his main functions coordination of the human abilities in his department. His job is to find and develop the achievers. A manager must have administrative skills. A successful manager is marked by his ability to plan and organize the work of others rather than by the amount of work he does himself. A tendency to deal too much in detail, inability to seek achievement, and lack of vision can contribute to the failure of managers. Ability to inspire and teach, ability to make decisions, and a creative imagination are important marks of a successful manager.[3]

Dr. Elwin R. Henry, Jersey Standard's adviser on employee-relations research, reported that evidence from his studies of managerial success had produced through statistical methods "six dimensions, or six factors, or six kinds of measurements" that distinguished "the hot rods" from "the least good managers." In order of importance they are: (1) initiative, assumption of responsibility, and leadership; (2) job knowledge and skill; (3) dependability, thoroughness, and follow-through; (4) getting along with people; (5) stability under pressure; and (6) fine personal qualities and work habits.[4]

A psychologist writing on the subject of executive qualities pinpoints ten qualities frequently found in the executive who has gained success:

Accepts himself	Can make decisions
Respects others	Has resiliency
Accepts responsibility	Welcomes work
Is self-confident	Has strong principles
Has patience	Has sense of proportion[5]

Auren Uris cites Stogdill and Washburne as follows:

Ralph M. Stogdill suggests that leadership traits can be classified under five general headings:

1. Capacity (intelligence, alertness, verbal facility, originality, judgment)
2. Achievement (scholarship, knowledge, athletic accomplishments)
3. Responsibility (dependability, initiative, persistence, aggressiveness, self-confidence, desire to excel)
4. Participation (activity, sociality, cooperation, adaptability, humor)
5. Status (socio-economic status, popularity)

Norman F. Washburne says that sociologists have found that there are certain things that good leaders do, and he cites eight such things:

1. A good leader initiates action.
2. He gives orders that will be obeyed.
3. He uses established channels within his group.
4. He knows and obeys the rules and customs of his group.
5. He maintains discipline.
6. He listens to subordinates.
7. He responds to their needs.
8. He helps them.[6]

Mandell's findings, covering 106 executives in five large organizations, indicate that:

. . . their greatest strengths were making decisions, effectiveness in dealing with people, dependability, taking responsibility for their actions, honesty in dealing with people, and integrity. Their greatest weaknesses were failure to delegate, inflexibility, ineffectiveness in judging people and in getting others' cooperation.

Such an authority as Chris Argyris has suggested the following qualifications, which seem to add up to self-confidence and emotional maturity:

1. Ability to take "knocks"
2. Ability to withstand frustration
3. Ability to be objective in judgments
4. Ability to set realistic goals
5. Ability to accept victory or defeat gracefully

Another authority, C. Wilson Randle, in reporting the results of a thorough study of 1,427 managers and executives, found the following characteristics significant for all levels and types of managers:

1. Drive
2. Intellectual ability
3. Leadership
4. Organizing ability
5. Initiative

Randle further found that dependability and high work standards were significant factors for top-, but not lower-level, executives. Technical knowledge was important in engineering, research, and financial management, but not in sales and manufacturing. In general, he found that inadequate executives showed lack of intellectual ability and initiative, and were performing poorly in their present jobs.

From these various survey results, the qualities of the effective executive may be deduced. He is a man who is interested in administration, is dependable, highly motivated, effective in dealing with people, has good judgment, and is emotionally mature.[7]

In a research study to determine the personal characteristics and skills that have the highest relationship to over-all management performance in U.S. Navy activities throughout the United States (282 line managers, including 60 Navy officers), it was found that:

1. There are a number of qualifications whose importance for executive success is related to the size of the unit being administered. The following characteristics were found in this study to be more important for the heads of larger units than for the heads of smaller units: ability to get the cooperation of other line units and of staff units; intelligence; working fast; self-confidence; careful planning; following through; and not neglecting management duties because of technical interests. Therefore, high level ability in smaller units may not be predictive of success in larger units.

2. This study identified, among others, some important qualifications not often stressed, such as:

a. the ability to work effectively under frustrating conditions
b. the ability to assign the right man to the right job
c. "would give an honest report even if it would hurt him personally"

d. administrative creativity

e. the ability to spot the key parts of complex problems and not get lost on minor points

f. correcting situations when they need improvement and recognizing the need for changes without waiting for an emergency or making excuses

g. the ability to set priorities effectively

h. the ability to handle a large number of different problems at the same time

A study of more than 1,400 executives in private industry confirmed the importance of three-quarters of the characteristics found important in our study.

3. Two of the most frequent errors made in describing the qualification requisites for management positions are the inclusion of items which, while relevant, are valueless because all the applicants have the necessary amount of the particular ability and the emphasis on factors specific to the situation and the concomitant omission of general and equally important factors.

4. A serious deficiency in any *one* important ability or characteristic can lead to managerial failure, in contradistinction to other types of jobs, such as, for example, engineering—the engineer with serious personality defects may still make an important contribution in the technical aspects of his work and the engineer who is technically weak may be effective in the selling phase of the work.

5. Management skills, such as the ability to handle many different problems at the same time, and setting priorities effectively, have higher validity than such general characteristics as level-headedness, self-confidence, ambition, or intelligence. The probable reasons for these differences are that any individual general characteristic must be accompanied by other characteristics in order to provide a basis for effective performance, and the evaluation of general characteristics is less reliable on a relative basis—subject as they are to the standards of the evaluator and based on inferences—than the evaluation of skills.

6. Management skills also have higher validity than items relating to the goals of executive work such as keeping costs to a minimum and obtaining high production. The possible reason for this difference is that the importance of these and other goals is not general; goals are determined by function and organization, while skills are more ubiquitous.

7. Management skills have higher validity for these positions (third-, fourth-, or fifth-level management) than such skills, often emphasized for supervisory positions, as the ability to gain the liking of subordinates, ability to get their cooperation, giving credit when deserved, and letting employees know how they are doing.

8. The research data obtained indicate that the frequent discussions

of the relative importance of intellectual abilities and personal characteristics for management positions are meaningless because most management skills are based on an intermingling of intellectual and personal characteristics and because many undersirable personal characteristics are heavily influenced by lack of ability. For example, ruthlessness—"would do almost anything to get ahead"—is directly related to having ambitions exceeding one's abilities. Being rated highly as a careful planner is associated with an ability which is partly intellectual, spotting the key parts of complex problems, and such a presumed personal characteristic as willingness to face up to unpleasant problems; setting priorities effectively is related both to being broadgauged and to working effectively under frustrating conditions; and following through to see that work is on schedule is related both to the ability to handle a lot of problems at the same time and to persistence —not giving up easily.

9. The data do not support the belief that neglect of management duties is caused by a high level of technical ability; this neglect seems to be mainly found among weak, inadequate executives who bury themselves in details in order to avoid problems they cannot handle well.

10. The data fully support the contention that decision-making ability is fundamental to managerial success. The failure to get facts before making a decision and not being able to withstand pressure are two of the major characteristics connected with poor performance in this area of the manager's work, while good decisions are associated with the ability to spot the key parts of complex problems and not get lost on minor points, facing up to problems, and keeping one's head in an emergency. This variety suggests why efforts to improve decision-making ability are sometimes of limited value—different people may have different reasons for their weakness in this ability and some of the reasons for the weakness are based on fundamental, nontrainable characteristics.

11. In this sample, at least, the extent of delegation to subordinates was not highly associated with performance. This finding may be primarily the result of the nature of these jobs—few outside relations, homogeneity of occupations, and location of all subordinates in a limited geographical area.

12. The data suggest a hierarchy of intellectual abilities: (a) the application of intelligence—e.g., "Good at spotting the key parts of complex problems"—has a higher validity than intelligence in the abstract —"Highly intelligent"; and (b) abstract intelligence has higher validity than its segments—e.g., memory.[8]

NEGATIVE VIEWPOINTS

In a series of articles appearing in *Fortune* magazine, Perrin Stryker has pointed out that the terms in the literature dealing with leadership are used so loosely in management circles that they appear to have been nearly drained of meaning. In the survey made by *Fortune,* seventy-five high-ranking executives wrote out detailed replies to a seven-page questionnaire asking for definitions and opinions on terms commonly used to describe executive traits. The following were considered indispensable:

1. Judgment
2. Initiative
3. Integrity
4. Foresight
5. Energy drive
6. Human relations skill
7. Decisiveness
8. Dependability
9. Emotional stability
10. Fairness
11. Ambition
12. Dedication
13. Objectivity
14. Cooperation

But such a listing revealed great confusion in terms. For example, the trait of "dependability" was defined by the seventy-five executives in terms of no less than 147 different concepts. Some executives furnished five or six different concepts; others gave as many as eight or nine.[9]

Stryker further points out that:

Real managerial competence could not be defined in terms of a standard list of specific qualities and aptitudes and skills, even if the terms used meant the same thing to all executives. Executive jobs and companies and industries are so varied and so changeful that no two executives are successful under exactly the same circumstances or by virtue of precisely the same traits or abilities.[10]

Along the same line, Harvard University Professor Myles L. Mace has written: "The lack of criteria as to what a good executive is, and the lack of uniformity in executive positions, would seem to deny the validity of any single list of personal traits."[11]

FUTURE SPECIFICATIONS

Professor Earl Brooks of Cornell University sets out some new performance goals and appraisal methods that he believes will be used in looking for managers in years to come:

1. Group analysis of performance will be less important.
2. Subordinate and superior will prepare more fully for discussions of what is expected and how both can improve.
3. Less attention given to personality traits and more to results.
4. Both long- and short-termed objectives will be considered.
5. Accent on future and areas for improvement will be stressed more than mistakes or shortcomings of past.

6. Less emphasis on how executive's job is done and more on end results.
7. Promotability and performance will be considered separately.
8. Forms, ratings, scales, graphics, adjective descriptions, forced-choice items, and over-all numerical ratings will receive less attention.[12]

CONCLUSION

In view of the conflicting evidence for and against traits, characteristics, personal qualities, etc., for managers and leaders, it might help the novice to have something on which "to hang his hat" when it comes to his own self-development. With this in mind, we have broken down leadership characteristics into the following manageable units for study and development in the chapters that follow: (1) intellectual capacity, (2) emotional stability, and (3) relations with others.

QUESTIONS AND PROBLEMS

1. Why are there so many pitfalls in attempting to codify leadership traits and characteristics?
2. If you were asked to evaluate the skills of a manager, what would some of them be?
3. What is your explanation of the wide variety of findings of research studies on managerial traits and characteristics?
4. Name two negative factors in the listing of personal traits found in leaders
5. Write out your concept of the perfect manager, taking into consideration both the affirmative and negative points made in this chapter.
6. Write out your evaluation of your own managerial traits and characteristics, making two columns, one headed "Weaknesses" and the other "Strengths."
7. Outline a program of self-development to strengthen the "Weaknesses."

REFERENCE NOTES

[1] Carl Heyel, *Appraising Executive Performance*, American Management Association, 1958, pp. 102-105.

[2] Robert Tannenbaum and Warren H. Schmidt, "How to Choose a Leadership Pattern: Should a Leader be Democratic or Autocratic with His Subordinates—or Something in Between?," *Harvard Business Review*, March-April, 1958, pp. 95-101.

[3] Morris I. Pickus, "What Must a Manager Be?," *Personnel Journal*, December, 1963, p. 580.

[4] Perrin Stryker, "On the Meaning of Executive Qualities," *Fortune*, June, 1958, p. 117.

[5] Mortimer R. Feinberg, "How to Measure Maturity," *Nation's Business*, February, 1963, pp. 40-41.

[6] Auren Uris, *The Management Makers*, Macmillan, 1962, pp. 77, 80.

[7] Milton M. Mandell, "How to Gauge Executive Potential," *Dun's Review and Modern Industry*, March, 1957, pp. 43-44.

[8] Milton M. Mandell and Sally H. Greenberg, "Analysis of Management Characteristics," unpublished study, U.S. Civil Service Commission, 1960.

[9] Perrin Stryker, *op. cit.*, p. 116.

[10] *Ibid.*, p. 118.

[11] Myles L Mace, *The Growth and Development of Executives*, Harvard University, 1950.

[12] Earl Brooks, "Yardstick for Future Managers," *Nation's Business*, August, 1959, pp. 54-56.

READING REFERENCE

An Analysis and Inventory of the Skills of Management and Supervision, Office of Personnel and Training, Federal Aviation Agency, Washington, D.C., March, 1963.

27

INTELLECTUAL CAPACITY

There is no doubt that a superior degree of intelligence is a desirable asset for a business leader. On the other hand, he should not be too far above average; a genius, for example, would probably lose patience with those he worked with and supervised.[1] In fact, an IQ above a certain point is probably not necessary.[2]

To prepare for business leadership in today's competitive world, the young man or woman must obtain a good basic education. In a survey of over a thousand young executives made by *Fortune,* it was found that:

First among the traits that distinguish the young executive today is his early desire for a thorough education. In high school or college the young man who was to become a member of this executive generation discovered the value of education as a tool, and he soon set about fitting that tool to his hand. According to *Fortune's* sampling, over 85 per cent of these men had graduated from college, one out of three of them with academic honors. Of the college graduates, over 40 per cent went on to take graduate degrees. Eighty per cent of the college graduates worked to pay for some part of their education's cost. One out of three of them went to school at night. As a group, these men are the best educated ever to emerge in positions of business importance. And, significantly enough, most of them spent some portion of their academic lives in the study of the useful disciplines, like engineering, economics, or accounting. Their education served to arm them for some kind of business activity.[3]

Management is thought by many to be approaching the status of a profession. If this is true, those who aspire to become

440

leaders in the business community must prepare just as diligently for business management as they do for other occupations. As an indication that they do, Kuehl reports:

The successful manager in our country is an intelligent and dedicated individual, who sees his function as a distinct profession, with its own set of ethics, its own body of learning, and its own classifications of work. Competence in management requires specific study and experience, plus the development of a philosophy and mode of action appropriate to the profession. The character of the professional manager is constantly changing. There was a time when ambition, vision, and ruthless determination were the primary requirements for managerial success. Education was secondary. Time was when business operations were run on a day-to-day basis. Today, a manager must anticipate the future and plan ahead, preferably five to ten years.[4]

The young executive today is ambitious to get ahead through the application of his knowledge and through his willingness to seek more knowledge. Guzzardi makes the point that:

To move onward and upward—to progress by the hard application of his knowledge—is a commonplace of his experience. Thus pragmatism becomes his guiding philosophy. The whole significance of his business life he measures by his effectiveness in the world outside himself, that external world of people, products, and problems that he moves in. For him, thought is analytic activity directed at solving the concrete business problem that comes before him at a given moment in time. His job is like the river of Heraclitus: it is never the same from one hour to another, and on its flux he can impose his formulas, his practical solutions that create new problems that require new applications of his highly applicable intelligence.[5]

From this we get a portrait of today's young executive as a deeply serious young man, intelligent, competitive, pragmatic, and totally committed to meeting the challenge and responsibility of his job. Guzzardi points out that this can ultimately get him into trouble:

He burns up his intellectual energies on his job and he has few outside interests that engage his intellectual curiosity: thus, culturally, he is a narrow man, and that narrowness may handicap him later on when he delves into the larger social questions about business and its grander designs.[6]

To clarify the meaning of intellectual capacity, we will discuss its component parts: perception, imagination, judgment, and expression.

PERCEPTION

The intellectual capacity of a person is certainly measured by his ability to perceive what is going on around him. The business leader must focus his attention in the proper direction if he is to be successful.[7] In addition, he should view the people with whom he comes in contact with freshness, penetration, and understanding so that he can properly evaluate them and their intentions.[8] Perception can be further analyzed under the following headings:

Interest

Perceptivity can be greatly enhanced by simply showing and taking an interest in people, things, techniques, etc. It is a psychological fact that the more interest we take in a thing, the more likely we are to perceive it in its entirety.

Observation

A mentally alert individual sees things, observes actions that others miss, with the result that he lives a richer and fuller life. An observant person will have the curiosity to ask "why" in order to ferret out the unexplained in any situation, and to arrive at new solutions.[9]

Listening

There is a difference between listening and hearing. Listening is constantly focusing our attention on a sound. Hearing is merely having our ears in good working order.

Hearing goes on all the time—but listening is "tuned in and tuned out" in much the same way that we turn our radios on and off.

When we listen, we are usually tuned in for about eight seconds at a time. What is important is the length of time that we are tuned out. We can be tuned out for just an instant—or for a lifetime.

The key to improving listening is reducing the length of the "tuned-out" periods.

Here are some of the common barriers to good listening:

1. Preparing an answer. Early in the talk, we may hear something we disagree with. We tune out and prepare our argument. Had we stayed tuned in, we might have found that we actually agree with the speaker.

2. Listening for facts only. Many people have a habit of "scanning the speech" rather than listening. They are scanning for facts. Most of these facts can be obtained in any library. Usually it is the conclusion

that the speaker draws from a standard set of facts that is unique.

3. Creating or tolerating distractions. Distractions cause us to tune out. Here are some common ones:

a. Noise—the popcorn sack in the movie.
b. Air—the smoke filled room.
c. Lack of visibility—the seat behind the potted palm.
d. Worry—"*Where* did he say the bathroom was?"
e. Facilities—"The mind cannot absorb more than the seat can endure."

4. Prejudice. "I know him—and he can't tell me a thing."

Now that we have looked at some of the barriers to our listening—some of the factors that increase our "tune-out" time—let's look at the other side of the picture, ways to improve our listening.

1. Note taking. Here are three general rates of speed—most of us write at about 20 words per minute—most of us talk at about 125 words per minute—most us think at a rate of 200 to 500 words per minute. These facts can help us with our note taking. Notes should be written like telegrams—short, to the point. Here is the way it works. We follow the speech along until we are sure of the speaker's point. Then we tune out. We turn on our thinking mechanism and condense down what the speaker said into a few words. We pick up our pencil and jot down the condensed idea. We then "tune back in."

By using this system, we are taking advantage of the speed of our minds and using it to compensate for the lesser speed of our handwriting.

2. Listen selfishly. Before going to a meeting, ask yourself what value the speaker can offer you. Here is an example. You may have no interest in road construction. However, you may be forced to go to a meeting concerning asphalt versus cement roads. Think of your position as a taxpayer—"Which will last longer?" "Which is cheaper?" Think of your own safety—"Which gives better traction in wet weather?" "Which offers better visibility?" Before long you can drum up some "selfish motivation" on most any subject.

3. Reach for the central idea. Your listening can be made more effective if you rapidly grasp the pattern the speaker is following. A number of them use the "tell them what you're going to tell them—then tell them—then tell them what you told them" system. Another pattern is a point followed by one or more illustrations. Once you have grasped the pattern of the talk, you can be discriminating about when to tune in and when to tune out or "scan" the talk.

4. Be fair. This point concerns prejudices. It would be absurd to tell you to do away with your prejudices. The message here is keep them—but keep them on ice. In other words, recognize your prejudices—

then lay them aside and *listen*. *After* hearing the talk, if you still have strong feelings on certain points, go talk with the speaker.

5. What is not said. This means listen with the eyes and the feelings as well as with the ears. Often it is the *way* a thing is said that is the real communicator. For example, the sentence, "He is a nice man" could be said to communicate, "He is a knight in shining armor," or "He should drop dead."

In a nutshell, listening is a conscious focusing of attention. It can be "tuned in and tuned out." The key to good listening is decreasing the "tuned-out" periods. There are barriers that cause us to tune out, and there are techniques and methods of motivating ourselves that enable us to listen more accurately over longer periods of time.[10]

Questioning

Either in a conference or an interview between two people, there are three types of questions:

Direct
Open-end
Loaded

The direct questions start with "do, don't, would, wouldn't, could, couldn't," etc. A response usually will be either "yes" or "no."

The open-end question starts with "who, what, why, where, when, or how." The response is open-ended—it can be anything.

Here is the important difference between direct and open-end questions. The direct gives opinion—the open-end can give facts. A direct question is, "Do you like your job?" Open-ended, the same question would be, "What do you like about your job?"

Recognize that there is nothing wrong with a direct question. There are many times when all we want is a yes or no answer. The point is merely that the direct question is designed to do a certain job—not all jobs.

The open-end question helps bring to the surface the background or viewpoint behind a simple yes or no.

The third basic question type is the loaded question. Actually it is two elements—an opinion or prejudice of the questioner—*and* a question.

"Has your mother stopped taking dope?"

"Do you people ever work?"

A less deadly variation can be:

"You can deliver on the 29th, can't you?"

These questions are designed to confuse or embarrass or "put on the spot." Usually, they do not bring out as good an answer as the other two types because the answerer must seek some way to defend or justify his answer. They rarely pay off. They are to be avoided.[10]

Reading

Competition with fellow executives within the organization and with outside companies literally force the modern executive to read a great deal both on and off the job.

A survey taken by a trade journal in the plant operations field indicates the priority of goals which executives set themselves in professional reading:

1. New equipment and materials
2. Business conditions
3. General news affecting business
4. Engineering and technical trends
5. Engineering and product techniques
6. Product and equipment design
7. Washington news
8. Research and development findings
9. Management methods
10. Prices, commodities, and supplies.[11]

Reading takes up so much of some executives' time, in fact, that many have resorted to learning speed reading techniques. A person aspiring to become an executive today who is a slow reader should make a concerted effort to improve his ability in this important skill.

IMAGINATION

Without imagination, American industry would not hold its enviable position in the world today. It is imagination that has made possible our present economy and continues to keep us "ahead of the pack" in most fields. American industry is more and more looking for imaginative young people to take over ultimate positions of leadership. Imagination, then, is a marketable ingredient in the job market place. We will examine it under the following headings:

Originality

Being original does not necessarily mean being different. As the word is used here, it means breaking out of traditional ways of thinking to discover original thoughts or ideas. It can, of course, be applied to a product, method, or technique that has already been created. Originality is a product of the imagination which, not being satisfied with the present, wants to originate something different or new.

One of the most practical techniques for bringing significant relationships to light is the check list. Alex Osborn has given us such a check list based upon his principles of "adaptation," "modification," "magnification," "minification," "substitution," "rearrangement," and "reversal."

In what *new* ways could this (object, item, whatever) be used *as is?*
How could it be *changed* to suit a new use?
What *else* could be made from it?
How could the *waste/scrap/excess* by-product be used?
Could the *shape* be changed to advantage?
Suppose it were *curved, straight, tapered, twisted, coiled, flat?*
How about a different *package* or *combination?*
What about *motion, power?*
How about another *part/ingredient/material* in place of this?
Should it be *stronger, weaker?*
What might be *added, subtracted, divided, multiplied, proportioned?*
What about more *light*, or less, or a different *kind?*
How about different *sound*, or more, or less?
Could it be more *compact, condensed,* or *enlarged, expanded?*
Should it be *lighter, heavier, denser, less-dense?*
What about *spacing* it, *interrupting* it, putting it *together?*
Should it be *wet, dry?*
Should it be *streamlined, blunt, rough, smooth, shallow, deep?*
Could it be put into *assortments, assemblies, knock-downs?*
Should it be *exaggerated, understated, emphasized, toned-down?*
What about *speed, sequence, timing, frequency?*
How about an *alloy, ensemble, blend, isolated form, merger?*
What might be done to *attract the eye, tickle the taste, please the ear, improve the feel, sweeten the smell?*
Should it be *bigger, smaller, fatter, thinner, taller, shorter, narrower, wider, lower, higher?*
Suppose it were *rearranged*; *placed differently*; different *layout*; *raised, lowered, tilted, leveled, supported, suspended?*
What if it were *transposed, interposed, juxtaposed, super-imposed, inside, outside, positive, negative, opposite, same, parrallel, diagonal, up-ended, turned around, inside out, other-ended, slanted, angled, perpendicular?*[12]

Certainly such a list piques the imagination and should be a great aid in originating ideas.[13]

Vision

The element of "vision" should not be confused with "dreaming" or other connotations. Vision has a place in the business world, and the person who can look ahead and "see" applications of his ideas in other situations, in the future, and in his planning has a quality that should be utilized to its fullest. Visionaries are as necessary to today's business world as are those who work with their hands. Perhaps the "Buck Rogers" of today will be the reality of tomorrow. Vision is the ingredient that helps us to project ourselves, our company, our community, our economy ahead in a way that proves practical and worthwhile.

Planning

While the skill of planning has been discussed elsewhere in this book, the act of planning calls upon a manager's every imaginative resource. This is particularly true when setting up new plans.

In discussing planning as an intellectual process, LeBreton and Henning have this to say:

A plan is almost invariably a product of some degree of creative thinking on the part of the planner. The creative thinking process is stimulated by the existence of a problem which must be solved or an objective which must be ascertained and set by the thinker. Obviously, the more complex the problem, the more complex must be the thought carried on to reach a solution to the problem. In the initial stages of thought, the complexity factor introduces an introspective problem, a problem in which the thinker is actually frustrated by his efforts to form and coalesce his thoughts as he carries on creative planning.[14]

Creativity

Creativity is apparently not something that just happens; it is the result of intelligent and purposeful thinking. The outstanding man is the one who can see and create possibilities and then project plans and anticipate results.

Since creativity varies so greatly among people, what are the characteristics of a creative individual? B. B. Goldner identifies them as follows:

1. Intelligence—the ability to apply what is already known
2. Experience—a rich, varied background that can be tapped for ideas
3. Imagination—the capacity to create alternatives or develop solutions
4. Flexibility—the faculty of being able to spin around on a dime to meet challenges
5. Problem-sensitivity—attunement with job and personal environment that makes it possible to foresee and solve problems before they reach the white heat stage
6. Curiosity—an eagerness for information

7. Originality—ability to create what will become acceptable
8. Independence—belief in self and the courage to withstand the pressures of a group, whether social, political, or business
9. Freedom from fear—the confidence to break away from traditional viewpoints

Goldner further points out what management must do to encourage creativity:

1. Develop a climate of creativity.
2. Wholeheartedly sponsor a continuing program.
3. Actively encourage daring and imaginative ideas.
4. Try to discover, encourage, and evaluate creative people.
5. Span the gap between policy and practice.
6. Insist on measuring results.[15]

Further expressions of creativity in the business environment are explored by Frederic D. Randall in his discussion of successful patterns for executive action. He makes the following points:

1. Creativity is the result of a delicate series of mental actions, all of which can be greatly influenced by the business atmopshere in which the executive works.
2. Creative thinking demands a genuinely free exchange of information among men at different levels of authority. Formal communication programs are not enough.
3. The "crash" or emergency approach discourages creativity and should not be applied any more than necessary to problems in need of solution, especially those of a vital and long-run effect.
4. In planning and control, the conditions that stimulate imagination should be taken into account.
5. A group's understanding about the consequences of failure is an exceedingly powerful force in determining creative potential.
6. Conditioned thinking, such as may stem from a strict policy of promotion from within, blocks the creative process, unless management takes countermeasures.
7. Creative process. How does the mind develop new thought? Most psychologists would agree that the creative process involves these five fundamental steps:

   a. Sensing (recognizing a problem)
   b. Preparation (gathering data pertinent to the problem)
   c. Incubation (mulling over the data)
   d. Illumination (recognizing a possible solution)
   e. Verification (testing the proposed solution)[16]

JUDGMENT

Judgment is defined by Heyel as "the ability to form a sound opinion, make an estimate, or reach a conclusion from the available facts and their surrounding circumstances."[17]

An effective business leader's judgment is not diluted by the unimportant facts and events of his environment; likewise, it does not ignore the important ones. It is guided by a strict discipline of thought.[18]

A special kind of judgment possessed by the business leader is a keen sense of timing. He puts theories into practice and new products on the market when the time is right.[19]

Following are some questions that can be asked in appraising the judgment ability of managers:

1. Does the appraisee have the rounded experience that should enable him to weigh the kind of factors important in the decisions that must be made by whoever holds the position in question? . . .
2. Again, has he evidenced a highly developed ability to recognize the significant variable?
3. How is his sense of timing? Does he look before he leaps?
4. Has he shown the ability to step out of his own shoes and visualize how the results of his proposals will appear to others? Is a sense of fitness and propriety inherent in his actions?
5. Does he have foresight—has he shown the ability to look ahead and gauge the probable effects of proposed actions?
6. Has he shown commercial sense in that he is able, without sacrificing essential quality, to temper perfectionism with a realization of what is required to market a product or to get something done on time?
7. Has he shown evidence of being conscious of the cost implications of his and his employees' actions?[20]

Common Sense

Judgment is often the result of practical experience. To most people, it implies the use of good, common sense to make something work. Using common sense can be thought of simply as thinking something through—a problem, a situation, a decision. The reputation of a business leader is often determined by his ability to demonstrate common sense in making major decisions. It is indeed a quality that all leaders envy and aspire to.

Understanding

The successful business executive is regarded as having a thoroughly developed understanding of people, things, and events.

His decisions are based on conclusions reached from analysis of the facts in relation to one another and to the problem as a whole. He fits the opinions of the experts into a complete picture, giving proper weight to each.[21] Understanding is the synthesis of a person's knowledge and information, intelligence, and experience.

Intelligence

As was pointed out earlier, too much intelligence may prove a business handicap. Albert Einstein was undoubtedly a genius, but he was not a business leader. From secondhand accounts of people who worked with him, he was difficult, to say the least. The intelligence of a genius, fortunately for most of us, is not a requirement for successful business leadership. With merely average intelligence a man may become a leader, provided he uses the intelligence he has.

Intelligent business leaders do not play hunches; they use their intellects to make decisions based on the facts and the opinions of people who know—the experts.[22] They are willing to think on their own, to ask "why"; they do not merely rearrange their prejudices. In addition, business leaders analyze, catalogue, codify, then synthesize their findings.[23] The most skillful managers are able to carry out a multiplicity of activities simultaneously.[24]

The executive also possesses knowledge of his own weaknesses and strengths, which allows him to discount his biases and increases his sensitivity to those about him. This helps him immeasurably in getting along with people.[25]

A final observation on the use of intelligence is that a junior executive has to think deductively—from principle to application; while a senior executive has to think inductively—from observation to relationships, to principles.[26]

Foresight

Foresight is distinguished from some of the other, higher-level intellectual traits in that it has to do with operational in contrast to theoretical pursuits. This is the leader's "sixth sense."

Foresight is neglected in management literature, and there is evidence that this neglect is reflected among managers themselves.[27]

It is clear that new thinking and different dimensions need to be established before we can clearly identify foresight in the smörgåsbord of qualities the manager must possess.

EXPRESSION

Peter Drucker has stated somewhere that the problem of communication is the major problem of management. If this is true—and it undoubtedly is—then those who aspire to become managers or who have already attained that pinnacle of success should put forth the effort required to become effective communicators, both oral and written. This problem is a large one for most people since speaking and writing the language do not always come easily.

While the subject of communications has been treated elsewhere in this book, we may well call attention here to what the American Management Association has to say about its importance:

Communication is today's "open sesame," the answer to every management problem from wordy reports to misconceptions of company attitudes and policy. The supervisor's role as a communicator is the strongest link in the line extending from the board of directors down to the newest clerk or watchman. Not only must he communicate management's thinking and decisions, but he must also feed back reactions and developments in the ranks. And there are barriers to the free flow of information: the organizational layers through which ideas must pass; the impossibility of talking personally with everyone; the feeling, prevalent among some managers, that the less said the better; unwillingness—or sheer inability—to listen properly; and the tendency to color information transmitted up and down until it loses much of its value. The supervisor must, therefore, be trained in the techniques of communication so that he can pass along, for example, management's views on the union's latest demands and, in turn, report back just how far the members are likely to go in support of their leaders.[28]

Oral Expression

Successful business leaders are usually good speakers because they:

1. Know for what purpose they speak.
2. Intend to say something meaningful.
3. Know what to say.
4. Speak up.
5. Bring their hearers into the speech.
6. Work on their best feelings.
7. Have a rich vocabulary.
8. Avoid mannerisms.
9. Use short sentences.

10. Know when to stop.
11. Inspire confidence.[29]

The business leader must be understood by both his peers and his subordinates. This is not easy in view of the varying backgrounds of the individuals involved. Henry Albers says, "The executive should understand the manner in which language and its usage may influence human behavior. He should consciously use the insights gained from semantics to improve the effectiveness of communication. Executives must contend with the 'realities' of human behavior and cannot assume that every man lives by the rules of semantics."[30]

Written Expression

It is equally important that the business leader be able to express himself in writing. He has to do so at almost every turn, in letters, memorandums, and reports, all of which become part of the permanent records of an organization. His ability to express himself effectively in writing is one of the most forceful and effective tools the business executive possesses.

QUESTIONS AND PROBLEMS

1. Besides good health, what is the most basic necessity for today's manager and executive?
2. What is the value of intellectual capacity? Can a person be too intelligent for his own good? Explain.
3. Give three examples of alert perception on the part of an individual.
4. Why should listening and reading be a part of intellectual capacity? Explain fully.
5. How can questioning add to intellectual capacity?
6. Outline a reading program for yourself to develop your intellect and perception.
7. Why is imagination such a valuable asset to a manager or executive?
8. Is it possible for a person to be too creative? Explain.
9. Explain the term "judgment" in your own language. How can you identify it in yourself?
10. Why is expression so important in operating management?

REFERENCE NOTES

[1] J. F. Bender, "Leadership—What Makes It?," *Sales Management,* August, 1948; and E. E. Jennings, "Some Leadership Fallacies," *Management Review,* December, 1952.

[2] Ernest Dale and A. Smith, "New Report Cards for Bosses," *The New York Times,* March 31, 1957.

[3] Walter Guzzardi, Jr., "The Young Executives (Part I)," *Fortune,* June, 1964, p. 184. Courtesy of *Fortune* Magazine.

[4] William J. Kuehl, "Manager in Transition," *Administrative Management,* September, 1963, pp. 72-74.

[5] Walter Guzzardi, Jr., *op. cit.,* p. 190.

[6] *Ibid.,* p. 184.

[7] G. U. Cleeton and C. W. Mason, *Executive Ability—Its Discovery and Development,* Antioch Press, 1946.

[8] U.S. Air Force ROTC, *Principles of Leadership and Management,* Air University, June, 1954.

[9] R. W. Heffner, "What Makes a Good Executive?," *Advanced Management,* December, 1954.

[10] William R. Davidson and James H. Healey, *Power Management,* Allegheny Power System and its subsidiaries, 1962, pp. 48-51.

[11] Auren Uris, *The Management Makers,* Macmillan, 1962.

[12] Alex F. Osborn, *Applied Imagination,* Scribner, 1957, pp. 274-321.

[13] Jack W. Taylor, *How to Create New Ideas,* Prentice-Hall, 1961, pp. 157-158.

[14] Preston P. LeBreton and Dale A. Henning, *Planning Theory,* Prentice-Hall, 1961, p. 256.

[15] B. B. Goldner, "Are You Flunking in Creative Thinking?," *Sales Management,* December 5, 1958, pp. 33-35.

[16] Frederic D. Randall, "Stimulate Your Executives to Think Creatively," *Harvard Business Review,* July, 1955, p. 121.

[17] Carl Heyel, *Appraising Executive Performance,* American Management Association, 1958, p. 109.

[18] P. B. Niles, "Six Standards for Executive Conduct," *Dun's Review and Modern Industry,* April, 1956.

[19] R. W. Heffner, *op. cit.*

[20] Carl Heyel, *op. cit.,* pp. 109-110.

[21] G. U. Cleeton and C. W. Mason, *op cit.*

[22] J. F. Bender, *op. cit.*

[23] Chris Argyris, "Research Trends in Executive Behavior," *Advanced Management,* March, 1956.

[24] Robert N. McMurry, "Man Hunt for Top Executives," *Harvard Business Review,* January, 1954.

[25] Auren Uris, *Developing Your Executive Skills,* McGraw-Hill, 1955.

[26] R. W. Heffner, *op. cit.*

[27] Stanley Stark, "Executive Foresight: Definitions, Illustrations, Importance," *Journal of Business,* January, 1961, pp. 31-44.

[28] American Management Association, *AMA Encyclopedia of Supervisory Training,* 1961, p. 94.

[29] J. F. Bender, *op. cit.*

[30] Henry H. Albers, *Organized Executive Action: Decision-Making, Communication, and Leadership,* Wiley, 1961, p. 336.

READING REFERENCES

Ewing, David W., Dan H. Fenn, Jr., eds., *Incentives for Executives,* McGraw-Hill, 1962.

Mason, Joseph G., *How to Be a More Creative Executive,* McGraw-Hill, 1960.

28

EMOTIONAL STABILITY

By emotional stability we mean the ability of an individual to stay on an even keel, especially under stress-and-strain situations. The person who is emotionally stable does not lose his temper in emergencies or when he does not get his own way. The person who has acquired stability is said to have gained *poise,* which is another way of saying that he is balanced. Balance and stability are desirable in the leader because any show of nervousness or lack of confidence is readily imparted to those who are looking to him for guidance.[1]

The part emotions play in personality comes out in Richard W. Wallen's description of three personality types:

Within all of us there are broad patterns of personality. These arise from the ways in which we handle two basic sets of emotions and impulses: the tender and the tough. The tender emotions are those that express affection, sympathy, and consideration for others. The tough emotions are those of aggression, pushing for action, and struggling against obstacles. Both sets of emotions are within each of us. But many people, as they mature, reject or deny one or the other; though they cannot obliterate their tender or tough feelings altogether, they do seek to disguise these impulses and to alter the ways in which they express them.

Top executives can find three distinct personality types in the ranks of almost any corporation. To recognize these types is no mere academic exercise: it is, in fact, a major asset for the executive who must select men for management posts. The three are: the modest helper; the strong achiever; the detached critic.

Modest Helper. These are the people who, for one reason or another, have determined to reject or deny their capacities for aggression and toughness. They are modest, unassuming, and they find their greatest satisfaction in helping others. In cases where these people have gone to extreme lengths to deny their aggressive impulses, they have great difficulty in being firm or standing up for themselves at all. These are the people who have gone so far as to reject even normal self-assertion, because they equate it with aggression.

Bias of an equal and opposite degree is the hallmark of the *Strong Achiever.* He accepts his tough impulses and rejects his tender ones. He views life as highly competitive, believes deeply that the best defense is a good offense, and to him an obstacle is something to be beaten down as rapidly as possible. Such a man usually makes a poor listener and a bad corporate diplomat or bargainer.

More complex is the personality of the *Detached Critic,* the man who rejects the display of both tender and tough emotions, who is determined to view all his associations coolly and logically. He seeks to be emotionally remote. Usually he has a passion for accuracy and orderliness, a dedication to facts and systems.[2]

Heyel provides us with some guides to measure emotional stability:

1. Does the subordinate executive appear rattled when unexpected or critical questions are shot at him?

2. What is his general reputation as to temper? Irritability? Flare-ups?

3. Is he subject to widely fluctuating moods—highly elated at one time, depressed at another? Everyone, of course, is subject to variations in the way he feels; the question here is twofold: (a) the violence and frequency of the up-and-down swings, and (b) any tendency to *show* one's feelings. Remember, we are confining ourselves to behavior on the job. The stable person is one who can be expected to keep off-the-job stress from interfering with work relationships.[3]

DRIVE

Drive is a deep inner compulsion to achieve, and is positively basic to the success of the business leader. It is usually accompanied by an apprehension of failure. To be satisfied with the job at hand is of course desirable, but discontent with present conditions is useful provided it does not upset one's inner balance.[4]

Some business leaders are self-oriented, seeking prestige in their own eyes; some are social-oriented, seeking recognition; some are material-oriented, seeking money; some are guided more by company interest than by their own.[5]

The type of *drive* discussed so far has been *positive drive.* There also exists *negative drive,* which, if allowed to become dominant, can disqualify a person as a leader. Negative drive is exhibited by the man who pursues the following:

1. Safety—originating often in fear and resulting in sticking to one's plans at any cost to others or oneself. Persons thus motivated often join people and causes only for personal advantage.

2. Popularity—but not really caring for either people or their tasks.

3. Approval—especially if it is sought constantly.

4. Authority—originating often in feelings of rejection and resulting in viewing everyone as a threat, hating people, and pigeonholing them according to their status and strength. As a subordinate, such a person would bootlick his boss, expecting his help in return. As a boss, he would reduce his subordinates' stature by applying inflexibly high standards.

Self-esteem is a drive that is often useful, but dangerous inasmuch as taking all the credit for oneself diminishes the drives of one's subordinates. It may also displace interest in one's job and in people.

The most desirable drive is that known as self-actualization, i.e., the drive to develop oneself to the fullest possible extent.[6]

The drives observable in today's young executive are commented on in Walter Guzzardi's *Fortune* magazine study:

> The men revealed here are not, however, the fictional stereotypes of souls bartered to The Organization for material reward. Today's young executive feels himself to be his own master. Through the organization, he gratifies his own drives. But he does not love it, find his security through conformity within it, or let it curtail any freedom he values. He will unhesitatingly move to another company if he sees a better opportunity to "create something." Promotion, expanding responsibility, new challenge—these are his chief motivations, and he's sure he can gain these goals by knowing enough and working enough. . . .
>
> The organization is the means by which he gratifies his own drives: he does not love it, he does not want to be loved by it, and he believes it is better for both of them if they do not love each other. He does not seek security through conformity. His security lies within himself.[7]

Drive in an executive is often motivated by his desire for advancement:

> But promotions are what hold real magic for him. They are the invisible sprigs of laurel that he cherishes. Promotions carry with them those twin excitements, "more challenge and more responsibility," and

toward those goals he drives with real ferocity. As he wins a larger share of them, one need is submerged, a higher need emerges, and the man presses on to gratify that new need. The basic requirements of life are met, but motivation remains strong.[8]

Motivation

Man's behavior patterns are motivated by both biological needs and learned goals. All biological motivation follows a pattern, such as: (1) A need mobilizes the energy necessary to reach a goal (need—behavior—goal). (2) As the need becomes more intense, the energy becomes more vigorous. (3) The behavior is selectively narrowed down to those actions that hold most promise of reaching the goal.

In everyday living, however, behavior is motivated by learned rather than biological needs. A man can never escape his biological limitations, yet he can use his human machinery (brain power) to satisfy needs that have little to do with mere survival.

Behind much of our behavior is the fear of failure, which is at the root of much maladjustment. As needs become more intense, they summon up more and more energy and, at some point, different for each individual and situation, shade into distorted perceptions and disintegrated behavior. So intense motivation may either facilitate or inhibit action.

A source of intense motivation is conflict between incompatible needs. The outcome may be either paralysis of decision or alternation of the conflicting needs, which in turn may lead to repression. The sources of conflict may be objects or people, such as those who enforce rules. Then we often "take out" our frustration on someone else, releasing a chain reaction which poisons the atmosphere. Unrealistic levels of aspirations, for example, nearly always result in frustration.

Everyone has a set of generalized motivations in the form of interests, attitudes, and values, which are responsible for both achievements and failures. Interests easily become frustrated when they cannot be expressed. Attitudes—persistent likes and dislikes —are made up of many special motives. Negative ones, such as prejudices and stereotypes, lead to a closed mind, frustration, and maladjustment. Values, the final standards of our behavior, underlie and tie together many attitudes. Many people have different sets of standards for different areas: ethical ones in their personal lives, but pragmatic and functional ones in their business and professional lives. Such dual allegiance may be a source of conflict. Intense and inflexible values may lead to disruptive behavior.[9]

Initiative

Individual initiative is what makes a man a self-starter, someone who gets things done without having to be prodded. A subordinate may, of course, display more initiative than is desired if he goes beyond the directives and authority given him. Without good judgment, action may be merely impulsiveness.[10]

A man with initiative has creativeness.[11] George Odiorne names five basic qualities that characterize the man who can get things done on his own:

1. Inner drive—doer has a single target.
2. Sorts out the vital from the trivial.
3. Taps and uses ideas of others—generates confidence in others.
4. Is tough-minded.
5. Takes obstacles in stride—assumes all problems can be solved.[12]

Another writer gives eight tests that spot a man's initiative:

1. Does he present problems or solutions?
2. Does he use available resources?
3. Does he know the facts?
4. Are his reports in proportion to results?
5. Does he get discouraged easily?
6. Does he finish the job?
7. Does he rattle?
8. Does he meet deadlines?[13]

Enthusiasm

Enthusiasm is a behavior characteristic that is highly valued by both peers and subordinates. Its greatest value is that it is contagious. A department manager, for instance, who shows enthusiasm in his work will probably be surrounded by enthusiastic workers.

Ambition (Industriousness)

Ambition, or industriousness, is not always understood by others because it varies from person to person. The industrious boss cannot understand a subordinate who does not have his ambition; likewise, an industrious subordinate cannot understand a boss who is not ambitious.

Ambition is closely linked to motivation. A person who is habitually lazy will be exceedingly difficult to motivate. It would seem that the best way to motivate people to be industrious is to exhibit ambition yourself.

Carefulness (Accuracy)

A leader with a great deal of drive needs to be extremely careful in how he performs his tasks. As used here, "carefulness" means care and judgment in the use of information, checking of sources of facts, and the stating of situations as they actually exist.

Endurance

A person may have many of the traits and characteristics necessary for success as a leader, but if he lacks the physical endurance necessary to carry out his work, then he will certainly fall short of his ultimate goals. People vary a great deal in this respect. Some tire easily, other are tireless. In any event, the person who aspires toward a top job in management should realize from the outset that there is no place in business today for physical weaklings. The modern executive's world includes his responsibilities to the job and organization, social obligations, recreation for both fun and business, and family responsibilities. Altogether these call for endurance of the first order.

STABILITY

The ideal leader accepts himself and others. He admits his shortcomings, shows little defensiveness, no hypocrisy, nor tendency to impress. He is unconventional, but he does not show it, except in important matters. He endures solitude and, in fact, may seek it. In the midst of the crowd, he can attain detachment. He maintains his dignity despite indignities and his happiness despite hardships. Reward, status, and love are less important to him than inner growth. In a grave situation, he can make vital decisions without letting his own fears get in the way.[14] Stability is that ability to maintain a stable façade in the face of difficulties.

As the commentator on one executive survey points out:

Stability is really a contradiction of terms: it is the nature of emotions to move and fluctuate continually, so man is naturally and continually unstable.

To many of the executives surveyed, stability is more often a matter of reacting evenly to stress and to frustrations than it is of rigidly suppressing the feelings; and, also, it is more often identified with objective judgment than with subjective self-confidence. . . .

Several executives in the survey made the point that a good executive knows how to blow off steam, as well as how to confine it.[15]

Stability in the business leader is an unbelievably valuable asset. Guzzardi observes:

The young executive is serious, with the abiding seriousness about his business that is a precondition to all business success. He is aggressive, confident, independent, and decisive—all qualities that seem to have been a part of his natural character and mental structure since he began to mature. He possesses an inquiring, acquisitive mind that he has trained and polished until it has become an extraordinarily effective instrument with which to attack the entwined problems of his business life. He works hard, partly because competitive fires burn within him, partly because he forever seeks "more challenge and more responsibility," and he believes hard work can attain for him those twin desiderata. He has a strong propensity toward pragmatism—he strives always to effect changes in the external world, changes that he can then hold out at arm's length and admire.[16]

Self-sufficiency

One of the most obvious characteristics of a leader is his self-sufficiency. He moves about under his own drive and initiative. He takes hold of the task to be performed and carries it through on his own, seeking assistance from others only as his good judgment dictates.

Self-sufficiency can easily be tested. Problem-solving, case studies, and task assignment are techniques used to "prove out" an individual's self-sufficiency.

Self-discipline

The ability to discipline oneself is the basis of all work effort. This trait is different from ambition in that it is an emotional quality. A person may have ambition but still not be able to discipline himself to carry out an assignment.

The effective implementation of self-discipline requires a high degree of personal organization. This embraces the control of one's time, one's work, and oneself. Further, it seems to be a prerequisite for leading others. Its absence tragically undercuts the most intelligent man, or else restricts him to mediocre or unprofitable pursuits. The organized man is dependable. He is the man who takes delegation, and who in turn earns the right to delegate. The substances of his work may require monitoring, but not its dispatch. He is orderly because through system he gets more and better results. Like a fine watch, he is not only made of good stuff, he functions efficiently, he keeps good time, and he does all of this with balance and precision.

Perseverance

This is the trait of stick-to-itiveness, the tenacity to see something through to its ultimate conclusion. It also connotes follow-through, which is so vitally important to the successful manager and leader. The amount of perseverance required of the manager varies greatly with the job at hand. In situations involving many frustrations, for example, it is of first importance.

Adaptability

Willingness on the part of the manager to adjust a course of action or a point of view to changing conditions is a sign of adaptability. The opposite of this quality is "bull-headedness" or an "I won't change" attitude.

Here are a few questions to ask about the leader's adaptability:

1. Has he shown reluctance to admit a mistake?
2. Is he overly sensitive to criticism?
3. Is he willing to accept suggestions?
4. Does he show evidence of keeping up with new developments in his field?
5. Has he displayed a cooperative attitude toward the study of new systems and procedures sponsored by staff and service groups outside his own department?
6. How readily has his division or department adjusted to drastic changes in budget or personnel assignments that may have been ordered as a result of company-wide adjustments to new conditions?
7. Does he personally accept in good grace changes beyond his control to which he must accommodate himself, or does he continually complain about them?
8. Is there a pattern of recent tightening up in his receptivity to new ideas and new ways of doing things? Is this attributable to age or perhaps to some other physiological condition?[17]

Decisiveness

This behavior trait is "not only the ability but the willingness to determine a course of action and carry it out."[18] The manager or leader must have the courage of his own convictions. If he does not possess it, he will make a mighty poor leader. In order to be decisive, a person must have confidence in his own abilities and those around him.

Decisiveness can, of course, be tested by analyzing the decisions a person has made. Have they stood up over a period of time? How specific have they been? Are they clean-cut and clear? Will others corroborate your opinion of them?

Dependability

To be dependable is to have proved time and again that you can get a job done without being checked upon by your superior. Initiative and drive can be fluctuating traits, but dependability is a pattern of *consistent* behavior, built up over a period of time, dealing with small as well as large matters. A few checks on whether a man possesses this behavior characteristic are:

1. What is his record on promises? Does he stall off accountability or the unpleasantness of facing up to shortcomings by making promises which he does not keep?
2. What clues to this trait are evident in his personal actions—such as being punctual for appointments? Does he turn in his reports on time, properly completed?
3. Does he follow through without dragging his feet on previously agreed-upon actions, even if they were contrary to his own expressed opinions? Have there been occasions when he indicated agreement on an issue at a meeting but later, in private, expressed a dissenting view?
4. Is he an "alibi-er"?[19]

Dependability is closely allied to habit. An habitually dependable person finds himself uncomfortable when he fails to measure up to his usual performance, and he makes certain that he does not fail again under similar circumstances. On the other hand, some people are always late and can be depended upon to be so.

Maturity

Maturity is not a matter of age, since some people are fully matured in their early years, while others remain basically immature all their lives. Maturity, fortunately, can be developed, provided a person exercises the necessary discipline. Heyel has this to say about maturity:

A mature person is in command of himself. He is well adjusted emotionally and does not panic easily. He is usually calm under great stress, displaying poise, confidence, and self-reliance. He doesn't let minor setbacks completely disrupt his ability to assess the changed situation or interfere with his ability to concentrate on other matters. His reactions are adult and not childish: He doesn't rely on tantrums and pouts to get his own way, has learned the value of persuasion and agreement, and is aware of the frequent need for giving in a bit to attain an end.[20]

The business leader, then, must be mature in his thinking and actions if he is to attain the pinnacle of success. He cannot hide his level of maturity from those about him; it is constantly on display.

Poise

A business leader who possesses poise is capable of remaining entirely calm under the most trying conditions. Such a person is not easily frustrated, does not make snap judgments, nor is he overanxious about decisions. He handles himself with complete ease and full confidence.

Poise is a trait that does not just happen. It is the result of a solid background of education and training, experience in being around and working with people, and good basic intelligence. It is one personal trait that does not come out of books, but from the inward soul of the individual.

High Standards

A person who knows what standards he wishes to attain and then sets out to maintain them has done much toward building his own stability and a reputation for stable behavior.

In the survey by *Fortune,* the importance of standards to the young executive is fully recognized:

Sharpening this inner compulsion are self-imposed standards that the young executive is dedicated to. Although they may coincide with the standards prescribed by the organization, they exist independently of those. In part, at least, they were inculcated in the man by his preparatory education. He is a professional manager, a member of the society of professional managers. From that brotherhood . . . he has adopted standards of professional performance, and they complement his own inner urge. One business school graduate explains: "I want to do more than the boss requires. Satisfactory performance is simply not enough to suit me. . . . My basic drive is for excellence—the standard I want to meet."[21]

INTEGRITY

A high degree of over-all integrity is required from a business leader because an executive position, even in a private organization, is one of public interest and responsibility. Integrity is directly related to ethics, which in turn have their roots in a value system. Any treatment of the subject tends to become extremely complex. Suffice it to say here that without integrity on the part of business leaders, business employees, and the great mass of the consuming public, the American economic system could simply not operate. This is especially true in the wide use of personal credit in the purchase of consumer goods, real estate, etc.

In discussing the integrity of executives, one writer says:

It is my opinion that businessmen do not have substantially more, or less, integrity than men in other occupations. But I think it is important that businessmen should have a higher sense of integrity than others, and should so conduct themselves that this is recognized by all.

In sum, it seems to me that if a man is to be truly a business leader, and not just an executive, he must have the persistence to ask himself about the strengths and weaknesses of his company and the courage to ask himself about his own integrity.[22]

In attempting to identify just what integrity is, the following reference may be helpful:

But what is integrity? This is a hard question to answer. We have indicated that one mark of integrity is consistency—that a man of integrity is one who acts or behaves in a manner which is consistent with the things in which he believes. But this isn't quite enough. A hardened criminal may well act in total consistency with his own, selfish values and antisocial beliefs. And we have previously considered the case of the bigot, who acts in rigid, unbending conformity with what he believes to be "right and proper." Yet we would scarcely call the hardened criminal or the bigot men of integrity.

Apparently then, true integrity demands something more than consistency. One additional requirement, obviously, is that the personal values which govern a man's behavior generally must be in harmony with the society in which he lives and acts. Meeting this requirement eliminates the hardened criminal, but still leaves the bigot—the one who brands all with whom he disagrees as immoral or stupid. He seeks integrity by sacrificing all to a superficial consistency, while avoiding the most difficult requirement of all. That requirement is to weigh and evaluate the different sets of values which are in conflict in each situation, looking always to the choice of the *greater* value, or the *greater* good.[23]

Integrity is certainly far more than financial integrity, which is what usually comes to mind when integrity in business is mentioned. Our code of ethics for everyday living could simply not function were it not for moral integrity, and there would be great turmoil were it not for intellectual integrity. The business leader, consequently, cannot forget or ignore any one of these.

Moral Integrity

Moral integrity stems from the ethics of the culture of which we are a part. Benjamin Selekman has this to say about it:

> Once businessmen invoke ethical and social values they are tampering with the most sacred symbols of human society. One can exploit a product or service, emphasize its style, utility, price, beauty, the prestige it may bring, and so forth. In the market place, materialism has its natural habitat. The consumer may buy or refuse to buy. But morality is the most treasured possession of a people, hammered out over history as man searches for some satisfying answer to the puzzlement inherent in his relationship to his fellow man and to his God. These values are the ones for which men die, for which martyrs have given their lives.[24]

The true test of moral integrity is that imposed upon us by the society in which we live, work, and play. From it come the moral guides, goals, and objectives that we, as individuals, must live up to and attain. The business leader is caught up in morality both as an individual and as a leader in his community. Much, therefore, in the way of moral behavior is expected of him.

Intellectual Integrity

The search for integrity within ourselves is often shunted off as unimportant, time-consuming, of no consequence. But the effective business leader must be honest with himself; he must be able to call a spade a spade and an ace an ace. He cannot fool himself—at least not for long. So the leader must search within himself and come to grips with the realization that his own intellectual integrity must be based upon solid ethical standards.

Financial Integrity

This category of integrity is the most familiar to everyone. It is the old-fashioned code of honesty that is taught from early childhood. Emphasis upon it probably stems from the fact that our society is primarily an economic and therefore a materialistic one. Material goods are capable of being stolen, expropriated, destroyed, or mislaid, and we are dependent upon the honesty of those who handle the moneys required in the conduct of normal business operations.

The business leader must as a matter of course practice financial integrity, and he has the responsibility of enforcing it upon those who work with and for him.

COURAGE

There is no doubt that inner security is needed to take the risks connected with business.[25] That security is supported by faith: faith in God, faith in one's fellow men, and faith in oneself.

In discussing the attributes of professional managers, Woodman says:

Faith can be in the form of religious faith or faith in the future of his company, or in the future uses of a product; but, however expressed, it is always sincere and intellectually derived. This faith gives the executive a firmness of conviction and permits him to formulate a plan, which is essential to accomplishment of its goals. It often means that the executive will discuss plans or proposals in an optimistic manner which, in turn, inspires the confidence of his employees. It also enables the executive to give unfaltering direction to his organization, which is necessary to attain success. As religious faith protects one from evil, business faith protects one from diversions and diffusion of effort.[26]

Risk-Taking

From the very beginning of a business venture, it is fraught with great risks. In fact, hundreds and hundreds of businesses fail each year. The business leader must have courage and intestinal fortitude to withstand the pressures that are certain to engulf him from time to time. Never for a moment should he minimize the risks he is taking, for to do so may lead to failure. Success comes when an individual assumes risks with full knowledge of the facts involved and a true conviction that the risks will be overcome.

Faith in God

First, let us fully recognize that there are some who do not believe in religious faith. It is not our intention to belabor the point. The stand taken here is that "Man cannot live without faith because his relationship with the future is an affair not alone of thought but also of action; life is a continuous adventure into the unknown . . . the prime requisite in life's adventure is *courage*, and the sustenance of courage is faith."[27]

In discussing the place of religion in business, Edward C. Bursk quotes from a statement made by a businessman at a meeting of business specialists at Harvard University:

We have been talking here this afternoon about the physical sciences, about the social sciences in general and some of them in particular. And yet we haven't mentioned one very important area of human activities—religion. I do not mean Religion with a capital R, or any particular sect or creed, and I don't think I mean the Church, with or without a capital. Yet, as I read history, as I observe the facts of life today, I cannot help but see that religion—or some spiritual force—is, in fact, part of the realities of life. I don't quite see how we can discuss the world's problems without recognizing it.[28]

Out of the inevitable maturity of experience, the business leader acquires a concept of charity, a sense of humility, and an unfathomable faith whether he has learned it from books, church, or religious meetings. In his *A Moral Philosophy for Management*, Benjamin M. Selekman points out:

. . . Unless the new and rapidly growing management group holds on to social and moral goals, it is doomed to lose what it now has in the way of authority and opportunity. Private enterprise in the form of the modern corporation has still to win the prize of legitimacy. The prize will continue to prove elusive without a growing faith in the community that, whatever the faltering, justice and the good life can best be realized through a decentralized industrial system manned by individuals of high purpose responsive to the ethics of our Judaeo-Christian tradition. . . .

Indeed, the great corporation executive, as any great governor of men, is he who so conveys justice and equity in all his bearing that his people know that righteousness prevails within his realm.[29]

Faith in Self

A person who aspires to a leadership position in even the smallest business organization is licked before he starts if he does not have faith in his own abilities. Such faith, of course, needs to be tempered with the quality of humility so that it remains under control.

An excellent statement pertaining to belief in self is contained in a brochure written by Perry L. Rohrer:

The man who is going to succeed has confidence. Many writers casually refer to this quality as self-confidence, but in our observation it carries a far broader implication. A man with this kind of confidence has a strong degree of personal stability and consistency. He tolerates only productive anxiety. He makes tension work for him instead of against him. He trusts himself. He has the courage to do what needs to be done. He is not overly dependent on the approval of others because he has personal security deeply rooted in his faith in himself. He has aggressiveness that is outgoing and initiating, not hostile or arrogant. He is free to be decisive. He accepts criticism objectively and constructively as a report on how he is doing. He is constantly seeking ways to test the effectiveness of his action.[30]

Of major concern to the potential business leader is the fact that faith in self is essential to having faith in others.

Faith in Others

A person who has become manager of a group of people doing work which he had formerly performed is likely to feel that he can do the job better himself. Learning to delegate to others, then, involves faith—faith in others. The manager must, of course, carefully choose the tasks which he delegates. Confidence is gradually built up with their successful completion until ultimately the subordinate and the manager find themselves working harmoniously together.

QUESTIONS AND PROBLEMS

1. Attempt to determine your emotional stability under the following circumstances: (1) your best friend turns out to be disloyal to you; (2) your house catches fire in the middle of the night and your telephone has "gone dead" from a storm outside; (3) you are told that you are no longer needed at your place of employment.
2. What is your analysis of the reasons that emotions have not been studied more fully in the past?
3. Which type of personality are you? Are you happy about it? What can you do to change your personality?
4. List five drives that affect your everyday life.
5. Give several examples of impulse motivation. Why are they dangerous?
6. Why must the manager or executive be a self-starter? Name some examples of self-starters in your locality.
7. What is the line of distinction between enthusiasm and ambition? Which do you have the most of?
8. Explain why the business leader must have endurance.
9. Give the reasons for being self-sufficient in performing a job assignment.
10. Explain the difference between perseverance and dependability.
11. Is there such a thing as being mature physically and immature mentally? Explain.

12. What has decisiveness to do with leadership?
13. What is your opinion of setting high standards of excellence for yourself? For others? For subordinates? For your peers?
14. Define moral integrity in your own words. Why is it so important in business?
15. Give an example of intellectual integrity. Of intellectual dishonesty.
16. Describe what faith is. What kinds of faith are there?
17. Evaluate religious faith in today's competitive business world. Is it necessary?
18. Do you have faith in yourself? How do you know it? Give examples.
19. How can you prove that you have faith in others?
20. How can you develop greater emotional stability?

REFERENCE NOTES

[1] Carl Heyel, *Appraising Executive Performance,* American Management Association, 1958, p. 114.

[2] Richard W. Wallen, "The Three Types of Executive Personality," *Dun's Review and Modern Industry,* February, 1963, pp. 54-56.

[3] Carl Heyel, *op. cit.,* p. 115.

[4] B. B. Gardner, "What Makes Successful and Unsuccessful Executives?," *Advanced Management,* September, 1948, pp. 116-125; W. E. Henry, "The Business Executive: The Psychodynamics of a Social Role," *American Journal of Sociology,* January, 1949, pp. 286-291; and S. F. Teele, "Developing Tomorrow's Business Leaders," *Management Review,* July, 1956, pp. 605-611.

[5] H. B. Moore, "Five Tips on Picking Young Executives," *Management Review,* December, 1951, pp. 729-730.

[6] A. H. Maslow, "Self-Actualizing People: A Study of Psychological Health," *Personality, Symposia on Topical Issues,* No. 1, April, 1950, pp. 11-34.

[7] Walter Guzzardi, Jr., "The Young Executives (Part I)," *Fortune,* June, 1964, pp. 97, 99. Courtesy of *Fortune* Magazine.

[8] *Ibid.,* p. 5.

[9] U.S. Air Force ROTC, *Principles of Leadership and Management,* Air University, June, 1954, pp. 42-45.

[10] Carl Heyel, *op. cit.,* pp. 110-111.

[11] Perrin Stryker, "I Want a Man Who's a Self-starter," *Fortune,* September, 1958, pp 147-149.

[12] George S. Odiorne, "Five Tests for Initiative," *Nation's Business,* June, 1959, pp. 76-78.

[13] Howard R. Dressner, "Eight Tests Spot Initiative," *Nation's Business,* March, 1960, pp. 104-106.

[14] U.S. Air Force ROTC, *op. cit.,* p. 104.

[15] Perrin Stryker, "What Makes an 'Emotionally Stable' Executive?,"

Fortune, July, 1958, p. 117.

[16] Walter Guzzardi, Jr., *op. cit.,* p. 98.

[17] Carl Heyel, *op. cit.,* pp. 113-114.

[18] *Ibid.,* p. 112.

[19] *Ibid.,* pp. 112-113.

[20] *Ibid,* p. 120.

[21] Walter Guzzardi, Jr., *op. cit.,* p. 97

[22] George Albert Smith, Jr., "Questions a Business Leader Should Ask Himself," *Harvard Business Review,* March–April, 1956, pp. 42-49.

[23] U.S. Department of the Navy, *Personal Values and Administrative Leadership* (AO Instruction P-12230.10), Government Printing Office, 1959, p. 11.

[24] Benjamin M. Selekman, *A Moral Philosophy for Management,* McGraw-Hill, 1959, pp. 16-17.

[25] Eli Ginzberg, *What Makes an Executive?,* Columbia University Press, 1955, p. 28.

[26] Roy H. Woodman, "The Attributes of Professional Managers," *Canadian Chartered Accountant,* February, 1962, pp. 157-160.

[27] Harry Emerson Fosdick, *The Meaning of Faith,* Abingdon, 1917, p. 3.

[28] Edward C. Bursk, *Business and Religion,* Harper & Row, 1959, p. 3.

[29] Benjamin M. Selekman, *op. cit.,* pp 218-219.

[30] Perry L. Rohrer, "It Takes More Than Intelligence," *The Management Psychologist,* March, 1961, pp. 10-11.

29

RELATIONS WITH OTHERS

Making every effort to get along smoothly with other people is worth all the trouble it may involve because, in addition to providing a livelihood, it also brings (1) increased personal satisfaction, (2) greater future security, and (3) better chance of promotion. Some individuals never achieve any great measure of these rewards, but they are available to anyone who appreciates their worth and understands how to achieve them.[1]

The success of a manager in business comes largely from his ability to develop an effective employee team. It is the group of managers and top executives who determine the company climate in which an employee has to work.

Eugene J. Benge, discussing the importance of the relationship between the manager and his subordinates and their ability to get along with each other, cites a comprehensive study which indicated that:

Seventy per cent of the companies queried said that the ability to get along with people was the most important attribute. This ability, they believed, consisted of six major traits:

1. Cooperation with others in the group, including acceptance of the surroundings in which the group had to work
2. Persuading others, teaching them, keeping in two-way communication with them
3. Enthusiasm, a contagious trait of great value in the group effort
4. Self-respect, reflecting an understanding of an individual's relation to other members of his group, and their relation to him
5. Emotional maturity, revealed by freedom from impatience, pettiness, fear, hatred, and instability

472

6. Leadership, the ability to plan work for others, to get them to follow the leader's plan[2]

Interestingly enough, the findings from this research were indirectly corroborated by another study which analyzed the personnel records of ten thousand employees. The conclusion was drawn that 15 percent of success results from technical training and 85 percent from personality development.

This all boils down to the fact that supervisors, managers, and top executives should make every effort to so set the work climate that effective results are realized.

FRIENDLINESS

The good leader has a special affection for his own group, even though they are at times foolish, weak, or difficult. He should be approachable by its members from the lowest to the highest, never making them feel that they are wasting his time.

The friendly leader attracts many friends, followers, and disciples; but he is also sought out by bores, scoundrels, and unhappy people. He must develop techniques to keep this latter group at a distance, while still being of help to them.[3]

Friendliness is also a form of recognition. A friendly greeting from the "boss" is always a welcome reminder to the subordinate that he is working for a human being like himself.

Cheerfulness

The person with a cheerful outlook on life is likely to get along well with his associates because they will enjoy working with him. The employee who remains cheerful when difficult situations arise is admired by his fellow workers for his stability and is the type of person others like to work with.

Sincerity

Give the impression that you believe what you say and that you can be counted upon to carry out what you say you will. Sincerity is the basis of others' confidence in you. Avoid unusual mannerisms, affected talk, and snobbishness. Work hard to be sincere for it will pay off handsomely in the long run.

Tolerance

Tolerance may be defined as the ability to bear with a person in a particular situation. It involves an understanding of another person's problem and allowing leeway in its solution.

One's degree of tolerance is, of course, related to the specific situation involved. A new employee, for example, may require a great deal of tolerance for the first few days on the job, but much less by the end of his first week. A show of tolerance would be entirely justified in the case of an employee with long years of uninterrupted service who suddenly asks for a day off to be with his sick wife in the hospital.

Good judgment in determining the degree of tolerance required in a given situation is imperative.

Respect

A business leader must win the respect of his subordinates. His position as boss may be automatically respected, but to gain the personal respect of a worker, he must put forth conscious effort.

On the other side of the coin is the respect the leader should have for his subordinates. One of the great things about American democracy is the constitutional right of every man to be treated fairly and with equality. This requires that he be handled fairly at all times and that his rights are respected.

Both manager and subordinate must do his part to establish a relationship that will command the respect of the other. When that is accomplished, a good working relationship will result.

Trust

One learns to trust another person through his acts, not in one situation but in many. The business leader who is trusted by his subordinates and peers has won for himself a coveted prize in the field of human relations. Earning the trust of all who work for and with him is one of a manager's finest goals.

Participation

Employees and supervisors like to feel that they can take the initiative in discussing problems and decisions which affect their particular job. Management must make every effort to establish an atmosphere in which participation is not just a theory but a reality. The business leader who is confident, sincere, and tolerant of others will get the participation of those about him. By so doing, he will add another edge to his sword of effectiveness with others.

Courtesy

Courtesy is actually an expression of kindness. It lubricates our daily contacts with others and keeps things running smoothly.

If you are courteous, you can often say and do things you could not possibly get away with if you said or did them without grace. That is why leaders mind their manners.

A student of the technique of executive leadership suggests the following building blocks of courtesy for business leaders:

C   stands for the *courage* to be kind when things go wrong.
O   stands for the *other* fellow's point of view, to keep in mind.
U   stands for the *urgency* to say and do pleasant things.
R   stands for *rules* of conduct that make us pleasant to be with.
T   stands for *temper,* to be held in check.
E   stands for *everyone,* to be treated politely.
S   stands for *sincerity*—of smile, handclasp, word that help so much.
Y   stands for *you* (and me) whose duty is to deal with others as we wish to be dealt with.[4]

Helpfulness

Any position in business leadership presents many opportunities to assist one's fellow workers. By taking advantage of those opportunities, you gain the satisfaction of helping others, in addition to showing them that you are interested in their welfare. You can help them by (1) assisting them with their work, (2) sharing their interests, (3) sympathizing with them, and (4) giving them due praise.[5] In return, they will come to know you better and think better of you.

SENSITIVITY TO OTHERS

A sensitivity to the needs of others is one of the most vital of all human qualities. The business leader who has developed it is sympathetic and responsive and is able to avoid both antagonism and being pushed around. He has a feel for selecting the right people for assignments under his supervision.[6]

In addition to personal sensitivity, he has social sensitivity to groups, such as his company, the community, his customers, and the nation; and he is able to interpret one group to the other.[7]

The sensitive business leader has developed his empathy to a high degree. He is able to assimilate, integrate, and evaluate the efforts of people.[8] Recognizing the other man's point of view, he is willing to compromise, or even take the loss of an argument.[9]

His sensitivity carries over to his dress as well. He is conventional in dress, neat, and carefully groomed.[10]

In summary, it may be said that the person who is sensitive

to the needs of others exhibits fairness in all his dealings, showing tolerance, impartiality, consideration, and equitableness.[11]

Recognition of Weaknesses

All of us have weaknesses and we are hesitant to admit them. The business leader who is sensitive to the needs of others ferrets out these weaknesses and *builds* upon them. He does this by helping the individual strengthen himself. This may be in the form of assignment to a different job where the worker can gain experience and thereby overcome the weakness; it may mean giving him personal counsel; or it may mean providing further training to remove the weakness. In any case, the fact that his weak points are recognized encourages him to do something about them.

Sometimes we imagine that others do not notice our weak points. This is a mistaken idea for, if we are aware of them, others will be also. We must maintain a constant vigil to stamp out and correct them just as quickly as we possibly can. It is not easy, but, as part of our self-development, we have an obligation to do so.

Recognition of Strengths

Most of us know and acknowledge our strengths. The business leader who has the ability to sense these strengths in his subordinates has a real key to his own personal success. This means, of course, that he must know his people, the work they do, the quality of that work, their interest in it, and their knowledges and skills. He capitalizes on every strength within his organization to build it to its fullest functioning capacity.

Recognition of Wants

To know and fully appreciate the wants of those working for you is a difficult task. Nevertheless, the leader who is truly sensitive to others will make it a point to know the needs and wants of those he supervises. Such information is obtained both directly and indirectly, much of it simply by listening. Satisfying those needs and wants to whatever extent is possible becomes a plus tool in the hands of the wise, knowledgeable, and sensitive leader.

AUTHORITY

The business leader conveys an impression of forcefulness by intellectual brilliance, physical mien and manner, and directness of action. He is clearly distinguished by decisiveness based on the best information available. Though he may seem to make snap judgments, most of them were actually made previously, when he anticipated the contingency.[12] Being sufficiently forceful, he becomes the natural rallying point, and he has the ability to hold together a disintegrating situation.[13]

Prestige

One of the driving forces of the business leader is the prestige and power of his position. This prestige aids him in his relations with others in the organization; it gives him power over some, power coordinate with others, and power with those above him. He has worked hard and devoted much time and effort to rise to a position of prestige, and he is willing to work even harder to maintain it.

Speed of Decision

The speed with which decisions are made by business leaders adds strength to the effectiveness of any organization. In appraising this aspect of executive performance, here are some check questions to ask:

1. Have there been serious bottlenecks because of inability to get decisions out of the man?
2. Is he ready to express his own viewpoint to his superior, or in staff meetings, when the occasion warrants?
3. Is he willing to have his decisions go on record?
4. Has he stood by decisions which proved unpopular?
5. Does he give the impression of having convictions of his own, or does he reflect the viewpoint of the advocate who most recently got his ear?
6. Is there a pattern of consistence in his decisions? Or has he frequent and sudden changes of mind?
7. Is there a spottiness, or change of mood, in his decision making; that is, are there periods when his decisions are forthright, prompt, and to the point, followed by other periods when the reverse is true?
8. Is he committee-prone? Does he seek to dilute responsibility for decisions which should be his by falling back upon group action?[14]

Definiteness of Decision

Making a decision is one thing; sticking by that decision is quite another. The business executive needs to make certain that decisions that are made by him will be backed up and followed through. On this subject, Roy H. Woodman has this to say:

The professional manager is usually decisive; he has the courage of his convictions and does not often compromise his objectives. His decisiveness is necessary in order to ensure his maximum contribution to an organization and to give clear direction to his employees. His decisiveness and direction are correct when based upon a breadth of knowledge and a sound appreciation of his objectives. The professional manager is particularly capable as an interpreter of facts. Business managers today have, literally, mountains of information available in the form of surveys, reports and historical information. The good manager has the ability to arrange problems in their proper perspective, direct his subordinates toward the solution of a series of small problems, and thereby avoid situations which create major problems.[15]

The making of decisions can be a source of emotional strain. The strain can be somewhat alleviated by understanding two elements involved: (1) Decisiveness. This is the manner or the *feeling* that surrounds the process of decision-making. (2) Selection of an alternative. This is the mental act by which you finally pick out one of two or more possible alternatives.[16]

The great enemy of decision-making is procrastination. To procrastinate on a decision can build up tremendous pressures and in the long run can be harmful to a manager. On the other hand, under certain circumstances to procrastinate is wise, especially when you need more facts and when there is no time pressure anyway.

Aggressiveness

As used here, aggressiveness has a favorable connotation. The business leader should, of course, not be too "pushy." But if he is to be effective, he must be wide-awake in his dealings with people and take hold of problems that face him with a positive aggressiveness.

Delegation

Delegated authority permits a leader to "Let George do it" and operate from the sidelines.[17] Also, it frees him from routine decisions and gives him time to concentrate on broader policy and planning matters.[18] The able business leader selects the best man to do the job, defines the task to be done, and then lets him select the means.[19] This lightens the leader's burden, increases efficiency, and gives greater assurance of good results. The real pay-off is that it gives the subordinate a sense of responsibility, a fuller understanding of the task at hand, and real job satisfaction. It makes him cooperative.[20]

RESPONSIBILITY

In an organization each person has certain definite responsibilities to help the whole enterprise attain a common goal. This is done through selective job assignment, the use of incentives, the building of morale, and the cooperation of all. It is the responsibility of the business leader to see to it that all these are utilized and accomplished.

Responsibility to the Organization

First, the leader should realize that the organization and all the people in it are bigger than he is. Consequently, he has a deep responsibility to it. He must do his part to manage the organization, or the organization will manage him.

The success of an organization is dependent upon each person within it, with greater emphasis upon those who are its leaders. The direction it takes will depend largely upon those who head it: top management, middle management, and supervisors.

Responsibility to Superiors

The business leader abides by the decisions of those higher in rank.[21] Furthermore, his loyalty to the organization is fundamental; otherwise management policies would not work.[22]

Realizing that one's superior is a part of the organizational structure, the leader must make every effort to ignore his personal feelings about him. Perhaps the most convincing argument for loyalty to a superior is one's own need for the loyalty of his subordinates.[23]

Responsibility to Peers

As a coordinator, the business leader must coordinate his task with all the other units of the organization that are affected by it, in order to secure the best possible interaction. This is referred to as lateral responsibility.[24]

For a platform of mutual understanding and cooperation, here are a few planks:

1. Give useful information.
2. Tie in your own performance.

3. Try to understand the other.
4. Make contacts outside your working hours.
5. Ask for help.
6. Offer help.
7. Show interest.[25]

Responsibility to Subordinates

The responsibility of a business leader to his subordinates corresponds to their dependence on him for their security and their self-realization. The subordinate must be told what his duties are, how to do them, and his relationship to them. Conflicting orders have to be prevented and superfluous orders avoided. The lines of authority have to be kept clear.[26]

One has to realize that the situation of a subordinate is similar to that of a child: his primary need is for security. He is given numerous fringe benefits, such as retirement rights, insurance, credit unions, etc. In addition, rules against arbitrary lay-offs and promotions are demanded by unions. In his workday relationships, a subordinate has to be given:

1. An atmosphere of approval, else he will develop resistance.
2. A knowledge of the company's general policy, its rules, of the requirements of his job, or impending changes, of the personality of his superiors, and of his own standing.
3. A consistent discipline, which would back him up when he is right and show disapproval when he is wrong, else he will tend to take advantage of the situation, develop a guilt feeling, and finally become antagonistic. In an atmosphere of approval, mild discipline will suffice; in one of disapproval, even severe discipline will not succeed. If there is security, a subordinate will seek self-assertive, but cooperative, independence; if there is none, reactive struggle will lead to friction.
4. Participation in decisions affecting the subordinate is essential. This is prevalent on higher levels of business administration and has proved fruitful. It is missing on the lower levels; efforts of "consultative supervision" have largely failed.[27]

If a subordinate differs with his superior radically and sincerely, a mechanism of appeal should be available. Something of that order is available for workers in the shops; but there always is the danger of retaliation, unless there is a union behind them.[28]

In addition to security and opportunity for self-realization, a subordinate expects status, attention, a feeling of belonging, decisiveness, direction, routine, and help.[29] The leader should also be interested in the inner conflicts of his followers, and not leave this matter solely to other agencies, such as the church.[30]

A large corporation provides for regular discussions by their supervisors with each of their immediate subordinates on (1) his major strengths; (2) the improvements he has made, those still possible, and those planned in the near future; (3) his over-all performance rating; and (4) his possible replacement.[31] The basis for this interview and "self-review" is a form previously filled out by the subordinate.

INSPIRATION TO ACCOMPLISHMENT

The leader in business must inspire those who work with and for him to high accomplishment. The ability to inspire others is recognized as an unusual and coveted one. The leader must nevertheless try to develop it.

If the leader is successful in making the goal itself satisfy his subordinates' wants, a high standard of performance will be "stamped in" as an autonomous need and training will become acceptable and attractive, even if it involves hardships.

In order to inspire subordinates to high performance, you must:

1. Establish goals, be accepted by your subordinates, reward attainments, create competition with both their previous accomplishments and other groups, rather than with individuals of the same group.
2. Rotate them on complementary operations, provide alternatives to their choice, and encourage attempts for improvement of the routine.
3. Allow fair margins in the chain of operations in which one group depends on the other; encourage their lateral communication.
4. Show that you expect a good job to be done; not that you are good.[32]

Former President Eisenhower defines inspiration in leadership as "the art of getting somebody else to do something you want done because he wants to do it."

Discipline

In order to inspire discipline, the leader must:

1. Realize that effective discipline is self-discipline, a matter of personal and team proficiency, which gives the individual personal satisfaction; it is his voluntary subordination to the welfare of the group.
2. Set up standards of behavior by consistent rewards and punishments, without whim or favoritism, and by conforming his own behavior to these standards. Punishment should never be general for failure of one or a few.
3. Praise in public, censure in private; praise generously but not in-

discriminately. Pass on outside praise, accept blame as your own responsibility. Give the group prestige; fight for their needs and rights.
4. Set immediate concrete goals in the successive stages toward the ultimate goal.
5. Never rely on your own formal status.

Teamwork

Teamwork is strong only if the members of an organization have a marked sense of identification with it. Identification with units within the organization is desirable if moderate; otherwise, it may create friction.

In order to inspire teamwork, the leader must (1) establish a well-defined and meaningful relationship between all members of the group; (2) avoid setting up one member against the other, but foster cooperation; (3) encourage social functions in the group, so that it will give them status and pride.[33]

Self-development

As managers determine what their individual needs are out of their own experience, they will inevitably try to satisfy those needs through a program of self-development. No one can do this for them; they must want to develop themselves first.

The outline followed in this book may well serve as a check list for operating managers and executives in determining their needs. For example, Part II discusses the framework of management, consisting of organization, human relations, and communications. As a manager, ask yourself what you need to know about organization. What do you actually know? What don't you know that you need to know? What are your strengths in human relations? In communications? What are your weaknesses? Based upon such an analysis, you can begin to develop a program of training and self-development to fill in the weak spots and to shore up your failings.

Gordon Lippitt, a faculty leader at the Executive Management Program at the Pennsylvania State University in the summer of 1964, suggested the following goals of self-directed executive development:

1. Self-insight
2. Situation sensitivity
3. Diagnostic skills
4. Role flexibility
5. Problem-solving skills
6. Management philosophy

Devotion to the Organization

A good part of the inspiration we get comes from our loyalty to the organization for which we work. We are proud of it, we anticipate its every success, and we feel deeply its every failure.

Devotion to the Leader

Loyalty and devotion to those who lead our organization is vital to our own success and to the success of the enterprise. It is upon this devotion that the organization heads depend for their follow-through on plans for the present and future.

As one of the leaders within the organization, you must strive to merit the devotion of those who work for you. You need them and they need you for your mutual success.

QUESTIONS AND PROBLEMS

1. Why is getting along with people so important in our business lives?
2. What would you say is the first job of the effective manager?
3. What ability appears to be most important in business today?
4. Why is friendliness so difficult to achieve? Explain.
5. Check yourself on the elements of friendliness: cheerfulness, tolerance, respect, trust, participation, courtesy, and helpfulness. How do you rate? How can you improve yourself in these elements? What is your program?
6. Why is the element of trust so important in business relationships? Give an example of this element out of your own experience.
7. Are you sensitive to the needs of others? How do you know? How can you test your sensitivity? Give examples.
8. List your weaknesses and strengths in your relations with others. Write out your program for strengthening your weaknesses.
9. Select one of your classmates and identify ten wants that you have observed him to have. Check with him to determine how accurate you were in diagnosing his wants.
10. Is authority ever taken advantage of in business situations? Explain and give an example.
11. Does prestige impress you? In what ways?
12. How decisive are you? How do you know? Give an example.
13. Have you ever delegated anything? What and for how long?
14. Why is responsibility to subordinates so very vital in managerial situations?
15. Have you ever been inspired? In what way? Who inspired you? What was the result?
16. What is teamwork? Have you ever been a member of a team? How well do you work with others?

17. What are you going to do about your own self-development after reading this book? What is your program?

REFERENCE NOTES

[1] Everett B. Wilson and Sylvia B. Wright, *Getting Along with People in Business,* Funk & Wagnalls, ʹ950, p. 4.

[2] Eugene J. Benge, *How to Become a Successful Executive,* Frederick Fell, 1960, p. 12.

[3] U.S. Air Force ROTC, *Principles of Leadership and Management,* Air University, June, 1954, p. 105.

[4] James F. Bender, *The Technique of Executive Leadership,* McGraw-Hill, 1950, p. 80.

[5] Everett B. Wilson and Sylvia B. Wright, *op. cit.,* p. 190.

[6] G. U. Cleeton and C. W. Mason, *Executive Ability—Its Discovery and Development,* Antioch Press, 1946.

[7] R. W. Heffner, "What Makes a Good Executive," *Advanced Management,* December, 1954.

[8] R. N. McMurry, "Man Hunt for Top Executives," *Harvard Business Review,* January, 1954.

[9] P. B. Niles, "Six Standards for Executive Conduct," *Dun's Review and Modern Industry,* April, 1956.

[10] *Instruction: Management Performance Review,* Reuben H. Donnelly Corp., 1950.

[11] Perrin Stryker, "The Executive Who Was Always Fair," *Fortune,* February, 1959, pp. 124-125.

[12] *Instruction: Management Performance Review, op. cit.*

[13] U.S. Air Force ROTC, *op. cit.,* p. 104.

[14] Carl Heyel, *Appraising Executive Performance,* American Management Association, 1958, pp. 78-79.

[15] Woodman, Roy H., "The Attributes of Professional Managers," *Canadian Chartered Accountant,* February, 1962, pp. 157-160.

[16] Auren Uris, *Developing Your Executive Skills,* McGraw-Hill, 1955, pp. 52-53.

[17] W. L. Ganong, "What Makes a Successful Executive?," *Management Review,* September, 1951, pp. 518-519.

[18] U.S. Air Force ROTC, *op. cit.,* p. 23.

[19] G. U. Cleeton and C. W. Mason, *op. cit.*

[20] Auren Uris, *op. cit.,* pp. 138-139.

[21] G. U. Cleeton and C. W. Mason, *op. cit.*

[22] P B. Niles, *op. cit.*

[23] U.S. Air Force ROTC, *op. cit.,* p. 59.

[24] *Ibid.,* p. 62.

[25] Auren Uris, *op. cit.,* p. 247.

[26] M. L. Blum, *Industrial Psychology and Its Social Foundations,* rev. ed., Harper & Row, 1956, p. 201.

[27] *Ibid.*, p. 202.

[28] *Ibid.*, p. 203.

[29] Robert N. McMurry, *op. cit.*, pp. 46-62.

[30] S. F. Teele, "Developing Tomorrow's Business Leaders," *Management Review*, July, 1956, pp. 605-611.

[31] G. U. Cleeton and C. W. Mason, *op. cit.*

[32] U.S. Air Force ROTC, *op. cit.*, pp. 17-18.

[33] *Ibid.*, p. 34.

READING REFERENCES

Albers, Henry H., *Organized Executive Action,* Wiley, 1961.

Bellows, Roger, Thomas Q. Gilson, and George S. Odiorne, *Executive Skills,* Prentice-Hall, 1962.

Davis, Keith, *Human Relations in Business,* McGraw-Hill, 1957.

Likert, Rensis, *New Patterns of Management,* McGraw-Hill, 1961.

Saltonstall, Robert, *Human Relations in Administration,* McGraw-Hill, 1959.

Sill, Sterling W., *Leadership,* Bookcraft, Inc., 1958.

Simon, Herbert A., *The New Science of Management Decision,* Harper & Row, 1960.

PART VI

ANALYSIS OF
INFLUENCES ON MANAGEMENT

Management is influenced on all sides by a number of forces outside as well as inside the company. They extend beyond the theory of management, and an experienced manager is well acquainted with them. Not to treat them here would be short-changing the reader considerably in his attempt to understand the *total* field of management as it exists both in theory and in practice.

The outside influences are identified figuratively as the economic, social, and political "roadway" on which our bicycle runs. They are changing daily as they are affected by state, regional, national, and international affairs, by the attitudes of customers, the community, and the general public, and by the action of previous managers who broke new paths through the "forest" of knowledge, insights, and creative analysis. The inside influences on management are identified as the objectives of the organization as a whole, the personal objectives and attitudes of each of its employees at all levels, and the transitory ideas, machines, and methods which nurture future business trends and practices.

30

OBJECTIVES AND THE
MANAGEMENT ENVIRONMENT

Historically, the role of business in American society has been that of turning out goods and services at a profit for owners or stockholders. Changes in the moral and social climate of our times have made it impossible for business leaders to let their responsibility end with the mere meeting of competition and the making of a profit. Indeed, the day is gone when business regarded labor as a commodity and the community as something beyond its concern. A major development of the past quarter-century has been the ethical awakening of business organizations, and a growing awareness of enlarged responsibilities in a changing management environment.

As a result, the objectives of business organizations have been greatly upgraded in recent times. The larger social responsibility of a business organization is now assumed, and its goals and objectives have been modified to conform to the newer concept. It has, indeed, become popular to manage by objectives. In so doing, management must relate its objectives to the organization's administrative functions of planning, organizing, motivating, directing, and controlling.

OBJECTIVES RELATED TO MANAGERIAL FUNCTIONS

Planning

Plans are meaningless unless directed toward a goal or objective. General company objectives give rise to a broad program, e.g., a power production expansion program. Each program or part of it has its own particular goal, which contributes to the over-all objective. Each program, in turn, breaks down into sub-programs or plans, each with its own goal consistent with and contributing to the next higher goal.

Dr. William H. Newman of Columbia University gives these reasons for translating operating programs and plans into anticipated results:

1. Purposeful and integrated planning is made easier. Formulating and crystallizing goals serve as a guiding light in directing subsequent planning. We plan from general objectives to a more specific one. The major goals provide the mission toward which subsidiary goals are directed, and so on down to the most detailed plans. Integrated planning is possible only through this method.

2. Divergent and unproductive work is more likely to be avoided. Emphasizing objectives and standards helps manager and operator keep their eye on the ball. There is a natural tendency for us to become involved so deeply in the work itself that we sometimes forget what it is that we are aiming for.

3. Operating goals can be used as bench marks or standards which can be used as building blocks in developing plans and programs.

Operating goals used in the past are used as the basis for future plans of action. They may be revised to fit the future expectations but they are, nevertheless, the point of departure.

Planning of the necessary functions cannot be done unless we know the purpose they are to serve. We cannot, furthermore, assign responsibility for performance unless we know what results are to be achieved.[1]

Organizing

An organization is a group of functions set up to accomplish a purpose. Unless we know what the goal or objective of each part or function is, we cannot properly decide its kind and amount of work, we cannot fit the various working parts together in an integrated way, and we cannot devise procedures which will permit all parts to work together without conflict. Good objectives are necessary for good coordination of the separate functions.

Each time the organization changes—expands, contracts, or alters its activity—it should achieve greater effectiveness in performance of functions, reduction of expenses of operation, and improvement of morale.

Motivating

People can only cooperate in achieving common goals when they have been informed of these goals and accept them as benefiting not only the company but themselves. Motivating includes persuading individuals to subordinate personal objectives temporarily to the objectives of the organization. Unless we know these objectives and agree on their importance and priority, we cannot expect such subordination by individual employees.

Directing

The objectives of the company can be used as guidelines in establishing the pre-employment training which job applicants must have had in order to be considered for employment.

To determine the additional training and development needs of each employee, a performance appraisal is made. In deciding what training to give the employee, we ask, "What sort of training will enable him to make a greater contribution to organizational objectives?"

Careful indoctrination in company objectives creates a frame of mind willing to accept the guidance of higher authority. If employees have high morale, i.e., high acceptance of company goals, managers must frame instructions and guidance in terms of company objectives for maximum effectiveness.

Controlling

Control is concerened with results. An objective is a desired result. Thus, without objectives, control cannot exist. To be able to tell whether work is going according to plan, we must be able to compare what is being done with what was planned to be done. Objectives, therefore, are standards by which we measure how much better or worse our operations are than planned. This kind of comparison is neccesary for proper control.

PRINCIPLES APPLICABLE TO OBJECTIVES

In any program of managing by objectives, five principles appear to be appropriate.

Principle of acceptability. An organizational objective, to be successful, must be palatable to the members of the organization. This means depicting the objective in terms which make it as acceptable as possible to employees. For example, we should state our objective of providing an adequate return on invested capital so as to appeal to all concerned with the enterprise:

It is the objective of this company to earn an adequate return on invested capital to the end that the enterprise may continue to prosper and grow; and thereby provide greater opportunities and benefits for an increasing number of employees.

It is difficult to make people want to work for the gain of others, in this case the stockholders. Showing how this benefits the employees as well increases their acceptance of the objective.

Principle of attainability. To be effective, an objective must be attainable within a reasonable time. If the people who work for its attainment cannot tell fairly soon whether or not they have achieved it, it will soon lose its effectiveness. Over-all, long-term objectives must be translated into short-term or immediate objectives. Thus: "The company must have 30 percent of its product market within five years, 50 percent in ten years, and 75 percent in twenty years." In five years everyone connected with the firm can know whether or not the short-term objective was attained. The goals may not be reached; the important point is that they must be capable of being attained.

The motivational principle. To be effective, an objective must have inspirational qualities which motivate all personnel to want to strive to achieve it. One objective of American Enka Corporation is: "to be the most highly respected company in the industry." This sort of objective inspires employees to act always in a manner that will reflect well on the firm.

If every firm fashioned its objectives so as to exploit the maximum motivational values, and did it honestly, there would undoubtedly be far more productivity in American business than there now is. A stroll through virtually any business firm will convince even the casual observer that most employees are not really motivated. A sharp contrast is afforded by those firms whose management has been successful in communicating objectives which have "caught fire" with the employees and have created a genuine interest in seeing the enterprise succeed. Most new firms display some of this spirit. In many cases this is because the owner-manager works with his employees, and communicates to them a sense of personal involvement. With growth in size and the separation of manager from employees, motivation is often reduced and productivity declines.

Principle of simplicity. To be effective, an objective must be stated as simply and clearly as possible. And there should be a minimum of objectives so far as the individual employee is concerned.

Principle of communication. To be effective, an objective must be communicated to all who are concerned with its achievement. Such communication must not only be initially effective, but must be continuously reiterated. In all its communications, oral and written, with employees, management must stress the basic purposes of the enterprise.

MAKING OBJECTIVES WORK EFFECTIVELY

Fundamental to the success of any program of managing by objectives is their wholehearted acceptance by all managerial personnel. Everyone must be made to realize that he is expected to meet the objectives of his position. And if the supervisor takes a casual attitude toward the objectives, what subordinate cannot be expected to do likewise?

In appraising the performance of a subordinate, it is dangerous to accept outstanding performance on one or two objectives as an acceptable excuse for less than reasonable performance on other objectives. This can lead to severe imbalance in the total operation. Managers must demand at least reasonable performance on *all* objectives, if the over-all company objectives are to be successfully attained.

Improved achievement of objectives can be logically expected when the subordinates participate in setting their individual standards. By such participation, a subordinate usually is more convinced of their fairness.

When a subordinate is asked to set goals for himself and his work, he will usually set tougher goals than if they were assigned to him. Unless too tough standards are cut to more realistic levels, the supervisor at the end of the period will find himself excusing below-standard performance because the subordinate set too high a goal for himself. At the same time, too obvious a reduction of standards will cause the subordinate to lose some respect for the objectives—and for management as well.

The basic technique of involving subordinates in goal-setting begins with the supervisor setting out goals for the unit as a whole and for the general managerial environment within which they must be achieved. He then asks the subordinate to develop the position objectives which he believes are realistic within this environment. These are usually established for one-year time periods. In an informal conference, the supervisor uses his best counseling methods to develop with the subordinate a realistic set of objectives—performance standards—for the specific position for the indicated time interval.

Periodic review must be made to make sure that basic

conditions have not changed which require revision of the standards. Adjustments for conditions beyond the control of superior and subordinate must be made. At the end of the period, an interview must be conducted by the superior with the subordinate to review the performance against the standards and to identify the corrective action—rewards or penalties—that must be taken.

Only by bringing company objectives down from long-range to short-range, from company level to individual position level, from preperformance to postperformance, and by penalizing for failure and rewarding for success can an effective program of managing by objective be accomplished.

RETREAT FROM THE HISTORICAL CONCEPT OF BUSINESS RESPONSIBILITY

The concept of the business firm as a highly individualistic institution with profit maximization as its sole responsibility has strong roots. Professor Selekman points out that the historic behavior of the laissez-faire capitalist was consistent with the basic philosophy that once dominated the nation.[2] This philosophy, according to Professor Selekman, was woven of four strands.

The first was the doctrine of Adam Smith, founder of classical economics, formulated in his book, *The Wealth of Nations* (1776). Self-interest, Smith maintained, was the best guide to personal and social policy. He held that the wealth of a nation would be increased if government kept hands off, and the energy and initiative inherent in individuals were mobilized in the pursuit of self-interest. If each man tried to maximize his own gain by competing in the market with others who were similarly motivated, then the right price would be determined by bargaining in a free market place. The market was conceived as a self-regulator of business activity. Under the prod of self-interest, each individual would try to produce as much as possible, and in this way the wealth of a nation would be enhanced.

The second was the contribution of Malthus (1798), according to whom population tended to increase in a geometric ratio, thus growing more rapidly than the food supply. This theory posed a dismal outlook for the average citizen. The working man was thus foredoomed to live close to a subsistence level.

Third, Ricardo (1817), building upon the market-place concept of Adam Smith and the population theory of Malthus, formulated the widely accepted "iron theory of wages." According to this theory, wages could never be more than that amount required to yield subsistence. Parenthetically, it may be noted that this "iron law" was later used by Karl Marx as proof of the exploitative nature of capitalism.

The fourth strand was developed from the work of Darwin. His statements about the struggle for survival in nature were used as the basis for what was called Social Darwinism. As expressed by Herbert Spencer (1850), this meant that only the fittest survived. The strong rose to leadership, and under concepts of a self-regulating market mechanism they benefited society by so doing, with no need for their being directly concerned with the social or environmental consequences.

This social philosophy became the accepted basis for an individualistic, self-centered, conception of business enterprises until the picture was altered by a wide variety of environmental changes and technical innovations, including:

Transcontinental railroads
Automobiles
Communications improvements by telegraph and telephone
Conquering of Western frontiers
Increasing emphasis upon machinery in industrial production
Concentration of capital
The development of the modern corporation
Absentee ownership
Facilities for mass distribution
Development of advertising as a business function and as an industry
Evolution of labor unions
An air transportation system

More specifically, it is common to attribute the business retreat from this historic conception of responsibility to two primary causes: (1) the hostility directed against business beginning with the Great Depression of the 1930s; and (2) the emergence of a new professional managerial class, as distinguished from the owner-manager of former days who founded his own business, was its principal stockholder, and operated it himself.

MODERN CONCEPTS OF CORPORATE RESPONSIBILITY

Today, when business executives get together and talk about corporate responsibilities, the conversation is rarely confined to the historic conception of the property rights of stockholders. It is more likely to involve a wide variety of claimants to whom corporate management feels some sense of responsibility. Moreover, the balancing of these often conflicting claims poses one of the most perplexing problems of corporate management.

Professors Richard Eells and Clarence Walton classify the various claimants on a corporation as follows:

Direct Claimants	*Indirect Claimants*
Security holders	Competitors
Employees	Local communities
Customers	General public
Suppliers	Government[3]

Direct Claimants

The nature of the shareowner's property rights in a corporation are quite distinct from those of a proprietor or partner. The property of the corporation is not owned directly by stockholders but by a nonpersonal entity, the corporation. Proponents of democratic capitalism advocate widespread distribution of corporate ownership so that more people will have a direct stake in private enterprise. The greater the distribution of ownership, however, the greater becomes the divergence between management and ownership. Moreover, the interest of many shareholders is passive or temporary, and many shares of corporate stock are owned by institutional investors which exercise little control over corporate affairs.

While adamant traditionalists argue that common stockholders alone have a legitimate claim on corporate earnings, the directors are more likely to act as "trustees for the institution," rather than as mere guardians of the stockholders' rights. Management's responsibility runs to the board, and not to the ultimate owners in a direct line.

Employees, being contributors to the corporation and contractually related to it, are direct claimants on the enterprise and look to it for financial as well as noneconomic rewards. They fall into two groups: those who manage corporate affairs and those who carry on operations. For the loyalty and solidarity of the latter, there is often competition between firm and union. To the extent that an employee's loyalties are polarized outside the firm, toward the union, the firm cannot be a cohesive group of men pursuing common objectives. Thus the struggle to achieve unity of effort, and the concessions that may have to be made to maintain it, become an exceedingly important aspect of corporate responsibility.

In line with the doctrine of customer sovereignty, Peter F. Drucker has written, "There is only one valid definition of business purpose: to create a customer." While the general consuming public and business customers do not usually directly control or determine corporate policy, as the main source of corporate revenue they have a substantial influence upon it. As actual or potential buyers of what the corporation has to sell, customers usually have a more direct line to management than stockholders do.

Suppliers are a diverse group, including all contributors of material, financial, and human resources. Sources of direct supply are of such vital importance to a firm that it often passes along to them the scientific and technological knowledge it generates in its own activities. Increased attention in industry to ethical and legal norms that apply to supplier relationships reflect a growing recognition of the interdependence of various kinds of economic units.

Indirect Claimants

The three most important categories of indirect claimants are competitors, local communities, and the general public as represented by government. Compared to the direct claimants, the relationships here are usually noncontractual, much more tenuous, and subject to considerably more controversy.

Competition in well-managed companies is construed broadly to include not only other suppliers of similar or substitute products and services but also suppliers of products which serve different purposes but which compete for available discretionary spending.

As stated by Eells and Walton:

A competitive firm has no obligation, strictly speaking, toward competitors; its obligation, if any, is to the competitive system and to the norms that organized society establishes for competitive conduct. All responsible business executives recognize that, quite aside from their legal obligation to obey antitrust laws, there is a moral obligation to competitors that arises independently of the rules of law. Some of this nonlegal obligation has its roots in enlightened self-interest to the extent that competition is regarded as the "life of trade," or as a stimulant to innovation and *esprit de corps* in the organization.[4]

Perhaps the most immediate of the indirect claimants is the local community. The contributions of such communities are many and varied, from schools that educate potential employees and churches that contribute to the moral environment to local governments that provide security and protection. Specific claims may take the form of support of local charities, local purchase of a reasonable part of a firm's supply requirements, and maintenance of a plant that is considered a good neighbor.

A question of considerable controversy is the proper nature and scope of corporate participation in the process of government. As a taxpayer, the corporation is clearly a direct contributor to government, and there is no question that it must bear a share of the burden of government.

A broader understanding of the political functions of business is evident today in the development of activities which go beyond the historic practice of lobbying, to include programs of communication between business firms, or associations of firms, and governments. A current major business problem is to define more clearly the extent and means of proper corporate participation in the affairs of government.

CONDITIONS OF SOCIAL RESPONSIBILITY

In meeting the claims of such a wide variety of claimants, executives must strive to satisfy three conditions so that they *can become responsible*. These are stated by Eells and Walton as (1) discretion as to courses of action; (2) the availability of resources to implement the plan of action chosen; and (3) the availability of knowledge about the probable consequences of the decision.

The first two conditions involve making available to corporate management adequate authority, the necessary structure of authority, and the necessary sanctions. The third condition is more perplexing. Adequate authority, properly structured, does not insure rational conduct. Also needed is greater knowledge of the potential effects of decisions upon the various claimants. This implies the need for the continuing education of managerial personnel and the creation of better informational sources.

EVOLUTION OF MANAGEMENT CONCEPTS

As early as men began to gather together in large groups, an orderly system of conducting business transactions was recognized. This was evident some two thousand years before Christ in the Code of Hammurabi, which contained the basis for many business and legal practices still in use today. From this earliest recorded

evidence of recognized management practices, progress has consisted of climbing a ladder of social perception. Lawrence A.
Appley, president of the American Management Association, has
illustrated this development in the following simple steps:

Savagery—the other fellow is my enemy and is to be destroyed.

Slavery—the other fellow is to be conquered and put at my service.

Servitude—the other fellow is to serve me for a consideration and to
ask for no more.

Welfare—the other fellow should be helped up when down, without
too much concern for what got him down.

Paternalism—the other fellow should be cared for, and I will decide
to what extent.

Participation—the other fellow has something to contribute to my
efforts and can help me.

Trusteeship—that for which I am responsible is not mine. I am developing and administering it for the benefit of others.

Statesmanship—the other fellow is capable of being far more than he is,
and, it is my responsibility to help him develop to his fullest potential.

QUESTIONS AND PROBLEMS

1. What purpose do objectives serve? Explain fully.
2. Describe the relationship between the objectives of an organization
   and the administrative skills of management.
3. Name the five principles applicable to the objectives of an organization.
4. How can objectives be made to work effectively?
5. Discuss the responsibility of the business organization in our present-
   day economy.
6. What is meant by the term, "modern concepts of corporate responsibility"?
7. Explain the evolution of management concepts.
8. What are the social responsibilities of modern business organizations?
9. What is the relationship between company objectives and personal
   objectives?
10. Discuss your own personal objectives and tie them into your plans
    for the future.

REFERENCE NOTES

[1] William H. Newman, *Administrative Action: The Techniques of
Organization and Management,* Second Edition. © 1951, 1963, by permission of Prentice-Hall, 1963, pp. 26-27.

[2] Benjamin M. Selekman, *A Moral Philosophy for Management,* McGraw-Hill, 1959, pp. 8-9

[3] Richard Eells and Clarence Walton, *Conceptual Foundations of Business,* Irwin, 1961, p. 136.

[4] *Ibid.,* p. 161.

READING REFERENCE

Davidson, William R., and James H. Healey, *Power Management,* Allegheny Power System and Its Subsidiaries, 1962.

31

THE SOCIAL, POLITICAL, AND ECO-NOMIC INFLUENCES ON MANAGEMENT

There are many outside influences on business organizations that create the external climate in which they must operate. These outside forces have much to do with long-range planning, decisions pertaining to capital expenditures, building programs, hiring practices, etc. The alert administrator today is cognizant of these forces and he makes good use of his knowledge about them. To ignore them would be fatal to the organization.

CONCEPT OF INTERNAL VERSUS EXTERNAL VALUES

Not infrequently, the role of management is viewed as an internal one only: the technical coordination of the factors of production, to achieve the most efficient, lowest-cost operation. Such a narrow view of the managerial function is not only inadequate, it is erroneous.

The error of this concept is clear at the most superficial level because most businesses engage in activities deliberately designed to influence the external environment. The most obvious example is that of advertising. Advertising that promotes a product probably comes to mind first. But there is another type of advertising whose aim is not to sell a particular product but rather to create a favorable impression of the firm itself. Institutional advertising was most prevalent during World War II when firms had little, if anything, to sell to the consumer but wished to keep their names before the public.

Not only do firms attempt to influence their external environment, but their own alternatives are circumscribed or enlarged by this environment; therefore an understanding of its social, political, and economic forces is essential.

SOCIAL INFLUENCES

Undoubtedly, the most dramatic recent social upheaval has been the civil rights movement involving our most underprivileged minority group. Many firms and their managers have found this a source of business problems. They have been forced to decide such questions as whether to alter employment policies, customer relations policies, expansion plans, and so on.

No firm has been immune from these questions, whether in the centers of ferment or elsewhere. No unequivocally advantageous decision seems possible. The decision to resist change may in the short run lead to boycott and in the long run to social and economic ostracism. But if change is not resisted, boycott and ostracism by opposing groups can be just as damaging since there is no certainty which of the contending social forces will ultimately hold sway.

As a manager, the executive must have a sufficient understanding of the social forces at work to make some estimate of the likely short- and long-run impact of alternative courses of action. Ultimately, the question he must decide is whether or not, and at what speed, the patterns of the past shall be altered, both in his particular region and on a national scale.

The manager, however, is also a citizen with his own scale of values. As a business administrator, he will be expected to evaluate alternatives dispassionately, thinking solely of the long-run implications for the firm. But if he reaches conclusions about business behavior which are incompatible with his own convictions, he may have to decide whether he can any longer implement those policies.

This is only a more dramatic and newsworthy example of the types of social forces which affect a firm's policy decisions. Social conceptions of appropriate working conditions, hours, and wages are equally potent forces. Another social trend which has had important implications for managerial decisions has been the changing role of women in our society and the resulting influx into labor of women with children, since more than half the female labor force is over forty-five years of age.

EDUCATIONAL INFLUENCES

The advancing educational level of the population has had its impact on the business firm, both in the degree of responsibility that can be expected from, and the degree of compensation that is expected by, this changing labor force. Only in the last generation has that force not consisted of a large proportion of the foreign born, a change that has eliminated a potential source of both skilled and unskilled labor.

POPULATION INFLUENCES

All manner of population changes and shifts also have their impacts on business. Population growth is a widely discussed and misunderstood social change since, in its present form, it seems to be uncorrelated with economic events and does not portend higher levels of living for the general population. Firms that take population growth into account in their planning should recognize the uncertainties that exist as to its continuance and effects.

Our population has grown at the extremes of the age distribution. We have more young people to support and educate and more older people to retire and support. This asymmetrical age distribution presents such problems as these:

1. The supply of labor in the vigorous working years is small relative to our population.
2. The growing number and proportion of the aged have increased the pressure for both public and private retirement programs, presenting firms with financial costs and the necessity of understanding the technicalities of myriad retirement program alternatives.
3. The young and the old both provide unique markets but also exact unique costs, the aged for retirement, the young for education.
4. The relative scarcity of labor in the prime working years has tended to increase somewhat its bargaining power, making it better able to enforce its demands for both higher compensation and increased leisure.

Population change may also be in the nature of geographic shifting, and the firm caught unawares may find it has lost either future opportunities and/or past markets. Many but not all geographic shifts have an economic base. For example, the ubiquitous-

ness of the motor car and the development of road networks
spawned the postwar growth of the suburbs. The firm that mis-
gauged either the social forces at work or their impact did so at its
peril. Not only have the suburbs drawn population from the cities,
but the average income and ancestry of the cities' population has
changed, although it has not, typically, diminished in size.

Other population shifts have been even more important for
some firms. In the postwar years, population movement has tended
to be in a westward and southwestward direction. Both basic industrial and consumer goods manufacturing firms, as well as
service and distributive enterprises, have found it increasingly
advantageous to tailor their operations to these shifts. As with all
social changes, the firm that foresees such trends enjoys an advantage, and no management can be fully effective that does not
take into account such evolving social trends and values.

POLITICAL INFLUENCES

Political developments of both major and minor propor-
tions can have profound effects on the firm. War and its attendant
dislocations provide a significant example. Far less profound alterations in the international environment can be of equal concern.
This is obvious in the case of a firm which engages directly in international trade. But it is also true for firms that have indirect
dealings with businesses engaged in international commerce. For
example, the retail establishment which services employees of a
supplier to an export firm would be rash not to keep abreast of
political events in the relevant importing countries.

If this is true of trade, it is all the more true in the case of
firms which have branches or subsidiaries abroad. They are subject
to two types of potential losses: (1) direct losses should these foreign
assets be expropriated; and (2) losses of extractive or fabricative
functions which take place beyond our borders. The very continued
existence of such firms is contingent upon foreign political
conditions.

All forms of foreign operation are dependent to some degree upon the type of relationship our government maintains with
foreign governments and international organizations. Business dealings with a nation with whom we do not maintain consular relations or with whom we have not joined in copyright or patent
conventions are made riskier by these omissions. Problems arising

from the international movement of business receipts are lessened by the adherence of governments to the International Monetary Fund, and business investment opportunities abroad have been enhanced by the existence of the International Bank for Reconstruction and Development. Yet the limitations of these international undertakings must be kept in mind by managers whose firms' operations are in any way dependent upon them.

National political events influence international operations as well. Dealings with certain nations are at times unpopular, as they are at present with Cuba. On the other hand, dealings with certain nations may be openly encouraged; for example, the relative ease with which Americans may travel throughout the Western Hemisphere.

Undoubtedly, the single greatest influence upon international operations are our tariff laws. Firms which still operate behind a protective tariff must be rare, since over the years the gradual reduction of our tariffs and economic development abroad have combined to alter the setting of business operations. As reciprocal tariff reductions are negotiated, foreign markets and new sources of supply of semifabricated or fabricated items become available. No firm can be both efficient and oblivious to these potentialities.

FOREIGN POLITICAL INFLUENCES

Political events abroad are not normally within the range of influence of American firms, but positions taken by our own government are subject to influence and these positions may induce desired alterations of foreign national policies. These possibilities open up the very large and troublesome question of the extent and methods by which business firms should attempt to influence political behavior.

Standards of ethics change, and the day of blatant corporate manipulation of political power is fortunately past. No longer do we accept with equanimity the influence of a Mark Hanna on a Presidential election or the reputed "ownership" of state legislators by railroad companies. A degree of control has been established through passage of such legislation as the Hatch Act, which limits the political activity of corporations in Federal elections. Ingenuity can evade legislation, however, and we are constantly forced to depend upon the democratic sensibilities of all citizens to save us from perversion of the political process. No responsible business manager can avoid settling for himself the limits of ethical behavior in the furtherance of his firm's objectives.

NATIONAL GOVERNMENT INFLUENCES

The impact of government on business affairs can be so pervasive that it virtually defies analysis. At one time in our history, government was presumably limited to providing a monetary system, a code of laws, a method of adjudicating disputes, police and military protection. But even in that heyday of laissez faire, government ran the post office, built roads, subsidized water and rail transportation, encouraged and protected foreign commerce and engaged in other activities which advantaged some and hindered other enterprises.

Gradually, the governmental role expanded, often in reaction to business practices themselves. (Adam Smith noted the tendency of business to conspire against the public interest.) Today we find it necessary to file a major antitrust suit on the average of once a day to preserve competition from those who extol it. Similarly, it was business practices that led to the regulations contained in the Food and Drug Act and in myriad other business regulatory laws.

Government not only preserves and regulates enterprise; it also encourages it. Research investments are stimulated by the potential monopoly that a patent grant permits, and uniform bankruptcy laws support credit relationships. Governmental research has been the source of progress in that industry which employs more people than any other, agriculture, and has, in fact, provided it with various subsidy programs. In addition, air, water, railroad and highway transport have been to some extent subsidized, as have newspapers and magazines and all who advertise in them.

Typically, firms are less cognizant of the subsidies they receive than they are of the taxes they pay, and, indeed, the outflow from taxes does exceed the inflow from subsidy. It should be recognized, however, that there are varieties of government expenditure which, though not subsidies, are sources of encouragement for enterprise and provide opportunities for profit. To be aware of this, all one need do is watch the expansion attendant upon the highway program. The relative cheapness of electric power in this country is also a product, in part, of government expenditure for both construction and regulation. Other instances could be cited, but the essential point is that central government activities both circumscribe and expand business opportunities.

STATE AND LOCAL GOVERNMENT INFLUENCES

This is equally true of state and local government. The local zoning law that prohibits or facilitates physical plant expansion with attendant changes in property values is only one case of profit or loss arising from legislative enactment. The level of taxation and the type of service provided by government at local levels are clearly of concern to business and are likely to be much more subject to its influence, raising again the question of limits of propriety. State and local governments have done much to influence labor conditions, labor relations, product quality, product pricing, and methods of distribution.

ECONOMIC ENVIRONMENT INFLUENCES

Few would dispute the contention that the economic environment is an important contributor to the relative success of any firm, yet many managers are ill-equipped to evaluate that environment. The general level of economic activity as measured by such conventional indicators as the GNP, the total employment figure, or the percentage of unemployed is familiar to all, but the forces that underlie swings in economic activity are rarely taken into account in the average firm's decisions. Suppose a firm is unaware that a gradual accumulation of inventories in the hands of manufacturers is taking place. Or suppose the importance of this warning sign is underestimated. Suppose, further, that its significance is overestimated and is not viewed with the proper caution. Competent management is of course concerned with both the level and movement of economic activity, but it also understands causes and does its best to anticipate trends.

The firm should not be operated on the assumption that high levels of economic activity are necessarily to its advantage. Certain enterprises, because of either the nature of their product or service or the income level of their customers, are in enhanced positions during periods of economic adversity. It is also true that prosperity can be achieved by various routes, each of which have different implications and ramifications for the firm.

In a time of high and rising economic activity, wisdom may suggest that a brake be applied to the economy. An informed management will attempt to evaluate the potential advantage of such a policy to the firm. If no brake is applied, would the short-run enhancement of the firm's position be greater or less than the costs associated with a potentially greater subsequent decline? And what about the way the brake is applied? Clearly, if the firm is heavily engaged in borrowing, restraint on the economy through higher interest rates and restricted credit would be far less satisfactory from its standpoint than restraint via higher tax revenues or decreased governmental expenditure.

Equally clearly, firms largely dependent upon governmental contracts would prefer monetary to fiscal restraint. But even within the fiscal and monetary areas, alternative courses of action affect firms differently. If monetary restraint is considered, should it operate through a general tightening of credit or through selective increases in down-payment requirements imposed on consumers? If tax increases are dictated, should they be at the corporate or personal level? The answers to these are not obvious but depend upon the nature of the clientele the firm serves.

All these questions can be asked in reverse about policies appropriate to a recession.

At various times in our history we have noted that the level of economic activity in an area or region may not conform to the national trend. The management of a firm cannot therefore rely totally upon impressions gained from national data. Those factors which make a region unique should be encompassed in planning. Parallel to this is the fact that national governmental policies do not bear uniformly on all regions or industries. Traditionally, for example, government programs to overcome recession have consisted of construction work, which has not had equal geographical distribution. Its direct effect will depend, therefore, upon the firm's connection with the construction or the area of impact. The shovel manufacturer will see the fruits long before the manufacturer of pianos.

THE COMPETITIVE ENVIRONMENT

The firm's efforts to adjust itself to competitive pressures— or to apply those pressures to others—are all part of the job of the manager. Whether the source of competition is foreign or domestic, certain questions should be asked and answered. For example, is the basis for competitive pressure to be found in the quality of the product, its price, the terms or conditions of sale, or the effectiveness of the distribution methods? Each of these general headings calls for a whole list of additional questions. To take but one, low foreign wages are frequently cited as a source of foreign competition, yet investigation rarely establishes this to be a dominant factor today. Low wages and low costs frequently prove to be antithetical, not synonomous.

Competition, however, may come from other sources and take other forms. While the cotton textile producers undoubtedly foresaw the inroads that synthetic fibers would make upon their market, it is doubtful that they recognized that the prevalence of home washing machines would reduce the average consumer's inventory of cotton goods. Similarly, it is doubtful if ten years ago our steel industry anticipated that there would be on the market an automobile with an all plastic body.

It must be remembered, however, that for every firm that is disadvantaged by competitive pressures, there is another which receives potential benefit; the very home washing machines which hurt textile producers proved a boon to both the soap and advertising industries. The potentialities of the chemical, aluminum, and other industries to make inroads upon steel's market had to be capitalized upon before they could be appreciated.

Another competitive element is that of relative cost, which involves two ingredients: (1) the cost of inputs into the firm's productive process and (2) the efficiency of that process. The fundamental questions are quite simple: Have we found the lowest-cost source of supply, are we using the lowest-cost combination of inputs per unit of potential output, and are we achieving that potential output? As long as any one manager is asking himself these questions, no other manager can afford not to do so.

The way inputs are combined is the heart of the productive process, and since World War II this process has employed fewer and fewer workers directly. If present trends continue, we will soon have more nonproduction workers employed by manufacturing firms than production workers. An alert management must be cognizant of the cost-reducing possibilities that technology develops, must recognize the personnel problems associated with significant changes in productive techniques, and must be alert to the potential dangers which exist from converting variable production labor costs into fixed capital and salaried labor costs.

LABOR INFLUENCES

The nature of the work environment and of the relationship between the supplier and purchaser of labor is more subject to political and social control than any other purchase the firm makes. Public policy strongly influences health and safety standards on the job, the nature and hours of work, minimum rates of compensation and the ability of the employees to combine for their mutual advantage.

The existence of combinations of workers makes one aspect of the managerial function easier. Through the union, management is kept fully informed of trends in worker attitudes and terms and conditions of work. But this is far from the entire story. The existence of the union makes it necessary for management to deal repetitively, sometimes daily, with still another source of pressure. Over the years, labor relations have followed an evolutionary path that has resulted in a reduction in strife, but have extended their sphere of interest to cover more than questions of wages, hours, and working conditions.

Effective management must be able to estimate labor's demands on the firm with a high degree of accuracy. Their impact is bound to be of a cost-increasing, and should be of a morale-increasing, nature. It is clear that one of the roles of management is to achieve the most of the latter for the least of the former.

The manager is subject to pressures from a variety of sources. To do his job effectively, he must reach a compromise which is at least minimally acceptable to all of them. Without an appreciation of the social, political, and economic factors in his firm's environment, he will be unable either to compromise satisfactorily or to capitalize on his opportunities.

QUESTIONS AND PROBLEMS

1. Why must a manager be aware of the social, political, and economic factors in his firm's environment? Explain fully.
2. Do you think there is a danger in a manager's concentrating on internal affairs and thereby excluding important external affairs? Explain.
3. Select a local industry and describe how the population growth is directly affecting that industry.
4. In what ways do national politics affect state and local political decisions? Local planning? Local decisions?
5. How does the foreign political situation influence you in your present situation? As a student? As a manager? As an employee of a business? As an administrator?
6. Explain what the term "economic environment" means. How does it affect you?

7. What influence do social factors have on management decisions? Locally? At the state level? At the regional level?
8. What consideration should be given to population growth in a business enterprise? As it affects the organization? As it affects its markets? As it affects you?
9. Give an example of a product that is affected by the competitive environment.
10. Why does labor influence management decisions? How does it do this?

READING REFERENCES

Baritz, Loren, *The Servants of Power,* Wesleyan University Press, 1960.

Brady, Robert A., *Organization, Automation and Society,* University of California Press, 1963.

Gellerman, Saul W., *Motivation and Productivity,* American Management Association, 1963.

Hart, Donald J., *Business in a Dynamic Society,* Macmillan, 1963.

Johnson, Rossall J., *Executive Decisions: Human Element Factors, Management Functions Social Responsibility,* South-Western Publishing Company, 1963.

Mee, John F., *Management Thought in a Dynamic Economy,* New York University Press, 1963.

Serbeien, Oscar N., *Educational Activities of Business,* American Council on Education, 1961.

Spates, Thomas G., *Human Values Where People Work,* Harper & Row, 1960.

32

ATTITUDES OF PEOPLE AND MANAGEMENT

One does not go far in the field of management before he realizes that, in addition to the technical knowledges and skills, the administrative skills, the "holy three" of management, and the personal characteristics of a manager, there is another force at work: our own attitudes and those of others.

How these attitudes develop and where they come from is a highly specialized subject combining the fields of psychology, physiology, and sociology. It is not within the purview of this book to delve into these complex fields. Nevertheless, we will attempt to deal with some of them in this chapter as they relate to the field of management.

In discussing human beings as the primary raw material in the business organization, Newman and Summer say:

One important set of influences arises from a simple and obvious characteristic of human behavior: Men live and work together. Their relationships soon result in patterns of behavior and belief; social scientists call such patterns "cultures." Every enterprise develops, within the broader national culture, its own "subculture"—that is, the belief and patterns of conduct that are associated with living and working together in that company. Two aspects of a business subculture of particular interest to a manager are:

1. The customs, habits, and ways of working together that develop *informally* in a growing enterprise. These customs, which grow up around normal company activities, elaborate and extend, or perhaps modify, formal organization.

2. The informal *social groups* among employees that strongly influence their attitudes, beliefs, and behavior. These informal groups often (though not necessarily) center on personal interests and non-company objectives.

Research on human relations in established organizations clearly demonstrates that informal social relationships have a marked influence on effectiveness and efficiency. Formal organization is essential, but we cannot possibly *prescribe* many of the spontaneous relationships that are sure to arise. Prescribed or not, these social patterns have a marked influence on how people respond to managerial action.[1]

Mason Haire throws an interesting light on the meaning of attitudes:

We often speak of someone "having" an attitude, as if the attitude were a tangible and separate thing, in much the same sense that he might have a Chevrolet rather than a Ford. This way of speaking about it has led us to try to change "his" attitude by persuasion, sweet reasonableness, or attack. Certainly all of us have been discouraged by the fact that we do not seem to change attitudes in this manner very often, and that, indeed, attack often seems to strengthen the person in the attitude he "has." If we look back over what we have said so far about the problem of an individual's making sense out of his complex environment, we see that we should not think of him as "having" an attitude but rather as having organized the world in a certain way. In this sense the word "attitude" should not be used as a noun, but rather as an adverb that modifies the verb "to see." An attitude is a way of seeing things. To attack it as "his" attitude is to miss the meaning of the organization of the other person's perception of the world. Instead, we must try to see the way in which he sees things and then help him to see other things there.[2]

We shall consider attitudes under the following groupings: (1) attitudes of employees, (2) attitudes of consumers and users, (3) attitudes of the community, and (4) attitudes of the general public.

THE ATTITUDES OF EMPLOYEES

To help an employee modify his attitude, management must know why he feels the way he does about certain things. If we accept Mason Haire's point that "An attitude is a way of seeing things," then let us consider some of the factors that "painted the picture" the individual "sees" as his total attitude. For example, in a business environment, an employee's total attitude may be influenced by his various attitudes toward:

1. Management, involving:

   Promotion policies; training programs; grievance policies; seniority policy; bonus and profit-sharing programs; pension plans; recreation programs; vacation policies; salary and wage policies

2. His immediate superior, involving the superior's:

   Knowledge of the job; ability to maintain discipline; opportunity to offer suggestions; impartiality in dealing with workers; empathy shown to workers; interest in workers and their families

3. The work task, involving:

   Number of hours worked; rate paid; interest in job; advancement possibilities; physical working conditions; work load; location of employment; dislike of job; preference for inside or outside work; productivity required

4. His fellow employees, involving:

   Familiarity with his fellow workers; employee recreational activities; type of workers desired; dislike of fellow workers

5. The public, involving:

   Customer courtesy; consideration of customer's rights; friendliness of contact with public; point of contact effectiveness

6. Organized labor, involving:

   Membership in the union movement; benefits derived from union membership; standards of work

7. Minority groups (those of a different race, color, or religion), involving:

   Worker-to-worker relationships; tolerance of others; expectancies from others; pride of relationship with others; loyalty to the group

8. Government—local, state, and Federal—involving:

   Influence on job and organization; personal opinions of candidates; effect changes of officeholders may have on organization

This list is far from inclusive, but suggests some of the factors that contribute to the total image of a person's attitude, or what he "sees."

Where the question of material rewards fits into the general framework of motivation, attitudes, and job satisfaction at the General Electric Company is related by that company's former vice-president Lemuel R. Boulware:

When we started our job-improvement, or "job-marketing," program, we found what was apparently a typical situation. We had paid high wages—usually well above others in our communities. We had voluntarily pioneered pensions, insurance, and other benefit programs. Work had been steady. Jobs had been doubled in the past decade. Working conditions were the best, and so, we hoped, were the manners of management.

But was all this understood? Had it resulted in approval of our accomplishments or even of our intentions and efforts? Had it resulted in job satisfaction? Generally, it had not. In fact, the harder we tried along the same lines, and the more we got done, the more misunderstanding and disapproval we seemed to experience.

So we decided to apply to employee relations what we had learned elsewhere about pleasing people. We tried, for instance, to develop satisfied job customers. Our efforts have been in the following four areas:

1. Good pay for good work. We have tried to demonstrate that we want to voluntarily do what is right about wages, benefits, working conditions, and other material aspects of jobs. We have tried to demonstrate that we do not have to be dragged unwillingly to do right, but need only to find out from any source what is right, for we are devoted to serving the balanced best interests not only of our employees but also of consumers, owners, other businessmen, and the public. We will not—and no one else should—even consider trying to get the better of the other in such an important matter of honor affecting close associates.

We have also reminded our employees continuously that in their own interests they, too, must voluntarily give value received by honestly applying their skill, care, and effort toward a full day's work as determined by reasonable modern standards.

2. Good human interest—both ways. We have tried to demonstrate that we want to do right—to take a deep personal interest—in the area of human association. We have tried to show—no matter what the failings of the moment may be—that our interest is high, our intentions are good, and our performance is improving. We have tried to have our attitude and actions indicate that we put human considerations first; that we respect and protect employee dignity; that we are trying to provide a sense of importance, significance, and genuine participation; that we want to help employees get every bit of extra human satisfaction possible out of their personal association with us, as well as out of the exciting productive activity we are all carrying on together.

We have, at the same time, reminded our employees that such two-way human relations depends for success on both management and employees doing their part.

3. Good understanding of jobs and of the economic relationships among interdependent specialists. We quickly found that to accomplish any of the goals that I have indicated, it was imperative that we in top management learn to understand—and then teach—where jobs come from, how free people act in a free market, how we all work for each other as interdependent specialists, and how in general our business and economic system operates.

We felt we had to learn and teach the facts about money; about taxes; about private enterprise as differentiated from collectivist systems; about the value of incentives, savings, technology, risk, competition, profit and loss, and other rewards varying with performance; and about war booms and readjustments.

We felt we must show employees and the public how much money comes into the business and how much of it goes to outside suppliers, to taxes, to employees, to reinvestment in growth and strength, and to shareholders.

We felt that the most startling change needed by us managers, not only in employee relations but in other fields, was in our understanding of economics and in our ability to make ourselves understood and convincing in this area.

We felt this knowledge would give us the cause to speak up boldly and confidently with the truth to employees and neighbors, no matter how unpalatable it might be at first to those in whose interests we were working and whom we wanted to respect and like us, and no matter who had to be contradicted among those of good or evil power.

We have, at the same time, urged the individual employee to learn in his own interest the economics, morals, and politics of his particular role as a contributor, claimant, and citizen—and to compare it with the roles played by his fellow citizens.[3]

Attitude Measurement

The importance of knowing the attitudes of our employees is neatly summed up by Beaumont when he says, "Only when the attitudes of workers are understood can their behavior be predicted with a reasonable degree of probability."[4] This predictive ability can be one of management's most important tools. To have some idea, in advance, of what the employee's reactions will be to a new policy, a changed regulation, etc., will quite obviously increase the chances of its success. Or if our prediction tells us that it will be met with hostility, management can reappraise the proposed change to determine whether or not there is any justification for the resistance.

Beaumont points out further that:

While the social and organic needs of the individual determine the goals he seeks to attain, his attitudes cause him to select certain types of reactions as more satisfying outlets for his energies and more desirable approaches to the goals he has chosen. These attitudes are acquired by past experiences of success and failure and by the acceptance of the standard code of the group with which the individual is identified. They are individual reactions of a highly personal nature and have nothing to do with a man's intellectual capacity or his skills.[5]

Thus standards and schedules set on the basis of a particular level of skill may be impossible of attainment because of attitudinal influence on production. Similarly, work assignments given on the basis of intellectual level may be inadequately accomplished as a result of these same attitudinal influences. Thus we may accept the fact that the planning phase of management may be seriously hampered without knowledge of employee attitudes.

But how can we determine employee attitudes? There are several methods of gathering data. Jucius classifies them as (1) direct observation techniques, (2) employee-initiated techniques, and (3) employer-initiated techniques.[6]

Attitude Development

Before we attempt to influence or develop employee attitudes, we must determine whether or not they are, by their nature, susceptible to change. Pfiffner sheds some light on this problem by stating: "The pattern of human behavior can be altered within limits much broader than previously supposed. The behavior of individuals can be altered as can the behavior of social groups in the work environment." He goes on to suggest a four-point program for those who attempt the task of attitude development:

1. The attitude developer is exhorted to have a sound basic knowledge of both individual and group dynamics. He must understand why people act as they do both individually and as members of either formal or informal organizations.

2. The individual is advised to thoroughly understand the people with whom he is associating—the people whose attitudes he is attempting to influence or develop. He must understand the make-up of both the formal and the informal group. He must further understand the ethics, norms, and group attitudes of the individuals with whom he is dealing as it is in the light of these ethics, norms, and attitudes that messages, instructions, and regulations will be received and interpreted.

3. Attempt to induce change should be based on persuasion and information rather than being fear-motivated.

4. When attempting to introduce radical change or change long-standing or deep-seated attitudes, it is often better to permit one of the group to introduce and champion the change. The group will be less apt to reject a change sponsored by one of their own number than one sponsored by an outsider as such a change carries with it a threat to the group security.[7]

In the opinion of several authorities, communications, counseling, and consultative management offer excellent opportunities for attitude development.

ATTITUDES OF CONSUMERS AND USERS

An organization doing business with certain consumers has little or no influence upon them except as it develops a company image in their minds. While advertising in all media is aimed at accomplishing this, the most positive, sure-fire way to create a good company image is to provide a quality product or service, build a reputation for follow-through on it, and back up claims with action. It has been said that "success breeds success," and in this case the adage is probably true.

One of the best recent examples is the success of International Business Machines Corporation (IBM). This is a relatively new company, yet in a few brief years it has made unheard-of strides in the business equipment field and built a most enviable reputation for itself. This organization truly has a company image and its customers will buy almost anything it produces. To build such an image has taken time, patience, and great investment. But above all the products they manufacture are good ones, there is a need for them, the financial arrangements for renting or purchasing them are favorable, their servicing is outstanding, and their follow-through with their customers is exceptional. Result: success!

ATTITUDES OF THE COMMUNITY

No longer can management ignore the community in which it operates. An organization must build a good local image so that it can recruit employees, support the community's competitive bids for industry, and provide good homes for its employees, especially those who have been brought in from other towns and cities.

Mr. Boulware says on the subject of community attitudes:

We quickly came to see that good pay for good work, good human relationships, and good economic, moral, and political teachings inside our business would not in themselves produce harmonious over-all employee-employer relationships.

The outside influences were too many and too strong. We were going to have to go out among our neighbors to get good community understanding, approval, and support of us and our activities.

So we have been seeking every available means to deserve and get a firm belief by the community that we are a good employer, a good customer of other businesses, a good supplier of goods and services to our customers, a good taxpayer who asks no bargains, a good contributor to charities and not a drain on them, a good citizen, and an avid worker in what our fellow citizens believe to be "for the good of the cause."

But we have understood from the beginning that this job in the community can be done by no one employer. So we have sought to join with other businessmen and interested citizens in being sure that we engage in proper business and professional conduct in the public interest and at the same time help with economic education, moral reawakening, and political sophistication among a majority of all citizens.[8]

ATTITUDES OF THE GENERAL PUBLIC

The day was when executives of business enterprises could ignore whatever impact their decisions might have on the general public. Today, however, American business executives must face up to many public demands for new actions, different policies, and changed attitudes in areas that were rarely considered business responsibilities. These new challenges are centered on the following areas:

1. Business initiative in supplying and maintaining the economic performance of the country.
2. Policy innovation in which business anticipates needs for new general rules and develops them.
3. A positive approach to the basic problems of function, structure, and accountablity of the enterprise.
4. Imagination, sensitivity, and courage with respect to the role, function, and conduct of the business executive.[9]

In addition to these challenges, the modern executive today must shape his attitudes and philosophy to the double role he must play: "businessman" and "professional." As a businessman, he must receive adequate rewards to stimulate his efforts for the future. As a professional, he must have public acceptance of his role. If he is to achieve both, business must understand not only the nature of his dual role, but also how the public perceives the risks he takes.

There is a still newer attitude evolving toward the role of business enterprise in our society. Business is private and is accepted as such. It is autonomous and operates under its own rules, pursuing goals set by itself. But it is not a private affair and the concern of its stockholders, executives, and employees alone. It is a community asset, public in its conduct, its mores, and its impacts.

In the pursuit of its everyday private business, and in performing its economic job, business is therefore expected to further human values and to serve national purpose. This is at the core of contemporary business ethics.[10]

QUESTIONS AND PROBLEMS

1. What is an attitude? Name one.
2. Do you believe that the attitudes of consumers have anything to do with their buying habits? Give some examples.
3. What are some of the things you like about the community in which you live? How have your attitudes been influenced by the policies determined by local government officials? Could community attitudes be improved? How?
4. What is expected of business in terms of values?
5. Make a list of your attitudes toward (1) school, (2) life in general, (3) state government, (4) your classmates, (5) your teachers, (6) study, and (7) business.
6. What has research found out about motivation in employee relations?
7. What is your understanding of the General Electric Company experience with motivation and job satisfaction? Discuss.
8. From what company do you purchase your school supplies? Why? Explain.
9. Discuss why the modern-day business executive cannot ignore the general public.

REFERENCE NOTES

[1] William H. Newman and Charles E. Summer, Jr., *The Process of Management,* Prentice-Hall, 1961, p. 138.

[2] Mason Haire, *Psychology in Management,* 2nd ed., McGraw-Hill, 1964, pp. 106-107.

[3] Lemuel R. Boulware, adapted from an address at the University of Michigan Industrial Relations Conference, unpublished, March, 1956.

[4] H. Beaumont, *The Psychology of Personnel,* Longmans, 1945, p. 25.

[5] *Ibid.,* p. 24.

[6] Michael J. Jucius, *Personnel Management,* Irwin, 1947, pp. 295-299.

[7] John Pfiffner, *The Supervision of Personnel,* Prentice-Hall, 1951, pp. 34, 185.

[8] Lemuel R. Boulware, *op. cit.*

[9] James H. Healey, "Developing a Personal Philosophy of Management," *Manage,* June-July, 1962.

[10] Peter Drucker, "Big Business and the National Purpose," *Harvard Business Review,* March-April, 1962.

READING REFERENCE

Newcomb, Theodore M., *Social Psychology* (Dryden Press), Holt, Rinehart and Winston, 1950, chaps. 3-7.

33

MANAGEMENT IN TRANSITION

AN INTRODUCTION TO QUANTITATIVE DECISION-MAKING

The purpose of this book has been to provide a basic introduction to classical organization and decision theory in the functional areas of management. Such a presentation would be incomplete without at least a short chapter on the quantitative techniques which pervade current management thought. Even the staunch advocates of the behavioral or interdisciplinary approach to organization theory find it impossible to ignore the avalanche of mathematical models inundating modern business specialists.

Collection, assimilation, and analysis of relevant information seem to be the critical factors in this new advancement in the science and art of managing. The utilization of electronic data processing equipment provides instantaneous planning and control data that permit sounder and more comprehensive decisions.

The almost unlimited capabilities of current and proposed data processing systems are nothing if not awe-inspiring. In fact, if one examines the area of cybernetics (complex, probabilistic, self-regulatory systems), it becomes evident that computer simulation is more and more approaching the human thought process itself. Closed-loop control systems are now capable of detecting and evaluating variations in a manufacturing process and subsequently initiating automatic corrective action which brings the process back within acceptable tolerances. Once the initial system is designed and implemented, human decisions become unnecessary.

However, even as the electronic "brains" are controlling

production, analyzing the works of Shakespeare, examining the Dead Sea Scrolls, and playing bridge with the masters, it seems highly improbable that a machine will ever be invented that will be capable of doing all our thinking for us. Consequently, while recognizing the future potentialities of technology, we must live and decide and judge in terms of the present. The purpose of this chapter will thus be to discuss some of the basic quantitative techniques that aid in the formalization of the decision-making process. The material should give the reader an insight into methods applicable to the mathematical approach to business management and organizational design, with the hope that interest will be stimulated toward further reading and study in the area.

MATHEMATICAL BACKGROUND

Correct utilization of the techniques to be covered in this chapter requires some knowledge of such basic mathematical tools as probability theory, straight line functions, rectangular coordinates, and simultaneous equations. More advanced work necessitates a background in Bayesian statistics, matrix algebra, and differential calculus, but none of these are necessary for the understanding of this chapter.

PROBABILITY AND EXPECTED VALUE

Very few decisions can be based upon perfect information where the decision-maker is absolutely certain of all the variables inherent in his problem. If this were the case, we would say that he was working under conditions of certainty where all variables could be assigned a probability of one. If such situations do arise, the only problem becomes one of ranking the feasible alternatives and selecting the one(s) which best enable the decision-maker to reach his chosen objective.

Examples of this type of decision are not easy to develop for the simple reason that very few things, outside of death and taxes, are certain. However, it is conceivable that some situations will so closely approximate conditions of certainty that for all intents and purposes they may be treated as such. Take, for instance, the entrepreneur who is changing over to an automated machine shop. He has an opportunity to purchase five different items of equipment that are fully guaranteed by their manufacturer. He has a limited amount of capital available and therefore must choose only two of the five new machines. His industrial engineers are given the task of determining the savings which could be realized from each piece of automated equipment over a given period of operation. By manipulating cost and revenue figures, the entrepreneur is able to rank his five alternatives in such a manner as to enable him to choose the two which would be most profitable. This would thus be a decision made under conditions of certainty where all cost and revenue figures are assigned probabilities of one.

Usually, however, the manager is confronted with problems involving risk and uncertainty. Risk exists when the decision-maker has partial knowledge regarding the probability of a given event taking place and uncertainty when he has no information at all concerning probabilities.

Before giving examples of these two types of conditions, it might be well to discuss briefly probability theory.[1] The probability of a particular event occuring may be defined as the ratio of the favorable to the total possibilities. By "favorable" is meant all the possible events that would satisfy some preconceived condition established by the decision-maker, and the "total" would be the sum of all possible outcomes. Putting it another way, probability is the proportion of times we can expect a certain event to take place. The traditional illustration makes use of the gambler's cube, commonly called a "die." Given a nonbiased die, the probability of rolling either an ace or a deuce on a particular throw is $1/3$ (i.e., 2:6 is the ratio of the favorable outcomes to the total possible outcomes).

The probability of an event must fall somewhere between zero and one, inclusive. A probability of zero implies that there is absolutely no possible chance that an event will take place, while a probability of one means that we are absolutely certain that the event will occur. The basic theorems which must be remembered when speaking of probability are:

The addition theorem: The probability of either one or another independent event occurring at a given time is equal to the sum of their separate probabilities.

The multiplication theorem: The probability of two independent events happening simultaneously is the product of their separate probabilities (i.e., given two unbiased dice, the probability of rolling 12 is $1/6 \times 1/6$ or $1/36$).

The sum of the probabilities of a set of mutually exclusive and collectively exhaustive events must be 1 (i.e., the probability of getting either a 1, 2, 3, 4, 5, or 6 when rolling a die, assuming, of course, it doesn't stand on edge, is $1/6 + 1/6 + 1/6 + 1/6 + 1/6 + 1/6 = 1$).

With this very limited but necessary summary of probability theory in mind, let us return to the decision-making process, which requires that we set an objective, delineate and analyze alternative ways of reaching that objective, and finally choose from them the one or ones which we feel will best help us reach the pre-established objective.

The environment within which we must make decisions is extremely complex due to the almost infinite variety of situations which may evolve as a result of our own decisions. In a democratic economic system, for example, there are innumerable combinations of alternative strategies which may be adopted by one or more of our competitors for each personal strategy that we may wish to analyze. Thus if a sales department is trying to develop a new marketing strategy, its manager must think not only in terms of his own budget allowances but also in terms of the amounts each of his major competitors may spend in retaliation.

However, all is not so black as might appear since risky and uncertain situations very often lend themselves to systematic analysis through use of the expected value principle. This principle makes possible the assignment of probabilities to competitive strategies (or states of nature) and by subsequent multiplication of the probabilities times the conditional values attached to our own strategies, we can arrive at an optimum decision rule. This rule is based principally upon the economic motive of profit maximization and states: Given a set of strategies, the decision-maker should always choose that strategy which yields the greatest expected value. According to the laws of statistics and probability theory, consistent use of this principle will yield long-run profit maximization.

The reader should be reminded that we are now speaking of decisions made under conditions of risk where probabilities can be assigned to the occurrence of applicable events. These probabilities may be either objective (based upon historical data or empirical evidence) or subjective (based upon the experience and/or intuition of the decision-maker, yet nevertheless expressed in objective terms to allow for quantitative evaluation).

One other concept that should be mentioned before discussing a practical illustration is that of the utility or usefulness of money. We say that money has a linear utility if the amount which might be lost is independent of the amount which might be gained. For example, if a decision could lead to a loss of $10,000 or a gain of $100,000 and the chances of loss or gain are

50-50, we would naturally say that the risk was a good one. However, if the $10,000 loss would be very detrimental to the decision-maker, such as wiping him out of business, we would say that money did not have linear utility for him. Another example of this concept might occur shortly before your payday. You might be more concerned about spending five dollars for a steak dinner the day before you got paid than the day after you were paid. In other words, the value or usefulness of money changes over time and usually depends upon the size of your bank account. In the following illustrative problem, it will be assumed that money has a linear utility to the decision-maker.

A small investor is attempting to decide whether he should erect a service station or a bowling alley on a particular piece of land. A reliable real estate broker has informed him that within five years there may be either a new interstate highway or a five-hundred-unit housing division constructed in the near vicinity. He attaches a probability of .2 to the former, .4 to the latter, and claims that there is a .4 probability that neither project will be implemented. The investor, after a study of projected profits, is able to construct the following table, which is often referred to as pay-off matrix, of conditional profits. For example, if he builds a bowling alley and the new subdivision is completed, he would realize a profit of $30,000 per year.

TABLE 4.   Pay-off Matrix

| | States of Nature | | |
Decision Strategies	New Highway $PR = .2$	New Subdivision $PR = .4$	Neither $PR = .4$
Build bowling alley	$ 5,000	$30,000	$4,000
Build service station	40,000	8,000	2,000

In order to make a decision as to which strategy he should choose, the investor must now calculate the expected values and accomplishes this in the following manner:

Strategy No. 1: .2(5,000) + .4(30,000) + .4(4,000) = $14,600
Strategy No. 2: .2(40,000) + .4(8,000) + .4(2,000) = $12,000

Thus, according to the principle of expected value, the investor should build a bowling alley since it is *more probable* that he will realize a greater return from it than from a service station.

If the decision-maker has no previous experience, subjective judgment, or objective data with which to assign probabilities to the outcomes of his various alternative courses of action, he is said to be operating under a condition of uncertainty. There have been decision criteria developed which enable the manager to lend some consistency to his decision-making under this state of insufficient knowledge. Some of these criteria—such as the Laplace, which assigns equal probabilities to all events; the maximax which assumes extreme optimism, since the decision-maker always chooses the best alternative; or the minima, which assumes the worst alternative is going to take place—seem to be losing significance.[2] However, there is a method, the Regret Model, which seems to be of some value in assisting the manager who is in a state of uncertainty. The Regret Model attempts to minmize the loss that can occur to the decision-maker if he were to choose from a given set of alternatives. Let us take a simple example to illustrate the method.

Suppose a small farmer is attempting to decide how to utilize a new section of land he has just purchased. He has eliminated all but three alternatives, which are (1) plant wheat, (2) convert to pasture land, or (3) grow evergreen trees. The farmer thinks that one of four possible types of weather will be predominant during the coming year but does not want to attach probabilities to any one or all of these weather conditions (i.e., states of nature). After a few cost and revenue calculations he arrives at the pay-off matrix (values expressed in thousands of dollars), shown in Table 5.

TABLE 5.   Pay-off Matrix

Decision Strategies	States of Nature			
	Very Rainy	Moist and Cold	Moist and Hot	Very Dry
Wheat	0	−1	7	0
Pasture	3	0	4	−4
Evergreen trees	4	6	−1	−3

Given the above information, the objective of the decision-maker is to minimize his maximum regret. "Regret" is defined as the best thing that could happen under any state of nature subtracted from all the other returns under that state. This definition calls for the construction of another matrix as shown in Table 6.

TABLE 6.   Regret Matrix

| Decision Strategies | States of Nature | | | | |
	Very Rainy	Moist and Cold	Moist and Hot	Very Dry	Maximum Regret
Wheat	−4	−7	0	0	**−7**
Pasture	−1	−6	−3	−4	**−6**
Evergreen trees	0	0	−8	−3	**−8**

If the farmer wishes to minimize the regret which faces him, he would convert his newly acquired real estate into pasture land. The reader will undoubtedly ask whether this form of analysis provides a guaranteed optimum solution and the answer must be an unqualified "no." However, the model does lend consistency and organization to the decision process.

Our discussion of managerial decision-making would be incomplete if some mention were not made of a most useful tool for evaluating investment alternatives, commonly referred to as the "present value method." This method enables us to express future cash inflows and outflows for all investment strategies under consideration in terms of the present. In this procedure, we can place all the strategies on the same basis (i.e., present dollar value) for comparison purposes. In other words, we take into account the time value of money (by "time value" is meant that a certain amount of money in our possession today is worth more than the same amount would be a year from now since we could invest today's amount and realize at least a small interest return upon it during the year's time) and thereby providing the decision-maker with a more realistic tool for analysis of his alternatives.

Many of the models currently used by managers in the analysis of investment alternatives, such as payback, return on investment (profit/net tangible total assets), first year performance, and full life performance, fail to take into consideration this time value of money. By not doing so the decision-maker's analysis is often distorted, especially when cash flows are significantly different from one alternative to the next. For example, if we were to calculate return on investment (ROI) for two proposals both costing $30,000, with one returning $1,000 profit per year for six years and the other returning $2,000 profit per year for three years, we would arrive at the same figure for ROI, 20 percent ($6,000/$30,000). By this type of analysis, it would appear that the alternatives are equally profitable. However, the present value method, which is more accurate, providing we know future cash flows, clearly says that the proposal returning $2,000 per year for the first three years is the more profitable since the return is being realized at an earlier point in time.

The present value method actually discounts all cash flows to the present, eliminating time as a variable factor in the analysis. The formula which is applied is

$$PV = \frac{A_n}{(1 + C)^n}$$

where PV = present value of a given cash flow

A_n = amount of the flow at the end of the nth year

C = cost of capital

n = number of years

Some assumptions are implicit in the present value technique and do offer limitations to the analysis in certain cases. These assumptions include the following:

1. Cost of capital is known or can be approximated by the firm.

2. The cost of capital will remain fairly stable over the life of the investment.

3. Future cash flows can be predicted to a fair degree of accuracy. It is realized that "fair degree of accuracy" says very little. However, the prediction of cash flows could be based upon objective probabilistic judgments, and thus we could incorporate the concept of expected value in the present value model and arrive at some form of expected present value model which allows us to operate under conditions of risk. Consider the following decision problem as an example of the present value method.

I. M. Grate, manager of the large construction firm, the Greater Grader Company, is contemplating the purchase of one of two new road graders. Due to the heavy use given these graders, their average life is only three years. The situation has been analyzed as one of risk since Mr. Grate is not able to predict his future cash inflows with certainty. He is, however, able to assign probabilities and conditional values to arrive at the nondiscounted ("nondiscounted" in this sense means that no consideration has been given to the time value of money) expected values of profits for each grader shown in Table 7.

TABLE 7.   Expected Profits from Graders

	Expected Cash Inflows	
	Grader 1	Grader 2
First year	$7,000	$4,100
Second year	3,200	3,000
Third year	2,300	2,000

It is further recognized that grader 1 will need a $2,000 overhaul at the end of the second year and that grader 2 will require $200 in maintenance at the end of the first and second years. The first cost of grader 1 is $8,000 and of grader 2 is $6,000. Based on the foregoing information, Mr. Grate must select from between one of two alternatives; that is, which grader to purchase. Using the present value principle, all cash flows would be discounted to the present time as shown in Tables 8 and 9. (Assume the weighted cost of capital for the firm is 10 percent. Ignore depreciation and tax factors.)

TABLE 8.   Net Present Value of Grader No. 1

Grader 1	Inflows		Outflows	
Year 1	$ 7,000 × .909* = $ 6,363		$ 8,000	= $8,000
Year 2	3,200 × .827* =	2,646	2,000 × .827* = 1,654	
Year 3	2,300 × .751* =	1,727		
Total		$10,736		$9,654
	Net present value of grader 1 = $10,736 − $9,654 = $1,082			

* These percentage figures are obtainable from any compound interest table.

Since the net present value of the second grader is larger, Mr. Grate should purchase it with the expectation of realizing greater profits through its use.

LINEAR PROGRAMMING

Another quantitative area which can be of great value to the decision-maker is that of linear programming.[3] This concept

TABLE 9.   Net Present Value of Grader No. 2

Grader 2	Inflows		Outflows	
Year 1	$ 4,100 × .909* =	$ 3,727	$ 6,000	= $6,000
Year 2	3,000 × .827* =	2,481	200 × .909* =	182
Year 3	2,000 × .751* =	1,502	200 × .827* =	165
Total		$7,710		$6,347
	Net present value of grader 2 = $7,710 − $6,347 = $1,363			

* These percentage figures are obtainable from any compound interest table.

was first developed and applied in 1947 by George Dantzig, who was called upon by the United States Air Force to investigate the feasibility of applying mathematical techniques to military planning and control problems.

The general linear programming problem evolves about the efficient allocation of limited resources in order to accomplish some pre-established objective. Resources may include land, labor, machinery, capital, etc., and the objective, or "objective function" as it is most often referred to, is usually to maximize profits or minimize costs. A problem that is amenable to linear programming methods may have a large number of feasible solutions which satisfy basic stipulated conditions or constraints, but the optimum solution is that which simultaneously meets the goal of the decision-maker and the limitations on available resources.

It is beyond the scope and intent of this chapter to explain the methods used in solving these types of problems, but a simple example will serve to demonstrate the usefulness of linear programming techniques. Suppose a small businessman is manufacturing screws and he receives orders for two different types, machine screws and wood screws. His profit margin is $0.02 each on the former and $0.03 each for the latter. He uses two machines to manufacture both types, a threading machine and a slotting machine. He has a limited amount of time available on each machine (i.e., forty hours per week for slotting; eighty hours per week for threading). In the manufacture of wood screws, three minutes are required for slotting and two for threading. Machine screws require five minutes threading time and three minutes on the slotting machine.

The question for the manufacturer is: "How many of each screw should be produced to maximize my profits?" The objective function thus becomes to maximize $.02M + .03W$ subject to the following constraints: $3W + 3M \leqq 2400$ min and $2W + 5M \leqq 4800$. The symbol $\leqq$ means that the total time spent in the manufacture of the two types of screws must be equal to or less than the total time available on the machines. Thus, in this problem, machine capacity becomes a limited resource and the manufacturer is seeking to maximize his profits subject to the constraint of time. If the reader is interested in the techniques used in the solution of problems similar to the one explained above, he may refer to the Reference Notes and Reading References found at the conclusion of this chapter.

Other problems which lend themselves to linear programming are so-called transportation problems, which received their name from their early applications to warehousing and distribution methods. For example, consider the manager of a distribution center who wishes to ship a number of units of a particular item from a group of warehouses to a group of retailers, each of which requires a specific amount of product. The problem in this case is to determine how many units to ship from each warehouse to each retailer in order to minimize total shipping costs. This type of decision process can be solved by using the transportation method of linear programming, a method that has been applied to various problems that are comprised of many variables (such as amounts to be shipped from a given source to a particular destination) but only two constraints (i.e., total amount available and total amount required).

One last example of a problem solvable by linear programming is the now famous diet problem. Given in this problem are the vitamin contents of numerous foods as well as the vitamin daily requirements of the average citizen. The objective function then becomes the determination of the minimum-cost diet that will satisfy the vitamin constraints.

Inherent in this programming technique for decision-making is a limitation found in the name of the method itself, "linear." Linear, or straight-line, relationships are assumed among the variables in order to make effective use of linear programming models. We also assume that cost, profit, and constraint functions are known "for certain."

INVENTORY CONTROL

Another area which has been constantly subjected to the rigors of quantitative analysis is that of inventory control since relevant variables, such as available warehouse space, productive capacity, demand, and order costs are relatively easy to quantify.[4] Probably the most widely used model in inventory control is the famous, or perhaps we should say infamous, EOQ (Economic Order Quantity) model. This model is supposed to tell the decision-maker how many units to manufacture or purchase for inventory in order to minimize his total inventory costs.

Before examining the model itself, it would be well to explain the components of inventory cost. First, there is an order cost, which is simply the cost of placing the order. This may be composed of the administrative or clerical time required to write up an order plus any shipping, receiving, or inspection costs associated with the purchase. Or, if we are manufacturing the item ourselves, the order cost would be expressed in terms of machine setup or retooling time.

The second type of cost is carrying cost, or the cost of carrying an item in inventory over a period of time. Included in this are such components as insurance, taxes, the obsolescence factor, damage in storage, and that ever-present opportunity cost of capital which says that the money we have tied up in inventory could be earning a return for us someplace else if it was available for investment.

Careful thought will show that we have two opposing forces at work in this situation. As we increase the size of our orders, we decrease the total ordering costs since we are reducing the number of orders we have to place. However, at the same time we are reducing ordering cost we are increasing carrying cost since the average amount of goods carried in inventory over a given time interval is increasing. A graphical representation of the two components of total cost, as well as the total cost itself (see Fig. 18), should clarify this.

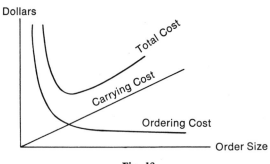

Fig. 18

The graph indicates that total cost decreases to a certain point and then begins to increase. Basic calculus says that we have a function which reaches a minimum at a single point of inflection, and it becomes our job to find this point. Further examination of the graph shows that the point of minimum total cost occurs directly above the point where the curves of the two components of total cost intersect. This means that total inventory costs can be minimized by solving for that value of Q (EOQ) which equates ordering costs to carrying costs.*

$$\text{Let carrying cost} = \frac{Q}{2} CI$$

where
$$C = \text{cost of an item}$$
$$I = \text{a figure calculated by management}$$
to express the percentage of the cost of an item charged to insurance, tax, and opportunity cost for carrying that item in inventory.

$$\frac{Q}{2} = \text{average inventory size}$$

$$\text{Let ordering cost} = \frac{R}{Q} S$$

where
$$R = \text{yearly demand}$$
$$Q = \text{lot size}$$
$$S = \text{cost of placing one order}$$

By setting carrying cost equal to ordering cost we arrive at the following formula:

$$\frac{Q}{2} CI = \frac{R}{Q} S$$
$$Q^2 CI = 2RS$$
$$Q^2 = \frac{2RS}{CI}$$
$$Q = \sqrt{\frac{2RS}{CI}}$$

where Q is called the Economic Ordering Quantity.

Earlier in this discussion of inventory control, the word "infamous" was used in referring to the EOQ model just developed. Can you see any reasons for assigning this rather derogatory nomenclature to such a seemingly neat little tool? The greatest danger in using quantitative models lies in accepting them as the gospel

* The intersection of two lines indicates the point at which both functions are equal; that is, the X and Y coordinates at the point of intersection are the same for both functions.

truth without recognizing their limitations. Many look upon the EOQ model as a beautiful cost-saving device (which it can be) without realizing that it is a *certainty* model. Remember what was said earlier about certainty? Consider the assumptions which must be made:

1. Demand must be known and constant.
2. The time between placement and receipt of an order (lead time) must be known and constant.
3. The opportunity cost of capital must be known or at least closely approximated.
4. Given 1 and 2, we automatically reach the assumption that we have no cost of lost sales (i.e., stock-out costs caused by the fact that there were not enough items in inventory to cover a sudden rise in demand).

It is good to know how to use techniques and models, but it is even better to recognize their limitations. Progress is being made in the area of inventory control mainly through the utilization of methods discussed earlier in this chapter; namely, probability theory. By assigning probabilities to the variables, we can change from a deterministic (certain) to stochastic (probabilistic) model and thus use a more realistic approach to problem solution.

SIMULATION

Further refinement to the decision-making process is added through the use of simulation, a fairly recent development that has done much to advance the field of scientific management. By definition, simulation means assuming the appearance of something without actually taking on the related reality of the entity being simulated.[5]

Simulation enables a person to gain experience by compressing the relevant variables of a real-life situation into a short-time period for the purposes of observation, analysis, and ultimate improvement of the decision process. Through the use of simulation, the manager and his staff are able to examine the results of interacting variables before a real-life decision is actually rendered. Performance can be appraised and capabilities recognized through training methods which use simulation or, as it is sometimes called, gaming techniques. A classical example of simulation is the military war game. Simulation models have been used for some time in training military personnel when it was not possible or too expensive to provide real-life situations. This training device can provide years of actual experience in a few short hours with a minimum risk to human safety.

The simulation model in business represents a complex organizational system or subsystem and the success of the simulation depends upon the attainment of planned objectives. Relevant variables are abstracted, but the relationships among them remain real so that results can be traced to decisions. Successful simulation of complex business situations is made possible through the use of high-speed computers, which have the capability of storing large amounts of information, performing lightening-like calculations, and finally rendering a decision which is based upon the information fed them.[6]

By using computers, the decisions and results of one period can be made to influence future conditions, thus providing a dynamic, moving decision framework as contrasted to the traditional static case study approach to executive training.

Simulation provides feedback through past experience and future trends. Decisions are based on all relevant data, and variances from planned courses of action are measured and noted and thus play an important role in determining subsequent real-life decisions.

THE COMPUTER

In the early 1950s, a revolution was begun, the impact of which has not yet been fully realized. This revolution was brought about by the operations research analysts and systems engineers with the help of their chief technological assistant, the computer. Solutions to the quantitative problems suggested in this chapter depend upon the efficient and accurate utilization of relevant information. This is where the computer plays a significant role since its high-speed, automatic, and electronic data processing capabilities provide a relatively lost-cost information retrieval and analysis system.

Also, as diversification and decentralization within industry continue to add complexity to the decision-making process, more and more reliance is being placed upon the computer to bring coordination and control to big business. Real-time (instantaneous) systems enable the manager to base his decisions on the most recent information from all corporate divisions. For example, inventory control or production scheduling can be based upon up-to-date sales requests from all parts of the country. American airline companies are currently utilizing real-time computer systems to schedule their flights all over the world.

It should be remembered, however, that no machine has yet been invented that can simulate the human thought process and, consequently, the computer will not yield decisions for which adequate programs (written instructions) have not been prepared. Neither can the machine make value judgments regarding the role of the corporation in society, or the role of the manager with respect to his human resources.

SUMMARY

This exploration into the area of quantitative decision-making has been brief and basic. It is hoped that the reader who has an interest and an aptitude for mathematics will pursue these fundamental ideas further and by so doing add to his understanding of the complex field of management.

QUESTIONS AND PROBLEMS

1. What are the three conditions under which a manager may be called upon to make decisions? Explain each of these conditions in relation to probability theory.
2. What is a basic limitation of the present value method of evaluating investment alternatives? What is one way of overcoming this limitation?
3. Define the term "model." What is an example of a model that you have used in your everyday life? How does this model abstract from reality?
4. Report on an industrial study that utilized simulation as a research technique.
5. Develop a way in which linear programming might be used in the more efficient allocation of capital funds.
6. What is the net present value of an investment which yields $200 a year for seven years and has a first cost of $850, given a cost of capital of 6 percent?
7. What is the expected value of a speculation which has a .5 probability of returning a $6,000 profit and a .4 probability of resulting in a loss of $5,000?

REFERENCE NOTES

[1] Harold Cramer, *The Elements of Probability Theory,* Wiley, 1955.
[2] C. W. Churchman, R. A. Ackoff, and E. L. Arnoff, *Introduction to Operations Research,* Wiley, 1957.

[3] Saul I. Gass, *Linear Programming*, McGraw-Hill, 1958.

[4] Harold Bierman, L. E. Fouraker, and R. K. Jaedicke, *Quantitative Analysis for Business Decisions*, Irwin, 1961.

[5] Stanley Vance, *Management Decision Simulation*, McGraw-Hill, 1960, p. 1.

[6] Zora Kukie, *Simulation and Gaming: A Symposium*, American Management Association, 1961, p. 61.

READING REFERENCES

Charnes, A., and W. W. Cooper, *Management Models and Industrial Applications of Linear Programming*, Wiley, 1961.

Churchman, C. W., *Prediction and Optimal Decision*, Prentice-Hall, 1961.

Clough, Donald J., *Concepts in Management Science*, Prentice-Hall, 1963.

Greene, Jay R., and Robert L. Sisson, *Dynamic Management Decision Games*, Wiley, 1959.

Miller, D. W., and M. K. Starr, *Executive Decisions and Operations Research*, Prentice-Hall, 1960.

Schlaifer, Robert, *Introduction to Statistics for Business Decisions*, McGraw-Hill, 1961.

Simon, H. A., *The New Science of Management Decision*, Harper & Row, 1960.

INDEX